GLOBAL PUBLIC HEALTH COMMUNICATION

Challenges, Perspectives, and Strategies

Edited by Muhiuddin Haider

Department of Global Health,
School of Public Health and Health Services;
The Elliott School of International Affairs

JONES AND BARTLETT PUBLISHERS

Sudbury, Massachusetts

BOSTON   TORONTO   LONDON   SINGAPORE

World Headquarters

Jones and Bartlett
Publishers
40 Tall Pine Drive
Sudbury, MA 01776
978-443-5000
info@jbpub.com
www.jbpub.com

Jones and Bartlett
Publishers Canada
2406 Nikanna Road
Mississauga, ON L5C 2W6
CANADA

Jones and Bartlett
Publishers International
Barb House, Barb Mews
London W6 7PA
UK

Library of Congress Cataloging-in-Publication Data

Global public health communication : challenges, perspectives, and strategies / [edited by] Muhiuddin Haider.
   p. ; cm.
Includes bibliographical references and index.
ISBN 0-7637-4776-9 (pbk.)
1. Communication in public health. 2. Health promotion. 3. World health.
[DNLM: 1. World Health. 2. Communication. 3. Health Promotion. 4. International Cooperation. WA 530.1 G5635 2005] I. Haider, Muhiuddin.
RA423.2.G56 2005
362.1—dc22

2004023581

Production Credits
Publisher: Michael Brown
Production Director: Amy Rose
Associate Production Editor: Tracey Chapman
Editorial Assistant: Kylah Goodfellow McNeill
Marketing Manager: Ed McKenna
Associate Marketing Manager: Marissa Hederson
Manufacturing and Inventory Coordinator: Amy Bacus
Design and Composition: Paw Print Media
Cover Design: Timothy Dziewit
Printing and Binding: Malloy, Inc.

Printed in the United States of America
09 08 07 06 05   10 9 8 7 6 5 4 3 2 1

Dedication

In memory of my teacher, mentor, and friend
Professor Everett M. Rogers,
a health communications pioneer.

Contents

Acknowledgments

To acknowledge all the driving forces and motivations for editing this book would be beyond the scope of these pages. However, I will take this opportunity to highlight the most salient impetuses behind such an undertaking. First are the tangible knowledge and lessons I gained by my life in Bangladesh from childhood all the way to my career as a health professional, and witnessing firsthand its health and development needs. In my early years as a student of Dhaka University in my native country, I had the opportunity to observe the role of radio communications in behavioral change of farmers and agricultural transition, social and technological development, and family planning. I am highly indebted to the growing field of communications across various disciplines—health, agriculture, and education—that plays a significant role in the processes of modernization, institutional and community capacity building, and health promotion.

Also foremost, I must extend my appreciation for key individuals and influences that served as inspirational milestones throughout my professional experience. Daniel Lerner visited Dhaka in February 1970 as a Ford Professor at MIT through USIS. He showed me the importance of health communications, particularly for developing countries, and introduced me to his Mobility Theory. I thank Everett Rogers for being an excellent teacher, mentor, as well as a friend, and for his esteemed contribution of the Diffusion of Innovation Theory. Without his example, contribution to communications, and sharing of wisdom, my purpose in editing this book would have been left incomplete. Invaluable experiences interacting with professionals in communications and other related fields of health, education, and development directly served as inspiration for this book. Of course, the current burden of disease also served as an important reason for its fruition.

I express my deepest gratitude to all the contributing authors who made this book possible and purposeful. Without their offering of extensive expertise, practical guidance, and lessons learned, the enhancement of health communications research and practice would have been less realized: Javed S. Ahmad, Kenneth Alibek, Sarah Al-Shoura, Nisha P. Aravindakshan, Kriss Barker, Ruth Berg, Chi Chiao, Mark Cistulli, Sue Clay, James W. Dearing, Edward Downs, Fariyal F. Fikree, Gayle Gibbons, Kristina Gryboski, Everold Hosein, Ross Kidd, Florence N. Kitabere, Gary L. Kreps, C. Kirk Lazell, Rita Leavell, Linda Lloyd, Gillian Lyon-Powers, Jessie Mbwambo, Dominique Meekers, Wendy Meltzer, Donald E. Morisky, Elaine Murphy, Linda Neuhauser, Gretchen

R. Norling, Rafael Obregon, Asiya Odugleh, Ranjeeta Pal, Will Parks, Dhaval S. Patel, J. Gregory Payne, Scott C. Ratzan, Elil Renganathan, Everett M. Rogers, Katherine E. Rowan, Anton Schneider, Skye K. Schulte, Kwa Sey, Anand Verdhan Sinha, Rachel A. Smith, William A. Smith, Leslie B. Snyder, Lisa Sparks, Mohammad Raili Suhaili, Dallas Swendeman, Taigy Thomas, Silvio Waisbord, William F. Waters, Kurt Wise, and Kim Witte. The efforts of all of these experienced individuals and their eagerness to share their knowledge are immensely gratifying. Their gifts to communications are invaluable.

I am very grateful for the dedication and resourcefulness of Ranjeeta Pal, my research assistant, in corresponding and collaborating with the authors on their chapters and providing technical support to the development of the book. She was responsible for organizing the content matrix, reviewing the formatting of all chapters in preparation for publication, and managing the logistics and all documents pertaining to the book. She also contributed her written ideas to the book's introduction, Diffusion of Innovation chapter, and epilogue. Her critiques, suggestions, and insights were instrumental from the incipient stages to creation of the final product.

A significant credit goes to research assistant Christine Demmelmaier for her wonderful job in revising, editing, and offering her constructive ideas on all the chapters. The project's undertaking would not have been feasible without her technical and communications proficiencies. Two of my health communications students, Kristin Harris and Lan Yu, contributed their valuable time and research for the Diffusion of Innovation chapter. I thank and praise them for performing exhaustive literature reviews, compiling useful case examples, and providing a solid foundation for evidence-based recommendations in that chapter. They went well beyond the call of duty.

Last but farthest from least, I sincerely thank the Jones and Bartlett team for their incredible support, patience, and enthusiasm for the project. In particular, Publisher Michael B. Brown and Editorial Assistant Kylah Goodfellow McNeill have been instrumental in the shaping, production, and refinement of several drafts of text. They stood by with confidence and commitment to the fruition of this work, and are the channel through which the message of the book is disseminated.

I now gratefully acknowledge you, the reader, for undertaking the task of reading this book and reaping from it lessons and insights to apply in your work for a lifetime.

—Muhiuddin Haider, PhD
Department of Global Health, Department of International Affairs
The George Washington University

About the Contributors

Muhiuddin Haider, PhD, is a Faculty member in the Department of Global Health at the School of Public Health and Health Services and in the Department of International Affairs at the Elliot School of International Affairs in George Washington University in Washington, DC. He received his Masters degree in Population Planning and Doctoral degree in Population Education and Communication from the University of Michigan, Ann Arbor. His major interests and expertise include health communication program development and evaluation; health infrastructure capacity building; family planning, HIV/AIDS, and MCH social marketing campaigns; national and global reproductive health capacity building; health reform via public private partnerships; and IEC/BCC programs for disease prevention and treatment. Dr. Haider has extensive field experience in 21 countries in South, East, and Central Asia, the Middle East, and Sub-Saharan Africa.

Ranjeeta Pal is a MPH candidate and McNair Fellowship recipient specializing in Global Health Promotion at the George Washington University in Washington, DC. She earned dual B.S. degrees in Physiology & Neurobiology and Psychology from the University of Maryland; assisted anti-malarial drug development and pharmacology research at the Walter Reed Army Institute of Research; and now works as a research assistant at the Center for Global Health, and as an intern at the NIH Office of Global Affairs. Ranjeeta has interests and experience in health communications to promote public wellness and prevent infectious and chronic diseases; reproductive health program development; maternal and child health; social marketing for behavior change in HIV/AIDS prevention and control; a partnership for anthrax vaccine education; and public health preparedness.

Javed S. Ahmad, MPH (Public Health Education, University of California, Berkeley) is a leader in Information Education and Communication (IEC). As a Technical Adviser in IEC, he has built capacity of Central Asian countries in modern reproductive health communication and advocacy approaches. He is committed to evidence-based communication strategies, low-cost – high volume – high quality IEC materials, and use of desk-top publishing techniques for in-house designing of print materials. He has pioneered education-entertainment approach on television and radio for family planning in Maldives, Uzbekistan, Azerbaijan and several other countries. His work experience in Africa, South and Central Asia has been mostly with the UN agencies, bilateral donor and nongovernmental organizations in the population and reproductive health fields. He has worked in Sri Lanka, Nepal and Slovakia with regional responsibilities, in USA to work internationally and in Kenya, Liberia, and Pakistan with national responsibilities. Mr. Ahmad is currently working as a freelance health communication consultant and part-time on Population Aging program of Columbia University, New York.

Sarah Al-Shoura, MPH, is the Chief Registrar of the National Genetic and Birth Defects Registry in the Kingdom of Saudi Arabia. She received her Master of Public Health degree from the George Washington University School of Public Health in 2003. She has co-written occasional paper series on public-private partnerships in HIV/AIDS Prevention, Control, and Treatment programs as well as on Anthrax Vaccine Education.

Nisha P. Aravindakshan is a Master of Public Health Candidate in Global Health Promotion at the George Washington University. She received her B.A. in Psychology from GWU in 2003 and currently serves as an Intern for the Partnership for Anthrax Vaccine Education and the Pan American Health Organization, Immunization Unit.

Kriss Barker, MPH, is Vice President for International Programs at Population Media Center (PMC). She has 20 years of experience in international development, specializing in behavior change communication, qualitative and operations research, monitoring and evaluation, and training. Currently, she directs country and regional program activities in Africa, Asia, and Latin America using the Sabido methodology for entertainment-education to promote behavior change. She holds a Masters Degree in Public Health with a specialization in International Health and Family Planning from the Tulane School of Public Health and Tropical Medicine. She has worked in over 20 countries worldwide.

Ruth Berg, PhD, is the Commercial Marketing Strategies (CMS) Research Director and is highly experienced in CMS research and evaluation.

Chi Chiao, ScM, MSPH, PhD Candidate, is a health demographer. She received her undergraduate degree and MS degree from the School of Public Health at National Taiwan University and an M.S.P.H. degree from the Department of Community Health Sciences, UCLA, where she is a doctoral candidate. Her research interests include women's reproductive health-related problems, such as HIV/AIDS, and breast and cervical cancer control for American Asian Pacific Islanders.

James W. Dearing, PhD, received his doctorate in Communication Theory and Research from the Annenberg School for Communication at the University of Southern California. Currently, he is Professor in the School for Communication Studies, Ohio University. Dearing's primary academic interest is the empirical testing and application of diffusion of innovation theory, the study of new ideas and their spread through social systems. His research teams investigate the use of diffusion and social marketing concepts by nonprofit organizations, system change initiatives and their community-level impact, formal and informal networks created to spread scientific innovations, and the activation of opinion leadership to spread best practices.

Fariyal F. Fikree, PhD, is a Program Associate in the Population Council's International Programs Division at the headquarters in New York. She participates in and directs research and program activities related to reproductive health, with specific emphasis on domestic violence, postpartum health care, refugee reproductive health, reproductive tract infections, safe motherhood, unsafe abortion, and other related reproductive health topics. Prior to joining the Council, Fikree was a country advisor on reproductive health for the UNFPA Country Support Team for East and Southeast Asia in Bangkok, Thailand. She provided technical assistance on reproductive health issues to the Philippines, Cambodia, Indonesia, China, Laos, and Vietnam. Fikree conducted one of the first community-based studies on maternal mortality in Pakistan, assessing maternal mortality ratios and defining many of the risk factors associated with maternal, perinatal, and infant mortality in that country. She also published a well-known paper on the development of children during the first two years of life, and defined the growth and development charts for Pakistani children. In addition, Fikree published a noted paper on domestic violence among Pakistani women. Fikree holds a medical degree from Shiraz University, Shiraz, Iran. She has also obtained a master of public health and a doctorate in public health from the Johns Hopkins School of Hygiene and Public Health, Maryland.

Kristina Gryboski, PhD, is the Program Coordinator for PATH, Program for Appropriate Technologies in Health in Washington, DC. She has worked globally as a researcher, program manager, and trainer in reproductive health on a broad range of topics, including family planning, qualitative research, nutrition, gender, female genital mutilation, and maternal and child health. At PATH, Dr. Gryboski is focusing on participatory and capacity-building methodologies that empower communities, policy makers, service providers, and other stakeholders to work collaboratively.

Everold Hosein, PhD, Communication Advisor (Communicable Diseases) at the Mediterranean Center for Vulnerability Reduction, World Health Organization (WHO), is an international communication specialist (born in Trinidad and Tobago) with 30 years of experience in strategic communication, integrated marketing communication, advocacy and public relations, health education, and IEC (information-education-communication) related to social development issues and behavioral impact/behavior change/behavioral development. His communication work has focused on the following fields: nutrition, early childhood education, children's welfare and girls education, water and sanitation, communicable diseases prevention and control, environmental education, general public health, reproductive health (including maternal/child health, family planning and HIV/AIDS/STD prevention), health promotion, university education, agricultural and rural development, population and development, and banking/monetary policies. He has completed over 160 consulting assignments around the world, from Africa and Asia to the Caribbean, Latin America, Europe, and North America. Dr. Hosein's expertise includes integrated marketing communication, public relations, advertising, social mobilization, health education, public education, public information campaign strategy planning, audience/market research, communication programme reviews/evaluation and new programme development, communication training, audio-visual and print materials production, radio-television-video-print media production and dissemination, media relations, and promotional special events. He has worked with, among others, various United Nations agencies including UNICEF, the World Bank, Inter-American Development Bank, Asia Development Bank, USAID, the German Government, national and international non-governmental organizations, and governments in developing countries. He contributes to the Communication Initiative and "Massive Effort," a global campaign against AIDS, tuberculosis, and malaria.

Florence Kitabere, MB, ChB, MMed, MPH, is experienced with the use of social networks in child survival and HIV/AIDS programming.

Gary L. Kreps, PhD, University of Southern California, is Professor and Chair of the Department of Communication at George Mason University (GMU) in Fairfax, VA, where he holds the Eileen and Steve Mandell Endowed Chair in Health Communication. He also holds a joint faculty appointment with the National Center for Biodefense at GMU. Prior to his appointment at GMU, he served for five years as the founding Chief of the Health Communication and Informatics Research Branch at the National Cancer Institute (NCI), where he planned, developed, and coordinated major new national research and outreach initiatives concerning risk communication, health promotion, behavior change, technology development, and information dissemination to promote effective cancer prevention, screening, control, care, and survivorship. He has also served as the Founding Dean of the School of Communication at Hofstra University in New York, Executive Director of the Greenspun School of Communication at UNLV, and in faculty and administrative roles at Northern Illinois, Rutgers, Indiana, and Purdue Universities. Gary's areas of expertise include health communication and promotion, information dissemination, organizational communication, information technology, multicultural relations, and applied research methods. He is an active scholar, whose published work includes more than 200 books, articles, and chapters concerning the applications of communication knowledge in society. He has edited several special issues of major national and international scholarly journals concerning health communication research and application. He has also received numerous honors, including the "2004 Robert Lewis Donohew Outstanding Health Communication Scholar Award" from the University of Kentucky, the Future of Health Technology Institute's "2002 Future of Health Technology Award," the Ferguson Report's "2002 Distinguished Achievement Award for Outstanding Contributions in Consumer Health Informatics and Online Health," the "2000 Outstanding Health Communication Scholar Award" from both the International Communication Association and the National Communication Association, and the "1998 Gerald M. Phillips Distinguished Applied Communication Scholarship Award" from the National Communication Association.

Rita Leavell, MD, PhD, is a physician with specialty in Pediatrics and an MBA in Marketing/Management. She has over 19 years of experience in strategic design, management, and evaluation of broad-based international public health projects in Asia and Africa, and has become skilled in the use of private sector infrastructure to achieve sustainable health goals. She has authored numerous publications on family planning, social marketing, vitamin A, and other topics. Until October 2004, she was the Commercial Market Strategies Project India Representative for Futures Group International, managing a staff of 110 professional and field staff in India, reaching over 65,000 clinics and pharmacies. She is now Principal Associate, Abt Associates in Bethesda, Maryland, as Project Director for the USAID-funded Private Sector Project Task Order One.

Linda Lloyd is a public health consultant who developed a pilot intervention project for dengue in Mérida in the mid-1990s with support from the Rockefeller Foundation.

Gillian Lyon-Powers, MPH, is the Program Officer for the Measles Initiative at the American Red Cross headquarters in Washington, DC.

Dominique Meekers, PhD, is a principal investigator at the Tulane University School of Public Health and Tropical Medicine, Department of International Health and Development.

Wendy Meltzer, MPH, is the Managing Editor of the *Journal of Health Communication*.

Donald E. Morisky, ScD, MSPH, ScM, is Professor and Program Director for Social and Behavioral Determinants of AIDS and TB Training in the Department of Community Health Sciences at the UCLA School of Public Health.

Elaine Murphy, PhD, is a Senior Associate and Professor in the Center for Global Health. She was the founder and Director of the Women's Reproductive Health Initiative at PATH. Dr. Murphy has worked in global health and behavior change communications for over 25 years, focusing on reproductive health, family planning, HIV/AIDS, maternal and child health, gender, and human rights. She worked for 11 years at Program for Appropriate Technology in Health, where she directed the Women's Reproductive Health Initiative, a policy project to improve women's lives by promoting their reproductive health within a gender and human rights framework. Prior to joining PATH, Dr. Murphy was Director of International Programs at the Population Reference Bureau, and implemented a USAID-funded project to communicate actionable population and reproductive health research findings to policymakers in developing countries. At USAID's Office of Population, she designed, monitored, and evaluated large-scale family planning communication and training projects. She has been active in the USAID Interagency Gender Working Group and for eight years cochaired the Client-Provider Interactions Committee of USAID's MAQ Initiative (Maximizing Access & Quality of Reproductive Health Services). USAID recently honored her with a MAQ Lifetime Achievement Award. She has also served on the Human Rights Committee of the American Public Health Association and is a board member of two organizations working to promote health and human rights in Turkey and Pakistan, respectively.

Gretchen R. Norling, PhD, is the Research Director for the Mid-Atlantic Region at the Mary Babb Randolph Cancer Center and Assistant Director, Cancer Prevention and Control, Robert C. Byrd Health Sciences Center of West Virginia University. In addition, she conducts health communication research with the National Cancer Institute's Cancer Information Service at the National Institutes of Health.

Rafael Obregón, PhD, is Communications Advisor in the Child and Adolescent Health Unit, Area of Family and Community Health, at the Pan American Health Organization, Washington, DC. He received his Masters degree in Communication and Social Development, with a concentration on Public Health, from Ohio University, and his Doctoral degree in Mass Communication from the Pennsylvania State University. His major interests and expertise include health communication program development and evaluation, and behavior change communication in child health, HIV/AIDS, and sexual and reproductive health. He also has worked on entertainment-education for development and in communication for development and social change. Dr. Obregon has extensive field experience in Africa and in Latin America. Prior to his involvement with the Pan American Health Organization, he was Assistant Professor of Communications at Universidad del Norte, Colombia, and consultant to various international organizations such as the U.S. Agency for International Development, UNAIDS, the Communication Initiative, and Population Communications International.

Asiya Odugleh, from the WHO Mediterranean Center for Vulnerability Reduction, located in Tunisia, assisted the county's social mobilization team. She is the Project Manager of The Global Elimination of Lymphatic Filariasis, Egypt.

Will Parks is a World Health Organization public health consultant experienced in the use of COMBI in the prevention of communicable diseases.

Dhaval S. Patel, PhD, MPH, is currently a researcher with the International Center for Research on Women and Population Services International under the AIDS Mark Programme. His previous post was with the United Nations Children's Fund as a Programme Officer for the 'Right to Know' Initiative. Dr. Patel has worked and collaborated with various countries in Asia, Africa, Europe, and Central America. His specializations include development communication, social and behavioral change interventions, research, monitoring, evaluation, and public health issues worldwide.

J. Gregory Payne, PhD, MPA, is an editorial board member of the *Journal of Health Communication*. His research interests include political and health communication. Dr. Payne received his doctorate from the University of Illinois at Urbana Champaign and his MPA from the Kennedy School at Harvard University. He is co-founder of the Center for Ethics in Political and Health Communication and a faculty member at Emerson College, Tufts University and Yale University. He has is an editorial board member of the *Journal of Health Communication, Media Ethics, Communication Studies* and has edited five consecutive editions of the *American Behavioral Scientist* on presidential campaigns and has publications and presentations in international academic and popular media. A National Endowment for the Humanities Fellow, he has been on expert panels for the Centers for Disease Control, Department of Defense, State Department, United Nations, as well as international organizations. He is the general director of the Saudi American Exchange, devoted to promoting public diplomacy in the aftermath of 9/11. He is the recipient of several awards including the first Distinguished Alumni Award from the Communication Department at the University of Illinois, the President's Award for the International Association of Business Disciplines, the Loftsgordon award for outstanding teaching, and SAE Formula One Service Award.

Scott C. Ratzan, PhD, is the Editor-in-Chief of the *Journal of Health Communication: International Perspectives*. He also is Vice President, Government Affairs, Europe for Johnson & Johnson. Dr. Ratzan was a former Senior Technical Adviser in the Bureau of Global Health at the United States Agency for International Development (USAID), and has also served on expert committees for the World Health Organization (WHO), the Institute of Medicine (IOM), and various other U.S. government agencies. He is the Founder and former Director of the Emerson-Tufts Program in Health Communication, a joint master's degree program between Emerson College and Tufts University School of Medicine. He is a faculty member at Tufts University School of Medicine and George Washington University Medical Center as well as the University of Cambridge and the College of Europe in Belgium.

Elil Renganathan, PhD, is the Director of the WHO Mediterranean Center for Vulnerability Reduction in Tunis, Tunisia. He is a leader in the WHO's COMBI approach, which integrates health education, information-education-communication (IEC), community mobilization, consumer communication techniques, and market research, all directed to specific behavioral outcomes in health. COMBI uses participatory research techniques adapted from marketing, communications, sociology, and anthropology to identify behavioral issues amenable to communication solutions.

Everett M. Rogers, PhD, served as Chair and Graduate Director for Communications & Journalism at the University of New Mexico from 1993 to 1997. He taught courses on introduction to communication, intercultural communication, diffusion of innovation, international communication, and statistical methods. He is the pioneer of Diffusion of Innovation theory and the author of several communication textbooks. He received his Regents Professorship in 1999 and retired in the summer of 2004.

Skye K. Schulte, MS, MPH, graduated from the Tufts University School of Medicine (epidemiology/ biostatistics and health communication) and Tufts University School of Nutrition Science and Policy. Ms. Schulte first began working at HealthGate as an editor/writer, and now serves as the Marketing Manager and does HealthGate's monthly health observances newsletter. Ms. Schulte has given presentations on a variety of health and technology topics for national conferences, governmental organizations, and academic institutions (MIT, Yale Medical School). She also gives presentations to health professionals and the public on improving interagency communication, dealing with the media, organizational capacity building, terrorism, and many health and nutrition topics.

Kwa Sey, MPH, PhD Candidate, is an epidemiologist at the HIV Epidemiology Program of the Los Angeles County Department of Health services and a doctoral candidate in the Community Health Sciences Department of the UCLA School of Public Health. He is currently a co-investigator on two CDC funded studies aimed at enumerating and characterizing newly diagnosed and newly infected cases of HIV in Los Angeles County service and evaluating the cost-effectiveness of 3 different methods of recruiting newly diagnosed HIV cases. His research interests include cost-effectiveness analyses of health-related programs, and structural HIV interventions.

Anand Verdhan Sinha has spent most of his career conducting social and market research, developing health communication campaigns, and advising on social and rural marketing. He lives in Delhi and works as the Country Director for Abt Associates Private Sector Project in India.

William A. Smith, EdD, is the Executive Vice President of the Academy for Educational Development, one of America's largest nonprofit organizations. AED supports more than 200 million dollars in programs every year—across the U.S. and in more than 80 countries of the world. AED has become one of the leading American institutions in the use of communication and social marketing to support public health.

Dr. Smith began his work in public health on infant diarrhea, immunization campaigns, and acute respiratory infections in rural communities throughout Africa, Asia and Latin America. In the mid-80's he became heavily involved in AIDS prevention both around the world and here in the U.S. Today Bill supervises health programs ranging from elder care to teen drug prevention – from policy advocacy to communication campaigns. Dr. Smith is also a co-author of the recently released Institute of Medicine's Report: Health Literacy: A Prescription to End Confusion Report and a co-founder of the Social Marketing Institute, a columnist and editorial board member of the *Social Marketing Quarterly, the International Journal of Health Communication and the Applied Environmental Education and Communication: An International Journal*. He authored a recent book entitled *Fostering Community Based Social Marketing*. He has published dozens of articles of how social marketing can be used to support social change on subjects from condom use to air pollution; from policy reform to fund-raising for non-profits. Dr. Smith has his doctorate in non-formal education with an emphasis on gaming theory from the University of Massachusetts. He is co-founder of the Social Marketing Institute, columnists for the *Social Marketing Quarterly*, and publishes widely on health, human behavior and social marketing.

Leslie B. Snyder, PhD, is an Associate Professor of Communication Sciences in the Department of Communication Sciences at the University of Connecticut. Her doctoral dissertation in Communication at Stanford University focused on "Learning and acting in a health communication campaign: Teaching rural women to prevent infant dehydration through diarrheal disease control in The Gambia, West Africa."

Lisa Sparks, PhD (University of Oklahoma, 1998), is an Associate Professor of Communication at George Mason University, Fairfax, VA. She serves as Director of Graduate Studies and Basic Courses for the Department of Communication. Her research primarily focuses on communicative behaviors of individuals across the life span with an emphasis on older adults; how older adults function in the health care delivery system; and how various relationships are maintained and negotiated during the aging process.

She has published several books including *Handbook of Communication and Cancer* (forthcoming), and *Cancer Communication and Aging* (forthcoming), both co-authored with H. D. O'Hair and G. L. Kreps. Dr. Sparks has published more than 30 journal articles and book chapters related to the intersection of aging, communication, and health/risk issues as well as more than 30 additional publications that focus on the scholarship of teaching and learning. Dr. Sparks currently serves as Editor of *Communication Research Reports* (2005–2007) and manuscript reviewer for a number of peer-reviewed journals, both in communication and gerontology. In 2003, she served as Guest Editor of *Health Communication: Cancer Communication and Aging*, a special issue that featured papers presented at a symposium held at George Mason University.

In addition, Dr. Sparks has served as a Cancer Communication Research Fellow and an External Scientific Reviewer for the Health Communication and Informatics Research Branch, Behavioral Research Program, Division of Cancer Control and Population Sciences, National Cancer Institute, National Institutes of Health, Bethesda, MD.

Mohammed Raili Suhaili, PhD, is the Deputy Director of Public Health, Malaysia. He has expertise in effective health communication.

Dallas Swendeman, MPH, earned his B.A. in Anthropology from the University of California, Los Angeles, his MPH. in Community Health Sciences at the UCLA School of Public Health, and is currently working on his PhD in Community Health Sciences at the same institution. He has been working in social and behavioral health research for the past 12 years in working roles ranging from field interviewer to project director. His primary research interests and work experience center around HIV/AIDS prevention intervention trials and evaluations, including work with sex workers, drug users, men who have sex with men, and other groups disproportionately affected by the HIV/AIDS epidemic in local and international contexts. Mr. Swendeman is currently a pre-doctoral fellow in the National Institute of Mental Health HIV/AIDS training program.

Taigy Thomas, MPH, received her Bachelor of Arts from the University of California, Irvine in 1997. She received a Masters in Social Ecology, with a Health Psychology emphasis, from the University of California, Irvine in 2000. Her thesis, titled Social Class Indicators and Beliefs about Environmental Risk referenced the risk perceptions of lay residents in Carson, California and Richmond, California. She is currently a doctoral student at UCLA in the School of Public Health, where she is pursuing a Dr.P.H. in Community Health Sciences, with a Biostatistics minor.

Silvio Waisbord, PhD, is Senior Program Officer with the CHANGE Project of the Academy for Educational Development (AED). Previously, he was Associate Professor in the Department of Journalism and Media Studies and Director of the Journalism Resources Institute at Rutgers University. He has written on development communication and journalism.

William F. Waters, PhD, is an Associate Professor of Global Health and International Affairs at the George Washington University in Washington, DC, and Senior Associate for the Center for Global Health. His work centers on the relationship between health and development; participatory, community-based research and capacity building; the impact of globalization on local populations; indigenous peoples; and health in the U.S. Latino community. His recent work includes a comprehensive assessment of health in the Latino community in Washington, DC, and research on barriers to care in the metropolitan Washington Latino community, a three-year field-based study of the impact of changing land use patterns and ethnicity on the environment and local health and food consumption patterns in the upper Amazon region of Ecuador, Colombia, and Venezuela; and applied research in Latin America and East Africa on relationships between microenterprise development and health.

Kurt Wise, PhD, APR, teaches public relations in health care at DePaul University, Chicago. Dr. Wise is the Coordinator for DePaul University's undergraduate Public Communications Track. He developed a course, Bioterrorism and Communication, that he teaches at DePaul as a Focal Point seminar. Dr. Wise's career in communications and education spans more than two decades. After earning his undergraduate degree from Indiana University, he worked in radio news and sports in three states. He hosted a radio public affairs show in Indiana for several years and earned a master's degree in broadcast journalism from Indiana University. Wise left the broadcast news business to pursue a career in public relations. He served as press secretary for a major political party during a successful gubernatorial campaign. He later edited an outdoor magazine and served in public relations management positions in the natural resources, gaming, and medical fields. Before seeking his doctorate in public relations at the University of Maryland, Wise was public relations director for Cook Incorporated, the world's largest privately-held medical device manufacturing company.

Kim Witte, PhD (University of California), is a Senior Program Evaluation Officer at the Center for Communication Programs, Johns Hopkins University, where she is providing technical assistance with conceptualization, design, evaluation, and analysis of international health communication research projects, on leave from her position as Professor, Department of Communication, Michigan State University. Her current research focuses on the development of effective health risk messages for members of diverse cultures and on health and development interventions. Dr. Witte is a past-Chair of the Health Communication Division of the International Communication Division and a past-Chair of the Health Communication Division of the National Communication Association. She sits on 8 editorial boards and has served as expert consultant to the National Libraries of Medicine, the Centers for Disease Control & Prevention, the National Institute of Occupational Safety and Health, and others. Her work has appeared in *Social Science and Medicine, International Quarterly of Communication Health Education, Communication Yearbook, Health Education & Behavior, Communication Monographs, Journal of Community Health*, and elsewhere. Dr. Witte has received funding from the CDC, the National Institute of Occupational Safety and Health, and the American Cancer Society, and elsewhere. Her work has been recognized by more than 12 "Top Paper" awards at both national and international conferences, as well as by the "Distinguished Article Award" by the Applied Communication Division of the National Communication Association, in recognition of the applied and practical value of her research. In 1997, Dr. Witte was awarded the "Teacher-Scholar Award" at Michigan State University, in recognition of excellence in research and undergraduate education. Recently, Dr. Witte was named the Lewis

Donohew *Outstanding Scholar in Health Communication*, awarded in recognition of outstanding research contributions to the health communication field made during the preceding biennium. She is the lead author of *Effective Health Risk Messages: A Step-by-Step Guide*, published in 2001 by Sage Publications, and was awarded the "2001 Distinguished Book Award" by the Applied Communication Division of the National Communication Association.

Foreword

Human behavior is essential for health, and effective health communication is critical for attainment of a broad range of health outcomes. These include the United Nations Millennium Development Goals, which have become the yardsticks for the effectiveness of health-related investments by multilateral and bilateral donors. Too often, efforts to improve the performance of health systems fail to take into account the human factor, including the behaviors of consumers and providers of health care services that can erode the effectiveness of initiatives aimed at improving health system performance. Effective health communication is increasingly recognized as one of the pillars of such efforts, along with better financing, organization, regulation, and stewardship.

Leading experts in the field have come together in this text to provide readers with a compendium of cutting-edge reviews of the theory, methodology, practice, and evaluation of health communications. The chapters emphasize the practical challenges and address a range of core public health issues, including reproductive health, HIV/AIDS, child health, and infectious diseases, as well as such new challenges as emergency preparedness for bioterrorism and the SARS outbreak. Key health communications tools, including social mobilization and social marketing, are also covered, along with methodologies to plan and assess which messages are appropriate and whether they are effective.

The text builds on interventions that are known to work and looks forward to improvements that are needed to address gaps that remain, as well as emerging challenges. Building public- and private-sector capacities to link health communication to service delivery and reach beyond the health sector to other sectors that influence health outcomes is addressed in the concluding chapter. Teachers, students, and public health practitioners should read and re-read the contributions in this text to build and strengthen their grasp of the essential elements of public health communications.

Thomas W. Merrick
World Bank Institute
The George Washington University
Washington, D.C.

Introduction

Public Health Communication: Utility, Value, and Challenges

Muhiuddin Haider and Everett M. Rogers

At the turn of the twenty-first century, communication is an integral element of public health practice, promotion, and preparedness. Over the years the arena of health communications has evolved into a powerful set of tools for reaching policy makers, politicians, and the public with messages to impact quality of life. This book offers a compilation of theoretical and practical ideas from experienced public health researchers, practitioners, and educators. The best judge of the utility and value of health communication will be the reader. Intended audiences are individuals who pursue research and theoretical frameworks, enhance applications of health communications models, cultivate program design and implementation, and conduct educational training.

The main focus of the text is the interaction, in practice, among health communications, health behavior, and health and health care services. Because several diseases are behavior oriented, communications to assuage their burden requires Behavior Change Communication. The interaction among health, behavior, and communication is important in the context of the global burden of disease. Lying heavily on developing nations, the global burden of disease is a product of interwoven demographic, economic, political, social, religious, and environmental factors. Major categories of risk factors that contribute to disease burden include maternal and child malnutrition and micronutrient deficiencies, physical inactivity, sexual and reproductive health risks, addictive substances, environmental risks, and occupational risks.[1] Effective communication, behavior change strategies, and health sector development are essential to address these risk factors and ultimately reduce the burden of disease.

A significant proportion of the world's disease burden is related to behavioral practices that can be influenced through communication. For example, anti-smoking social marketing campaigns target tobacco as a risk factor for multiple cancers and cardiovascular disease. As a result, the global burden of disease related to use of tobacco can be further alleviated. The ultimate challenge for health communications is to mobilize its resources to have an impact on behavior change in order to mitigate HIV/AIDS, other communicable diseases, and chronic diseases. The key here is that communications can have impacts on health behaviors that in turn affect the burden of disease.

The interaction among health, behavior, and communication is heavily influenced by the socioeconomic circumstances of targeted individuals, groups, or communities. The burden of disease and associated risk factors differs among high-mortality and low mortality developing countries, and those in developed countries, covering a spectrum that ranges from primarily communicable diseases to chronic diseases. Often the basis of many behaviors such as risk taking, risk reduction, or health promotion practices is a person's socioeconomic status (SES): a complex interaction among income, profession, ethnicity, and location. Communications interventions must take these characteristics into account in their design and implementation in order to have optimal effect on health behavior. Communications must also be constructed to consider disparities between groups with respect to SES in tailoring messages to target the same problem in different groups.

Moreover, the interaction among health, behavior, and communication conveys the applications, contributions, and lessons of various health communications programs that address such topics as reproductive health, family planning, infectious diseases and HIV/AIDS, social marketing, crisis management, and health literacy. Health communications programs have the potential to prevent the loss of healthy life due to both infectious and chronic diseases such as diarrhea, tuberculosis, pneumonia, respiratory infections, malnutrition, cancer, and heart disease.

The role of communications research is evidenced in the United Nations Millennium Development Goals, eight of which were to be achieved by 2004. The goals are to eradicate extreme poverty and hunger; achieve universal primary education; promote gender equality and empower women; reduce child mortality; improve maternal health; combat HIV/AIDS, malaria, and other diseases; ensure environmental sustainability; and develop a global partnership for development. Of these goals, four specific health challenges are to eradicate extreme poverty and hunger, reduce child mortality, improve maternal health, and combat HIV/AIDS, malaria, and other diseases. To solve the problems posed by these development goals and offer readers a comprehensive understanding of the interaction among health, behavior, and communications, this book is organized into five categories according to the primary subjects of the chapters. These are:

1. Theoretical Perspectives in Public Health Communication
2. Methodological Perspectives in Public Health Communication

3. Evidence-based Perspectives in Public Health Communication
4. Public Health Communication: A Practical Guidance
5. Notes from the field

Each category devotes several chapters to the experience-based rationale for different public health communications programs and their development, implementation, and evaluation. The contributing authors come from diverse academic and professional backgrounds and share their thoughts and recommendations with great faculty and alacrity.

Each chapter brings its own uniqueness and ingenuity to explain the interrelatedness between health status and communications components. These components include channels, messages, target audiences, positioning, and intended behavioral changes. The papers also demonstrate how intervention complexities are associated with the desired health outcomes. Such complexities include variables associated with channels and factors affecting the scope of messages. These include environment, socioeconomic status, organization, planning, and management. It is important to keep in mind that the relationship between these factors and health outcomes cannot easily be identified as causal. Today's practice of following "pattern variables" to explain intervention complexities and health outcomes poses future challenges and can determine the level of utility and demonstrated values attached to existing theory, methodology, and evidence in communications. These challenges include accounting for confounder variables beyond the intervention, and ensuring that health outcomes are actual effects of the interventions and not attributable to external factors. Because of external factors such as SES, we cannot hastily conclude that any changes in health status are due to the communications interventions themselves. To this effect, communications require rigorous monitoring and evaluation of processes, results, and impact. The chapters examine how theories, methodology, and evidence explain the interwoven elements of intervention that affect the health of a population. In doing so, the interactions among health, behavior, and communication are illuminated.

Focus of this Book

The context for the content of this book is a triangular interplay among three components: health, behavior, and communication, as shown in Figure 1. These components represent major challenges in public health communication and service delivery, which will be addressed at length by the individual chapters.

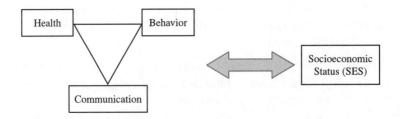

Figure 1. The Interplay among Health, Behavior, and Communication in Relation to SES

The health component considers issues related to the present burden of disease, behavioral aspects of disease, access to services, and cost of services. Its relationship to behavior and communication is critical in that health-promotion messages often focus on the adoption, alteration, abandonment, or altogether rejection of particular behaviors that have an impact on health. Communication can affect attitudes and behavior, which in turn influence health. Summary measures of population health include mortality, disability, and survival free of disability. It is important to remember, however, that health is not an outcome in itself; rather, it is actually a part of all the processes that result in the ultimate aim of high human functioning, productivity, and good quality of life.

The behavior component takes into account factors such as social context, individual characteristics, environmental factors, economic development, and cost-benefit ratios, as well as beliefs, rituals, and practices. These can enable, deter, or reinforce behaviors. Behaviors such as drug use, smoking, and exercise can often be influenced by persuasive information. For example, successful anti-tobacco campaigns in Poland, Thailand, Brazil, and South Africa show that—even amid powerful advertising and lobbying by tobacco companies—multi-level leadership, resource mobilization, and education campaigns can significantly overcome tobacco use.

The communications component addresses the importance of message design and dissemination, the role of theory; evidence-based best practices, products, and media materials; and social marketing strategies. The behavioral impact, scalability, and sustainability of communication programs will be discussed. In the effective communication of health messages, public health professionals must continue to surmount significant hurdles. These include inadequate infrastructure, political obstacles, and the use of Behavioral Change Communications, and information education communications to affect health promoting behaviors.

The five sections presented in this book analyze how to effect solutions to the above challenges within the context of public health theory and practice. Many of the experiences highlighted here are the fruits of years of best practices and lessons learned. Based on these analyses, recommendations are provided to meet the challenges in the interest of health promotion.

Several issues are intimately linked with the utility, value, and problem solving of public health communications. The questions at the start of each chapter are posed to address them.

Public Health Communications Utility, Value, and Challenges

Overview

The role of theory in health communications is to provide a sound framework on which health campaigns can be based and evaluated. Theories applied in health communications programs include the Health Belief Model, Precede-Proceed Model, Transtheoretical Stages of Change, Theory of Reasoned Action, and Diffusion of Innovation. In this section, Chapter 1 deals with the FOMENT model and Diffusion of Innovation (DOI) as a synergistic theoretical framework in public health communications. FOMENT is proposed as an addition to the DOI theory, to complement DOI's effectiveness at organizational and managerial levels, and to increase adoption of innovations. FOMENT can combine with DOI to address social change, economic development, and sustainability by analyzing the lack of adoption and support of innovations by organizations. FOMENT has the power to build capacity for organization and planning at a management level, as well as boost diffusion of innovation on the level of public health organizations. Thus, it focuses beyond simply the individual to encompass groups, and allows individual characteristics to be integrated into organization, planning, and management levels of groups.

Chapter 2 reviews social marketing and its potential contributions to a modern synthesis of social change. Social marketing is, "The use of marketing principles and techniques to influence a target audience to voluntarily accept, reject, modify, or abandon a behavior for the benefit of individuals, groups, or society as a whole."[2] Genuine social marketing focuses on both external (access to resources, new services, and fewer barriers) and internal (clever or persuasive messages) influences on behavior.

Chapter 3 discusses the *Push and Pull Factors in Changing Health Behavior: A Theoretical Framework*. The author describes systematic approaches used to influence knowledge, attitudes, and behavior. He also explores the critical role of what he terms "push and pull" factors that increase the rate of adopting new health behaviors.

Chapter 4 assesses social change interventions that are geared to produce attitudinal and behavioral change to improve a group's wellness. Social change is defined as an iterative process in which community dialogue and collective action produce a shift in a community that improves the health and welfare of its members. In this process, a catalyst sparks community dialogue, which leads to collective action. The model of social change can be applied to reducing HIV/AIDS-related stigma and discrimination.

The second chapter (Chapter 5) deals with applications of observational research in global health communications. Observational research can prove invaluable for defining problems, formulating research questions, and analyzing data. This approach can be applied to key health issues at the global level.

Chapter 6 speaks to social mobilization as a tool for outreach programs in the HIV/AIDS crisis. Social mobilization is a process for uniting multi-sectoral community partners to raise awareness, demand, and progress for the initiative's goals, processes, and outcomes. As background, concepts of social mobilization will be illustrated by examples from the field, as well as a discussion of good practices, and lessons to be learned on social marketing..

Chapter 7 focuses on the use of social networks in child survival programs and HIV/AIDS. Social networks, or interactions and linkages among people in a community, and their resultant social capital have become increasingly incorporated into research and implementation programs. Social networks contribute to positive care-seeking behavior by linking health facilities with communities. Use of identified networks at the community level can increase demand for health services such as vaccinations, health information dissemination, HIV/AIDS treatment and prevention, and effective disease surveillance.

Chapter 8 examines Sex, Soap, and Social Change: The Sabido Methodology. The Sabido Methodology is a behavioral change communications approach to develop mass-media serial dramas to promote social change, favorable attitudes, and healthful practices. A circular model of communications and a two-step flow theory of communications are applied to behavior change within the community. Key steps in developing a Sabido-style serial drama include formative research, literature reviews, media analysis, social services infrastructure analysis, moral framework, plot and character construction, episode production, scripting, and summative research. The entertainment education product can have lasting health impacts.

Chapter 9 focuses on quality communication during a public health crisis. Establishing and maintaining pre-crisis relationships and public relations are vital to help organizations effectively manage/respond to a crisis. Relationship maintenance strategies include access, disclosure or openness, assurances of legitimacy, networking, sharing of tasks, and integrative strategies of conflict resolution. Critical elements of relationships that involve an organization and its constituents are control mutuality, trust, satisfaction, and commitment.

Chapter 10 explores Community-Assisted Marketing Strategies and how they can broaden a community's role in health behavior change marketing interventions. This theme underscores the importance of active community participation in program design, implementation, and evaluation, because it increases the effectiveness of behavior change campaigns.

Chapter 11 examines "Reproductive Health: A Communication Challenge in the Twenty-first Century." Communications processes underlie changes in knowledge, attitude, and health behavior (preventive and curative) via personal channels, family, health sector (governmental or nongovernmental organization), and mass media. Various case studies (Safe Motherhood, Emergency Contraceptive, and Nonpermanent Contraceptives) show that an evidence-based framework is critical for communications strategies to effectively confront the reproductive and sexual health challenges of the twenty-first century, such as family planning, antenatal care, and the HIV/AIDS pandemic.

Chapter 12 deals with expanding the market for low-dose oral contraceptives in urban North India. Programs such as Goli ke Hamjoli (Friends of the Pill) engage the private sector (doctors, chemists, opinion leaders, civic groups, professional organizations, and the media) to expand the use of commercially available birth control pills. Goli ke Hamjoli shows great health impact, namely the increased use of oral contraceptive pills among urban women.

Chapter 13 assesses the "Importance of Client-Provider Interactions (CPI): Evidence from Family Planning Programs." The key processes in CPI are interpersonal communications; confidentiality/privacy; informed choice; individualized care; dynamic interaction; avoidance of information overload; and the provision and use of memory aids. Courtesy and responsiveness to the client's needs (i.e., the client being someone who seeks contraceptives) leads to increased awareness of contraception, its effective use, the continuation of family planning methods, and increased client satisfaction.

Chapter 14 examines ways to develop a more strategic approach to monitor reproductive health social marketing programs in developing countries. Now that reproductive health programs include a broad range of health products and services including Behavior Change Communications), in contrast to the family planning initiatives of yesteryear, the attendant social marketing programs must keep up with this evolution. This requires a product market shift from the focus on condoms and birth control to also encompass behavioral change.

The AIDS pandemic has taken a severe toll on human life, human resources, and the global economy. Though strides are being made in treatment of HIV/AIDS in the developed and developing world, prevention is a critical step to curb the pandemic's human toll. Thus, HIV/AIDS prevention interventions warrant greater application of communications strategies. To respond to this growing need, Chapter 15 focuses on "Improving Program Effectiveness Through Results-oriented Approaches: An STI/HIV/AIDS Prevention Program in the Philippines."

Child health is another area in which health communications can be powerfully harnessed to bring about health promotion and disease prevention interventions. Each year more than ten million children in low- and middle-income countries die before they reach their fifth birthday. Seventy percent of these deaths are due to just five preventable and treatable conditions: pneumonia, diarrhea, malaria, measles, and malnutrition.[3] Chapter 16 examines "The Role of Communication in the Integrated Management of Childhood Illness (IMCI): Progress, Lessons Learned, and Challenges in Latin America." IMCI is an approach to child health that focuses on the well-being of the whole child; reducing death and disability; and promoting improved growth and development among children under five years of age. IMCI care includes preventive and curative elements implemented by families, communities, and health facilities. Strategic components of IMCI are improving case management skills of health care staff, overall health systems, and family and community health practices.

Child health is heavily impacted by adult health behavior. Chapter 17 takes a look at "Linking Communication for Campaign and Routine Immunization: In Need of a Bifocal View." Chapter 18 reviews some state-of-the-art recommendations for communications campaign design for both chronic and emergency health problems. Health communications campaigns that address chronic and emergency conditions can efficiently change the health behaviors of masses.

Infectious disease holds a high priority position in public health, with the majority of the developing world still undergoing the epidemiological transition from infectious disease to chronic illnesses. Chapter 19 reviews "A Case Study" of WHO's experiences with strategic social mobilization and communication in the prevention and control of communicable diseases.

Effective communications is vital for an orchestrated response to a public health crisis. In hazardous situations where the risk level is high and affects a large and vulnerable audience, such as during the September 11 attacks, crisis communication serves as an important source of information and helps the public weather the fear, despair, and stress that accompany crises. This art is inextricably linked with risk communications, which includes crisis management and public relations. Chapter 20 touches on the development and implementation of the art of crisis communication.

Emergency preparedness has taken on a newfound significance following the September 11 terrorist attacks. The threat of bioterrorism, such as the use of anthrax as a biological weapon against the United States, has presented novel challenges for public health communications. Emerging is a need for health literacy for emergency preparedness, as in cases of SARS, West Nile virus, malaria, and Lyme disease. Accordingly, Chapter 21 examines emergency and risk communications to prevent and respond to biological threats. Vital to risk communications efficacy are information accuracy, credibility, and channels. Communication to prepare for biological threats involves careful planning and dissemination of messages.

Not only in crises and during emergencies, health communication also faces challenges during times of relative peace—when prevention is recommended. Communication for a nationwide anthrax vaccination program, for example, is explored in Chapter 22. Protecting the public from potential risk is no easy task and involves overcoming barriers in risk perception, levels of public trust, and message delivery. The SARS outbreak in 2003, for example, also provides useful lessons for program implementation.

Chapters 23 through 26 serve as a window into the processes involved in real-world communications programs. The work presented is more process-oriented than results-oriented, and provides practical guidance for health communications programs and policy. Topics explored include cancer communications, behavior change, reproductive health, HIV/AIDS programming, and anthrax vaccine education.

Chapter 23 in the Notes from the Field section describes a case study of "Cancer Communications Research for Health Promotion" at the National Cancer Institute. Health communication can reduce cancer risk, incidence, morbidity, and mortality, while enhancing the quality of life throughout cancer care (prevention, detection, diagnosis, treatment, survivorship, and end-of-life care). Regional Cancer Information Services and Centers of Excellence in Cancer Communication Research address the needs of patients.

Chapter 24 provides a thorough content analysis of anthrax in the media. The analyses in this chapter offer relevant insights into adequacy of the media's response to the threat of anthrax.

Chapter 25 speaks to building rapport between clients and providers and the implications of good rapport for medical education and the physician-patient relationship.

Chapter 26 in this section examines AED-USAID Strategies for Innovation and Behavioral or Social Change. The remainder of the section deals with patient safety and communication barriers, the promotion of reproductive health through television dramas, analysis of media content on the anthrax vaccine, and HIV/AIDS campaigns.

The epilogue discusses potential future directions in public health communications. An emphasis is on *Focused Behaviors, Innovations, and Organizations*. Issues discussed include improving program effectiveness through theory, evaluation, and results-oriented approaches. Furthermore, value is placed on integrating communications with service delivery. Other areas of priority are building indigenous capacity to maximize expertise in supporting multi-media and multi-sector initiatives; public-private partnerships; and the responsiveness and communications of national governments, donors, and programmatic agencies to incorporate public health agendas.

The collection of writings, reports, and analyses presented in this book can shed some light on how to overcome the communications challenges as they relate to health. It provides practical guidelines for implementation of effective health communications campaigns in several areas, including emergency situations and health crises. This problem-solving approach allows questions on three major levels—theoretical, methodological, and evidence-based—to be answered regarding the potential of communications in changing behavior and ultimately having an impact on health to improve the quality of life.

Each section of the book addresses a unique and major issue that challenges effective health communications. For theoretical perspectives in health communications, the overwhelming challenge is the predictability of health behaviors and outcomes based on experience-tested theories and models. For methodological perspectives in health communications, the highest hurdle is to ensure the robustness and comprehensiveness of planning and implementation strategies. For evidence-based perspectives in public health, a significant challenge is the replication of evidence. For practical guidance in health communication, the goal is to provide direction on a micro level—based on relevant lessons learned. These challenges in health communication not only offer practitioners a platform to brainstorm and develop innovative strategies, but they also open the door for building upon the foundations that have already been established. As the wealth of information in this book shows, each challenge can be met in an imaginative and singular way.

Notes

1. M. Ezzati et al., "Selected Major Risk Factors and Global and Regional Burden of Disease," *The Lancet* (2002).
2. P. Kotler, N. Roberto, and N. Lee, *Social Marketing: Improving the Quality of Life*, 2d ed. (Thousand Oaks, CA: Sage Publications, 2002).
3. WHO, *Millenium Development Goals*, United Nations Development Programme, 2004. http://www.undp.org/mdg/Millenium%20Development%20Goals.pdf

Diffusion of Innovations and FOMENT: A Synergistic Theoretical Framework in Health Communication

Muhiuddin Haider, Ranjeeta Pal, and Sarah Al-Shoura

Chapter Questions

1. How is Diffusion of Innovations theory relevant to public health?
2. What are the five key principles of Diffusion of Innovations theory that indicate a program's success? How are these principles applied to the examples given?
3. What are the main weaknesses of Diffusion of Innovations theory and how does FOMENT address these weaknesses?

Diffusion of Innovations: From Theory to Practice

The success of public health interventions, especially those promoting behavioral change, rests on effective communication. Communication of messages involves creation and sharing of information among people to reach mutual comprehension. Diffusion is a special type of communication in which the messages are about new ideas, behaviors, or products. Diffusion of Innovations (DOI) theory, after 40 years of application and testing by public health professionals, is widely used in countless health promotion and disease prevention projects as well as in programs outside of the public health field. This chapter discusses the theory's contributions and drawbacks with field evidence collected by public health experts over the years, based on the basic concepts of the DOI model. Several case studies will be presented to examine the effectiveness of and any weaknesses in the theory. Finally, newly proposed and complementary segments of DOI will be examined.

Effective communication is essential for every health promotion and disease prevention project. The promotion of good health often requires changes in perceptions, attitudes, behaviors, and practices among target populations. In doing so, many questions can be raised: How can social norms and traditions influence behavioral changes, and how is communication produced so that ideas and practices can be quickly and permanently adopted? After all, human behaviors are heavily influenced by beliefs, assumptions, and ideologies as well as by environment. In essence, appropriate communication methods, when suited to the audience's worldview, are crucial components of the efficacy of any public health intervention. Every new idea or practice introduced to a population can be viewed as an innovation by public health specialists.

Successful adoption of innovations begins with successful diffusion. A handful of people can have a significant influence on a larger group of people, resulting in a change in their behavior by modifying social norms or a value system. DOI is one of the most robust models that demonstrates such advances in health promotion and disease prevention programs as well as in many other global behavioral change interventions. DOI is primarily a sociological theory that uses social roles, norms, and networks to explain behavior and behavioral changes.[1] Its applications are vast and valuable in the public health field, ranging from education to behavioral change communication. The DOI model can be leveraged for successful interventions.

Background of Diffusion of Innovations

DOI theory was introduced 40 years ago by Everett Rogers. Diffusion is defined as a process by which an innovation is communicated through certain channels over time among the members of a particular social system. This includes both the planned and spontaneous spread of new ideas.[2] Diffusion is also a type of social change, that is, a process by which change occurs in the structure and function of a social system.[3] Social change (including decisions that affect public health) can occur as a result of certain consequences due to the invention, diffusion, and adoption or rejection of new ideas (i.e., innovations).

DOI theory has four main interacting factors: the innovation, which is a new idea or practice; a variety of communication channels; certain social systems; and a period of time. With these four basic elements, DOI works in five main stages. *Knowledge*, the first stage, happens when an individual acknowledges the existence of the new idea and begins to have some understanding about it. *Persuasion*, the second stage, happens when the person starts to hold a certain attitude or emotion toward this new idea that may be either positive or negative. The third stage is *decision*, in which an individual engages in activities that lead to a choice of the adoption or rejection of this new idea. After decision, *implementation* occurs, when an individual exploits an innovation. In other words, a person is actually applying this new idea or practice in his or her daily life. Finally, *confirmation* occurs when a person is seeking reinforcement or confirmation of the innovation when inconsistent messages appear.[4]

Innovations in public health have defining characteristics that affect and help to explain their differential rate of adoption. These are relative advantage, compatibility, complexity, ability to be sampled as a trial run, and ability to be observed. The utility and value of DOI in this field can be further appreciated in light of the fact that the optimization of these five qualities allows an innovation to be adopted more rapidly than others that lack them. Thus, health promotion or disease prevention programs can follow these guidelines to be more useful and productive for the targeted group of people.

DOI categorizes people into five separate types depending on their roles in this innovation adoption process. These are innovators, early adopters, early majority, late majority, and laggards. Rogers states that innovators are the small group of society members that adopt a new innovation at the very beginning.[5] These people, who serve as the gatekeepers of an innovation to the population they lead, are generally more educated, open-minded and exploratory.[6] Early adopters, a less adventurous group than the innovators, are next to adopt innovations. The early majority adopt the new practice just before the average population. The late majority involves one-third of the population that adopts innovations just after the early majority; these are the people who are most likely to adopt an innovation as a result of peer pressure. The last group of adopters in the process are termed laggards and are usually suspicious of the new idea, resulting in the increased time between knowledge and adoption.

These fundamental concepts, coupled with change agents, result in people's innovation-decision process leading to behavioral changes over time. Some examples of change agents are health workers from nongovernmental organizations (NGOs), government health officers, and educators in the field. Change agents are responsible for developing community communications regarding the need for change when a behavior or mentality is present that is detrimental to the welfare of the people. Change agents also function to establish information exchange relationships with community members, to diagnose health-related problems, to motivate clients to change, to translate intent into action, to stabilize adoption and prevent discontinuance of the innovations, and to achieve a terminal relationship.[7]

DOI theory has also made a significant contribution to the understanding and promotion of behavioral change. For example, DOI allows people to use innovations to fit their public health needs, which may vary by culture, economic conditions, abilities, and other circumstances. Thus, it is increasingly important to study how different innovations can affect the physical and psychological health of people in various ways. It is equally important to assess why a certain innovation, such as boiling water prior to human consumption in countries with unsanitary drinking water, is adopted or rejected.

Another aspect of DOI that is particularly useful to public health is the identification of societal norms—that is, the value system and accepted practices of a target community. For example, recognizing a community's cultural and religious principles that seem to oppose a health innovation is crucial to the adoption of that innovation, because such factors inevitably affect the innovation-decision process. Designers of public health campaigns need to identify these potential barriers prior to introducing the innovation into the community. Understanding the reasons behind these established norms enables the designer to circumvent major impediments to the diffusion process. Thus, emphasizing the benefits of a particular innovation, and catering to the societal norms of the community by making it complementary to those norms, leads to a greatly improved rate of diffusion and adoption of the innovation.

With the knowledge of the significant elements of the theory, it is essential to recognize the momentous role that DOI can perform in health promotion efforts, especially in raising health awareness, education, decisions, practices, and care.[8] One of DOI's particularly useful aspects as related to public health is its ability to identify the social norms and value systems of a target population. DOI also helps improve and customize innovations so as to fit a people's unique cultural needs. As stated previously, people depend on their social values, learned in childhood, to function in this world. These values give rise to a particular worldview that cannot be easily changed and can limit the human mind. In other words, people's value systems sometimes prevent them from seeing the truth or making the right decision. Understanding the reasons behind these established norms enables the program designer to avoid major obstacles to the diffusion process. For example, in the Philippines, designers of family planning projects must realize the influences of the Catholic Church's opposition to modern contraceptive methods. In this situation, to ensure the program's success the emphasis of the innovation must be shifted away from promoting modern contraceptives as a means to avoid having a child, to the more palatable message of using contraceptives as a way to plan for each child's future.[9] Emphasizing the benefits of a particular innovation, and changing the communication to coincide with the societal norms of the community leads to a greatly improved rate of diffusion and adoption of the innovation.[10] The adoption of modern methods of family planning by millions of men and women in the third world is already a proven success—with credit given to the DOI model. Given the diverse cultural backgrounds and complicated social structures, the Population Reference Bureau estimated in 2002 that 60 percent of married women of reproductive age in developing countries use some form of family planning, compared with 68 percent in developed countries during the same year, since the first family planning project launched in India in the 1950s.[11]

In the area of public health, the consequences of innovations have a significant impact on the wellness of communities and populations. Consequences are the changes that occur to an individual or to a social system as a result of the adoption or rejection of an innovation. Therein lies a significant value of DOI in public health. An essential link in health promotion and disease prevention is the successful communication of messages to enhance the wellness and decision-making capacity of populations and communities. Thus, disseminating effective messages regarding health education and health behavior is a critical component of most public health programs. DOI theory serves as an invaluable tool that can be utilized to promote adoption of health messages within a community.

The results of the adoption of innovations, as part of the application of the DOI theory, have significant impacts on the wellness of the communities and populations. These outcomes are the changes that are observable in an individual or in a social system as a result of the adoption or rejection of an innovation. In a Nepal vitamin A promotion project using the DOI model, certain households grew kitchen gardens. These households demonstrated, as innovators, the great improvement in well-being that can be achieved from increased vitamin A intake provided by kitchen garden products. The neighbors of the innovative households observed the changes resulting from the adoption of vitamin A-improved gardens, and began to keep kitchen gardens themselves. At the end of the first two years of the project, there were fewer than 100 kitchen gardens among the target families. However, within one year after initiation of the communication campaign, the number of target families increased tenfold.[12] Effects from innovations can be more persuasive than many other tactics because, for many cultures and societies, results that can be seen are more trusted than those that cannot.

This also explains why programs with only a few innovators serving as role models can still be successful in leading a large community to positive behavioral change.

With all of its strengths, DOI also has limitations in certain areas. As Haider and Kreps assert, DOI tends to blame the individual for his or her rejection of a new behavior, rather than take into account that the person is part of the social system.[13] Also, whether people from different socioeconomic classes are equally affected by the benefits of the innovation is an issue that has not been thoroughly addressed. Additionally, DOI faces the pro-innovation bias that assumes a program should be diffused and accepted by all members of the community. This bias leads researchers to ignore the rejections that emanate from sectors of the population and thus fail to notice anti-diffusion elements that prevent people from adopting the new ideas.

CASE STUDIES

1. The Guy-to-Guy Project: Innovators in the Diffusion Process. This program, conducted by PROMUNDO, a Brazilian NGO, demonstrated how to involve young men as change agents in gender-based violence prevention and in sexual and reproductive health promotion interventions. According to PROMUNDO baseline research of 749 men from Rio de Janeiro ranging from 15 to 60 years old, 40 percent had witnessed some form of violence by men against women in their home, and 25.4 percent had used violence against women at least once.[14] Twenty-eight percent of 225 young men aged 15 to 24 years had already fathered at least one child. Starting from 1999, this program worked with young men from low socioeconomic classes through peer education. The results showed significantly reduced violence against women in the area as well as an increase in child-caring activities and prenatal care among young fathers.

In order to prevent violence against women, the innovation created for this project was education to counter stereotypes of men as the superior gender that deserves to have power over women. The first step in the project was to recruit young men from this district who were interested and willing to help prevent violence against women and promote reproductive health. After gaining awareness and knowledge from the project, these young men also became innovators for the program. They then served as change agents for the program; as peer educators, these young men were trained to reach other young men, using mainly interpersonal communication channels with the help of educational materials, condoms, a lifestyle magazine, and a play about reducing violence against women.[15] Working with peer educators, more young men became knowledgeable about gender equality and reproductive health issues. Consistent with the five steps of the innovation-decision process, the target audience gained awareness and formed a favorable attitude toward the new idea after observing the positive changes in the peer educators' lives. This persuasion phase can also leverage the influential capacities of the change agents in a target community. Furthermore, the interpersonal communication methods used in this program allowed more potential to convince late adopters and laggards to adopt the innovation.[16]

People decide to adopt a new idea or an innovation mainly based on their perception of the innovation, what they think others' perceptions of the innovation are, and their beliefs about the innovation as compared to other innovations, according to Dearing.[17] In this particular project, young men were encouraged by their peer educators to discuss frustrations, barriers, and emotions about violent behaviors and reproductive health in small discussion groups. By sharing this information, "minorities" became "majorities," as more people identified their feelings with those of each other. Potential adaptors, who often shared similar frustrations such as childbearing at a very young age and domestic violence, could also identify with this group, allowing them to gain positive attitudes or bonds toward this innovation. On the other hand, social influence was strong, especially when communicating through an informal network (in this case, an all-male group from a relatively isolated social class). This was an example of using a small-group approach to recruit leaders to organize further small group meetings, in a kind of self-sustaining diffusion process.[18]

2. Communication Impacts: Philippines Family Planning Projects. Created by the Philippines' Department of Health between 1993 and 1996, a series of communication programs significantly increased modern contraceptive usage in the Philippines from 40 percent to 48 percent, an average increase of 2.66 percentage points per year.[19] Basic components of the campaign encouraged couples to visit their family planning providers, as well as to select modern family planning methods of their choice. Facing great opposition from the Catholic Church, programs carefully chose slogans and messages to show that the aim of family planning is not so much to avoid having children, as to provide the opportunity to love each child better by planning for each appropriately. Thus, the mass media campaign also focused on presentations by both professional and nonprofessional community members discussing the value of a planned family as a way to have more time to love and enjoy one's children. Also included in the communications were a series of radio and television advertisements representing the "voice of the people" on why they support family planning.

According to Smith, at least five key principles of DOI theory have proven to be powerful indicators of a program's success: relative advantage of the new idea over what people are already doing, compatibility with their constraints, behavior that is easy to accomplish, behavior that can be completed in installments, and observable results.[20] The Philippines family planning projects can be analyzed in these five categories. First, modern contraceptive methods are clinically proven to be effective in preventing unwanted pregnancies. Mass media campaigns in this program used testimonials from actual users and professional health providers to communicate this fact to the public. The benefits of modern contraceptive methods also served as reinforcement of the innovation, which helped to spread favorable attitudes toward family planning methods. As Haider and Kreps indicate, the effects of innovation have significant impact on the wellness of communities because all interventions are trying to achieve the outcome of adoption of an innovation.[21] Secondly, careful selection of the main message encourages more people to obtain contraceptive products without any opposition from their religious traditions or the social system. This demonstrates another beneficial aspect of the DOI model: the identification of the social norm prior to project design and implementation, resulting in an efficient diffusion process that avoids resistance stemming from social circumstances. Thirdly, the mass media was used along with interpersonal communication methods in order to make information and products widely available and easily accessible. Lastly, as the use of modern contraceptive methods began to show an obvious decrease in the number of unwanted pregnancies among the users, more people came to adopt the new methods.

Research shows that people usually do not take any action, especially with regard to something new, unless they have sufficient knowledge of it, have a positive attitude toward it, and have talked to others about it.[22] Through organized communications (such as the mass media), and through interpersonal communications of the new idea (such as social networks and natural diffusion processes), an increasing number of couples became familiar with the modern methods. This result carried the extra benefit of showing real-life, widespread positive results inside the community, triggering the later adopters to be convinced that modern contraceptive methods are an option worth subscribing to—and so they did.

3. Diffusion Theory and Drug Use. In 2001, Roberta Ferrence published a study evaluating the application of the DOI model to a number of drug-related health projects.[23] The projects under scrutiny focused on illicit drug use (mostly opium, some tobacco) and included programs that used spontaneous diffusion, and planned diffusion. Spontaneous diffusion in this situation refers to the natural, unplanned proliferation of drug use in a specific community. Planned diffusion refers to interventions that aim to change behavior by diffusing programs to targeted populations.

Studies of natural diffusion in the health field began principally with a study conducted by Coleman, Katz, and Menzel in 1966 of the diffusion among physicians of a new antibiotic.[24] The results showed a method of adoption consistent with the DOI's proposed categories for types of adopters (innovators, early adopters, early majority, late majority, and laggards). The epidemic model of diffusion, used in many programs, uses the language of epidemics instead of that of communications, describing the individuals of the population as "susceptible" or "not susceptible" to the diffusion.[25–29] This sort of study shows diffusion spreading through the same networks by which a disease would disseminate: schools, places of work, neighborhoods, prisons, friendship networks, and so on. For example, new drugs and tobacco use have been shown to distribute through friendship networks,[30–32] supporting the factors of diffusion proposed by DOI theory. Rates of smoking, for example, have been found to vary greatly between different economic, age, and education cohorts.[33] These studies did not plan the spread of the innovation through the DOI model, but the findings did show, in retrospect, that the dissemination of the product or behavior did concur with the processes proposed by the DOI theory. Studies of planned diffusion, on the other hand, utilized the DOI theory in the design of their interventions. These more recent projects, usually in the public education and health fields, showed success by focusing on social construction through the use of the DOI model to accomplish rapid changes in behavior in a population.[34–35] The use of mass media campaigns has proven to substantially improve results when compared to campaigns void of mass media utilization, for example, in needle exchange programs.[36] Geared toward a segment of the population with higher education, Oldenburg and colleagues researched the progress of diffusion when applied to primary care physicians' hazardous alcohol use.[37] The study's implementation of increased training and support resulted in higher rates of related screening and counseling. The DOI model has also been applied to programs focused on policy. Klingemann and Klingemann encouraged the adoption of a "medically controlled prescription of heroin."[38] This program, though successful in the aspect of diffusion, showed the strength of societal traditions and beliefs when it proved "countries whose values were more compatible with heroin trials were more likely to adopt them."[39] Many peer-led programs have also demonstrated success in applying DOI theory to peer systems.[40]

This research review shows substantial evidence for the DOI theory's accuracy "as an empirical model that describes the initial introduction and spread of a new substance or a new form of a substance."[41] Ferrence added to this critique, "the exception to this, in many of the studies, is the lack of consideration of economic and other forms of availability. Perhaps this could be inferred as part of relative advantage or reduced risk, but a case could be made that these attributes should be included explicitly." Ferrence also pronounced that rates of diffusion and adoption beyond those occurring at the initial diffusion are difficult to accurately predict by use of DOI theory. It is suggested by Ferrence that a combination of natural diffusion and planned diffusion be utilized in order to maximize both implementation and maintenance of programs. In other words, one should research the diffusion mechanisms already in place in a population and plan to target those systems. This concept is addressed by Everett Rogers's notion of communication channels and social systems as factors to be identified and addressed through DOI models. Ferrence concluded in her study that DOI theory has been proven to deserve "an important place in the repertoire of those who study changes in drug use and interventions directed at reducing harm."

4. Putting Empirically Supported Treatments into Practice: Lessons Learned in a Children's Mental Health Center. Schmidt and Taylor formed their study based on the need to implement proven quickly and thoroughly treatments in order to improve service accountability rates in the mental health field.[42] The plan is to develop cooperation with the clinicians, administrators, and innovators in order to disseminate the use of the empirically supported treatments (ESTs) in the organization's daily practice as part of their full-service delivery system. Schmidt and Taylor take the position that "behaviorally oriented therapies make up the vast majority of outcome studies that meet rigorous scientific standards for most childhood disorders." Lonigan and Elbert provide reviews.[43] Schmidt and Taylor reference the successful and empirically supported Incredible Years Parenting Program (see Webster-Stratton[44]), which was adopted in an applied setting.

The initial implementation process was conducted over a three-year period and included clinician training, the actual intervention, and a one-year follow-up with the families. The training used only clinicians motivated to implement the EST, and included education on social learning theory in terms of disruptive behavior in children, training on exact methods to utilize, modeling activities, peer-learning, and a workshop. To implement the EST treatment program, Schmidt and Taylor emphasize, "developing a collaborative working group,... making the decision process clear,... and pilot testing and organizational commitment to EST use."[45] In the development of the working group, the study emphasizes that clinicians and administrators must be united toward the same goal and work with an innovator, who will champion the project and oversee all implementation and adoption processes. In the statement of the decision process, the authors claim that sometimes practitioners rely on "clinical judgment" and "clinical opinion" instead of scientific evidence; this subjective practice needs to be avoided in order to conduct the implementation using "objective and relevant criteria of success." The process of implementation begins with a pilot group of early adopters who perform a trial program, which is then evaluated by the collaborative group (clinicians, administrators, and the innovator) and sent out for broader adoption. The processes of development, implementation, and evaluation of this project led to the creation of a "lessons learned" list authored by Schmidt and Taylor of key points for each member of the trio working group to focus on throughout the course of the execution of the project. The authors also strongly suggest that an innovation be surrounded by the proper infrastructure to ensure success. These recommendations are advisable in using the DOI model across the mental health settings and possibly in other situations as well.

Key Recommendations for the Successful Adoption of ESTs in a Clinical Setting

INNOVATOR

- Possess a legitimate influence and opinion in the adoption process.
- Have the time needed to network with external experts and obtain background information and research on the EST model.
- Provide information about the EST within the organization and advocate for the benefits of the model to the clients and the organization.
- Encourage early adopters of the EST to take on the role of "change agents."
- Support clinicians in taking the step from the "ideal" use of ESTs to the real-world of clinicians.
- Provide organization and communitywide training on the EST model.
- Build in community linkages to support and also participate in EST use.
- Advocate for and support program evaluation of EST intervention.

CLINICIAN

- Take the time to thoroughly learn the theoretical model and content of the EST program.
- Participate in a peer-learning group and discuss issues regarding the EST adoption.
- Obtain supervision and consultation from someone with expertise in the EST program.
- Emphasize a slow, comprehensive learning process.
- Initially conduct co-therapy with someone who is familiar with the EST model.

- Examine how the EST can best be adapted for use with the client base.
- Personalize the EST for the individual clinician while maintaining treatment integrity.
- Find ways to maintain enthusiasm and emotional energy in using the EST program.

ADMINISTRATOR
- Allocate special money for training in EST model(s) and to pay for external consultations.
- Allow for a slow adoption process.
- Give clinicians extra time to competently learn the EST approach.
- Have an all-or-none attitude about EST implementation.
- Take care of administrative issues, thereby freeing clinicians to do the clinical work.
- Build in organizational incentives and rewards for using the EST model.
- Choose early adopters who are enthusiastic and natural leaders within the organization.
- Provide informal or formal recognition to an innovator who will support the adoption process.
- Take an active "clinical" role in EST implementation.
- Proactively deal with destructive criticism and gossip.
- Provide open channels of communication to deal constructively with legitimate problems and issues.

Examples from the Field

The following are selected examples to illustrate the application of DOI to public health.

Romania's Love Plus Campaign to Improve Safe Sex Practices and Prevent HIV/AIDS

- Adoption of regular condom use by Romanian youth was not demonstrably incorporated into sexual practices initially.
- By incorporating the DOI model into the social marketing intervention, Population Services International was able to close the gap between raising awareness of condom use and the actual implementation and ongoing use of that innovative product.

Application of DOI to the RESULTS Advocacy Approach

- The RESULTS innovation in the advocacy field via volunteer action is to empower ordinary citizens to change their attitudes (from indifference to activism) toward government policies that harm the poor and hinder their transition out of poverty.

- The process of individual transformation from political apathy and hopelessness to action and involvement as leaders is considered a form of behavioral change, which results in the perception that "I can make a difference or do something about it." The adoption of this innovation impacts global health issues related to poverty such as control of AIDS, tuberculosis, and malaria, and effective interventions.

DOI and the ISHI (*Ishi* means *"Live"* in Kiswahili) Youth HIV/AIDS Multi-media Campaign in Tanzania

- The ISHI campaign emulates the DOI model in an HIV/AIDS prevention effort to diffuse the innovation of condom use among 14–25-year-olds in Tanzania. The main objectives of the ISHI campaign were to (1) increase perception of risk of HIV/AIDS among youth in Tanzania, (2) increase the number of youth delaying sex or abstaining, and (3) increase the number of youth seeking sexual health services including voluntary counseling and testing. These objectives include the challenge to reduce stigma associated with HIV/AIDS and to increase the number of youth who use protective measures (condoms) if they are sexually active.

- The recognition of a problem or need stimulates research and development activities designed to create an innovation to solve the problem or meet the need. Similarly, the ISHI campaign was deemed critical due to the immense research evidence indicating that despite being sexually active, many youth in Tanzania do not believe that they are at risk for infection with HIV/AIDS.

- The ISHI campaign clarifies myths and misconceptions about HIV/AIDS by using new social marketing messages geared for youth, the most vulnerable population. The campaign combines mass media advertising, community mobilization, and sports programs to send the message, "You can't tell by looking that someone has the virus. Abstain or use a condom."

- The innovation in this campaign is the use of mass media and youth trendsetters to promote abstinence or condom use, incorporating behavior change communication materials with messages to increase risk perception and youth outreach. The communication channels in this campaign included four main components: (1) mass media, media advocacy and contests including radio and TV jingles, press releases; (2) music concerts with popular local musicians and hip-hop stars; (3) educational behavior change communication materials including the billboards, posters, flyers, and information pamphlets with tested messages and factual information; and (4) community initiatives including road shows, university events, sporting events, and so on. This campaign initiative includes monitoring and evaluation of the process, outcome, and impact.

- One vital communication tool in the ISHI campaign was the change agent, who is an individual who influences clients' innovation-decision process in the desirable direction. This role was fulfilled by the ISHI Youth Advisory Group (YAG). The YAG group was composed of young trendsetters and professional youth who meet annually to design and review campaign implementation strategies, materials, and events.

- The most important lesson learned was the need to select very carefully the change agents who will influence the adoption rate of this challenging innovation to change sexual behavior among youth. Motivated change agents will influence the diffusion of the innovation.

DOI in the "Abandonment of Female Genital Cutting" Campaign in Senegal

- DOI was developed to address the gap between the introduction of a new behavior and the actual adoption of the behavior by a community or group.

- The innovation promoted here was the replacement of female genital cutting (FGC) with alternative rites of passage (ARP) that were culturally acceptable but nonviolent substitutes for genital mutilation. The *Tostan* educational program in Senegal succeeded in lowering rates of mutilation by encouraging community participation and educating all members of the group—with emphasis on the women in the group—as a means of ending FGC.

- Rights-based information and the health benefits of ending the practice of FGC were communicated to women who, once convinced of the message, then served as diffusers of the behavior change (replacing FGC with ARP) to other women, men, and the community at large. According to DOI theory, Tostan felt that societal context was crucial to success, so it employed an integrated approach to improve the socioeconomic status of those involved in the project, as well as developing other life skills recognized by the women as being important.

- Participants were empowered to break through existing personal or societal barriers and adopt the abandonment of FGC. The culturally appropriate methods to teach new concepts were based on African traditions of dancing, singing, poetry, music, and theater. These modes of information dissemination were transferred into the women's own communication techniques, in order to maximize the efficacy in transmitting the idea of abandoning FGC to other members of their community.

- By instilling a sense of dignity and power within the group, FGC practices were abandoned. Tostan was also successful in fostering women's ability to discuss taboo issues in a nonthreatening environment. It also made the issues surrounding FGC more visible to the entire community, thus conveying the message of the innovation.

Conclusion

As vital as a theory's or model's components are to the theory or model, true testing of the hypothesis cannot be accomplished unless the format is understood and followed with a course that was intended by the model's author. The previously described case studies follow the DOI model in its general intentions, identifying and incorporating the components and processes of the theory that were detailed in the model. This brought success to each study and survey, even with the compilation of projects highlighted here that are widely varied in purpose and even cross professional fields. The implications of this documented achievement in using the DOI model are widespread and diverse; multiple fields (especially in the social sciences) can incorporate DOI into policy, media, and community programs or aspects of their programs. Policy aspects that can be addressed in this manner include dissemination to gather support for policy advocacy and building awareness of the need for that policy; the diffusion of education regarding current policy; and the uniform enforcement of policy through multiple organizational structures. Aspects of DOI can use mass media outlets to spread the diffusion of public education; disseminate awareness for community policies that affect community services; encourage socially positive beliefs toward an innovation; and promote a product or behavior (possibly also modeling) by innovators. Community applications of DOI theory include improving efficiency and long-term results by spreading information through communication channels and social systems that are already present. In addition, focusing on established practices and behaviors of the target population that relate to the innovation can make the process of a population's adoption of that innovation easier—if they have a current behavior they can modify as opposed to fully adopting a practice or product that is foreign to them.

In the spirit of constant evolution, criticisms of the DOI theory/model must be addressed. The following is courtesy of Schmidt and Taylor's 2002 "lessons learned" portion of the publication relating their DOI-based program concerning a children's mental health center:

> Part of the difficulty in evaluating the diffusion model in planned diffusion studies relates to our inability to isolate the reasons for lack of success in certain studies. If the intervention does not work, is this due to lack of efficacy of the intervention or to a failure of the diffusion model? A larger body of rigorously designed studies with ample information on process as well as outcomes would increase our ability to evaluate the diffusion model.[46]

This frame of thought can potentially be applied to many social theories as well, especially those that are not so grandfatherly in age and use, and should be a reminder that all theories and models are in need of constant evaluation, modification, and varied application due to the ever-changing world and societies that scientists examine and strive to alter. Other criticisms of the DOI theory include a pro-innovation bias, the equality issue, a recall problem, and the individual blame bias.[47] Haider and Kreps identify needed improvements with the theory as:

> ...determining how to speed up the decision-making process, identifying appropriate change agents optimized for reaching different target populations, increasing understanding of adopter categories, making DOI more sustainable, building assurance for funding, and ensuring prospective rather than retrospective assessments of how different people respond to innovations.[48]

This critique spawned a concept created by Dr. Muhiuddin Haider of The George Washington University, based on his field experience in health communications. In order to maximize the rate and scope of diffusion, the public health field needed an operational paradigm to apply DOI. This is where Haider's new concept, FOMENT (focus, organization, management, environment, network, technology), can fill gaps in the translation from theory to practice. Haider proposed a strategy to improve the innovation-decision process of DOI as used in public health programs through the FOMENT system. The word "foment," as defined by the Merriam-Webster dictionary, means "to promote the growth or development of." The six components of foment are as follows: *"focus* on a specific behavior change; *organization* of the behavior change program; *management* that supports and approves of the behavior change plan; *environment* that is conducive to behavior change; *network* to diffuse innovations at individual and organizational levels; and *technology* available to diffuse innovations."[49]

FOMENT and DOI: A Synergistic Theoretical Framework in Health Communication

FOMENT is not proposed as a change, but a complement to the DOI theory, in order to supplement DOI's effectiveness at the organizational level and increase adoption overall. FOMENT's purpose is to combine with DOI to address social change, economic development, and sustainability by addressing the lack of adoption and support of innovations by organizations. To date, Haider's FOMENT shows great promise; its use has accomplished improvements in public health communications projects and is also applicable to programs utilizing other social theories that lack an organizational focus. Further research is encouraged to precisely determine the scope of relevance of the FOMENT strategy in additional public health communications campaigns, programs addressing other health aspects, and related social fields beyond the public health sector.

FOMENT has the power to build capacity for organization and planning at a management level, as well as boost DOI on the level of public health organizations, aside from that of the individual. FOMENT is a synergistic complement to DOI, and thereby a facilitator of its efficacy, in the organizational setting. For example, FOMENT aims at adoption of an innovation at the group level, whereas DOI focuses on the individual level. Haider explains that modifying a behavior change innovation for a group is easier than for an individual. Moreover, FOMENT analyzes interventions before implementation of a program whereas DOI examines the intervention after the program is already implemented. Thus, FOMENT minimizes problems in applying the intervention prior to its implementation, and thereby can maximize its effectiveness.

FOMENT is a strategic response to the challenge of how to integrate individual characteristics into organization, planning, and management levels. Whereas DOI explains these characteristics well, FOMENT actually serves to apply them in practice. The term "foment" itself means to promote the growth of, or incite, an idea. It also implies an attempt to stir up public opinion, thereby enabling proactive involvement of various organizations on multiple levels in a given public health initiative.

FOMENT is a strategy for the innovation-decision process; and this strategy serves to facilitate DOI in public health organizations. An organization is defined as a stable system of individuals who work together to achieve common goals through a hierarchy of ranks and a division of labor. One of the goals of diffusion programs can be to raise the level of good that potentially exists in a system or is accelerated by such an organization.

There are several areas of overlap between FOMENT and DOI that allow them to enhance one another's efficacy. The elements of the former can enable the elements of the latter to optimally leverage individual characteristics and thus improve the adoption of an innovation. For example, Focus can be correlated with Innovation. Organization and Management can be correlated with Communication Channels. Environment and Network can be correlated with Social System. Finally, Technology can be correlated with Time. Thus, FOMENT and DOI are complementary because they can be cooperatively assimilated into a powerful, optimized combination.

There are also consequential differences between FOMENT and DOI that allow each to productively supplement the other. As previously stated, DOI's main thrust is to bring about change at the individual level, whereas FOMENT strives to bring about adoption of ideas at an organizational (or group) level. Ideas concerning health behavior change are more easily modified and communicated by aiming at a group rather than an individual. Therefore, if innovations are adopted by organizations, which constitute the social system, the diffusion process gets a head start. In addition, DOI analyzes interventions after the innovation is in play. FOMENT, however, works before the intervention goes to the field. It acts as a means of revamping the entire planning process, from the time when a problem is identified or there is a need for a new behavior to be introduced into a society.

Furthermore, the concept of FOMENT has the potential to strengthen and build the capacity of DOI. This complementation is reflected among three different levels: (1) strengthening of theoretical and methodological bases; (2) capacity-building in organization, development, planning, and management; and (3) increased rate of innovation-adoption among individuals. Addressing each of the six aspects of FOMENT through DOI can greatly enhance the rate of innovation adoption within an organization.

This capacity for synergistic collaboration between FOMENT and DOI brings to light the need to minimize the gap in DOI theory for organizations in the public health setting. A divide that also needs to be bridged is between communities/individuals and governments/organizations. By means of FOMENT, the necessary theoretical tools can bridge this gap and facilitate the communication of innovations through public health organizations.

Potential limitations of DOI research can be overcome by incorporating concepts of FOMENT into the diffusion framework. As a result of this synergistic combination, FOMENT can catalyze the effectiveness of DOI and lead to a greater rate of adoption among individuals.

First, individual-blame bias in DOI can be overcome by integrating organization and management from FOMENT. Individual-blame is the tendency to hold an individual responsible for his or her problems, rather than the system of which the individual is a part.

Second, pro-innovation bias can be reduced by people and ideas coming from an organizational and management perspective. The pro-innovation bias is the implication in diffusion research that an innovation should be diffused and adopted by all members of a social system, that it should be diffused more rapidly, and that the innovation should be neither re-invented nor rejected.

Third, recall of innovations can be strengthened by Network, whereby messages are reinforced through interaction with other people, some of whom may be innovators. Diffusion research is dependent on recall data from respondents as to their date of adoption of a new idea.[50] Usually, the respondent is asked to look back in time in order to reconstruct his or her history of innovation experiences.

Fourth, how the socioeconomic benefits of innovations are distributed within a social system is an issue of equality. This can be addressed by the Environment component of FOMENT.

DOI in harmony with FOMENT needs to penetrate every aspect of capacity building, public and private health sectors, and collaboration with the government/donor planning process. The interactive relationship between FOMENT and DOI has tremendous potential to improve the capabilities of health-promotion intervention planning as well as implementation, to accelerate innovation adoption, and thus enhance the success of health campaigns.

It can be observed that the more successful innovations contain a greater degree of FOMENT's six components. In addition, the mutual and synergistic interaction between FOMENT and DOI can be leveraged by public health organizations and ventures to promote the efficacy of various innovations. As a result of such a productive complementation, the rate of adoption of health-promoting innovations, including preventive health behaviors and risk-reduction interventions, can be greatly enhanced to improve the wellness of communities.

The theory of DOI can serve as a powerful way to achieve favorable behavior changes for the sake of public health. Two pathways to accomplish this goal include a more thorough consideration of individual

characteristics in the innovation-decision process, and the incorporation of FOMENT into organization, planning, and management of public
health promotion programs.

Examples of the application of FOMENT to the prevention of birth
defects, to upholding patient safety, and to organizational relations will
be explored. In all cases, clinics at the organizational level must understand the innovations and incorporate them into their practice. This
requires collaboration from the planning and management sides. The
first case is the use of genetic counseling as a behavior change approach
to prevent birth defects due to consanguinity, biological, and chemical
agents in Saudi Arabia.

The second case illustrates how to overcome communication barriers between patients and service providers to promote patient safety.
Factors that contribute to error, such as patient factors, personal
impairment, and organizational or system failures can be surmounted
by communication strategies that address patient-provider characteristics at the organization, planning, and management levels. Innovations
can be targeted to hospital administrators and clinical directors to solve
system problems and improve patient care.

The third case is the functional relationship among NGOs, international donors, and the Government of Bangladesh as promoted by the
Bangladesh Rural Advancement Committee. This committee is an
example of an NGO whose micro-credit, women's education, and rural
development programs can benefit from the co-application of FOMENT
and DOI to planning and management levels.

The efficacy of various innovations within particular settings or contexts must be further evaluated and modified. DOI, along with FOMENT,
must be placed within the context of social change, economic development, and sustainability. By allowing flexibility of the diffusion theory to
cater to different target populations throughout time, environment, and
special circumstances, the DOI can reach a deeper and longer-lasting
impact in the scope of health behavior change.

It is important to keep a multi-level approach in mind when pursuing
social or individual change. A person's world consists not only of the
individual, his family and peers, and his community. It also is heavily
affected by the bigger picture that includes his community service
providers, the organizations and institutions in his country, his government, and the governments (and the populations that influence them) of
other countries that form foreign policy affecting the individual's socioeconomic situation, rights and freedoms, and daily life. These broader factors directly impact each individual's amount of opportunity for choice
of behaviors. Every community- or individual-based behavior change
project must keep this multi-level, multi-variable, cause-and-effect chain

in mind when developing plans for intervention. A focus on solely the individual or the community is a focus on a temporary fix for a diagnosed problem with multiple symptoms and confounding etiologies. Sustainable solutions must involve all levels of governments, organizations, health systems, community leaders and members, and smaller social systems in order to create a product for change that holds a lasting impact on individual and community health.

Acknowledgment: *Special thanks to GWU Master of Public Health graduates Lan Yu and Kristin Harris for their research and written contributions to this chapter.*

Notes

1. J. T. Bertarand, "Diffusion of Innovation and HIV/AIDS," *Journal of Health Communication* 9 (2004): 113–121.

2. E. M. Rogers, "Diffusion of Drug Abuse Prevention Programs; Spontaneous Diffusion, Agenda Setting, and Reinvention," in *Reviewing the Behavioral Science Knowledge Base on Technology Transfer*, eds. T. E. Backer et al. (Rockville, MD: NIDA Research Monograph 155, 1995), 90–105.

3. Rogers, "Diffusion of Drug Abuse Prevention Programs; Spontaneous Diffusion, Agenda Setting, and Reinvention."

4. M. Haider and G. L. Kreps, "Forty Years of Diffusion of Innovation: Utility and Value in Public Health," *Journal of Health Communication* 9 (2004): 3–12.

5. Rogers, "Diffusion of Drug Abuse Prevention Programs; Spontaneous Diffusion, Agenda Setting, and Reinvention."

6. Haider and Kreps, "Forty Years of Diffusion of Innovation: Utility and Value in Public Health."

7. Haider and Kreps, "Forty Years of Diffusion of Innovation: Utility and Value in Public Health."

8. Haider and Kreps, "Forty Years of Diffusion of Innovation: Utility and Value in Public Health."

9. D. L. Kincaid, "Social Networks, ideation, and contraceptive behavior in Bangladesh: A longitudianl analysis," *Social Science and Medicine* 50 (2000): 215–231.

10. Haider and Kreps, "Forty Years of Diffusion of Innovation: Utility and Value in Public Health."

11. E. Murphy, "Diffusion of Innovations: Family Planning in Developing Countries," *Journal of Health Communication* 9 (2004): 123–129.

12. K. Barker, "Diffusion of Innovation: A World Tour," *Journal of Health Communication* 9 (2004): 131–137.

13. Haider and Kreps, "Forty Years of Diffusion of Innovation: Utility and Value in Public Health."

14. PROMUNDO. Guy-to-Guy Project. Retrieved from http://www.promundo.org.br/download/Case%20Study.pdf, on March 10, 2004.

15. PROMUNDO. Guy-to-Guy Project. Retrieved on March 10, 2004.

16. Haider and Kreps, "Forty Years of Diffusion of Innovation: Utility and Value in Public Health."

17. J. W. Dearing, "Improving the State of Health Programming by Using Diffusion Theory," *Journal of Health Communication* 9 (2004): 21–36.

18. E. M. Rogers, "A prospective and retrospective look at the diffusion model," *Journal of Health Communication* 9 (2004); 13–19.

19. J. G. Rimon, Philippines Communication Outreach Accelerates Family Planning Use in 1993–1996 (Hopkins, 1998). Retrieved from http://www.jhuccp.org.pubs/ci/3, on March 19, 2004.

20. W. Smith, "Ev Rogers: Helping to build a modern synthesis of social change," *Journal of Health Communication* 9 (2004): 139–142.

21. Haider and Kreps, "Forty Years of Diffusion of Innovation: Utility and Value in Public Health."

22. Rimon, Philippines Communication Outreach Accelerates Family Planning Use in 1993–1996. Retrieved on March 19, 2004.

23. R. Ferrence, "Diffusion Theory and Drug Use," *Addiction* 96, no. 1 (2001): 165.

24. J. S. Coleman, E. Katz, and H. Menzel, *Medical Innovation: A Diffusion Study* (United States: Bobbs-Merrill, 1966).

25. H. Brill, *Sociological Aspects of Drug Independence in the U.S.A. and Great Britain: Importance of the Dimension of Social Contagion* (Amsterdam: Excerpta Medica International Congress, 1966), Series No. 129, 267–270.

26. N. Bejerot, *Addiction: An Artifiically Induced Drive* (Springfield, IL: Charles C Thomas, 1972).

27. P. H. Hughes and G. A. Crawford, "A Contagious Disease Model for Research and Intervening in Heroin Epidemics," *Archives of General Psychiatry* 27 (1972): 149–145.

28. M. H. Greene et al., *An Assessment of the Diffusion of Heroin Abuse to Medium-sized American Cities*, Special Action Office Monograph, Series A, no. 5, Special Action for Drug Abuse Prevention, October 1974.

29. J. G. Hunt, *Recent Spread of Heroin Use in the United States: Unanswered Questions* (Washington, DC: Drug Abuse Council Inc., 1974).

30. S. Einstein and A. Epstein, "Cigarette Smoking Contagion," *International Journal of Addiction* 15 (1980): 107–114.

31. M. Pfau, S. Van Bockern, and J. G. Kang, "Use of Inoculation to Promote Resistance to Smoking Initiation among Adolescents," *Communication Monographs* 59 (1992): 213–230.

32. A. Von Gernet, "Nicotine Dreams: The Prehistory and Early History of Tobacco in Eastern North America," in *Consuming Habits: Drugs in History and Anthropology*, eds. J. Goodman et al. (London and New York: Routledge, 1995), 67–87.

33. J. M. Borras et al., "Pattern of Smoking Initiation in Catalonia, Spain, from 1948 to 1992," *American Journal of Public Health* 90 (2000): 1459–1462.

34. E. H. Howze and L. J. Redman, "The Use of Theory in Health Advocacy: Policies and Programs," *Health Education Quarterly* 19 (1992): 369–383.

35. M. Dignan, P. Tillgren, and R. Michielutte, "Developing Process Evaluation for Community-Based Health Education Research and Practice: A Role for the Diffusion Model," *Health Values* 18 (1994): 56–59.

36. W. N. Elwood and A. N. Ataabadi, "Influence on Interpersonal and Mass-mediated Interventions on Injection Drug and Crack Users: Diffusion of Innovations and HIV Risk Behaviors," *Substance Use and Misuse* 32 (1997): 635–651.

37. B. F. Oldenburg, D. M. Hardcastle, and G. Kok, "Diffusion of Innovations," in *Health Behavior and Health Education: Theory, Research, and Practice*, 2d ed., K. Glanz, F. M. Lewis, and R. Rimer, eds. (San Francisco: Jossey-Bass Publishers, 1997), 207–286.

38. H. Klingemann and H. D. Klingemann, "National Treatment Systems in Perspective," *European Addiction Research* 5 (1999): 109–117.

39. Ferrence, "Diffusion Theory and Drug Use."

40. J. A. Kelly et al., "Randomized, Controlled, Community-Level HIV-Prevention Intervention for Sexual-Risk Behavior among Homosexual Men in U.S. Cities," *Lancet* 350 (1997): 1500–1505.

41. Ferrence, "Diffusion Theory and Drug Use."

42. F. Schmidt and T. K. Taylor, "Putting Empirically Supported Treatments into Practice: Lessons Learned in a Children's Mental Health Center," *Professional Psychology: Research and Practice* 33(5) (2002): 483–489.

43. C. J. Lonigan and J. C. Elbert, eds., "Empirically Supported Psychosocial Interventions for Children," *Journal of Clinical Child Psychology* 27(2) (1998).

44. C. Webster-Stratton, *The Incredible Years Parenting Program* (Seattle, WA: Seth Enterprises, 1992).

45. Schmidt and Taylor, "Putting Empirically Supported Treatments into Practice: Lessons Learned in a Children's Mental Health Center."

46. Schmidt and Taylor, "Putting Empirically Supported Treatments into Practice: Lessons Learned in a Children's Mental Health Center."

47. Rogers, "Diffusion of Drug Abuse Prevention Programs; Spontaneous Diffusion, Agenda Setting, and Reinvention."

48. Haider and Kreps, "Forty Years of Diffusion of Innovation: Utility and Value in Public Health."

49. Haider and Kreps, "Forty Years of Diffusion of Innovation: Utility and Value in Public Health."

50. Rogers, "Diffusion of Drug Abuse Prevention Programs; Spontaneous Diffusion, Agenda Setting, and Reinvention."

CHAPTER TWO

Social Marketing and Its Potential Contribution to a Modern Synthesis of Social Change

William A. Smith

Chapter Questions

1. What are the essential elements of a social marketing program?
2. How is a social marketing program different from concepts of traditional health education, social advertising, or social communication?
3. What role does social marketing play in social change?
4. What are the differences between social marketing and social advocacy?

Introduction

Social marketing has been in the literature since the 1960s.[1] Variations of social marketing are applied to promote childhood immunizations, diarrheal disease control, family planning, improved nutrition and diet, and environmental behavior. Too often, however, social marketing is used as a label for programs that are really social communications or social advertising activities. Media campaigns and the development of clever slogans and messages characterize these narrower applications. They often include sophisticated consumer research and targeting messages to populations, and are therefore often confused with social "marketing."[2] But genuine social marketing focuses on both external (access to resources, new services, and lower barriers) as well as internal (clever and persuasive messages) influences on behavior.

Social marketing is defined as:

A program management process (implies sequenced action steps);

designed to influence human behavior (not just knowledge or attitudes);

through consumer-oriented decision making (marketing);

leading to increased societal benefit (as defined by somebody).

Social marketing is characterized by five basic activities that constitute the basic project development process. It is these characteristics that make social marketing applicable to a broad range of social behaviors and programs.

Continual and iterative process of research, planning, action, assessment, and replanning.[3] Like many other program planning models, marketing uses a sequenced framework of assessment, planning, setting objectives, pre-testing, application, monitoring, reassessment, and modification. Unlike some social planning models though, there is a fundamental recognition in marketing that this is a *permanent* cyclical process. No one at Coca-Cola would argue, "Marketing Coke is something you do once, and then you don't need to promote it again because everyone knows about, and likes Coke." Selling Coke is something the company has to do every day in ever-new ways to meet an ever-changing consumer. There is, in many social programs, an assumption that behavior change is something to be "accomplished," and once in place, behavior should sustain itself through some natural reward or the power of some cognitive process. This leads to a linear planning model that is inconsistent with behavior change.

People and communities change over time. There are very few natural rewards for many of the behavioral changes that social marketing helps promote. Safer sex behaviors, for example, face continual competition from unsafe behaviors. People and communities need a permanent program of behavior change to reinforce existing adopters, as well as to help people at high risk become new adopters. Social marketing provides a framework for programs to continually assess, plan, and provide new support to meet the demands of those changes.

Consumer research.[4] People and their behavior are sufficiently complex to warrant a multifaceted (qualitative plus quantitative) and iterative research process to identify and track changes in people's knowledge, attitudes, and behavior that may influence the outcomes of interest to program managers. The key contribution of social marketing here has been *multifaceted research*—a skillful integration of qualitative and quantitative methods to produce practical answers to program design questions. Rather than asking, "What is it we don't know about a specific social behavior?", market research is focused on the answers to practical questions leading to program decisions; questions such as:

> "How are people different so that we can target their specific wants?"
>
> "What benefits do people care about most?"
>
> "Where are people most likely to want to go to get our products and services?"
>
> "What barriers are the toughest for people to deal with, and how can those barriers be lowered?"
>
> "How important is the price of a new behavior to different users?"
>
> "What messages (language, metaphors, images) break through the clutter of other messages and resonate as authentic for them?"

Audience segmentation.[5] People and communities are different, but can be grouped in ways that maximize certain similarities that often go beyond risk behavior or demographics. Programs can take advantage of these meaningful similarities and develop specific interventions to address for each segment identified. For example, all men who have numerous sexual partners are not alike. Consumer research can help make distinctions that are useful in reaching different sub-sets of this audience with greater precision and efficiency.

Exchange.[6] People do things in exchange for benefits. Behavior change often involves a cost to individuals or audiences (e.g., giving up a familiar behavior, or spending time, etc.). To give something up might require a program manager to offer some benefit in order to achieve a desired change; or successful behavior change agents must understand that people value many things other than health or wealth in this process of exchange.

Marketing mix.[7] A belief that people's behavior is influenced by four domains that people weigh against competing alternatives when choosing a social behavior: *Product/Service* (an idea, service, or behavior that offers a benefit); *Price* (the financial, emotional, social, temporal costs of the product); *Place* (distribution channels where the product/service is offered); and *Promotion* (methods for motivating or encouraging individuals to use the product).

To be considered social marketing, a program should demonstrate that the program planners gave serious consideration of all five factors. It is particularly this strategic consideration of the full marketing mix that differentiates social marketing from the concepts of traditional health education, social advertising, or social communication.

What about the Role of Social Marketing in the Use of Force and Social Sanctions?

The use of force to modify and shape human behavior is well understood. Through law and law enforcement societies shape the behavior of their people. But, in a democratic society, how can force be exercised? Isn't it necessary to market laws to the public? Even when it is proposed to make a law more equitable, doesn't the proposal have to be marketed to the politician, that is, the notion that force will be acceptable to the electorate? The regulation of alcohol through the prohibition law in the United States did not have popular support. Therefore, it failed. It has been common knowledge over the past few decades that cigarette smoking needs to be regulated, but it can't be done without popular support.[8]

Social marketing's principal contribution to social change is the notion that voluntary human behavior is achieved through an exchange of value. It argues that people change not because they are forced into action, but because they get something they value in return. The social marketing paradigm can be thought of as, "Let's make a deal." And therefore, the process of social change is to determine what the least costly item of exchange is that will produce the most change. The least costly, obviously, does not only apply to the dollar cost of exchange for either the provider or the consumer. It includes costs such as time or energy, and often subjective costs such as self-esteem, power, or prestige. Social marketing does not assume that the only motivating force in human behavior is money, but rather a wide variety of costs and benefits that vary from setting to setting.

Social marketing typically starts from a point where the change agent is clear about the desired change. The change agent wants to achieve a goal. The consumer is viewed as someone who must also benefit from the exchange and therefore must be understood. But the goal of social change is often established by the change agent and not by the consumer.

The change agent often has an established social mission— environmental protection, public health, or transportation safety. There is more often a specific behavioral goal such as: (1) get young gay men to use a condom with every partner; (2) get policy makers to increase the tax on cigarettes; (3) increase the number of parents who actively participate in parent-teacher organizations; or (4) increase the number of women in developing countries who breast-feed their child exclusively for the first four months after birth. The marketer often starts from the point where some behavioral goal is already established.

It is true that in some cases the specific behavioral goal can change as the marketer learns more about the target audience and about the problem. Take, for example, the history of the fight against infant mortality in developing countries.[9] The goal was to reduce the number of children dying from preventable causes. Diarrheal dehydration was the major cause of infant death in many countries, so the social marketing of oral rehydration was targeted as the specific goal. But social marketing programs that addressed diarrheal dehydration alone were ineffective in reducing infant mortality, because diarrhea was only the first threat to the infant's life. After surviving a bout of diarrhea, that infant went on to die of respiratory infection or some immunizable disease.[10] It was learned over time that to achieve the goal of lower mortality it was necessary to have a package of interventions. But the consumer did not arrive at this conclusion; rather it was once again the marketer.

Social marketing is often labeled manipulation. The argument is that the claim to consumer-orientation made by many social marketing advocates is indeed hollow because the marketer is the one who establishes the goals. The rest of the process is one to manipulate or "trick" the consumer into adoption. In a very real sense this can be true. But at the same time, the marketer's primary belief in exchange suggests that the "trick" must involve giving consumers something they *want*, not something the public health or environmental or transportation activist believes they *need*. Social marketing accepts the right of consumers to be as banal or as wise as they want to be.

The history of social marketing has been marked by the practice of social advertising and social communication. The reasons for this are multiple, including the presence of so many former advertising and public relations professionals in the field and the demands of the public sector clients for campaigns that raise awareness. At the same time there has been a significant growth in strategic marketing in a few government agencies[11]—the U.S. Institute of Medicine; the Centers for Disease Control and Prevention (CDC); the Environmental Protection Agency; the U.S. Agency for International Development; and more recently the U.S. Department of Transportation as well as many private agencies, associations, and nonprofits.

The history of social marketing in the U.S. public sector has been limited too often by an emphasis on social advertising. Fundamental barriers to marketing in public sector agencies remain. There is no true brand manager, no marketing executive, nor any integration of product development, pricing, distribution, and promotion in the public sector. Each of these functions is dispersed, often among agencies competing for public dollars. The National Institutes of Health develops vaccines. The Agency for Healthcare Quality and Research advises physicians. The CDC detects failures in the vaccine system. And state and local public health officials administer programs. Until this diffusion of responsibilities is remedied, social marketing will remain prey to the notion that marketing is nothing more than merchandising, advertising, and other forms of promotion.

The same has not been true of the nonprofit sector, however. Many of the major nonprofit organizations—from the AARP to the American Cancer Society—have demonstrated an ability to integrate strategic social marketing to influence not only what they say but what they do, how they do it, and for whom they do it.

Can Social Marketing Contribute More Than the Marketing of Products or Services?

Commercial marketing is not a tool with a single carefully designed purpose. Commercial marketing has changed from production-oriented marketing of the 1930s–1950s to price-oriented marketing in the 1960s to consumer-oriented marketing through the 1980s. With the emergence of new technologies in the 1990s, product focus became dominant again. Marketing morphs into new forms to absorb new knowledge and meet new needs in the marketplace. That is its primary strength.

The fundamental framework of both commercial and social marketing is supple, allowing new ideas and approaches to be integrated toward the single-minded end of influencing individual behavior, but it recognizes fully that social context is one of the primary influences on that behavior. In a democratic society where voluntary choice must be influenced to achieve results, and where the use of force has severe limits, marketing has arisen as perhaps the most pervasive unifying theory of social change. Social marketing adapts the capacity for change inherent in marketing to meet a changing set of social needs.

What Is a Benefit?

In social marketing, a benefit has three characteristics.[12]

- It is something the audience wants in comparison to something else that is already giving benefit.
- Of those things, it is something that social marketers can deliver to them.
- And finally, it is something that social marketers can convince people will be delivered, given the enormous skepticism prevalent among modern Americans.

The first characteristic is pretty obvious, but not always so obvious to determine. People do not always know what they want. Defining benefits is one of the greatest challenges of consumer research. How can social marketers distinguish between what people say they want and what they are willing to accept, given the trade-offs they know they have to make? People make wishes, but they also live in a real world where they compare one benefit against another. They also are not aware of all the possible benefits. How many people say, "I want a toothbrush that is battery operated and has my favorite cartoon character molded in three dimensions in the handle"? Creating a benefit often means putting two very distinct things together to make a surprising package the consumer would never have imagined. Good consumer research should focus on the broader interests and pleasures of the audiences—not just their attitudes toward health.

The second characteristic of benefits—"Can it be delivered?"—is perhaps the most challenging of all. Given limited resources, especially compared to the private sector, the ability of change agents to add a benefit (like molded cartoon characters) to services offered is hindered. Benefits need to be found that are either intangible or affordable. Partnerships with corporate America have become one vehicle for making benefits affordable. By working with Babies R Us, the National Highway Traffic Administration managed to offer promotional coupons for baby seats and get the word out about their importance at the same time.[13] But this kind of partnership is more difficult to imagine when dealing with a nonspecific product or service, as is often the case with behavior change promotion.

The third characteristic of benefits—"Can it be sold?"—has to do with credibility. Do people believe what change agents say? Do they believe that social marketers can deliver on their promises? It has to do with the ability to find an approach to communication that breaks down the natural skepticism widespread in a commercial America where everything is promises. The following scenarios take a look at some social and commercial marketing strategies that demonstrate some of these characteristics in action.

- Imagine a picture of a car seat installed in the front seat of a car. Beneath it, in large letters, are the words **LOVE SEAT.**

What is the benefit in this example? It is not safety—at least not explicitly. The benefit ties into what the seat represents, that is, love. It offers something that adults want to give—and want to be seen as giving. The result? New parents can call their own parents to say that they just bought little Joey his "love seat" instead of his car seat.

- Imagine an old wooden fence. Posted to the fence is a handwritten sign that reads something like this: "Children caught destroying this courtyard will be shot. Please protect your child from this tragic fate. Thank you. The Gardener."

Here's a twist. The benefit is how to avoid a negative consequence. This is done all the time; people are told they will become sick if they do X, Y, or Z. This message is somehow strangely credible because it is proximate. The implication is that there is a gardener and he may not be too educated, but he is serious. He might not be a child killer, but it is worth wondering, "Would he hit my kid?" Proximity and lack of "slickness" can attach credibility to a message and make a negative benefit more likely to be heeded.

- Here is a good, and probably familiar, example. It is a picture of an overweight 60-year-old man, lying out sunning himself in a two piece—yes, that is a two piece—bathing suit. Behind him are the words: *NO WONDER TOBACCO EXECUTIVES HIDE BEHIND SEXY MODELS.*

What's the benefit here? Well, the anti-tobacco folks tell the (almost naked!) truth while the competitor tells lies. But is it credible that this is a real tobacco executive? After all, this man is a model, too. So where is the truth? The truth is in the perception that the anti-tobacco people have it right and are clever. Arguably, the real benefit is the fact that the anti-tobacco folks are as smart as the competition and that it's good to be on their side. This ad says, "If you become an anti-tobacco person, you will be with a smart bunch of do-gooders, not some old bunch of fuddy-duddies."

- Hold onto your hats. This next one is pretty strong stuff. Imagine a young woman holding her bathrobe open with her right hand and her back to a wall. Kneeling in front of her is a transgender figure—perhaps a young woman; perhaps a young man. The woman in the bathrobe is pulling her panties down with her left hand to reveal a Gucci "G" shaved into her pubic hair.

Wow, this one is strong, and it is kind of obvious: sex. But what's sexy about a sad looking young man gazing at the shaved pubic hair of a boyish looking model and finding a Gucci label? Sexy? No, I don't think so. Gucci's reputation is to push the envelope. The benefit here might be, "Gucci will do anything for you. Gucci will be everywhere you want to be. Gucci will take any risk to make you happy." This also has the benefit of maintaining the brand's image and catching attention—breaking through the clutter of fashion messages Gucci competes with in magazine after magazine.

HITS HIM BELOW THE BELT

After too many, he'll offer much less. The facts of MIT life, based on experience — like the, um, lame side of wasted guys (5+ drinks). Find it in the MIT Tip Book: How to hold your alcohol, find condoms (fast), escape a roommate, avoid the freshman 15 and more. Written by MIT students for MIT students.

The Book of MIT Survival Tips. *after you really read it here*

Figure 2–1. "Hits Him Below the Belt"

Here's an example, as seen in Figure 2–1, of turning a negative consequence into a benefit if you don't engage in the behavior. "After too many, he'll offer much less...Written by MIT students for MIT students." And here's the second benefit: "Somebody like me"—another student—"came up with this campaign." This is a good example of how to sell a benefit that does not have any credibility unless it comes from one of your own.[14]

Confirmation Bias

In risk communication there is an interesting concept of confirmation bias that helps explain why some benefits are chosen over others. Conformation bias proposes that when confronted with information about a topic on which people already have a strong opinion (like paying too much for energy costs), most people divide the information into one of four categories and then deal with it in a particular way. For example:

- If I get some new information, I try to make it fit my previous conception.
- If I get contrary information, I filter it out.
- If I get complex information, I simplify it to fit my previous ideas.
- And if I get consistent information, I accept it as positive proof of my original position.

Imagine how helpful this set of concepts can be in terms of developing benefits that work. The predisposition to remain convinced of a previously held position is often the case, in which case, efforts to introduce contradictory information naturally fall on deaf ears.

What Benefits Do the Commercial Folks Use?

There is a well-accepted list of benefits that are used regularly by the commercial sector. These benefits are useful starting points to find ways to associate the newly proposed, less-than-pleasant behavior with something the target audience finds more appealing. They include:[15]

Taste	Romance	Rest
Comfort	Approval of others	Curiosity
Beauty	Superiority over others	Durability
Attractiveness	Physical well-being	Peace
Family well-being	Security	Excitement
Adventure	Fear	Risk
Social status	Fun and games	Sympathy
Efficiency	Economy	

There are several benefits on this list that are also old favorites of social marketers, for example, physical well-being, approval of others, and well-being of others. The key to success is to find a benefit or a set of benefits that can successfully compete against the benefits that compete with the new behaviors offered.

In Figure 2–2, Boxes A and B contrast two views of how social change takes place. In Box A Social Benefit is the result of forces that act through the individual, and the other acting through society. In this model, marketing is seen as targeting exclusively the individual, with advocacy marketing for external forces in society to provide benefits to deserving individuals. In Box B society and external changes are just as critical, but they act through changes in perceptions of people of their rights and the responsibilities of those in power or to blame for the social problem.

The dichotomy between A and B in Figure 2–2 has been reflected for years in the argument between advocacy and marketing. Advocates argue that marketing focuses exclusively on individual behavior, which results often in "blaming" the individual. Advocates further argue that advocation focuses on the institutional and environmental culprits that actually control individual behavior.

Exhibit

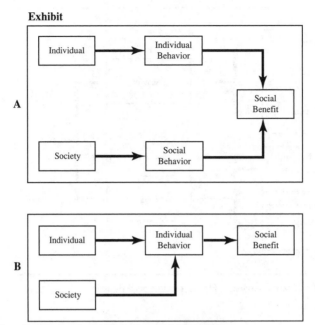

Figure 2–2. Contrasting Social Marketing with Social Advocacy

Marketing recognizes that there are institutional and environmental culprits, but they are seen as factors that influence individual behavior, not independent paths to social benefit. A lawsuit against the tobacco industry works not only by putting the tobacco industry out of business, but also by making it more difficult for a smoker to get a cigarette. But does anyone doubt that the moment cigarettes are banned universally, there would an illegal and violence-ridden trade in cigarettes? Smoking rates might come down temporarily, but like the prohibition of alcohol, some individuals will find a way to criminalize smoking and make a buck off segments of society who suffer from tobacco addiction.

It is important to get the logic right. Program planners must be cautious of these false either/ors. There is a search today among implementation agencies for clarity among the competing models of change. They want to compare risk communications, health education, social marketing, social capital, behavioral economics, advocacy, health communications, and on and on. The question is often posed: What works best for what problem?

The following, Figure 2–3, is a logic framework that might help. *A* represents the ultimate goal: improved societal benefit. *B* represents changes in human behavior necessary to achieve that goal (e.g., using

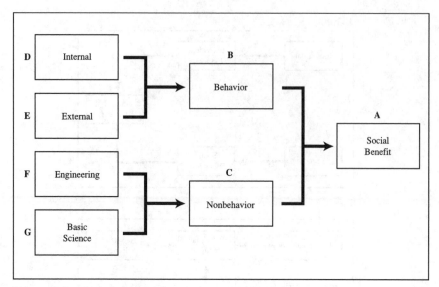

Figure 2–3. Logic Framework for Improved Social Benefit

seat belts, exercising, putting iodine in food consumption to avoid goiters.) C represents nonbehavioral means to achieve the same goal (e.g., air bags, a genetic modification in human susceptibility to obesity, and a law that requires salt to be iodized). D represents all the internal cognitive and attitudinal factors that influence human behavior (e.g., perceived benefits, self-efficacy, *perceived* social norms). E represents all the external, cultural, and structural factors that influence individual human behavior (laws inhibiting behavior, incentives, socio-economic status, discrimination, injustice, etc.). F represents the engineering capacity of society to produce nonbehavioral solutions. Salt can be iodized, for example, but it is not yet possible to manipulate genetic predisposition to obesity. G represents society's investment in basic science that will allow scientists to engineer specific solutions. A primary example is the enormous scientific effort to find a vaccine for HIV/AIDS.

Each of these domains represents potential targets of opportunity. In an effort to eliminate goiter in Nepal, the Nepalese can be taught to add iodine to their food. But wouldn't it be simpler to achieve this goal by iodizing salt and thus avoid the enormous complexity of changing individual behavior? This logic model provides a common frame of reference to debate whether choices made by change agents are sound, in their efforts to implement interventions. That is, by launching an attack on the largest target of change—the population at large—are changes being made to effectively integrate these interventions being addressed to the core problem?

What does social marketing contribute to any modern synthesis of social change? Its primary contribution is to show that the key principles of commercial marketing work on complex social issues. The concepts of exchange, competition, and segmentation are far more fundamental to human behavior than is usually assumed. They are supported by basic science emerging from psychology and sociology. Here are three suggested concepts that are fundamental for social marketing's contribution to the need for a modern synthesis.

Exchange. People do things in exchange for things they value. Understanding what people value is a key to influencing their behavior.

Segmentation. Individuals value different things at different times in exchange for different values. Therefore, grouping or segmenting people by their values related to a specific behavior increases the likelihood of identifying and offering a group the benefits they value.

Competition. People have choices. Therefore, almost all behaviors compete against other behaviors to provide competitive value to the individual. This suggests that the benefits offered must not only satisfy a value held by the individual, but they must compete effectively with other alternative behaviors open to that individual.

Tactically, social and commercial marketing can offer a plethora of tools and techniques, processes, and systems to address these three principles. But it is these fundamental notions that underlie effective social marketing and contribute perhaps to modern synthesis of social change.

Notes

1. P. Kotler and A. Andreasen, *Strategic Marketing for Nonprofit Organization* (Englewood Cliffs, NJ: Prentice Hall, 1991).

2. R. Rice and C. Atkin, eds., *Public Communication Campaigns* (Thousand Oaks, CA: Sage Publications, 2001).

3. A. Andreasen, *Marketing Social Change: Changing Behavior to Promote Health, Social Development, and the Environment* (San Francisco, CA: Jossey-Bass Publishers, 1995).

4. A. Andreasen, *Cheap but Good Marketing Research* (Homewood, IL: Dow Jones-Irwin, 1988).

5. R. Hisrich, *Marketing* (Hauppauge, NY: Baron's Educational Series, Inc., 1990).

6. Kotler and Andreasen, *Strategic Marketing for Nonprofit Organization.*

7. W. Smith, "Social Marketing: An Evolving Definition," *American Journal of Health Behavior* 24(1) (2000): 11–17.

8. R. Kluger, *Ashes to Ashes: America's Hundred-Year Cigarette War, the Public Health, and the Unabashed Triumph of Philip Morris* (New York, NY: Vintage Books, A Division of Random House, Inc., 1997).

9. Academy for Educational Development, *Results & Realities: A Decade of Experience in Communication for Child Survival* (Washington, DC: 1992).

10. Academy for Educational Development, *Results & Realities: A Decade of Experience in Communication for Child Survival*.

11. R. Hornik, *Public Health Communication: Evidence for Behavior Change* (Mahwah, NJ: Lawrence Erlbaum Associates, Publishers, 2002).

12. D. McKenzie-Mohr and W. Smith, *Fostering Sustainable Behavior: An Introduction to Community-Based Social Marketing* (Gabriola Island, B.C., Canada: New Society Publishers, 1999).

13. The Babies R Us coupon was created and distributed in February 2003 and February/March 2004 as part of the Buckle Up America campaign promoting safety belt and child safety seat use and is implemented by the Academy for Educational Development for the National Highway Traffic Safety Administration. More information can be found at *www.buckleupamerica.org*.

14. Save TFP, a student group on the MIT campus, oversaw the creation of the Celibacy Deviance campaign and the Conquer MIT guidebook, both of which carry messages about avoiding binge drinking. Implemented by the Academy for Educational Development in 2003 for MIT Medical, the group and its campaigns were part of an effort to reduce binge drinking among MIT students. More information can be found at *www.mit.edu/savetfp/index.html*.

15. R. Kaatz, *Advertising & Marketing Checkists: 77 Proven Checklists to Save Time & Boost Advertising Effectiveness* (Lincolnwood, IL: NTC Business Books, 1992).

CHAPTER THREE

Push and Pull Factors in Changing Health Behavior: A Theoretical Framework

Javed S. Ahmad

Chapter Questions

1. What are push and pull factors and how do they affect behavior change?
2. What is the purpose of a Broad-Base Health Communication Strategy (BBHCS)?
3. How does BBHCS address push and pull factors?
4. How are different communications theories and models integrated into BBHCS?

Introduction

Changing an individual's knowledge, attitudes, and behavior concerning an aspect of health demands a sound conceptual framework and a systematic approach. The process of health behavior change is complex. Some excellent conceptual models explain the process from different perspectives. The change in a target audience's knowledge, attitudes, and practice follows in stages. The framework described in this chapter builds on several theories and models—especially the Diffusion of Innovations theory. Additionally, this chapter outlines the "push and pull factors" that play a critical role in increasing the rate of adoption of new health behaviors and their implications for action programs.

In the last two decades, most likely as a result of rising concern about the HIV/AIDS pandemic, the topic of public health promotion and health behavior has come into the limelight. The severity and speed of the morbidity and mortality associated with HIV/AIDS worldwide defy conventional curative and preventive approaches that mostly rely on interventions such as vaccination, chemotherapy, quarantine, and hospitalization. During the early years of the HIV/AIDS epidemic in the United States, it became all too clear that unless disease-related behaviors of the high-risk population were changed, the disease would continue to spread like wildfire. This was the time when traditional health education methods were reviewed with the help of media agencies, and various information and education campaigns were launched to target high-risk populations.

These campaigns succeeded in slowing down the spread of the disease. But it was not fast enough. Practitioners of public health education were well aware that there was a gap between disseminating health messages and changing behavior. The size of this gap depends on many factors as the recipient of the message undergoes a process of comprehension and evaluation of the message before deciding to act on it. This process involves numerous factors such as the personality of the recipient, his or her wants and felt needs, perceptions, social, psychological and environmental influences, and an understanding of the perceived threat or risks. To a degree, the way messages are constructed, delivered, and reinforced also plays a critical role in the adoption of the suggested behavior.

HIV/AIDS poses an unprecedented challenge to the health authorities. The disease is as serious as malignant cancer, in addition to the added danger that it is communicable. It is unlike other communicable past epidemics such as plague, cholera, and tuberculosis, all of which were readily contained or treated with curative measures. HIV/AIDS is associated with sexual practices of largely young and middle-aged men and women. These practices involve values and norms of friendship, love, and strong sexual drives that are not easily influenced through health education alone. What is needed are better and more effective approaches, programs, and designs to get millions of men of all ages to wear condoms for each sexual encounter and to practice safe sex in general. There is also a need to change behavior of the drug addicts who use syringes to inject drugs and often share the needles. This group poses the biggest challenge for health professionals.

While the epidemic of HIV/AIDS in the United States led to an infusion of an unprecedented amount of cash for research and experimentation, health education theories and behavior change models have been in the making for over half a century. Almost every public health issue that involves a change in human behavior demands a well-planned and organized educational intervention. Over time, the practitioners began to evaluate and analyze what works and what does not, and why. Some of the large-scale, successful public health campaigns in recent history, including the use of seat belts and anti-smoking campaigns, yielded a wealth of information, research findings and many models of behavior change. Glanz, Lewis, and Rimer cited 51 distinct theoretical formulations in a review of 116 theory-based articles in two health education journals during a period spanning 1986 to 1988. "At that time, the three most frequently mentioned theories were: Social Learning Theory, the Theory of Reasoned Action, and the Health Belief Model."[1] Subsequently, the same authors reviewed 526 articles from 24 journals in health education, medicine, and behavioral sciences (from mid-1992 to mid-1994) and identified 66 different theories and models, of which 21 were mentioned eight times or more. When preparing for the third edition of their book, Glanz, Lewis, and Rimer concluded that 10 theories or models clearly emerged as the most often used. These were: Social Cognitive Theory (SCT) (sometimes referred to as Self-Efficacy Theory), social support and social networks, patient-provider communication, the Transtheoretical model, the Health Belief Model (HBM), the Theory of Reasoned Action, stress and coping, community organization, the Theory of Planned Behavior, and Diffusion Theory. They also included others such as social marketing and *PRECEDE-PROCEED* model for their practical applications.

It seems that there is a wider agreement in recognizing some of the theories and models, as evidenced in U.S. Department of Health and Human Services publications. In the latest edition of its publication, *Making Health Communication Programs Work,* social science theories, models, and constructs are categorized under: *Individual Level* (Behavioral Intentions; Communication for Persuasion, Stages of Change, HBM, and Consumer Information Processing Model); *Interpersonal Level* (Social Cognitive Theory); and *Organizational/ Community/Societal Level* (Organizational Change Theory, Community Organization Theory, and Diffusion of Innovations Theory).[2]

A Brief Description of Selected Theories and Models

The HBM is based on the hypothesis that "behavior depends mainly upon two variables: (1) the desire to avoid illness—or if ill, to get well—and (2) the belief that a specific health action will prevent or ameliorate illness. Specifically the HBM consists of the following dimensions: perceived susceptibility (subjective perception of the risk of contracting a condition); perceived severity (feelings concerning the seriousness of contracting an illness); perceived benefits; and perceived barriers (e.g., cost-benefit, side-effects, unpleasantness, convenience, etc.). It was determined that some stimulus was necessary to trigger the decision-making process. It was assumed that diverse demographic, socio-psychologic, and structural variables might, in any given instance, affect the individual's perception and indirectly influence health-related behavior.[3] However, the reviewers felt that evidence from 46 studies was strong for the "perceived barriers" aspect of the theory and weakest for "perceived severity" as a stimulus for action. This was, however, attributed to possible methodologic difficulties rather than a weakness in the model.

The Theories of Reasoned Action and Planned Behavior

Fishbein and Ajzen's theory of Reasoned Action originated from their work in 1975, which described that behavior change followed a person's intentions, while the intentions were based on his or her attitudes, which in turn were rooted in his or her beliefs.[4] The theory provides a framework to study attitudes toward behavior. According to the theory, the most important determinant of a person's behavior is **behavior intent**. The individual's **intention** to behave in a certain way is a combination of **attitude** toward the behavior and the **subjective norm**. The individual's **attitude** toward the behavior includes: **behavioral belief**, **evaluations of behavioral outcome**, **subjective norm**, **normative beliefs**, and the **motivation to comply**. If a person perceives that the outcome of performing behavior is positive, he or she will have a positive attitude toward using that behavior. The opposite can also be stated if the behavior is thought to be negative.[5]

Fishbein and Ajzen's theory gained popularity and has been applied in different settings for over two decades. Ajzen observed that the theory was particularly valuable when suggested behavioral change was in full control of the audience. When a person did not have the required resources, skills, and opportunities, the control was considered totally lacking. In most situations, behavior is located within this spectrum. To take into account such limitations, whether real or perceived, Ajzen added a third element to the original Fishbein and Ajzen model—the concept of perceived behavioral control.

Godin and Kok, in a review of The Theory of Planned Behavior, a companion theory of the Theory of Reasoned Action, stated that the former extends beyond the Theory of Reasoned Action. They observed that "perceived behavioral control can influence intention, as can the attitudinal and normative components. It can also influence behavior directly."[6] These theories underscore the importance of perceived social influence on behavior change. According to the National Institutes of Health, the theories support the idea that individuals' and society's (perceived) attitudes are an important predecessor to action.[7]

This is an important point that will be covered later in the chapter under the discussion of "push and pull factors."

The transtheoretical model, *Stages of Change*, states that behavior change is a process and not an event and that individuals are at varying levels of motivation, or readiness to change. Hence, different interventions are needed to suit their information needs. "Individuals do not change their behavior all at once; they change it incrementally or stepwise in stages of change. The stages most commonly used across research areas include: precontemplation, contemplation, preparation, action, and maintenance. Individuals do not typically move from stage to stage in a linear fashion, but often progress and then regress back to a previous stage before moving forward again. This change process is conceptualized most meaningfully as a spiral, which illustrates that even when individuals do regress to a previous stage, they can still learn from their prior experiences."[8] The model states that by knowing an individual's current stage, the change agent can help set realistic program goals. Tailored messages, strategies, and programs can be constructed to suit the appropriate stage.

Some of the theories and models that have gained popularity in recent years include SCT, *PRECEDE-PROCEED* Planning Model, Social Marketing, The Extended Parallel Process Model (EPPM), and Diffusion of Innovations.

Alfred Bandura's SCT describes behavior as being dynamically determined and fluid, influenced by both personal factors and the environment. In contrast to earlier behavior theories, SCT views the environment as not just a variable that reinforces or punishes behaviors, but one that also provides a milieu where an individual can watch the actions of others and learn the consequences of those behaviors. Bandura's major premise is that people learn by observing others. He considers vicarious experience to be the typical way that human beings change. He uses the term modeling to describe Campbell's two midrange processes of response acquisition (observation of another's response and modeling), and he claims that modeling can have as much impact as direct experience. Social learning theory is a general theory of human behavior, but Bandura and others concerned with mass communication have used it specifically to explain media effects. Bandura warned that "children and adults acquire attitudes, emotional responses, and new styles of conduct through filmed and televized modeling."[9] Processes governing observational learning include: attention, retention, reproduction, and motivation.

EPPM is based on fear appeal used in health behavior change messages and the response it elicits in the recipient of the message. In general, the model suggests health risk messages initiate two cognitive appraisals—an appraisal of the threat and an appraisal of the efficacy of the recommended response. Based on these appraisals, one out of three outcomes result: no response, a danger control response, or a fear control response.[10] During the first cognitive appraisal, a recipient of the message thinks only about the threat and evaluates its relevance and seriousness to him or her. If the threat is perceived to be not so serious or non-serious, it is simply ignored. On the other hand, if people perceive the threat to be serious and real, they become fearful and thus motivated to act. At that point, people appraise or think about the efficacy of the recommended response. Depending on the efficacy appraised, people perform either a danger control or fear control response. Witte and colleagues argue that when people perceive low efficacy (ability to adopt recommended action) and the perceived threat is high, they avoid action and instead try to control their fear.[11] The danger control responses are usually changes in attitude, intention, and behavior in line with the message's recommendations. Individual differences influence perception of threat and efficacy, but do not directly influence the outcome. However, fear appeals can and do fail if used improperly. And sometimes even the best fear appeal messages (or any other kind of persuasive messages) simply do not work because of cultural or personality factors.

The Diffusion of Innovations theory by Everett M. Rogers has survived decades of testing and critique. It offers a comprehensive explanation of how new ideas or products (referred to as innovations) are introduced and diffused in a society. The model applies to health behavior change as well as to other development-related innovations. "Diffusion is the process by which an innovation is communicated through certain channels over a time among the members of a social system."[12] The main elements in the diffusion of new ideas are: (1) an innovation, (2) which is communicated through certain channels, (3) over time, and (4) among the members of a social system. The innovation-decision process is the mental process through which an individual (or other decision-making unit) passes from first knowledge of the innovation to form an attitude toward the innovation, and then to a decision to adopt or reject the implementation of the new idea—and confirmation of this decision. Rogers conceptualizes five steps in this process: (1) knowledge, (2) persuasion, (3) decision, (4) implementation, and (5) confirmation. Speed of adoption is a major concern of Rogers. People adopt an innovation at different rates. Those who are first to adopt are categorized as innovators, or adventuresome. The next group of adopters are called the early adopters. The next groups are the early majority and late majority. The last to adopt, if at all, is the group of laggards. In other words, the reason people adopt an innovation immediately after learning about it, or later, depends on their socioeconomic status, personality variables, and communication behavior (e.g., discussion with peers). Change agents have a special role in speeding up adoption of innovation. However, these variables can influence the adoption process positively or negatively.

Planning Systems and Frameworks

The *PRECEDE-PROCEED* framework is an approach to planning that examines the factors that contribute to behavior change. These include predisposing factors, enabling factors, and reinforcing factors. Predisposing factors are the individual's knowledge, attitudes, beliefs, and values before the intervention that can affect his or her willingness to change. Enabling factors are those in an individual's environment or community that facilitate or present obstacles to change. Reinforcing factors are the positive or negative effects of adopting the behavior (including social support) that influence an individual to continue the changed behavior. These factors require that target individuals be evaluated in the context of their community and social structures, and not in isolation, when change agents plan their communication or health education strategies.

The *PRECEDE-PROCEED* framework for planning, as shown in Figure 3–1, is founded on the disciplines of epidemiology; the social, behavioral, and educational sciences; and health administration. Throughout the work with precede and proceed, two fundamental propositions are emphasized: (1) health and health risks are caused by multiple factors, and (2) because health and health risks are determined by multiple factors, efforts to effect behavioral, environmental, and social change must be multidimensional or multisectoral, and participatory.[13]

Social Marketing approaches to behavior change are rooted in the marketing techniques used in businesses, including publicity, promotion, and advertising. Social marketing is different than commercial marketing to the extent that while a "business's goal is to make profit by promoting, pricing, and distributing products for which there is a market,"[14] social marketing is subsidized by donors and public sectors, because it is aimed at serving socially desirable goals. Subsidies are typically provided (as is widely practiced in the case of farming) to supply products and services to consumers who would not be able to afford them at market prices and marketplaces. In other words, social marketing of contraceptives (where social marketing got its start), or other health-related products and services, aims to reach one or more segments of a consumer population who cannot afford to buy the same or similar products from open and competitive markets. This approach

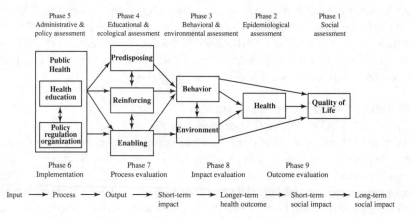

Figure 3–1. Precede-Proceed Model for Health Promotion Planning

has certain advantages. It not only makes contraceptives accessible to a wider target population, but it also helps to wean consumers away from free products and services that are available from charities and public sources. At least theoretically, the success of social marketing ultimately leads to self-sustenance in countries where social marketing was first introduced.

Social marketing, as a behavior change model, is distinguished by the commercial marketing techniques it employs straight out of the business world. The treatment of social marketing as a new, and perhaps excellent, behavior change strategy is a relatively recent phenomenon,[15] whose special merits are not always obvious. But it is likely that social marketing can be responsible for changing behaviors in the use of contraceptives to the same extent as commercial marketing has influenced consumers in the use of soap, brushing teeth with certain toothpastes, and taking aspirin—without receiving any subsidies.

Is There a Need for Another Model?

So far, this chapter has noted that behavior change is a function of beliefs, attitudes, and intentions. These in turn are influenced by external factors such as observation of peers, socioeconomic circumstances, and environment. People change behavior but go through different stages from knowledge to actual adoption. It is much better to approach a person with appropriate messages in accordance with his or her stage level. People are also influenced by role models as seen on television or heard on the radio. The time it takes to adopt an innovation depends on the personality, communication behaviors, and the socioeconomic status of the individual.

The models and theories of behavior change have other characteristics in common as well. These generally focus on changing an individual's behavior by concentrating on the existing knowledge, attitudes, and beliefs of the individual. They mention external factors, such as the role of peers, socioeconomic status of the target audience, and communication processes as they relate to behavior change. Diffusion of Innovations points out, perhaps more than other theories, the significance of the rate at which an innovation is adopted. The push and pull factors framework (PPFF) advances this concept a step further by proposing that change strategies should be comprehensive. In addition to focusing on the target individuals, they should also focus on external factors that play a positive or negative role in influencing the individual's behavior.

Push and Pull Factors in Changing Health Behavior

Push and pull factors are important to the extent they retard or speed up adoption processes. It is well known that not every new idea, intervention, or innovation is adopted by the intended target population at the same rate.[16] Behavior change literature is full of examples of interventions that took a long time before being adopted by a majority of the population. The practice of contraception in South Korea, for example, increased between 1970 and 1996, from 33 percent to 79 percent (on average, roughly at 1.84 percent annually). While South Korea's family planning program was regarded as successful in 1973, the increase in an unsuccessful program of Nepal was from 3 percent in 1970 to 23 percent in 1996 or on average about 0.8 percent annually.[17] In the United States, a large-scale National High Blood Pressure (BP) Education Program was launched in 1972. It galvanized all available resources of private and public sectors, and civil society in a concerted effort to educate the target population and urge action to control high BP. The National Heart, Lung, and Blood Institute's publication in 1997 reported that since the inception of the program the mortality from stroke declined by 60 percent, mostly due to the education program.[18] In other words, this remarkable success took a quarter of a century. It must be noted that rate of change is a function of adequate communication efforts as much as availability and access to promoted services and products. For example, in countries where family planning practice did not increase rapidly, it was partly due to a lack of access to contraceptives and services.

To elaborate further, health-related behaviors change for one of two reasons. Either the individual concerned wanted to or felt the need to implement the change and sought out information, or a change agent sent a marketing message that was a good fit with the wants or perceived needs of the individual. In other words, a change in behavior takes place only if the change (proposed or self-induced) is relevant and meets a person's needs or wants. If a proposed change is not wanted or not in line with perceived needs, the individual is likely to ignore the message. Consequently, to begin a process of behavior change, which a person might need but not perceive the need, it is necessary to first make him or her feel the need. Often, information campaigns are used to create awareness and to make target audiences feel the need.

The Push and Pull Factors Framework

There are many factors that affect behavior change and the speed at which it takes place in the target population, as illustrated in Figure 3–2. These factors can have either a positive (pro-behavior change) or negative (anti-behavior change) role. These are called push and pull fac-

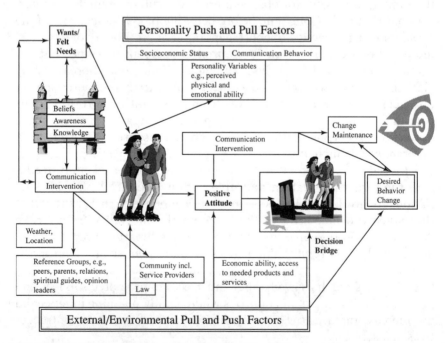

Figure 3–2. Push and Pull Factors in Behavior Change Communication

tors. These factors are grouped in two broad categories: (1) Personality factors and (2) external/environmental factors. Personality factors include: socioeconomic status in the society, communication behavior, and personality variables (such as a person's perceived ability to change) and psychological motivations and barriers. This category is similar to Rogers's characterization of people as innovators, early adopters, early majority, late majority, and laggards. The external/environmental factors include: reference groups (peers, parents, relations, friends, spiritual guides, opinion leaders, models, etc.); community (health leaders, service providers, institutions); laws (legal restraints, barriers); and the economic ability to obtain access to the needed products and services. An important variable, "prior experience with the suggested behavior change," comes into play for individuals who tried a behavior change but dropped it (for example, contraceptive users who for one reason or another discontinued use).

Personality Factors

The PPFF starts with the premise that all individuals have wants and emotional needs. It proposes that behavior change is in conformity with those wants and/or needs and it is likely that messages that address the relevant change will be noticed and recognized quickly and help form positive attitudes in a shorter time, leading to a decision to adopt the recommended behavior. If a proposed change is not congruent to a perceived need or want, it is likely that any kind of message sent will be ignored. In these circumstances, the first task of the communication program is to create awareness so that need is felt by the relevant segment of the target population.

As previously mentioned, there are numerous other personality factors. All theories and models list these personality factors as the key to the adoption of behavior change. Communication behavior, such as communication between peers, husband-wife, and with other reference group members can be influential, even critical, in either pulling off or pushing the proposed behavior change. When confronted with a fear-arousing health message, individuals appraise it in terms of their ability or inability to cope with the threat (efficacy). This is also a personality factor.

External/Environmental Factors

While personality factors play a major role in the adoption of behavior change, external and environmental factors also play a significant role. The research findings of the international Demographic and Health Surveys reveal that for women surveyed in many developing countries, factors such as religious opinions, husband's approval, and opposition of other members of the reference groups are the reasons for not practicing family planning. For example, in Mauritania, almost 22 percent of women said that because of religious opposition, they did not accept family planning.[19] This percentage was 17.3 percent in Yemen (1997), 16 percent in Pakistan (1990 to 1991), and 14.9 percent in Guatemala (1995). The husband's disapproval was cited, for example, by 9.3 percent of respondents in Guatemala, 7.9 percent in Uzbekistan, and 5.9 percent in Nigeria. Opposition by others in the women's family societal groups was mentioned by less than one-half percent of the women interviewed in several countries. Similarly, economic ability to pay for and lack of access to contraceptive products and services were mentioned by the respondents as the reasons for not practicing family planning by 2.7 percent in Paraguay (1990), 2.2 percent in Haiti (1994 to 1995), and 3.3 percent in Burkina Faso (1998 to 1999). Because in most developing countries contraceptives and related services are provided free at public health facilities, or are highly subsidized, cost is not the major reason for the low numbers of people practicing modern birth control. In other innovations, this might not necessarily be the case.

In the United States for example, Stephen Mumford found that before men decide to get a vasectomy, they take a year or longer to make their decision, consulting peers who have already been vasectomized.[20] The opinions of peers work either way: as pull or push factors. Similarly, when friends, husbands, and in-laws support a woman's intention to use contraception, it is considered a push factor. Realization of the man's role in the adoption of contraception came early in the family planning programs. Hence, most communication programs targeted men to either adopt contraception or approve adoption by their wives.[21] Although surveys have not yielded precise data, it is logical to assume that there are larger ratios of women who practice family planning than those not practicing, due to the external/environmental factors.

Economic costs or incentives can also play the role of pull or push factors. There are well-known examples of product promotions and incentives in health programs that can be considered as push factors. Good examples are when free syringes are made available to drug addicts and free or subsidized condoms are offered in HIV prevention programs. Free or largely subsidized contraceptives and related services in much of the developing world are clearly push factors. Monetary incentives to couples for accepting permanent contraception and targets set for service providers, particularly in South Asia, are other examples of push factors.

If the desired goal is to speed up the rate of change, consideration of pull and push factors is critical. The purpose of the communication effort should not only be to dispense messages in the most efficient and effective manner to reach the target individuals, but also to influence the factors responsible for pull and push on those individuals, in order to speed up adoption. The more comprehensive the communication approach is, the faster the behavior is likely to change and be sustained. Generally, communication interventions are directed at the personality factors only. However, depending on the nature of the desired change, all factors that pull or push individuals from decision making should be addressed. In the family planning field for instance, when research findings showed that one reason for slow adoption of contraception was that couples were not discussing birth planning and methods of contraception, national campaigns were launched to encourage husband-wife communication.[22]

In Bangladesh, in order to minimize the pulling influence of religious leaders (external factor) on the adoption of family planning, program managers began a serious effort to win the support of the clerics. The impact of reaching out to the religious leaders in Bangladesh cannot be underestimated, because contraceptive prevalence rate (CPR) jumped from 4 percent in 1970 to 41 percent in 1999 to 2000. On the other hand in Pakistan, where 16 percent of women cited religious opposition as the reason for not adopting family planning, and the efforts to sway the opinions of religious leaders were unrewarded, the CPR largely snail-paced from 6 percent in 1970 to 8.7 percent in 1990 to 1991, 12 percent in 1996, and 17 percent in 1999.[23-25]

Law and community can also pull or push a person from adopting a new behavior. For example, laws that prohibit a person from smoking in public places are a critical factor to change smoking behavior. Laws that require the use of seat belts for car drivers and passengers play a "push" role for many individual who adopt this behavior. Communities can also, at times, be influential in changing behavior by exerting social, legal, communal, and procedural influence on individuals. By threatening heavy fines for littering, communities push people to adopt better garbage disposal practices. By organizing health fairs, communities promote good health behavior such as blood donation, blood pressure checkups, and so on. Communities of health professionals pull and push behavior change on numerous issues, mainly by expressing their professional opinions, which are considered credible and trustworthy.

Attitudes are a precondition of the next step an individual takes before adopting a suggested behavior. This vital step is taken when an individual finally decides to adopt a new behavior. This step is called the decision-making bridge between positive attitudes and actual adoption of a new behavior. This is the point in the adoption process where a lot of individuals procrastinate. Decision making can be pushed through communication interventions by disseminating appropriate messages.

The desired behavior change is often the end-result of the change process. Individuals are most vulnerable at this stage and often procrastinate. Push and pull factors, including appropriately designed messages, can make a difference for a person taking the first step to cross the decision bridge.

Maintenance of behavior change is often the ultimate goal of a health program because many behaviors require sustained, long-term habits (e.g., brushing teeth, using condoms for every sexual act, completing several months' long treatment for tuberculosis (TB), etc.). This stage also requires use of appropriate communication interventions (CIs). If individuals who enter the maintenance stage are ignored, some people will relapse, or drop out, as is a frequent problem in family planning programs, TB treatment, or the use of condoms.

The Role of Communication Interventions

Communication Interventions are push factors at every stage of the behavioral change process. These interventions are made to create awareness of felt needs concerning proposed behavior change, and to provide information and the knowledge necessary to understand the change and adopt it. CIs are needed to change attitudes, cross the decision bridge, adopt the behavior change, and finally to sustain the change. Evidence-based communication strategies are the best insurance for timely interventions. CIs are the main tool for facilitating the change, whether through change agents (in person) or through messages.

The PPFF, therefore, emphasizes the importance of researching all factors (external, environmental, and personality related) to determine their relative role in influencing the proposed behavior change or adoption of an innovation. The research findings should lead to formulation of a communication strategy focusing on the key influencing factors. Research is continuously needed to monitor the progress of the implementation plans and to evaluate outcomes.

Broad-Base Health Communication Strategy (BBHCS): A Multipronged Approach

The significance of the conceptual framework is its potential to translate into action programs designed to address particularly difficult and challenging health issues, such as the pandemic of HIV/AIDS, malaria, TB, sexually transmitted infections, potential threats of new and unprecedented diseases (e.g., SARS, Anthrax) and even the prevention of disabilities among aging populations. The framework enlarges the focus of communicating health messages directly and exclusively for the target audience to include interventions designed to influence major push and pull factors affecting the speed of adoption indirectly. This approach is referred to as Broad-Base Health Communication Strategy (BBHCS). This strategy is likely to increase the speed of attitudes and sustainable behavior change, as both push and pull factors are studied and addressed appropriately.

BBHCS is developed by interwoven elements of various theories and models, based in particular on the Stages of Change model and Diffusion of Innovations. The strategy is compatible with Bandura's Social-Cognitive Theory and basic principles of the PRECEDE-PROCEED model.

The BBHCS blueprint for action comprises nine steps.

1. **Identify the main issues that require attitudes and behavior change. This should relate to the quantitative and qualitative goals set in the health program/agenda.**

   The first step in designing the strategy is to identify the evidence-based problems and issues to be addressed. This exercise should also include identification of any goals that have been defined by the health organization, ministry, or department. For example, in country X, the national Department of Health plans to reduce HIV/AIDS infection rate among the teenagers by 50 percent in five years. This kind of policy statement can help crystallize the parameters of the strategy such as the target audience, the time span, and the realistic goals. If policy or plan statements are not available, it is necessary for the organization entrusted with for-mulation of the strategy to produce them.

2. **Identify relevant policies, procedures, resources, including external/environmental, legal, economic, social, and other push and pull factors affecting or likely to affect proposed behavior change.**

   Once the goals are stated, it is necessary to analyze and identify the barriers and opportunities (social, economic, legal, environ-mental, human, and financial resources) with regard to the com-munication strategy. This can involve consultation with stake-holders, networking, and literature search on the identified issues. This is the step where the size and location of the target population are also defined.

3. Identify the specific target audience whose knowledge, attitudes, and behavior need to be changed and the stage they are at in the adoption process, as described here. This should also include audiences that indirectly influence the adoption process through push and pull factors.

Push and pull factors propose that the target audience be grouped into the following five segments:

1. *Avant-garde* or innovators. These are persons who have already adopted the proposed behavior change. In the context of family planning, for example, these are satisfied users. In the case of an HIV/AIDS prevention program, these are persons who, for example, practice safe sex, use clean needles, or ensure uninfected blood transfusions. In the case of TB patients, it means the patient regularly receives prescribed treatment.

2. *Experimenters* are those who tried the change but reverted. (See Stages of Change theory.) In the case of family planning or TB treatment, they are considered dropouts. It is assumed that this segment of the target audience previously had knowledge and positive attitudes toward proposed change. Dropping out can be intentional (such as for birth spacing in case of family planning), or due to dissatisfaction, or for circumstances beyond their control such as sickness, running out of funds, or breakdown in services and supplies.

3. *Procrastinators* are persons who have knowledge and positive attitudes toward the innovation or proposed behavior change yet cannot make up their minds to start practicing. Maybe they need more information and perhaps consultation with peers, reference groups, or service providers, before they cross the decision bridge.

4. *Opponents or unconvinced* are those who are knowledgeable but not convinced, or are against the innovation for personal, religious, cultural, political, and other reasons. These are people who admit having knowledge of the health action needed but do not have a favorable attitude or they disapprove of the proposed action.

5. *Hard-to-Reach,* or laggards, are not informed or ill-informed. When asked in a survey, they are likely to admit no knowledge of the health action being proposed. In addition, they do not appear eager to learn.

Baseline research should identify ratios of each group listed here in the entire target population. Moreover, the large groups can be further segmented by variables such as age, marital status, parity, residence, and socioeconomic status, depending on the innovation.

4. **Determine knowledge, attitudes, and practices of the target audience concerning the intervention, through analysis of the findings of existing and new research.** Research questions/variables should particularly be designed to identify the relevance and intensity of push and pull factors for the intended audience. This research enables communicators to design custom-made strategies for each group. For example, it will be more meaningful to inform patients about various HIV/AIDS treatments available to them than dispensing mere advice on safe sex practices. Often qualitative research yields adequate information on each subgroup.

5. **Specify communication objectives for each segment of the intended audience in terms of knowledge, attitudes, and practices.** The objectives should be specific, measurable, attainable, realistic, and time-bound. Since each target group is expected to be at a different stage of the adoption process, specific educational objectives will vary. For example, the specific objectives regarding the group of procrastinators might be: "By the end of the project, at least 30 percent of the sexually active men in this group, residing in area X, when asked in a survey, will report using condoms for each sexual encounter." The actual percentage can vary depending on the duration and intensity of the communication campaign, prior experience, access to the product, and other factors.

6. **Design appropriate messages that will help achieve the objectives.** Messages should be based on research findings pertaining to the information and motivational needs of the audience. Time-tested and effective approaches in message design should be considered as appropriate (e.g., messages that arouse fear, messages that ensure trustworthiness and credibility of the source, messages that elicit danger control response, messages from well-known and respected role models for the target group, or messages that specifically address questions and concerns of the group).

7. **Determine cost-effective and efficient channels of communication and approaches and methods to deliver selected messages to the target audience.** For greater effectiveness, use a multimedia approach that includes inter-personal communication. Selection of the media depends on the stage of the target audience in the adoption process. For example, those in the early stage of aware-

ness will easily benefit from mass media or one-way channels of communication such as television or radio. Those who are knowledgeable, but either lack positive attitudes or are procrastinators, will benefit most from the inter-personal approach or two-way channels. Those already practicing the suggested behavior change will need reinforcement messages—these can be delivered effectively through one-way channels such as mass media.

8. **Develop a detailed management plan.** This includes planning for financial and human resources, training, production of media and materials, timelines, and identification of responsible persons and institutions for various activities. Quantification and determination of the geographical location of the target audience are prerequisites of realistic media planning. Because resources are always limited, optimum blend of various media is necessary. When more is known about the reach and effectiveness of various media for the intended audience, better utilization can be made. Media should be developed prior to training in-the-field functionaries. Communication campaigns should also support field staff and enhance their image. There should be distinct materials and messages for each of the chosen target segments. It is not necessary to address all of the five segments for each campaign. For example, a focus on procrastinators can yield faster results.

9. **Design and implement a monitoring and evaluation system.** It is important to set benchmark information at the outset, preferably by instituting a management information system, involving recordkeeping and reporting on a periodic and consistent basis. This system can also make provisions to collect baseline information about the target audience, through a sample survey or focus group discussions, as resources permit. If behavior change is the ultimate goal of the strategy, there must be a reliable source of data on the relevant indicator. Ideally, there should be a systematic collection of these data by related institutions, for example, the Department of Health. Ad-hoc data collection (e.g., surveys) is an expensive alternative to monitor progress and the success of the program.

Notes

1. K. Glanz, F. M. Lewis, and B. K. Rimer, *Health Behavior and Health Education: Theory, Research and Practice* (San Francisco, CA: Jossey-Bass Publishers, 1997), 30.

2. National Institutes of Health, U.S. Department of Health and Human Services, *Making Health Communication Programs Work* (National Cancer Institute, NIH publication, September 2003).

3. N. K. Janz and M. H. Becker, "The Health Belief Model: A Decade Later," *Health Education Quarterly* 11(1) (1984): 1–47.

4. M. Fishbein and I. Ajzen, *Belief, Attitude, Intention, and Behavior: An Introduction to Theory and Research* (Reading, MA: Addison-Wesley, 1975).

5. Theory of Reasoned Action/Theory of Planned Behavior. Available at University of Southern Florida, http://hsc.usf.edu/~kmbrown/TRA_TPB.htm. Accessed on March 12, 2004.

6. G. Godin and G. Kok, "The Theory of Planned Behavior: A Review of Its Applications to Health-Related Behaviors," *American Journal of Health Promotion* 11(2) (1996): 87–98.

7. National Institutes of Health, *Making Health Communication Programs Work*.

8. C. A. Redding et al., "Health Behavior Models," *The International Electronic Journal of Health Education* 3(Special) (2000). Accessed on March 14, 2004 at: http://www.kittle.siu.edu/iejhe/3special/redding.htm.

9. A. Bandura, "Social Learning Theory." Accessed on March 14, 2004 at http://tip.psychology.org/bandura.html.

10. Bandura, "Social Learning Theory."

11. K. Witte et al., *Effective Health Risk Messages: A Step by Step Guide* (Thousand Oaks, CA: Sage Publications, 2001).

12. E. M. Rogers, *Diffusion of Innovations*, 4th ed. (NY: Free Press, 1995).

13. "The Precede-Proceed Model of Health Program Planning and Evaluation." Accessed on March 15, 2004 at http://lgreen.net/precede.htm.

14. P. R. Cateora, *International Marketing*, 9th ed. (Chicago: Irwin, 1993).

15. Accessed on March 15, 2004 at http://www.aed.org/health/health_social.html.

16. Rogers, *Diffusion of Innovations*, 4th ed.

17. P. T. Piotrow et al., *Health Communication: Lessons from Family Planning and Reproductive Health* (Johns Hopkins School of Public Health, Center for Communication Programs, 1997).

18. K. Glanz, F. M. Lewis, and B. K. Rimer, *Health Behavior and Health Education: Theory, Research and Practice* (San Francisco: Jossey-Bass Publishers, 1997).

19. Accessed on March 17, 2004, at http://www.measuredhs.com.

20. S. D. Mumford, *The Decision-Making Process That Leads to Vasectomy: A Guide for Promoters* (San Francisco, CA: San Francisco Press, 1977).

21. M. Flood, *The Men's Bibliography: A Comprehensive Bibliography of Writing on Men, Masculinities, Gender, and Sexualities*, 11th ed., 2003. Home URL: http://mensbiblio.xyonline.net/.

22. Piotrow et al., *Health Communication: Lessons from Family Planning and Reproductive Health*.

23. Accessed on March 17, 2004, at http://www.measuredhs.com.

24. Family Planning Association, Bangladesh (FPAB), "Support to Muslim Religious Leaders for the Promotion of Reproductive Health and Family Planning among Muslim Communities of Partner Countries." A South-South Partnership Project.

25. "Asia: Religious Leaders Call for End to U.S. Population Projects," *The Baobhab* (Pakistan: 1993).

CHAPTER FOUR

Social Change Interventions in Public Health Communications

Rachel A. Smith, Kim Witte, and C. Kirk Lazell

Chapter Questions

1. How is social change defined?
2. What are the phases of social change? Is this process used to understand community influences on attitudes, beliefs, and actions in the example of Namibia?
3. What are the main differences between a community-level process and an individual behavior change process?

Introduction

Imagine that a community hears on television and radio about a new virus called GBV. At the local market, neighbors begin to talk about GBV. Who has GBV? How is the virus contracted? How serious is it? How can it be treated? At the next meeting of a neighborhood social club, friends learn that someone in the group contracted GBV. There is no known cure for GBV, and the infected neighbor is a single parent with children who will be orphaned within a matter of time. Imagine this scenario takes place in a community that places a stigma on those with GBV. How can any given member of the community react? What information will people learn about GBV? How will information and influence flow through a community? How would a community's knowledge, attitudes, and actions change if no stigma existed? What would it take for the community as a whole to work together to prevent transmission of the virus or to mobilize resources to help those who have contracted it? Although GBV does not exist, this story plays out in communities around the world every day as new health concerns appear. As the story illustrates, the community at large has a substantial impact on how any given person in a population reacts to a new health issue. Many current health theories focus on reactions at the individual level. This chapter will describe a framework to look at communication as a process for social change with community-level variables.

The Variables of Community Communications

Community-level variables differ significantly from individual-level variables. The variables at the community level comprise group and social components such as leadership, equity, social norms, and social influence. In contrast, individual-level behaviors focus on personal attitudes, knowledge, perceptions, and interactions. By identifying the social processes and activities in a region, government leaders, health program planners, and health care workers are better equipped to understand how communities as a *whole* react and respond to an epidemic.

The guiding model for this report is a framework of communication for social change that focuses on community dialogue, debate, leadership, and negotiation.[1] Taking a page from reactions at the individual level, this framework speaks to influences on *collective* attitudes, beliefs, and actions. Community interactions and how they support or hinder public health programs, knowledge, and actions form a framework for social change. The framework offers a guide to community dialogue, debate, leadership, and negotiation. To illustrate the use of the framework, some preliminary results will be provided from current projects that describe community reactions to HIV in Namibia, a country in southern Africa.

A Framework for Social Change

Social change is defined as, "An iterative process where 'community dialogue' and 'collective action' work together to produce social change in a community that improves the health and welfare of all of its members."[2] When social change occurs, people's actions shift effortlessly to fulfill new or altered community norms and collective actions. These collective actions can come in the form of community norms, social cohesion, information equity among various groups in a community, mobilization of organizations, and a collective capacity to address health concerns.

The process of social change proceeds in three phases: (1) a catalyst that leads to (2) community dialogue, which leads to (3) collective action. Figure 4–1 depicts this model.

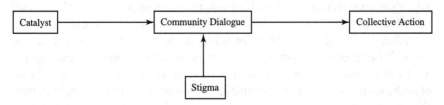

Figure 4–1. Model of the Social Change Process

A *catalyst* is something that sparks dialogue within a community. Taking an HIV test, learning the results of a loved one's HIV test, mass media programs, talks with health care workers, community mobilization campaigns, workplace programs, the cultural arts, church sermons, and parliamentary debate are all examples of catalysts that get people talking to each other about HIV/AIDS. When people in different regions in Namibia tested positive for HIV, the community faced a new health threat. Namibians learned about HIV and AIDS through their own experience, through interpersonal contact with loved ones who contracted HIV, or through mass media notices, news shows, and health campaigns that provided information on HIV transmission or AIDS-related treatment and care. Each of these events can serve as a catalyst for people to begin talking to each other about HIV/AIDS. The more people who are personally affected and reached by the catalyst, the greater the motivation to begin the second phase of social change—community dialogue.

Community dialogue is a three-step process first involving the recognition of a problem (step 1), followed by identification of and involvement of leaders (step 2), and concluded by community clarification of perceptions about the problem (step 3). This community dialogue can occur either in formal meetings, such as an organized class, or in informal settings, such as at the local bar. Figure 4–2 depicts these three steps of community dialogue.

The first part of community dialogue in the process of social change is *recognition* by some segment of the community that HIV poses a threat to the community and its members. For example, community members

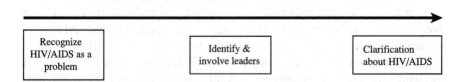

Figure 4–2. Three-step Process of Community Dialogue

might say that HIV is a serious problem that affects people they know and talk about who they suspect has HIV or an AIDS-related illness.

After a critical mass of residents recognize that HIV poses a threat to the well-being of their community, formal or informal *leaders* emerge (or are formally identified by community members) to take the responsibility of addressing HIV/AIDS. For example, community members might expect the leader of their church to provide guidance on how to react to HIV/AIDS issues or they might look to their health care workers for advice on how to prevent transmission or how to choose treatment options.

In the final community dialogue (step 3), *perceptions are clarified* about HIV and AIDS issues. Community members want to reduce their uncertainty about HIV, AIDS-related illnesses, transmission of HIV, caring for orphaned or vulnerable children, and anything else related to HIV and AIDS with leaders and other community members. During this stage, myths are refuted or supported; beliefs about HIV/AIDS are formed and cemented. Although the model depicts a sequential process, community members attempt to clarify their perceptions of HIV or AIDS in this linear fashion (as depicted in the model) or occur at any time in the community dialogue phase (e.g., during problem recognition or leader identification).

Not all community dialogue serves to promote supportive collective action. In some cases, discussion about HIV or AIDS generates or reinforces stigma. Stigma influences both the types of issues discussed, as well as the frequency and the length of such discussions. It is important to note that stigma influences each step in community dialogue by enhancing or inhibiting each step and the content of community dialogue. As stigma associated with HIV/AIDS issues increases, the community dialogue about these topics should become more prescribed and restricted.

One goal of a community intervention can be to provide a forum to discuss HIV or AIDS that addresses and lowers a stigma attached to preventing the transmission of HIV, treating AIDS-related illness, or supporting those living with HIV and their dependents. If an intervention can lower the stigma, then more people can feel free to talk about HIV or AIDS, because they no longer face social repercussions. Thus, stigma and community dialogue interact to influence the type and extent of collective action.

Collective action is defined as people addressing a common problem as a group.[3] Communities can pull together and help each other in the face of AIDS, or they can split apart and become more critical and hostile of those with AIDS (e.g., throwing them out of the community).

In summary, the framework for social change suggests that after a catalyst enters a community, community members talk about the catalyzing issue. This leads to community dialogue where recognition, leadership, and clarification of the catalyst emerges. Stigma can develop during the community dialogue phase, helping or hindering the call to some collective action. Framing communication as a process of social change represents a shift away from individual-level models of behavior change. Social change focuses on community-level variables that combat stigma, increase dialogue, and lead to collective action.

Namibia Findings

Namibia has the fifth highest HIV rate in the world, with 22.5 percent of the population estimated to be HIV positive, and was selected as a focus country for the U.S. President's Emergency Plan for AIDS Relief (known as the Emergency Plan). After interviewing 1,200 residents living near three different hospitals in three different regions of Namibia (Oshikuku, Onandjokwe, and Rehoboth), these regions can be described in the following way.[4]

Community dialogue appeared to begin. Respondents generally recognized HIV/AIDS as a problem, although it was viewed as less of a personal problem and more a countrywide problem. Leadership identification and clarification of perceptions varied across communities. Stigma, known to affect community dialogue when directly assessed—with questions like, Would you buy food from someone with HIV or AIDS?—appeared to be low. However, more subtle measures of stigma, like questions linking negative social attributes with HIV/AIDS, suggested a moderate level of stigma, especially in Rehoboth. For example, 30 percent of respondents in Rehoboth refused to answer if they had talked about the prevention of mother-to-child transmission of HIV within the confines of their formal group meetings.

In terms of collective action, again, the results differed substantially by community. Findings showed that knowledge deficits existed in all communities in specific groups. Most group members believe that they have the ability to take *collective action* to help those living with HIV and their dependents without the help of other groups. Oshikuku is the most interconnected community, because most people participate in groups and these groups share leaders and members. The majority of respondents in Oshikuku report that their groups have taken some action to help those living with HIV, yet this action typically takes the form of prayer, preaching, and moral support. In Rehoboth, fewer people participate in groups, and these groups are connected only through shared leaders. A third of respondents reported that their groups did *nothing* to help those with HIV, and their help, when provided, came in the form of food, prayer, and preaching. Onandjokwe shows high participation in groups, yet these groups are connected only through shared group members. Over half of the respondents reported that their group did *nothing* to help those with HIV, yet their help, when provided, came in the form of counseling and education. The kinds of actions taken in Rehoboth and Oshikuku provide some evidence that residents link morality and religion with HIV and AIDS. The average group member in the central, large groups in Oshikuku and Onandjokwe express interest in being tested for HIV, yet most members in the central, large groups in Rehoboth do not.

Group mobilization efforts might have greater success in Oshikuku and Onandjokwe, because they have previous experience and social resources to discuss HIV/AIDS issues. Grassroots group mobilization can be most effective in Onandjokwe, while leader-driven projects can be most effective in Oshikuku and Rehoboth (because of patterns of networks). Group mobilization efforts in Rehoboth face pressures from the community not to discuss HIV/AIDS issues publicly in their group meetings; however, interventions provide someone for residents in Rehoboth to talk to privately to clarify any confusion about HIV/AIDS. The only other concern in Rehoboth is to find another way to disseminate information and influence to 30 percent of respondents who do not participate in social groups.

In summary, an examination of a community's reactions to HIV and AIDS in Namibia provided insights into community-level processes that help design community programs in a way that is unavailable through individual-level theories and analysis. Through continued theoretical work and testing in the field, research will reveal what it takes for a community as a whole to work together to prevent transmission of diseases or to mobilize resources to help those facing health concerns.

Sources

Figure 4–1. Adapted from M. E. Figueroa et al., *Communication for Social Change: An Integrated Model for Measuring the Process and Its Outcomes* (New York: The Rockefeller Foundation, 2002).

Figure 4–2. Adapted from M. E. Figueroa et al., *Framework and Indicators for Measuring Social Change Process and Outcomes* (Baltimore, MD: Johns Hopkins University Center for Communication Programs, 2001). Figueroa et al.'s model is a ten-step flowchart depicting the process of social change. The model presented here is a condensed version of their complete flowchart.

Notes

1. M. E. Figueroa et al., *Framework and Indicators for Measuring Social Change Process and Outcomes* (Baltimore, MD: Johns Hopkins University Center for Communication Programs, 2001).

2. Figueroa et al., *Framework and Indicators for Measuring Social Change Process and Outcome.*

3. Figueroa et al., *Framework and Indicators for Measuring Social Change Process and Outcome.*

4. R. A. Smith et al., *Community-Level Patterns and Indicators: Strategic Information for Emergency Plan Programs in Oshikuku, Onandjokwe, and Rehoboth (Wave 1, Round 1)* (Baltimore, MD: Johns Hopkins University Center for Communication Programs, 2004).

CHAPTER FIVE

Observational Research in Global Health Communications

James W. Dearing, William F. Waters, and Everett M. Rogers

Chapter Questions

1. What are the advantages and disadvantages of observational research in global health communications?
2. How can observational research enrich the understanding of a subject when combined with other approaches?
3. What is the difference between participant and nonparticipant observational research?

What Observational Research Is and Where It Came From

Observational research is an approach to understanding phenomena in their own setting and on their own terms. The researcher systematically observes behaviors of individuals and groups and, in particular, is interested in patterns of behavior that reflect the shared norms and values of the group. While the sense of sight is most often employed, other senses are also important, especially the sense of sound, because observation includes listening to what is being said by the subject of the research. Observation often supplements more structured techniques such as interviewing individuals and groups because this allows the researcher to distinguish between what subjects say and what they do.

In many ways, observation is central to all scientific research, whether it be in the laboratory, the clinic, or field settings such as homes, workplaces, or communities. Observational research provides insights into social processes, such as communication as perceived and experienced by different actors in the study. Often misunderstood as unstructured and unscientific, observational research is not the same as casual vision, which is part of everyday life, although to the untrained eye, it can admittedly be very similar. The principal differences between mere sight and observational research are that the latter has a purpose, uses specific techniques, and involves both the systematic recording of data and the analysis of that data. As the following discussion shows, observational research has both advantages and disadvantages; it provides a powerful lens with which to study complex phenomena; at the same time, it is incumbent on the researcher to limit or eliminate sources of bias that can interfere with either the collection or the analysis of data, so that the scientist does not simply see what he or she wants to see.

Observational research is particularly relevant to communications in global health study because of the fundamental importance of shared insights among researchers in the field. How messages are developed and sent have essential cultural, social, and political underpinnings, and the ways that communications are understood and acted on likewise depend in large part on shared norms, values, and symbols (including, but not limited to, language).

Why use observational research? Compared to other methods—such as physiologic response experiments, close-ended survey questionnaires, and archival-based content analysis—observational research can be designed to produce a wide range of data, from the qualitative to the simple numeric recording of the frequency of events. Observational research can be used to define problems and to formulate research questions as an alternative to formal testing of hypotheses. It is especially appropriate for the investigator who is not yet well informed about the research problem or about the social system of study. Thus, observational research methods are often utilized relatively early in the scientific process. For example, Samuel Coleman, an American anthropologist, used methods of observation in several Japanese scientific laboratories to understand career mobility, relationships among scientists and lab administrators, and how female scientists fare in these work settings. Coleman started his work without preconceived questions or explicit hypotheses about these issues; rather, he let his observations and informal interactions with Japanese scientists in their places of work guide his study. Eventually, his insights as a participant observer led to 110 structured interviews.[1]

Alternatively, observational methods at times can be the only method used to gather data. Observational studies that are rigorously carried out provide a depth of comprehension, although at the expense of much breadth (that is, little or no external validity or ability to generalize the findings to other settings). Properly collected and documented, observational data can provide a wealth of information about specific phenomena because this approach allows for research subjects to express their experience of the phenomena in their own terminology.

Ultimately, the decision as to why and how to employ observational data collection and analysis depends on the researcher who should, like a competent carpenter, select the best tool for the job from a tool kit of research methods and techniques. Observational data can lead investigators to reformulate their perspectives and gain insights about the problem at hand. In this way, observational research can be very powerful.

The Roots of Observational Research

The use of observational research methods evolved mainly from investigations by ethnographers and anthropologists. Until recently, some scholars referred to the process as anthropologic methods. Ethnography involves the observation of peoples in their daily lives and social context. The ethnographic researcher sometimes lives in the community, and for extended periods of time. The goal of ethnographers is to understand the symbolic world of their subjects—through their eyes, perspective, and experience. This form of research is fundamentally observational, but frequently employs informal interviews of individuals and groups, because what individuals say is part of behavior, and language is the way that they express their perceptions.[2]

Among the best-known (and frequently cited) works from the ethnographic tradition of research into small, non-Western cultures is Mead's investigation of the sexual behavior of adolescent women on the island of Upolu, Western Samoa.[3] As a young graduate student, Mead took up residence within the local social system, learned the language, and recorded daily observations. She began her research with a particular interest in the transition of Samoans from youth to adulthood, which in European cultures was a stressful period. Was this stress during adolescence universal?

Mead began her research without formal hypotheses, but rather with a good grasp of the general phenomena and the curiosity necessary to explore these phenomena in a specific setting. She observed the daily life of her research subjects, and learned about their key institutions such as family, community, education, and religion. Mead was especially interested in observing the coming-of-age rites of young males and females. (Anthropologists often find it particularly useful to observe birth, death, marriage, and religious ceremonies, because on these occasions cultural values are especially evident.)

Like most anthropologists who use observational methods, Mead was a participant observer. She took part in the daily life of the people she observed, but at the same time tried to have as little impact as possible on their lives. She was undoubtedly aware that her mere presence might have affected behavior in ways that could never be fully known. This kind of research requires great patience, and endurance for a lengthy process whereby the researcher attempts to fit into and be accepted by the society that is observed. Acceptance is of paramount importance in order to observe phenomena that might otherwise be guarded by the society against an outsider. For example, the coming-of-age rites that interested Mead occurred only once a year. But by stint of patience and perseverance, she found that adolescence was in fact not a stormy transition in Samoan society, but was in fact a peaceful, happy stage of life. Similarly, Malinowski, one of the pioneers of anthropologic observational research, spent four full years among the Trobriand Islanders in the Southwest Pacific to achieve the goals of his study.[4] Mead's landmark study provides global health communications with an important lesson. Her methods gave her access to the intimate behavior that people in most cultures would be loathe to discuss openly. Too often, public health strategists base their programs on incomplete information, which results in a limited knowledge of cultural underpinnings pertinent to a community's shared beliefs and behaviors. Consequently, the culture is viewed as an obstacle to effective communications strategies rather than the essential feature around which programs should be constructed. True cultural competency is based on the kind of understanding that only observational research can provide.

Anthropologists also conduct observational research in small social systems of a domestic setting. A legendary example, which illustrates the principles of participatory observation, is William Foote Whyte's *Street Corner Society*.[5] As a graduate student, Whyte lived with an Italian-American family in Boston and participated in the activities (legal and sometimes illegal) of the Norton Street gang, observing small group structure and behavior. He found that the leadership structure of the gang affected behavior and communication, even in unexpected venues, including the bowling alley. The gang's leader (who was also a key informant) consistently achieved high scores, in part due to the support of his social followers. Others underachieved because of the criticism and badgering they endured from the rest of the gang. Over the years since Whyte's book was published, a number of street corner gangs have been studied using observational research methods.

Examples are Elliott Liebow's *Tally's Corner*[6] and Simon and Burns'[7] *The Corner: A Year in the Life of an Inner-City Neighborhood*.

Strengths and Weaknesses of Observational Research

Observational techniques are well suited for global communications research for several reasons. The methods are highly flexible, and they are not limited to the testing of formal hypotheses. Observation is one of the best ways to develop pertinent research questions and can also be used to confirm findings developed through other methods, which sometimes lack the intrinsic ability to incorporate the perceptions of research subjects. It is also unique in its ability to systematically assess perceptions and behaviors from the perspective of the actors themselves, so that culture becomes a fundamental aspect of the research rather than simply an additional factor to be considered.

Nevertheless, several weaknesses of observational research should be considered and actively addressed in order to reduce their potential to affect findings. Particularly relevant in this respect are the issues of validity and reliability, both of which are crucial considerations in quality control. *Internal validity* refers to the ability of research to measure what it purports to measure. Some researchers believe this is the true hallmark of observational research, given that it can optimize depth of inquiry into specific behaviors.[8] For instance, in-depth observations on how a given group obtains and exchanges information about health might be considered in order to provide a high degree of internal validity. Others caution that potential biases can affect the findings. Selection bias can result when different groups are not comparable. Information bias can come into play if different information is collected from different groups, or at different times. And confounding influences can result from the mixing or blurring, of effects, or if the influence of unaccounted-for factors is not considered.[9]

A related but separate question is the issue of *external validity* or the degree to which research findings can be generalized to other settings. Those who concede that observational research provides depth in understanding the behavior often suggest that this advantage comes at the cost of breadth. For example, Mead's observations were limited to the single social system in which she lived. She did not claim that findings from her village of study could be generalized to other groups. Derek Freeman, who began his study of Samoa 15 years later and in a different locale, found Samoan life fraught with sexual repression.[10] Whyte gained deep understanding into the behavior of about 25 people (including the 13 Norton Street Gang members) in Boston's North End.[11] But could he say that what he learned applied to anyone else, including the other 20,000 Italian Americans in the community, or even other street corner gangs? Limits to which findings can be generalized are usually assumed to be a weakness of observational research because a limited group is intensively researched. Even within that limited scope, subjects of study are not randomly selected and therefore findings cannot be inferred to a larger universe.[12]

On the other hand, most researchers hope that their findings will be of greater relevance beyond the study group, and that the data will reveal something of interest about a wider population. To one degree or another, this actually happens; otherwise why would the work of Mead, Malinowski, and Whyte still be cited as relevant, even if interest in Samoans or Trobrian Islanders who lived so many years ago has subsided, or for that matter, Italian Americans of the late 1930s? By reading these works and others like them, researchers can learn something about the human condition, and this adds to the catalog of knowledge of other groups, even if the ability to draw inferences is lacking.

Related to the issues of internal and external validity is the question of *reliability*, that is, the ability of studies to be replicated. This is where laboratory research shines, of course, and clinical research is also highly reliable because given the same conditions, other researchers who repeat the same steps should be able to obtain the same findings and arrive at the same conclusions. But in the social world, conditions constantly change, and in order to successfully address the many potential sources of bias (some of which are elaborated here) that can threaten reliability, the observational researcher must be careful to conduct the study with the utmost rigor and honesty. In the collection of data, this is best done by thorough training of data collectors and, whenever possible, complete note taking (to be discussed later in this chapter), and the electronic recording of raw data, especially interviews. In the analysis phase, the researcher might endeavor to make multiple observations at different times of the day, different days of the week, or even several seasons in order to optimize the strength and consistency of relationships. The reliability of analysis can be enhanced by using several different people to code data as well as through the use of software applications.[13–14]

Other Issues of Observational Research

Two quality control issues are important to observational research. The first is the importance of observing different cultures in a nonjudgmental manner, free of ethnocentrism. The ability to empathize (i.e., to take on the role of others) is a vital skill to be an effective observational researcher. For example, Mead found that the youth of Samoa engaged in free sexual activity prior to marriage, which many Americans at the time viewed with disapproval.[15] She was, however, nonjudgmental in her observations and analyses.

The second issue is the degree to which the presence of the researcher affects observed behaviors. For example did Mead, as a foreigner living in a small village, alter what she was there to observe? Did she inadvertently induce her respondents to behave in a manner that they would not have if she were not present? There are at least two reasons for thinking that this could be the case. First, research subjects might not want outsiders to observe parts of their shared experience that they believe should not be shared with strangers. Sacred rituals and other intimate forms of social behavior are examples of this. Conversely, subjects might try to act in ways that they believe the researcher expects them to, in an effort to be helpful—or in ways that will benefit the subjects themselves.

The problem of bias caused by the process of observation itself is called the *Hawthorne effect* in honor of a classic study, carried out in the Hawthorne plant of Western Electric by Rothlisberger and Dickson.[16] These scholars of organizations were asked by Western Electric, a major producer of electric lightbulbs, to investigate the importance of illumination in the workplace. A small assembly line was observed and, not surprisingly, when the level of illumination was increased, productivity increased. But when the level of illumination was decreased to the approximate equivalent of bright moonlight, productivity increased again. How could this be? Further observation revealed that the relationship between the level of illumination and worker productivity was mediated by the presence of observers: The employees perceived the presence of the researchers (and possibly their bosses), and they increased their work rate in response to the special attention they were receiving.

Similar findings come from research of even smaller groups. For example, Rokeach studied three psychiatric patients who each believed himself to be Jesus Christ.[17] Rokeach wanted to know whether, by forcing the three to meet regularly, they would have to confront the impossibility that each of them was Christ, and thereby be cured of their delusions. Alas, Rokeach's form of observation was highly intrusive; he wrote them letters "from God" and "from Dad" to "my Sons" and asked them questions that affected the patients in negative ways, and therefore much of what he observed was their reaction to him, not to each other. Twenty years after this experiment, Rokeach conceded that the study had been as much about him as about the other men. In fact, there had actually been been *four* Christs in the room.

Finally, there are important ethical issues in observational research. What if the scholars who observed the Hawthorne workers had worked beside them covertly, disguising themselves as regular employees? Melville Dalton overcame the Hawthorne effect by working as a checker on the piece-rate incentive system in a steel mill.[18] Thus Dalton became a covert observer of organizational behavior in the plant. What if they had made their observations through a one-way window? What are the ethical aspects of such covert observation? For example, should Whyte in *Street Corner Society* have participated in illegal acts (like gambling, and voting several times in an election) with his respondents? To what extent would rapport with his respondents have been damaged by his refusal to take part in illegal activities? Should he have used a concealed tape recorder, instead of taking notes in the privacy of his residence? Findings about domestic violence in indigenous Ecuadorian households were revealed to have been based on surreptitious tape recording; the author claimed that this was the only practical way to "interview" the respondents, who would never have agreed to being taped, even if confidentiality were guaranteed.[19] Was this ethical?

A related issue, which is specific only to observational inquiry, poses another ethical question. If subjects are promised confidentiality, is the researcher able to conceal their identity? The approach adopted by Whyte exemplifies this conundrum. Should the identities of observed individuals, including those committing crimes, always be protected by the observer? Whyte thought so, and he used pseudonyms for his respondents. Nevertheless, because of the intense, highly personal—but at the same time, often unique nature of information that can be gathered using observational techniques, the researcher might find it difficult to conceal the identity of respondents, because they might be recognized by other members of the group under study. For example, researchers who conducted an observational study of an upstate New York community, identified only as "Springdale," assured residents that they would not be publicly identified. After the study was published in a book titled *Small Town in Mass Society*,[20] the community's annual Fourth of July parade featured a float with an enlarged copy of the book's jacket, followed by masked residents riding in cars labeled with the fictitious names given them in the book. The float was followed by a manure spreader and an effigy of "The Author."[21] Because of the roles the residents played in the community, and because the researchers themselves were known to the community, the real name of the community was not hard to guess, and the true identities of respondents were not hard to establish. Consequently researchers were unable to study "Springdale" for the next 25 years. In spite of this failure, the use of pseudonyms for individual respondents and even communities is standard practice and should be employed by all observational researchers who promise anonymity to their study subjects.

The Nature of Observational Research

There are many kinds of observational research. The cultural anthropologist and the ethnographer use two tools: diaries or journals to record observations and impressions of the research as process, supplemented with systematic notes that include specific information about observed behaviors and interactions among subjects of study, including what is said. Here, the researcher can benefit from the interpretive insights of one or more informants. The point is that the researcher enters the world of the subjects with a specific agenda, but nevertheless remains open to where observations lead and to the successive refinement of interpretations. The researcher thus becomes the student, and the subjects of study are the teachers. In many ways, this approach is the hallmark of ethnography.[22] The researcher in this mode of analysis does not attempt to structure the situation of study, as Rokeach did in his contrivance to bring the three Christs face to face. In effect, the researcher works to produce a high degree of internal validity in the analysis of observations (i.e., to accurately measure what the research is intended to measure) while at the same time revealing the complex meanings associated with behaviors as understood by the subjects themselves and taking into account, as well, the effect of the observation on the processes being studied. By and large, cultural anthropologists have reconceptualized the problem of reactivity, from trying to minimize their influence on the subjects of study to become aware of their own effects and accounting for these.[23] The account will usually be qualitative and interpretive based on direct, reactive observation.[24]

In contrast, communications researchers who are more quantitatively inclined, including community psychologists, sociologists, industrial anthropologists, and public health professionals, might approach a field setting quite differently. Rather than becoming participant observers, they might opt to observe without participating, and enter the social system with a prestructured data-recording instrument, such as quantitative coding sheets or highly structured interview instruments. Whereas social interaction with informants and the people studied is central to the cultural anthropologist's endeavor, it might be less useful to the social scientist who does not attempt to understand the worlds of shared meaning of research subjects.[25] Their interest is the systematic collection of a much narrower, restricted range of data that are likely to be quite reliable, although possibly less valid.

The nonparticipant observation study by Cheadle and colleagues exemplifies this approach.[26] Webb and his colleagues refer to this as "simple observation."[27] They wanted to know how effective a health communication campaign had been to encourage people to consume low-fat rather than high-fat foods. Rulers in hand, they repeatedly measured the amount of shelf space devoted to low-fat foods such as 2 percent milk in the grocery stores in communities where the campaign took place. They reasoned that grocery managers would respond to heightened consumer awareness in their purchases of low-fat foods by stocking more of those foods. The team compared these nonparticipant observational data with data gleaned from grocery stores in similar communities where the campaign had not taken place. Using this technique (as opposed to, say, a questionnaire or participant observation), Cheadle virtually eliminated the Hawthorne effect because there was no way for consumers or even grocery store managers to react to the research team's presence. If the team had used a questionnaire, socially desirable responses ("Oh, I don't buy candy, but my friends do.") might well have obfuscated the true effects of the communication campaigns.

In some cases, though, nonparticipant observation is not feasible. Whereas Cheadle could walk into grocery stores and measure shelf space, Mead could not hide for extended periods to observe sexual behavior among adolescent women. Following the Cheadle example, the researcher can openly record observations on notepads, laptop computers, or handheld counters. The researcher's presence can be minimally invasive or even unnoticeable because there would simply be one more person among many in public settings, most of whom only informally take note of their surroundings. The sight of a person taking notes, speaking into an electronic device (e.g., a tape recorder or a cell phone), or using a laptop computer would be unlikely to arouse suspicion or even interest. Specifically, the social situation determines the degree to which the researcher's presence will cause people to behave in ways that they otherwise would not, unless perhaps the researcher is visibly different (e.g., from a different culture) than the subjects of the observation.[28]

In general, the more obtrusive the presence of the observer, the more reactive subjects will be to that presence. For certain types of physical data, a high degree of obtrusiveness of the person doing the data collection can produce zero reactance. A physician drawing blood is very obtrusive from the patient's perspective, yet the characteristics of the blood are not affected. Psychologic variables (such as anxiety), communicative variables (such as talkativeness), or other physiologic measures (such as heart rate), on the other hand, spike when observation is obtrusive. Reactance bias must be stressed as a potential problem in observational research because it is usually difficult to reliably estimate how much of what the researcher learns is because of normal field conditions, and how much is due to reaction to the observer. Forms of reactance include people doing what they think the researcher wants them to do, retreat from the setting, and exhibit overt or covert hostility.[29]

It might be assumed that the researcher can minimize reactance by not participating in the setting, but reactance can also be related to the degree of validity inherent in the data that are collected. This inverse relationship that characterizes different ways of collecting observational data is referred to as a "validity-reliability dichotomy." That is, the observer's participation (which allows for a deeper understanding than would otherwise be the case, by drawing the researcher closer to the "true scores" or highly valid data) also poses threats to validity. The more a data collection protocol or instrument is structured and standardized, the less valid data collection is a reflection of true attitudes, behaviors, and beliefs.[30] But unobtrusive observation, which eliminates threats to validity due to reactance, can raise a host of ethical issues.

Observational research suffers from another major source of bias. Systematic errors in the estimation of true (valid) scores derive from data-gathering instruments as well as from the person doing the observation. Coding schemes can be poorly designed, thus missing key aspects of observed constructs. And even highly trained observers vary over time in what they see. For example, they can become bored or inattentive, which will affect the quantity and quality of their observations.[31] And in spite of good training and experience, not all observers see the same thing. Nevertheless, objectivity can be optimized by employing accepted interviewing and observing techniques, being able to critically analyze information, retaining an active interest in research as a tool for understanding, allowing sufficient time, maintaining a nonjudgmental attitude, and being at ease when talking with others.[32]

In summary, the use of observational techniques has two advantages for global health communication research. First, they can confer very high internal validity because they can accurately capture the nature of the phenomena being observed. Second, they allow the investigator to avoid problems of reactance on the part of the subjects of study, thereby effectively eliminating entire classes of bias from consideration.

Combining Observational and Other Methods

As discussed thus far, observational techniques can be used alone. Observational research can also be used in combination with other approaches.[33-34] It is quite common to include observational methods in a broader research agenda, which might include quantitative methods, because the complementary sets of findings have different strengths, and thus allow for greater confidence that the findings are reliable. The desirability of combining dissimilar methods of data collection acts to inform a researcher's orientation to the phenomena of study. For example, a researcher might want to apply a combination of positivistic with interpretative epistemologic approaches to the same data set as autonomous teams assessing the same data.[35] The greater the difference in assumptions and research approaches, the greater the promise of interesting analysis and results.[36]

It has been found that using observational methods to offset the biases (also called systematic errors) that are inherent in self-reported quantitative approaches such as survey research leads to a fuller, more complex understanding of the topic of interest. Observational data can be used to validate survey results by either lending support to or casting doubt on quantitative findings. Consider the following example.

A study was conducted on the extent to which employees of a large organization had incorporated the new chief executive officer's (CEO's) vision for change. The CEO wanted her field staff, many of whom had been with the organization for many years, to work in a less directive fashion and more collaboratively with their clients. Data were collected to learn what the field staff thought and how they behaved by using three instruments: questionnaires; content analysis of monthly e-mailed report summaries written by field staff; and participant observation of workers in the office and field staff when they drove around the state to meet with clients.

By analyzing the survey results, it was learned that field staff liked the CEO's vision of collaborative interaction with clients and had put it to use. Results of the content analysis of written summaries of field visits supported the survey results. New collaborations were developed with clients, and the field staff stated that they valued listening to and learning from their clients. But then came the disquieting results from the participant observations. After the researchers acclimated to the roles as participant observers (as a ruse, for several months the observers brought their own work to the office and carried out requested tasks and errands), the office staff were heard making jokes about the new CEO and her mission. They made it clear that business as usual would continue in the organization, and they would outlast the new CEO, just as they had outlasted the previous CEO and his ideas for change. Moreover, the research observations revealed that in contrast to their written reports, field staff shared office staff resistance to change. Observations of the interactions between field staff and their clients revealed that field staff did not act at all collaboratively, and instead openly instructed their clients as to what needed to happen. (In many cases, the clients seemed to appreciate the directive approach.) The researchers' discussions with field staff on the issue of collaboration revealed they thought that they had acted collaboratively, even though their behavior indicated the opposite: They were assertive, directive, fact-finding, and autonomous in suggesting solutions to client problems.

How could these conflicting results be reconciled? The survey and content analysis said one thing, the two sources of participant observation, another. After discussing the strength of each set of data, it was concluded that the participant observation data provided the greatest validity and reliability. Because the new CEO wanted respondents to behave in a new way, and since they knew that the researchers had been hired by the CEO, staff members had a strong motivation to provide what they perceived to be acceptable responses. The survey answers and the self-written reports were both subject to self-reporting bias, because they responded to perceptions of the researchers' (and perhaps, perceived corporate) expectations. The participant observation data, while certainly subject to reactance, still provided greater internal validity and, probably, reliability. To paraphrase a cliché, in observational research, seeing can be believing.

Data Collection and Management

Observational researchers have several tools at their disposal to record data. It is worth emphasizing, first, the importance of rigorous data collection and management. To the untrained eye, observational research can appear to be very similar to simply watching people and talking to them. But it is not similar, and one of the main differences lies in the systematic collection and interpretation of data. Thus, field notes are typically detailed and voluminous. Data collection can include photographs, videotapes, and audio recordings as well as written material. The problem the researcher then faces is to translate large quantities of materials into succinct and tangible findings. Cultural anthropologists and ethnographers can spend several years analyzing their observational data; most researchers do not have that luxury; in fact, analysis can readily be done in much less time.

Much of what the researcher observes will be jotted down in the form of notes. In addition, it is often advantageous, when possible and appropriate, to supplement written material with tape recordings or videocassettes, particularly when observations include interviews that are unstructured, unplanned, and at times serendipitous, or more structured and planned. Audio recordings should always be transcribed; the text is then coded and relevant categories are developed, as discussed below. Tape recordings together with notes can be used to associate comments with specific participants, while video recordings can be used to code nonverbal communication, which can add interpretive power to the analysis.

Researchers take different kinds of notes; the alternative that is selected ultimately depends on what is most appropriate, most efficient, and least intrusive. The choice may well depend also on the circumstances of particular observations. Different techniques vary in the degree of completeness (e.g., how much is recorded at the time of the observation) and when the notes are actually written.

Field jottings are brief notes that are usually written during the observation to help the researcher remember observations or thoughts in order to stimulate later analysis. They are brief because there might not be sufficient time to record all that is seen or said, and the observation perhaps was not even planned. Usually recorded in small pocket notebooks, jottings are reviewed and expanded upon as soon after the observation as possible, and certainly the same day, while the experience is still fresh in the researcher's mind, and relevant details that were not included at the time can be fleshed out.

Diaries are regular, personal, and generally extended notes, in which the researcher records as much as possible of the data collection experience itself in order to stimulate critical thinking about the participants, settings, and other factors related to interactions during the research process. Just as in other diaries, entries are usually made on a daily basis.

Field logs include written schedules of what the researcher plans to do, along with extended annotations about what was actually done. Entries are recorded before events take place, and notes are added later to show the relationship between what was planned and what actually occurred. Logistical and contact information is often recorded in field logs, for example, so that the researcher can both document findings from the field and get in touch with relevant informants as needed.

Finally, *descriptive notes* are the mainstay of participant observation and the primary form of documentation. They are critical because if done well, they can lead to thoughtful analysis and will help answer research questions developed at the beginning of the study process. They are used for any type of observational research, and thus include information derived from structured or unstructured observations, individual interviews, group or focus group discussions, or archival sources. Notes can be taken to supplement a tape recording; if no recording is made, notes should record the exact words as spoken by the person rather than an interpretation. The reason for this will become clear when data analysis and coding are discussed. Briefly, these notes are the raw material that is later subjected to analysis. Good notes might include a quotation like, "I think you are right, because ....." Here, the thinking of the interviewee can later be analyzed. A notation that simply says "He agrees" cannot.

Descriptive notes include observations about behavior and the setting in as much detail as possible. Decisions can be made later as to what is relevant and what is not. Notes also include any developing ideas about research methodology in progress including, for instance, indications of reactance by subjects of the observations as well as ideas about why the things that are being observed are occurring in the way that they are.[37]

Descriptive notes can be derived from field jottings, or they can be written out in full. In either case, they should be reviewed as soon after the observation as possible, because there are often gaps that can easily be recalled in the short term but later forgotten. Gaps in notes are almost inevitable, even when taken by experienced researchers. This is often because it is essential to pay strict attention to what is happening at the moment, and writing at the same time might be either out of the question or can only be done sporadically. This can be the case in conducting interviews, when unplanned observations are made, or when things simply happen faster than the researcher is physically able to write. Also, there may well be occasions where, for ethical or practical reasons, taking notes is not feasible. In general, people who are interviewed usually expect the researcher to take notes or tape record the conversation; even so, permission to do so should be requested first. Also, it might be physically impossible to take notes at the same time as when observations made. For example, automobile safety is an increasing global health problem, and if the researcher drives in traffic in order to observe and understand driving behavior that leads to collisions, it would be foolhardy to take notes—this would only contribute to the problem (or ironically, add to the data). Sometimes, jottings can be made while observations are being made, but not full descriptive notes. Either way, it is essential to write out complete descriptive notes as soon as possible. Detailed, descriptive notes should always be made on the same day that the observations were made.

Observational research takes time. Particularly at the beginning of the process, the researcher might be unsure as to what is relevant and what is not. As observations become increasingly structured, though, the researcher can employ "optimal ignorance," which, like a horse's blinders, simply forces the observer to restrict the observation to phenomena related to the research, rather than to images that can be extraneous to the research question. One approach to structuring observations is time or event sampling. Rather than trying to capture as much as possible in a research setting (i.e., "around the clock"), the researcher could observe at selected times or settings[38] that allow for observation along a known range. For example, patient and family behavior in hospital waiting rooms can vary by time of day, day of the week, and type of hospital. Rather than spend extended periods of time in many waiting rooms, the researcher can identify blocks of time (e.g., early morning, mid-day, evening, and late night) and select one or more of different kinds of facilities (e.g., public hospital, private hospital, or smaller clinic).

For some kinds of research, notes involve some degree of quantification, if only the counting of frequencies of the occurrence of some behavior. For example, coding sheets can be used to record the frequency of observations in predetermined categories in order to calculate percentages for each category and to develop descriptive statistics such as mean scores per unit of time. For behavioral indicators, these kinds of simple calculations can be quite informative.

James W. Dearing conducted research to determine the degree of local involvement in public meetings of community coalitions. The community residents included retirees, chronically or terminally ill individuals, and ethnic minorities of low socioeconomic status. Coalition advocates hoped that the residents would add their own perspectives to discussions about access to health services. Most of the early contributors to the discussion, however, were physicians, hospital administrators, financial executives, insurers, business owners, and corporate officers. Would community residents speak up in the presence of highly skilled, high-status professionals? If they did, would the higher status professionals listen and respond? Would community residents continue to attend the meetings and stay active in the dialogue over time?

The participant observers were trained to recognize the affiliation of coalition members. With coding sheets in hand, they sat in the back of meeting rooms during the coalition's monthly meetings. Each time someone spoke up, a check mark was made on the coding sheet. If a related comment followed, another check mark was recorded in another category. In this way, observers were able to describe which type of person spoke the most, and the degree of interaction related to each type of comment. Frequencies were compared month by month to track changes in degrees of participation.

Data Analysis

Even when the principle of optimal ignorance is applied, observational research often produces large amounts of raw data, so that there is the danger of data overload when the time comes for analysis. The challenge is to reduce the amount of data without losing the essence (i.e., to separate the wheat from the chaff). Pages of notes represent a potential gold mine of information; at the same time, the very volume itself can make it difficult to see the connections among variables and events, or to tell a succinct and accurate story. How is data reduction accomplished? To begin with, the challenge is not very different than that faced by quantitative research. If several hundred structured interviews were conducted with written questionnaires, there would be a stack of questionnaires that in themselves do not allow the researcher to understand the phenomena of interest. The data must first be processed and analyzed. In quantitative analyses, the process is well understood: Simply enter the data in a spreadsheet and subject it to appropriate statistical procedures.

Qualitative data derived from observational research are handled in an analogous manner in that appropriate procedures are used to process the information. It is worth noting in passing that it is incumbent on the observational researcher to be explicit in describing these procedures. Too often, public perception is that observational research is based on a haphazard and wholly subjective management of information. In reality, though, there is a process; following the collection of observational information, the data are subjected to a multi-step process of analysis, usually referred to as coding. For purposes of this discussion, it is assumed that observational data in the form of complete notes of observations (or better yet, transcripts of informal or formal interviews) have been prepared.

The first step in data analysis is *pre-processing*. This phase actually begins before data collection even begins, and it continues through the different phases of fieldwork.[39] Pre-processing is based principally on the framework that guides the research, even if formal hypotheses have not been stated. Even studies that begin with relatively unstructured research questions are based on initial interests, expectations, and perceptions so that data collection is never completely random. The interactive relationship between data collection and the development of a conceptual framework is at the heart of grounded theory, the essence of which is that the data drive the theory. That is, theory emerges from the research process rather than as a product of formal hypothesis testing.[40]

At this preliminary point in the analysis, tentative categories related to the topic of the research are identified. These categories might well have emerged during the course of the observation. For example, research on women's refusal of sexual advances might begin with a set of categories that include strategies or actions related to the act of refusal as well as the contexts within which advances are made.

The second phase in the analytic process is the *identification of themes*. This phase is particularly important when the research is in its preliminary stages and when research questions have not yet been fully defined. This process, also called *concept mapping*, centers on making preliminary determinations on the potential relationship among categories. At this point, more concrete research questions can be formulated, even if they are still somewhat informal,[41] and adjustments can be made later in data gathering instruments. Once the data have been collected, the third phase, referred to as *data processing*, can be initiated. During this step, the researcher (or a trained coder) tries to understand the meaning of individual data points, which consist of discrete elements of field notes, including phrases that appear in transcripts of things that were said. During this phase of analysis, referred to by Strauss and Corbin as *open coding*,[42] notes and transcripts are read several times, and short annotations are written near each data point. These annotations can consist of several words, part of a sentence, or several sentences which, in the judgment of the analyst, has a single interpretation. The codes can be a product of the categories established earlier and, in fact, some codes will invariably be related to specific questions asked. For example, a study related to barriers to health care might produce codes related to observed cultural, linguistic, economic, or legal barriers as experienced by the subjects. Similarly, in discussing which communications media are most effective in providing information to a certain segment of the population, several categories might emerge (e.g., print media such as magazines or newspapers, broadcast media such as radio or television, or the Web). Careful analysis can reveal not only which of these media are most effective, but under what conditions, and with which caveats or exceptions. For example, a variety of factors, including gender, level of education, and income can be important qualifiers to reveal how a group of people, who otherwise appear to be homogeneous, have access to and use health information in different ways.

These codes are the basic building blocks of emerging theory, and the focus at this point is less to establish relationships or define categories than to understand underlying concepts through this process of labeling or naming what is said or observed. Sometimes, a phrase that is actually spoken or heard becomes the "in vivo" code.[43] The kinds of codes that emerge will differ depending on what has been observed or said, as well as the interests of the coder. For example, some categories might describe properties, including general or specific characteristics; an example is the kinds of attitudes expressed by patients or reasons why people have difficulty accessing health care. Other codes can indicate dimensions or location on a range of possible responses, often described in terms of amounts or frequencies, which may actually be numeric or more categorical (e.g., "rarely" or "almost always").

The number of codes that are written down is usually quite large at this point, although as the coding proceeds, emerging trends and tendencies become apparent to the researcher or coder; these can be noted as memos directly on the transcripts or notes for later confirmation. Quality control can be established to maximize reliability by having several people code the same data and then comparing notes to develop a unified set of codes. Establishing reliability among coders by comparing code decisions, datum by datum, is called *inter-coder* (between coder) *reliability*. This process also allows for optimizing *intra-coder* (within-coder) *reliability*. Establishing high inter- and intra-coder reliability ensures greater objectivity in analysis that can follow one observer and limited units of observation.

Once the initial stage of data sorting or open coding has been completed, the next step is *developing dimensions of interest*, referred to by Strauss and Corbin[44] as *axial coding*, or, when frequencies are calculated, *tallying data*. If frequencies are counted, this step usually involves entering each instance of previously categorized behavior into a computer, using a software spreadsheet such as Microsoft Excel. The data can then be imported for analysis into a statistical software program such as SPSS, which can produce summary descriptive statistics.

In more qualitative approaches, axial coding involves the analysis and interpretation of codes produced during the first phase, by establishing relationships among the codes. This is done in different ways. When similar phrases were used to articulate the same concept, codes can be restated, thereby eliminating different phrases that say the same thing. Also, during this phase, it will become clear that some codes or groups of codes will be related to others, often as subcategories. Axial coding allows the researcher to actually get at the underlying structure of observations and stated perceptions; at this point, the researcher essentially looks for ways to systematically explain what was observed or heard. For example, the researcher can identify similarities, differences, and trends, as well as intervening or mitigating factors and even exceptions to the rule. As relationships among codes become increasingly clear, it is often useful to draw diagrams with boxes or circles, connected by arrows or lines. This helps the researcher to think through the emerging relationships and assists the reader to better understand the research. By the end of this process, the researcher will have uncovered basic explanatory factors related to the phenomena of interest. For example, Hayward and Madill wanted to understand perceptions of organ donation among native inhabitants in England and Muslim immigrants, of Pakistani origin, in northern England.[45] The purpose was to learn how to communicate, in different ways, the need for matching organs. They found that different factors emerged among male and female natives and immigrants. For Muslim women, perceptions of organ donation were shaped by perceived costs and benefits as well as beliefs, rules, and understandings that mediate relationships with God, and the sense of self. For Muslim men, the relevant factors were perceived code of conduct for living as a Muslim and social effects of organ donation. The relevant factors among native English women were sense of self, issues of control over distal systems, and family issues. For native English men, the issues were the meaning of the body and issues of choice, control, power, and authority. These factors, in turn, could be used to develop appropriate messages.

While coding is initiated manually, and can be done entirely by hand, software programs such as Ethnograph, Hyperqual, NUD*IST, N-Vivo, and Atlas-ti are often used to facilitate the process.[46] Qualitative software programs are especially efficient when dealing with large amounts of text-based data because they allow for the grouping and regrouping of data based on previously identified criteria. Analysis of qualitative data without a computer program is also feasible—and is done anyway because the important decisions about categorization and codes must be done by the researcher, not a computer program.

The final step in data analysis is *interpretation*. This phase, sometimes called *selective coding*[47], integrates categories in order to refine theory. It is here that data are converted into a final product, whether it is theory or a set of recommendations for action. Specifically, interpretation results in one or more statement about the central category as revealed during the previous phases. In quantitative research, individual findings are usually presented in tables and charts, which must then be interpreted in order to arrive at an encompassing statement about the meaning and importance of the findings. Similarly, observational research, once analyzed, has to be interpreted in terms of one or more central categories.

Interpretation is crucial because of the researcher's duty to understand and explain the data's significance, not only in terms of simple responses to hypotheses and research questions, but also its relationship to the relevant literature. While the goal of quantitative studies is generalization to a larger universe through statistical inference, observational research has often served as the basis for analytical generalization, whereby the researcher uses the empirical study results to speculate about other groups, whether similar or different.[48]

The final step in the interpretation of observation data is often referred to as *circular validation*, whereby the tentative results and interpretation of the study are shared with the research subjects as a check on the accuracy of a written account. Feedback of research findings can help to correct facts, add nuance to the interpretation, and confirm or qualify what has been observed.

Conclusion

Like any communication research method, observational research offers many advantages and suffers from certain disadvantages. Moreover, the different techniques it encompasses are not always the most appropriate. As William Foote Whyte suggested, "Participant observation offers learning opportunities that cannot be duplicated by any other method. On the other hand, the method is not suitable for everyone and has its own limitations."[49] While sole reliance on observational research is not required, the approach has enormous potential to enrich other methods of data collection.

Notes

1. S. Coleman, *Japanese Science: From the Inside* (London: Routledge, 1999).
2. C. Pope and N. Mays, *Qualitative Research in Health Care*, 2d ed. (London: BMJ Books, 1998).
3. M. Mead, *Coming of Age in Samoa* (New York: Blue Ribbon Books, 1928).
4. B. Malinowski, *Argonauts of the Western Pacific* (London: Routledge and Keagan Paul, 1922).
5. W. F. Whyte, *Street Corner Society: The Social Structure of an Italian Slum* (Chicago: University of Chicago Press, 1943).
6. W. Liebow, *Tally's Corner* (Boston: Little, Brown, 1967).
7. D. Simon and E. Burns, *The Corner: A Year in the Life of an Inner-City Neighborhood* (New York: Broadway Books, 1997).
8. Pope and Mays, *Qualitative Research in Health Care*, 2d ed.
9. D. A. Grimes and K. F. Schulz, "Bias and Causal Associations in Observational Research," *Lancet* 359(9328) (2002): 258.
10. D. Freeman, *Margaret Mead and Samoa: The Making and Unmasking of an Anthropological Myth* (Cambridge, MA: Harvard University Press, 1983).
11. W. F. Whyte, *Learning from the Field: A Guide from Experience* (Thousand Oaks, CA: Sage Publications, 1984).
12. Grimes and Schulz, "Bias and Causal Associations in Observational Research."
13. Grimes and Schulz, "Bias and Causal Associations in Observational Research."
14. Pope and Mays, *Qualitative Research in Health Care*, 2d ed.
15. Mead, *Coming of Age in Samoa*.

16. F. J. Rothlisberger and W. J. Dickson, *Management and the Worker* (Cambridge, MA: Harvard University Press, 1939).

17. M. Rokeach, *The Three Christs of Ypsilanti* (New York: Columbia University Press, 1981).

18. M. Dalton, *Men Who Manage* (New York: Wiley, 1959).

19. K. A. Stolen, *A Meda Voz: Relaciones de Genero en la Sierra Ecuatoriana* (Quito, Ecuador: Centro de Planificación y Estudios Sociales, 1987).

20. A. Vidich and J. Bensman, *Small Town in Mass Society* (Princeton, NJ: Princeton University Press, 1958).

21. Whyte, *Learning from the Field: A Guide from Experience*.

22. J. P. Spradley, *The Ethnographic Interview* (Austin, TX: Holt, Rinehart and Winston, 1979).

23. J. Cassell and M. L. Wax, "Editorial Introduction: Toward a Moral Science of Human Beings," *Social Problems* 27 (1980): 259–264.

24. H. R. Bernard, *Research Methods in Anthropology*, 2d ed. (Walnut Creek, CA: Alta Mira Press, 1995).

25. R. M. Emerson, "Observational Field Work," *Annual Review of Sociology* 7 (1981): 351–378.

26. A. Cheadle et al., "Community-level Comparisons between the Grocery Store Environment and Individual Dietary Practices," *Preventive Medicine* 20 (1991): 250–261.

27. E. J. Webb et al., *Nonreactive Measures in the Social Sciences* (Boston: Houghton Mifflin, 1981).

28. S. Bochner, "Observational Methods," in W. J. Lonner and J. W. Berry (eds.), *Field Methods in Cross-Cultural Research* (Thousand Oaks, CA: Sage Publications, 1986).

29. C. Argyris, "Some Unintended Consequences of Rigorous Research," *Psychological Bulletin* 70(3) (1968): 185–197.

30. L. Suchman and B. Jordan, "Interactional Troubles in Face-to-Face Survey Interviews," *Journal of the American Statistical Association* 85(409) (1990): 232–241.

31. Webb et al., *Nonreactive Measures in the Social Sciences*.

32. A. G. Smith and A. E. Robbins, "Structured Ethnography," *American Behavioral Scientist* 26(1) (1982): 45–61.

33. J. Brewer and A. Hunter, *Multimethod Research: A Synthesis of Styles* (Thousand Oaks, CA: Sage Publications, 1989).

34. A. Tashakkori and C. Teddlie, *Mixed Methodology: Combining Qualitative and Quantitative Approaches* (Thousand Oaks, CA: Sage Publications 1998).

35. J. W. Dearing et al., "Social Marketing and Diffusion-Based Strategies for Communicating Health with Unique Populations: HIV Prevention in San Francisco," *Journal of Health Communication* 1 (1996): 343–363.

36. L. H. Kidder and M. Fine, "Qualitative and Quantitative Methods: When Stories Converge," in *Multiple Methods in Program Evaluation, New Directions for Program Evaluation*, eds. M. M. Mark and R. L. Shotland (San Francisco: Jossey-Bass, 1987), 57–75.

37. Bernard, *Research Methods in Anthropology.*

38. Bochner, "Observational Methods."

39. M. B. Miles, "Qualitative Data as an Attractive Nuisance: The Problem of Analysis," *Administrative Science Quarterly* 24 (1979): 590–601.

40. A. Strauss and J. Corbin, *Basics of Qualitative Research: Techniques and Procedures for Developing Grounded Theory* (California, London, and Delhi: Sage Publications, 1998).

41. Miles, "Qualitative Data as an Attractive Nuisance: The Problem of Analysis."

42. Strauss and Corbin, *Basics of Qualitative Research: Techniques and Procedures for Developing Grounded Theory.*

43. Strauss and Corbin, *Basics of Qualitative Research: Techniques and Procedures for Developing Grounded Theory.*

44. Strauss and Corbin, *Basics of Qualitative Research: Techniques and Procedures for Developing Grounded Theory.*

45. C. Hayward and A. Madill, "The Meanings of Organ Donation: Muslims of Pakistani Origin and White English Nationals Living in Northern England," *Social Sciences & Medicine* 57 (2003): 389–401.

46. E. Babbie, *The Practice of Social Research*, 9th ed. (Belmont, CA: Wadsworth Thomson Learning, 2001).

47. Strauss and Corbin, *Basics of Qualitative Research: Techniques and Procedures for Developing Grounded Theory.*

48. R. K. Yin, *Case Study Research: Design and Methods*, rev. ed. (Thousand Oaks, CA: Sage Publications, 1989).

49. Whyte, *Learning from the Field: A Guide from Experience.*

CHAPTER SIX

Social Mobilization as a Tool for Outreach Programs in the HIV/AIDS Crisis

Dhaval S. Patel

Chapter Questions

1. What is social mobilization?
2. How does the Right to Know (RTK) initiative use social mobilization tools? What lessons can be learned from the RTK program?
3. How does RTK involve young people in all aspects of the program?

The Nature of the HIV/AIDS Crisis

Epidemiology and Impact

The HIV/AIDS crisis has devastated people throughout the world. By the end of 2003, an estimated forty million were living with HIV/AIDS, with an additional eight million who either acquired the virus or died from AIDS.[1] Young people aged 15 to 24 are at the center of this crisis, with approximately one-third of the people globally who live with HIV/AIDS being youth. Due to a variety of reasons, the regions of Sub-Saharan Africa, the Caribbean, and Asia have been hardest hit with the most severe consequences of the epidemic.

In addition to grievous loss of life caused by HIV/AIDS, it is fiscally destructive to communities by the reduction in human capital and investment. Socially, the epidemic increases stigma and discrimination, and places burdens on governments, families, educational institutions, and health care organizations. This crisis also threatens societal security, especially in war-torn, politically unstable countries where HIV transmission is exacerbated by violence, armed conflict, and human rights violations. Most alarming is the negative correlation between HIV/AIDS and life expectancy. For example, in sub-Saharan Africa, the average age is now 47 years as compared to 62 years before the emergences of AIDS.[2]

Considering the international, national, and community-level efforts that have addressed or are currently addressing the global HIV/AIDS crisis, future outlook should hold promise. However, the projected statistics for the epidemic depict a bleak picture that predicts an additional forty-five million people becoming infected by 2010 unless effective global efforts are developed, implemented, monitored, and evaluated.

Different Approaches

Over the course of the last 20 years, researchers, politicians, health specialists, programmers, donors, and other stakeholders have introduced a plethora of different strategies to address the HIV/AIDS crisis with varying success. Ranging from micro- to macro-level approaches and internally motivated to externally driven approaches, HIV/AIDS interventions have evolved with time. For example, early on "information-only prevention" efforts (e.g., information programs, behavior change communication, health education) were employed commonly.[3] More recently, efforts have expanded and progressed to include "holistic community-based, social change" processes (e.g., entertainment-education, social marketing, community dialogue as well as norms, advocacy, poverty reduction, capacity building) to overcome the limitations of education-only initiatives.[4] Regardless of which approaches are utilized, the struggle against HIV/AIDS mandates the need for comprehensive, novel approaches.[5–6]

Even with a full arsenal of tools, many efforts are still hampered by the ability and degree to which HIV/AIDS risk behaviors can change. For example, recent meta-analyses of domestic and international health communication programs show that people change their behavior by as much as 10 percent after exposure to large-scale campaigns, indicating that a number of factors and strategies must be considered in order to achieve even those results.[7–9] One potentially effective strategy, which is being more visibly used in HIV/AIDS prevention, is *social mobilization.*

Due to an increasing need to respond to HIV/AIDS globally, *social mobilization* efforts are becoming much more commonplace as they are implemented in many countries because they have been shown to be effective in a number of ways.[10] For example, domestic and international social mobilization programs have favorably changed attitudes and behaviors, increased community dialogue, and positively increased care and treatment for HIV positive individuals.

To better understand how *social mobilization* outreach programs and their tools can effectively address the HIV/AIDS crisis, this chapter will (1) provide a conceptual background, (2) discuss a global case study, the Right to Know initiative, where social mobilization is used, and (3) illuminate To-Do actions and recommendations for the future.

Social Mobilization

Definition

The idea of social mobilization is not entirely new, but subjecting the concept to the rigors of academic scrutiny started primarily with the pioneering efforts of the United Nations Children's Fund (UNICEF) in the early 1990s.[11] A review of academic literature reveals a multitude of definitions, primarily because different terms are used somewhat interchangeably to mean the same thing. For example, the word "social" is often replaced with national, community, global, organizational, or local. At the same time, "mobilization" sometimes is exchanged with campaign, effort, response, initiative, action, movement, gathering, or activity.

With the different terms for social mobilization come a number of permutations that all still refer to similar concepts, processes, tools, and techniques associated with social mobilization initiatives. Although it is most likely unfair to categorize all of these different terms under the same rubric of social mobilization, this chapter does not intend to delineate all of the fine conceptual boundaries between social mobilization and its cousins. However, to ensure a common language for this chapter and the reader, a working definition is offered.

Social mobilization is the process of bringing together multisectoral community partners to raise awareness, demand, and progress for the initiative's goals, processes, and outcomes. Stated in a slightly different way by UNICEF, social mobilization is a broad-scale movement to engage people's participation to achieve a specific development goal through self-reliant efforts. This working definition is an apt one because it nicely ties together and umbrellas a set of common key tools that comprise social mobilization interventions, particularly HIV/AIDS outreach programs.

Key Tools

Social mobilization affords designers and programmers a package of different tools, or techniques, to consider and use in HIV/AIDS outreach efforts, regardless of the purpose of the initiative (e.g., prevention, care and support, services, communication). The key techniques, listed in no particular order, are partnerships, diversity, participation, leadership, and activities.[12] Although other tools can be documented and discussed depending on the specific social mobilization approach, the ones included in this chapter are those that are most commonly used. Other tools might already be subsumed into those discussed here.

Partnerships: By definition and perhaps the most critical of all social mobilization tools is the formation of partnerships between stakeholders in the community. Functioning as the foundation of most social mobilization efforts, partnerships create a collective synergy for the achievement of goals by the use of existing resources, which ordinarily would not be possible by independent individuals or groups. Reid explains that some existing resources that social mobilization partners can tap into include skills, knowledge, and information.[13]

Diversity: One of the most important keys to partnership development and maintenance is the need to bring together, or mobilize, a wide array of community stakeholders with different backgrounds, strengths and weaknesses, missions, and resources. A multisectoral, comprehensive set of partners is required to create effective action, including the continuum of national, societal, and local stakeholders from the arenas of politics, religion, education, nongovernment, media, health care, and families.[14] In addition to societal and institutional roles, diversity can also be defined, for example, in terms of sociodemographics, differences in HIV/AIDS risks and behaviors, and health status.

Participation: Field experiences have shown that HIV/AIDS outreach programs that utilize a participatory approach (e.g., internal, grassroots, ground up, involvement) have a better probability of success. With increased participation in all phases of the social mobilization cycle—design, implementation, monitoring, and evaluation—stakeholders are involved, and they build common identity and consensus, make decisions, and develop a sense of programmatic ownership, thereby leading to sustainability of behavioral outcomes. More important, increased involvement and participation expand the response calls for social change as an effective mechanism for reducing risks associated with HIV/AIDS.[15]

Leadership: Most successful social mobilization programs responding to the HIV/AIDS epidemic strategically appoint or establish solid leadership in the form of an individual, a group or organization, or steering committee composed of diverse stakeholders. This tool serves different purposes, such as developing awareness of the issues; setting up the processes for implementating the social change activities; encouraging feedback from lessons that stem from activities; motivating participation; allowing for decision making among all partners; identifying strengths and limitations; facilitating the creation of an identity; and building consensus.

Activities: As with other strategies used in the fight against HIV/AIDS, social mobilization develops, uses, and implements many activity-level tools to reach and work with participants. Whether it be town hall meetings, mass media communication messages, participatory action research, networking, capacity building trainings, rallies, street-level outreach efforts, or public events, this tool ensures that some type of mobilization activity is available for everyone.

With the delineation of the five tools of social mobilization interventions (i.e., partnerships, diversity, participation, leadership, and activities), a case study can be presented that illustrates these techniques.

Case Study of The Right to Know Initiative

Overview

To appreciate how different social mobilization tools can be effective in the struggle against HIV/AIDS, many different field examples—both in and outside the United States—could be discussed. Instead of citing and describing a subset of these social mobilization efforts, the author elected to use a UNICEF-designed, global initiative called Right to Know (RTK) as a case study. Keep in mind that although RTK does not operate in the United States, the tools discussed previously are still applicable and found in domestic social mobilization strategies. The abbreviated case described is based on work that the author of this chapter, along with many others, performed. For an in-depth discussion, please refer to Alexis, Patel, and Milicevic.[16]

The Right to Know (RTK) Initiative: Background

Right to Know is a global communication and outreach initiative designed to inform young people, aged 15 to 24, about HIV/AIDS and related issues. Over the past few years, RTK has addressed the needs for information, knowledge, and understanding of HIV/AIDS in 15 countries:

Bosnia-Herzegovina, Côte d'Ivoire, Serbia-Montenegro, Macedonia, Fiji, Ghana, Guatemala, Haiti, India, Jamaica, Malawi, Namibia, Nigeria, Thailand, and Zambia.

Generally, the main objectives of RTK are to (1) provide relevant information to all adolescents so they can make informed decisions to prevent HIV infection and lead healthy lives, (2) strengthen the capabilities of young people, communities, and stakeholders, and (3) foster partnerships for the participatory planning and implementation of appropriate HIV/AIDS youth communication strategies.

Specifically, four central themes govern how the initiative works:

- Genuine youth participation and development of country-specific efforts that ultimately help build capacity and develop social skills
- Youth mobilization and partnerships at every level of society for community ownership and support
- Participatory action research that guides communication strategies and at the same time builds capacity and mobilizes young people
- Participatory development communication strategies based on participatory action research that (a) address HIV/AIDS and related issues, (b) facilitate participation in youth development programs, and (c) support learning and growth of stakeholders

With this brief background, the second core theme, youth social mobilization, is discussed.

The RTK Initiative: Social Mobilization and Its Tools

Part of the success of this global initiative in various countries can be attributed to the use of different social mobilization tools, including **participation, partnership, diversity, leadership,** and **activities**.

By mobilizing, involving, and allowing young people to **participate** as key players in the design, implementation, and evaluation of country-specific HIV/AIDS communication strategies, RTK helps to ensure the relevance of the activities to the real needs of the youths themselves. Using the transformative power of young people from different walks of life, the initiative utilizes young people as researchers, creators, communicators, evaluators, and partners.

Through their active involvement, young people's participation in RTK can be witnessed in three ways: (1) participatory action research—see Wadsworth,[17] (2) HIV/AIDS communication approaches, and (3) monitoring and evaluation. The baseline HIV/AIDS data that the youths collect and analyze with their peers during the participatory action research phase serve as the foundation for the interactive design and implementation of HIV/AIDS outreach activities. Afterward, the young people even participate in the monitoring and evaluation of their efforts, becoming activists for the cause and thereby mobilizing other interested peers.

For example, the RTK initiative in Ghana primarily uses novel, participatory peer-to-peer HIV/AIDS outreach activities during the second level of participation. RTK-Ghana partners with the Dutch-based Feyenoord Football Academy there, which trains young Ghanaian boys aged 12 to 17 to be future footballers. By working with the academy, the young people aged 15 to 24 participating in RTK train the footballers at the academy to become HIV/AIDS peer educators, who in turn provide other footballers with HIV/AIDS information at tournaments. By using sports as an entertaining entry point to address the HIV/AIDS crisis, RTK mobilizes different young people and involves them from the start, thereby stimulating interest, empowerment, and ownership of the initiative in Ghana.

Another set of social mobilization tools used in the global RTK initiative is **partnership, diversity, and leadership**. Across the 15 countries, the broad array of multisectoral partners includes universities, social and religious groups, youth networks, youth-serving nongovernmental organizations, research institutions, media, governmental ministries, UNICEF country offices, and health care facilities. Because these partnerships are forged with young people's involvement, voice, and input, they raise the demand for entertaining and educational communication programs, as well as the sustainability of HIV/AIDS prevention strategies.

In each country, the establishment of an RTK steering committee is needed for leadership, guidance, direction, and oversight of the initiative at the outset. Through this diverse committee, the different partnerships are strengthened while increasing interaction, decision making, communication, and resource sharing. In most countries, the diversity of the partnerships means that some stakeholders take on different roles during different phases of the effort, which in the end results in greater collaboration and support of RTK activities.

Although all fifteen RTK countries create diverse partnerships (see Table 6–1), Thailand has perhaps one of the most unique set of stakeholders. By bringing together approximately 30 youth groups under the supervision of AIDSNet, Khon Kaen University, Chiangmai University, and the Program for Appropriate Technology for Health, RTK reaches out to and brings together individuals from all walks of life who are stigmatized or suffer from discrimination. For example, hard-to-reach groups, like out-of-school youth, youth in detention, men who have sex

Table 6–1. Some Multisectoral Partners in Various RTK Country Steering Committees

COUNTRY	PARTNERS
Macedonia	UNAIDS, Photovoice, MIA, HERA, Institute of Philosophy, UNFPA, UNDCP, UNESCO, WHO
Jamaica	UNDP, PAHO, UNICEF, UNESCO, UNFPA, USAID, CIDA, JAS, Jamaican Foundation for Children, Children First, Jamaica Red Cross Society, Hope for Children
Ghana	UNFPA, Ghana AIDS Commission, Ministry of Education, Ministry of Health, Johns Hopkins University, Save the Children, Planned Parenthood Association of Ghana
Malawi	UNFPA, National Youth Council, Center for Education, Research, and Training, Coordinators of Regional Youth Networks
Thailand	AIDS-NET, Chiangmai University, TYAP, UNAIDS, UNFPA, UNESCO, WHO

with men, drug users, scooter gangs, and at-risk school children, are included as partners in the initiative in Thailand.

Finally, the effectiveness of any social mobilization can be attributable to another important tool, namely **activities**. While forming partnerships from cross sections of society is mandatory for RTK success, without the aid of innovative activities that appeal to youth, the success of the social mobilization effort can be limited. RTK is no different with respect to its need to implement a multitude of HIV/AIDS activities that are youth appropriate.

Take for example some of the diverse activities that arise from the RTK social mobilization efforts in Jamaica, Macedonia, and Malawi.

- Jamaica: The RTK-Jamaica initiative focused on correcting misinformation about HIV/AIDS. The young people there adapted the *Ten Facts for Adolescents* to the local setting and created a colorful, entertaining wall chart. They utilized other information channels as well, including text messages in cell phones, music by local reggae artists, and radio broadcasts of music.

- Macedonia: The RTK-Macedonia team and partners found that young people lacked basic information about the risks associated with HIV/AIDS. To reach disadvantaged youth, the initiative employed multiple communication channels and formats, including a national television show, photography, comic strips, hip hop music, theater, and the Web.

- Malawi: The RTK-Malawi activities promoted the use of youth-friendly health services in order to encourage young people to participate in voluntary counseling and testing, HIV/AIDS prevention, and prevention of mother-to-child transmission. The significant sources of outreach and information were recreational activities, music, parental involvement, media coverage, and clubs for those living with HIV.

Clearly, RTK uses innovative, youth friendly approaches and activities during and after the process of mobilizing and bringing stakeholders together. Depending on the country and the various HIV/AIDS needs of the young people, the RTK social mobilization activities and communication messages are created, tested, implemented, and evaluated in order to disseminate HIV/AIDS information.

Recommendations for Future Social Mobilization Efforts

The case study of the RTK initiative, along with ample other campaigns documented in the scholarly literature, provides a set of actionable recommendations for future HIV/AIDS social mobilization interventions.

First, program designers need to consider the quantity of partners when using social mobilization tools. Although multisectoral stakeholders and leaders are needed, sometimes having too many players at the table can inhibit HIV/AIDS prevention efforts. Leaders should weigh the added value (e.g., resources, political clout, access to other partners) before inviting new stakeholders to join. Sometimes programs benefit more by working with and strengthening existing stakeholders, alliances, networks, and practices rather than developing new partnerships, which requires high levels of personal and organizational investment. Regardless of the number of stakeholders, the partners must articulate goals, inputs, processes, and outcomes so that the community recognizes what it is working toward and has the leverage to tackle problems—all of which could not have been done alone.[18]

Second, often those infected with HIV are the very same individuals who are not welcome to participate in addressing the crisis due to the stigma and discrimination attached to their illness. However, social mobilization efforts should include those with HIV/AIDS to put the name, face, words, and imagery of those who are infected or ill. This adds credibility and visibility to the effort and can counter stigmas by opening dialogue, showing respect, sharing stories of success and change, as well as sensitize the community as support increases.[19] Programmers should actively recruit and develop the involvement of people living with HIV/AIDS to create a better, internally driven initiative.

Next, social mobilization initiatives must effectively use the tools of traditional as well as modern communication venues, such as social clubs or broadcast media, in order to reduce HIV/AIDS risks. Six good practices can be offered for future social mobilization campaigns based on the global RTK Initiative.[20] These are,

1. Tailor programs to specific groups and their needs
2. Design messages for each group that are relevant and based on participatory action research findings
3. Use community resources, existing social networks, and available partners
4. Ensure that activities are innovative, entertaining, educational, and culturally acceptable
5. Allow for participant input, feedback, and interaction
6. Link up with other sectors and stakeholders involved in the HIV/AIDS crisis

Fourth, because the social mobilization tools can be applied in different ways to deal with HIV/AIDS (e.g., prevention, care, treatment, support, services), depending on the purpose of the campaign, designers should think about ways to integrate responses and efforts rather than construct stand-alone independent approaches. Through integration, different partners can be mobilized in different ways with a common vision, thereby sharing and reducing costs, energies, resources, and time.

Fifth, the limitation and failure of many HIV/AIDS prevention efforts—non-social mobilization and even social mobilization in nature—are the result of the lack of sustainability of favorable outcomes. One of the culprits for this lack is the inability to build community capabilities. Even if individuals, communities, and nations are ready for social mobilization approaches, many times they still must be taught how to plan and manage programs; effectively measure success; transfer skills from one partner to the next; adequately utilize resources; decentralize roles and responsibilities by allowing everyone to participate; and a host of other program management skills. In the future, programmers and researchers must devote ample time and energy to build capacities in order to ensure the sustainability of HIV/AIDS prevention methods using the social mobilization tools.

Finally, social mobilization outreach programs and their tools, as a way to address the HIV/AIDS global crisis, must be researched, monitored, and evaluated through participatory methodologies. While the value of assessment activities is self-evident in terms of providing program guidance during intervention and for the next phase of the initiative, the purpose of social mobilization is to bring together people and allow them to learn, discuss, and participate on their own. Naturally, these types of efforts should not leave assessment exclusively to external agencies only when the development of appropriate, sustainable strategies for HIV/AIDS prevention is paramount. Through capacity building training, future planners of social mobilization outreach programs should utilize participatory action not only for the creation of strategies, but also to monitor and evaluate them.

Conclusion

This chapter presented, discussed, and summarized some methods to design, implement, and evaluate social mobilization outreach efforts in order to tackle the devastating HIV/AIDS crisis around the world. A conceptual background on social mobilization was offered, followed by a study of the RTK Initiative. By considering the explicit set of To-Do actions and recommendations, planners of HIV/AIDS social mobilization interventions can now be better positioned in the future to deal with the challenges of HIV/AIDS.

Acknowledgment: The author would like to acknowledge the individuals involved with UNICEF's "Right to Know" Initiative. Their work is described in this chapter as an abbreviated case study of HIV/AIDS social mobilization efforts.

Notes

1. Joint United Nations Programme on HIV/AIDS, "Question & Answers II: Basic Facts about the HIV/AIDS Epidemic and Its Impact," *UNAIDS Questions & Answers* (2003).
2. Joint United Nations Programme on HIV/AIDS, *UNAIDS Questions & Answers*.
3. E. Clift, "IEC Interventions for Health: A 20-Year Retrospective on Dichotomies and Directions," *Journal of Health Communication* 3 (1998).
4. M. E. Figueroa et al., *Communication for Social Change: An Integrated Model for Measuring the Process and Its Outcomes.* Working Paper developed for the Rockefeller Foundation (2002).
5. J.-M. Alexis and D. S. Patel, *The Role and Effectiveness of Information and Counseling in HIV Prevention among Young People.* Report prepared for the World Health Organization (2003).
6. G. Dowsett, "Living 'Post AIDS,'" *National AIDS Bulletin* 10(2) (1996): 18–23.
7. R. Hornik, *Public Health Communication: Evidence for Behavior Change* (Hillsdale, NJ: Lawrence Erlbaum, 2002).

8. L. B. Synder and M. A. Hamilton, "Meta-analysis of U.S. Health Campaign Effects on Behavior: Emphasize Enforcement, Exposure, and New Information and Beware of the Secular Trend," in *Public Health Communication: Evidence for Behavior Change*, ed. R. Hornik (Hillsdale, NJ: Lawrence Erlbaum, 2002), 357–383.

9. L. B. Synder, N. Diop-Sidibe, and L. A. Badiane, *Meta-Analysis of the Impact of Family Planning Campaigns Conducted by Johns Hopkins Bloomberg School of Public Health/Center for Communication Programs*. Paper presented at the International Communication Association Annual Meeting, San Diego, May 2003.

10. A. Malcolm and G. Dowsett, "The Contexts of Community Mobilization and HIV/AIDS Prevention," in *Partners in Prevention: International Case Studies of Effective Health Promotion Practice in HIV/AIDS*, eds. A Malcolm and G. Dowsett (Geneva, Switzerland: Joint United Nations Programme on HIV/AIDS, 1998), 5–9.

11. Tulane School of Public Health and Tropical Medicine, *The ICEC and Global Social Mobilization*, 2004. www.tulance.edu/~icec/socmob.htm.

12. J. Robb, M. Samati, and S. Mwanza, *Social Mobilization Campaigns: An Affirmative Strategy for Involving Communities*. Paper presented at the Comparative and International Education Society Annual Meeting, Washington, DC, March 2001.

13. E. Reid, "Approaching the HIV Epidemic: The Community's Response," *AIDS Care* 6(5) (1994): 551–557.

14. Tulane School of Public Health and Tropical Medicine, *The ICEC and Global Social Mobilization*.

15. Joint United Nations Programme on HIV/AIDS, *Expanding the Response*. UNAIDS Briefing Paper (1996), 9–13.

16. J.-M. Alexis, D. S. Patel, and A. Milicevic, *The "Right to Know"Initiative: Good Practices Report*. Report prepared for the United Nations Children's Fund (2003).

17. Y. Wadsworth, *Everyday Evaluation on the Run*, 2d ed. (Australia: Allen and Unwin, 1997).

18. K. Panday, *Social Mobilization: Concept and Application for Poverty Reduction and Self-Governance*. Paper presented at the Regional Workshop on Promoting Effective Participation of Civil Society and Local Governance and Poverty Alleviation in the ECIS Region, May 2002.

19. E. Reid, "The Global Spread of AIDS," *National AIDS Bulletin* 6(7) (1992): 30.

20. Alexis, Patel, and Milicevic, *The "Right to Know"Initiative: Good Practices Report*.

CHAPTER SEVEN

Use of Social Networks in Child Survival, Infectious Diseases, and HIV/AIDS

Florence Naluyinda Kitabere

Chapter Questions

1. What defines a social network?
2. What is the difference between homogeneous and heterogeneous social networks?
3. How can social networks be used to achieve behavior change?

Introduction

Social networks and their resultant social capital have increasingly been incorporated into research and implementation programs. Social networks are interactions and linkages among people in a community. They are key channels of communication through which communities acquire information beyond the mass media. These interactions include connections among individuals through friendship, kinship, sexual contacts, and often involve exchange of information or services. The information, ideas, and support that people exchange within these networks are referred to as the social capital, or social resources. The individuals in networks, including who interacts with whom, how often, and what issues are discussed, all have a strong influence on the flow of resources within that network. People with strategic positions in these networks are said to have more social capital than their counterparts because their position gives them more and better resources.[1] Thus, social capital characterizes the various ways in which a given community's members interact. The extent and nature to which a person is involved in various informal networks and formal civic organizations affects his well-being in the community,[2] not forgetting the influence brought by the broader social, cultural, and physical environment into the network's structure and function.

Social networks are multidimensional by nature, and it is crucial to find out the types of networks that poor people can utilize and in what ways they contribute to each other in these interactions. Measurement of social networks can be done in various ways, including use of either egocentric or sociometric systems. Important factors in an assessment include the size and how close the network is, its homogeneity, heterogeneity, density, its duration and reciprocity, the variety of activities, and resources that flow among the members. The more heterogenic the network is, the higher the yield of benefits among the members. The more homogeneous groups find it easier to have collective action especially if they are democratic in their decision making.

Identification of either strong or weak ties is also important because each plays a significant role in the network. A weak tie can act as a bridge from one network to the other (connecting people with an almost equal status), or act as a link to people in authority such as the police, political parties, or private institutions such as the bank (connecting people across different status). Access to linking networks is essential to the well-being of an individual, especially in the low income countries and communities where public institutions are often corrupt, and bankers charge high interest rates.[3] Another important connection links leaders of poor communities to external assistance for development of their local areas, for example, urging the government to bring health programs into the community.[4]

On the other hand, it should be noted that networks can promote negative behavior, which can hinder instead of help the individual's well-being. For example, some networks refuse to allow girls to attend school; others encourage hidden populations to indulge in high-risk sexual activities such as interactions among IV drug users. Therefore, social networks that serve the public good should be encouraged and those that promote unhealthy behavior should be deterred.

Social Networks and Child Survival

Over the last three decades, several international organizations, led by the World Health Organization and United Nations Children's Fund, have implemented child survival programs, which led to a significant impact in reducing infant and childhood mortality and morbidity, especially in developing countries. Although child mortality rates have shown substantial and consistent reductions in most regions of the world since 1960, in recent years these declines have leveled or even reversed in many countries in sub-Saharan Africa.[5] One of the Millennium Development Goals is to reduce child mortality by two-thirds by the year 2015. However, the United Nations update on progress toward child survival goals, released in 2001, revealed that unless new resources and efforts are provided by affected countries and their assisting partners, this development goal will not be met.[6] Several studies have also shown that child mortality increases significantly in children infected with HIV mostly through vertical transmission from their mothers. After adjusting for competing causes of mortality for those under 5 years old, HIV infection caused 7.7 percent of under-5 years deaths in 1999, a substantial rise from 2 percent in 1990.[7–8] Therefore, sustaining goals for child survival and HIV/AIDS requires viable social networks within the various communities, to support behavior change at the grassroots level. This would work in synergy with other development strategies such as investing in human and physical capital.

Acceptance of routine immunizations, growth monitoring, promotion and protection of breastfeeding, use of oral rehydration therapy, and other positive health care behavior needs strong linkages between health facilities and the communities through social networks to be successful. Use of identified networks at the community level could increase demand for health services such as vaccinations, dissemination of health information, and effective disease surveillance. For example, the types and locations of social interactions such as marketplaces and community drinking wells can influence the local epidemiologic features of infectious disease, especially measles. In addition to this, the identified risk factors for enteric infections and acute respiratory infections significantly overlap and include poverty, overcrowding, lack of parental education, malnutrition, low birth weight, and lack of breastfeeding. Most of these are difficult to change in the absence of social change.[9]

Approaches to primary prevention of diarrheal disease, including provision of a community source of clean drinking water, improving sanitation through providing latrines, and promoting hand washing and other personal hygiene habits, have been found to be effective at reducing the rate of diarrheal disease in the community, when done under well-funded research studies. However, the reality of sustaining such improvements among large populations is directly linked to accessibility and availability of financial resources and a strong political will to do so, which in turn relies heavily on viable networks of community members.[10] These approaches will succeed only when the community is committed to making them work; and the interventions need to be introduced to the people in a culturally acceptable framework.

Other habits that can be influenced by the individual's social inter-action include medical care-seeking behavior by the parents/guardian of a sick child, access to appropriate care in a timely fashion, and ade-quate treatment and follow-up. Identification of indigenous interactions within a community, who the leaders are, and how information flows within the members can enhance development and sustenance of the beneficial health behavior needed to improve child survival.

Social Networks and HIV/AIDS

HIV/AIDS is a socially propagated illness with a transmission that often requires intimate contact between individuals, and thus it is strongly influenced by the social networks in which a person circulates. These networks can shape high-risk behaviors that enhance the spread of the disease. Therefore, social interactions are crucial to understand and fight the HIV/AIDS epidemic. The networks help to develop prevention plans and to formulate social policies.

These social networks can be utilized to help assess the facilitating factors or barriers to the spread of HIV infection in specific popula-tions. The networks within which a person interacts are important channels to introduce and sustain health-protective behavior change. Latkin and colleagues analyzed the interactions between condom use, condom norms, and social network characteristics among a sample of 105 urban poor individuals at risk of acquiring and transmitting HIV, in a drug-using community in the United States in which 17 percent were HIV positive.[11] This group found that condom use or lack of use was significantly associated with peer norms and strongly influenced by how friends talked about or used condoms. Intravenous drug use was negatively associated with condom use, while going to church posi-tively affected condom-promoting norms. The study also revealed that the size of financial support and health advice among the networks of the drug-users most positively related to condom norms. Therefore, interventions at the level of social networks can promote and normal-ize the use of condom in a given population.

Methodology for Use of Social Networks

A pre-tested questionnaire has been compiled, with focus on applica-tions for developing countries. The change agent can use these ques-tions to obtain data on the different types of networks an individual with a household has access to in a given community. Social networks have been assessed at different levels such as individual, household, regional, and entire societies. The most accurate of these is believed to occur at the household level. The integrated Questionnaire for Measurement of Social Capital [12] has questions to generate quantitative data on several aspects of social capital including groups and networks; trust and solidarity among neighbors and service providers' collective action and cooperation within the network; information flow and access to communication infrastructure; social cohesion and inclusion in the everyday interaction; and empowerment and political action. Questions about empowerment assess personal efficacy and ability to influence local and wider political decisions. These questions are obtained from earlier survey work done on social capital in several developing countries including Tanzania, Burkina-Faso, Bolivia, and Indonesia. The questions were used to collect data on subjective well-being, political engagement, sociability, community activities, and communication. They have been pre-tested in the field and subjected to external critique and panel advisers, and have been proven reliable, valid, and useful.

The questions can be incorporated into large national household surveys such as the Demographic and Health Surveys, or used for collection of social network data within the design and implementation of projects and programs at regional or district level that target households. Social network data can be collected as part of the baseline information prior to launching a project in anticipation for future evaluation of the project's impact, and several rounds of data can be collected as the project progresses. Thus, at each level of implementation, the analysis of the questionnaire answers helps assess the impact of the project on the social structures and make several comparisons between types of networks and project uptake.

The questions about groups and networks include the nature and extent to which members of a household participate in the different informal networks and social organizations in their community, what they contribute to these associations, and what they get from them. Other questions are formatted to assess the diversity of the networks, how their leaders are observed, and how their involvement as members evolves over time.

Data should also be collected about the trust an individual has toward his or her neighbors, community service providers, and strangers and how these perceptions change with time.

Collective action and cooperation is a strong attribute among network members. Thus, information should be sought on how household members interact with their community on joint projects or when responding to a crisis in the neighborhood and assess if there are any penalties the community gives if a person does not participate in this community effort.

The sample size and selection for such questions should be chosen for the bigger household national survey or for a baseline situational analysis, and the data analysis could be incorporated into the rest of the survey.

When using these questions,

- Adapt them to the local situation, which includes a detailed review of the questions and their coded answers to check their relevance to the local context and whether they are culturally sensitive.

- Translate them into the written local languages, to help maintain the quality and comparability of the data collected. Words such as organization, networks, and trust should be given special emphasis to clarify their meanings in the context of the native languages, with the help of local language experts. Then translate the questions back to English before analysis.

- Train the interviewers to have a similar approach, and conduct pilot testing to check the applicability of the questions. As a rule, use different households from those in the survey for the pilot study.

- During the analysis, assess the different dimensions of social networks across different groups.

- Identify any bridges, linkages, the extent of homogeneity and heterogeneity within the networks, membership in associations, the degree of trust and adherence to norms, and the extent of collective action as an output measure. (Collective action is critical because provision of many services including health activities requires committed action by the community members.)

- Cross-tabulate these results with other variables such as the household's welfare, poverty, access to health services, and other development indicators.

- Incorporate some multivariate models to assess other relationships between social networks a household has, and with other aspects such as land ownership, education, health, goods consumption, and physical capital.

The questions include:

I. Groups

1. What groups or organizations, associations, or networks do you belong to? (These can be formal or informal, where people get together regularly to do some activity or discuss things.)

2. Of the groups mentioned, does he/she participate actively in decision making? On a scale of 1 to 4 choose the appropriate level of involvement:

1 = Leader
2 = Very active member
3 = Somewhat active member
4 = Does not participate in decision making

3. How does one become a member of this group?

4. What is the main benefit of joining this group?

5. Does the group help you get access to any of the services listed here?
   a. Education or training
   b. Health services such as immunizations, HIV voluntary counseling and testing, health promotion messages, anti-retro-viral therapy
   c. Water supply or sanitation
   d. Credit or savings
   e. Agricultural input, irrigation, or other

6. Describe your group in terms of diversity in households, kinship, religion, gender, age, ethnicity, occupation, education level or background, political viewpoint, socioeconomic status, and how the group membership has changed over time, e.g., over the last 5 years.

7. How are leaders selected?

8. How effective is the group's leadership?

9. When the group is ready to make a decision, how does it go about it?

10. Does the group interact with other groups with similar goals within the neighborhood/village?

11. Does the group interact with other groups with similar goals outside the neighborhood/village?

12. Does the group interact with other groups with different goals within the neighborhood/village?

13. Does the group interact with other groups with different goals outside the neighborhood/village?

14. What is the source of funding for the group?

15. What is important source of advice that the group receives?

II. Networks

1. How many close friends do you have (i.e., people you feel at ease with, can discuss private matters, or call on for help)?

2. How many of these are able to lend you money?

3. How many people beyond your household could you ask to lend you some money if you suddenly needed it to feed your family for at least a week?

4. Could you count on your neighbors to take care of your children if you suddenly had to go away for a day or two?

III. Trust and Solidarity

1. In general, would you say that most people can be trusted or not? (Scale it from 1 to 10, with one being the least and 10 being the most.)

2. How much do you trust the different types of the following people? (Scale it from 1 to 5, with one being the least trust and 5 being the most.)
    a. People from your tribe or ethnic group
    b. People from other tribes or ethnic groups
    c. shopkeepers
    d. Local government officials
    e. Central government officers
    f. Police
    g. Teachers
    h. Nurses and physicians
    i. Strangers

3. Do you think that over the last five years, the level of trust in this neighborhood/village has become better, worse, or the same?

4. How well do people in your neighborhood/village help each other out these days? (Scale it from 1 to 10, with 1 being the least helpful, and 10 being the most.)

5. If a community project does not directly benefit you, but benefits many other members of the village/neighborhood, would you contribute money or time to the project?

IV. Collective Action and Cooperation

1. Over the last year, have you worked with others in your neighborhood doing something for the community's benefit? If yes, was participation required or voluntary?

2. Are the persons who do not participate in such community activities punished, criticized, or sanctioned? If so, how, and what do they do to them?

3. If a community problem occurs, such as a main water supply breakdown, how will the people respond collectively to try to solve the problem?

4. If something unfortunate happens to someone in your neighborhood, such as the death of a parent, how likely is it that some people in the community will get together to help him/her?

V. Information and Communication

1. How much time does it take for a household member to reach the nearest working post office? (Scale it from 1 to 10, with 1 being the shortest time and 10 being the longest time.)

2. How often does a household member read the newspaper or has had one read to him or her in the last one month?

3. How often does a household member listen to the radio?

4. How often does a household member watch television?

5. How long does it take to get to the nearest working telephone?

6. How often does a household member make or receive a phone call during one month?

7. From the following list, circle the three most important sources of information about what the government is doing (e.g., health services such as immunization, family planning, agricultural extension, HIV/AIDS)?
   - Relatives, friends and neighbors
   - Community bulletin board
   - Local market
   - Community or local newspaper
   - National newspaper
   - Radio
   - Television
   - Groups or associations
   - Business or work associates
   - Political associates
   - Community leaders
   - A governmental agent
   - Nongovernmental organizations
   - Internet
   - Other, specify

8. During what season is your house easily accessible by road?

9. If you live in a rural area, how many times have you traveled in the past 12 months to a neighboring village or town? If you live in an urban area, how many times have you traveled in the past 12 months to another part of the city?

10. Compared to five years ago, has access to information improved, deteriorated, or stayed about the same?

Most of the answers to the questions need to be coded for the questioner to enter the data easily. When the questions are used properly, the quantitative data collected provide immediate information that is useful to project managers, implementers, policy makers, and researchers.

Notes

1. R. Burt, "The Network Structure of Social Capital," *Research in Organizational Behavior*, eds. R. Sutton and B. Straw (Greenwich, CT: JAI Press, 2000), 345–423.

2. R. Putman, *Bowling Alone: The Collapse and Revival of American Community* (New York: Simon and Schuster, 2000).

3. D. Narayan, *Voices of the Poor: Can Anyone Hear Us?* (New York: Oxford University Press, 2000).

4. A. Krishna, *Active Social Capital: Tracing the Roots of Development and Democracy* (New York: Columbia University Press, 2000).

5. O. B. Ahmed, A. D. Lopez, and M. Inoue, "The Decline in Child Mortality: A Reappraisal," *Bulletin World Health Organization* 78 (2000): 1175–1191.

6. United Nations. *We the Children*, End-Decade Review of the Follow-up to the World Summit for Children: Report of the Secretary General. A/S-27/3. http:www.unicef.org.

7. N. Walker, B. Schwartlander, and J. Bryce, "Meeting International Goals in Child Survival and HIV/AIDS," *The Lancet* 360 (2003).

8. C. A. Latkin et al., "Norms, Social Networks, and HIV-Related Risk Behaviors among Urban Disadvantaged Drug Users," PMID: 12570967 (Pub Med, indexed for MEDLINE).

9. A. L. Reingold and C. R. Phares, "Infectious Diseases," in *International Public Health: Diseases, Programs, Systems, and Policies*, eds. M. H. Merson, R. E. Black, and A. J. Mills (Gaithersburg, MD: Aspen Publishers, 2001), 139–201.

10. Reingold and Phares, "Infectious Diseases."

11. Latkin et al., "Norms, Social Networks, and HIV-Related Risk Behaviors among Urban Disadvantaged Drug Users."

12. C. Grootaert et al. The World Bank Social Capital Thematic Group: Integrated Questionnaire for Measurement of Social Capital (SC-IQ), 2003.

CHAPTER EIGHT

Sex, Soap, and Social Change: The Sabido Methodology

Kriss Barker

Chapter Questions

1. What is the difference between the Sabido methodology and other types of entertainment-education?
2. How are characters and plot developed in a Sabido-style serial drama?
3. How do you think the Sabido methodology could be used to achieve behavior change at the community level?

The Sabido Methodology

The Sabido methodology is an approach to development of mass-media serial dramas. However, unlike typical "soap operas," Sabido-style serial dramas are not used to sell sex or soap, but rather, social change.

This chapter explores the Sabido methodology and the reasons why this theory-based approach to behavior change communication has been so successful. How do Sabido-style serial dramas differ from "soaps" and how does the Sabido methodology differ from other entertainment-education approaches? Why do audiences from the Philippines to India, from Tanzania to Ethiopia, and from Mexico to Bolivia find these dramas irresistible—and much more than merely educating in an entertaining way? And what does the future hold for the application of the Sabido methodology in rethinking the very foundation of comprehensive behavior-change communication programs?

Miguel Sabido: "Entertainment with Proven Social Benefit"

Miguel Sabido was Vice President for Research at *Televisa* (Mexican television) during the 1970s. While at *Televisa*, Sabido developed a theoretical model for eliciting pro-social attitudinal, informational, and behavioral change through commercial television programming. He called this model "entertainment with proven social benefit."

Between 1975 and 1981, Miguel Sabido produced seven social content serial dramas in Mexico:

- *Ven Conmigo* (Come with Me) provided specific information about a study program offered by the Secretary of Public Education in 1975.

- *Acompaname* (Accompany Me), Sabido's second entertainment-education soap opera, contained a family planning message (broadcast from August 1977 through April 1978).

- *Vamos Juntos* (Let's Go Together) promoted responsible parenthood and the active development and integration of children in the family and in society (July 1979 through March 1980).

- *El Combate* (The Struggle) promoted an adult education program launched in several communities outside of Mexico City (April through September 1980).

- *Caminemos* (Going Forward Together) tackled the theme of sex education for adolescents (September 1980 through April 1981).

- *Nosotros las Mujeres* (We the Women) ran through April to October 1981. It was designed to counter traditions associated with machismo and to encourage women to become aware of their important role in the family and society.

- *Los Hijos de Nadie* (Nobody's Children) addressed the issue of street children.

During the decade 1977 to 1986, when many of these Mexican soap operas were on the air, the country underwent a 34 percent decline in its population growth rate. As a result, in May 1986, the United Nations Population Prize was presented to Mexico as the foremost population success story in the world.

Thomas Donnelly, then with United States Agency for International Development in Mexico, wrote, "Throughout Mexico, wherever one travels, when people are asked where they heard about family planning, or what made them decide to practice family planning, the response is universally attributed to one of the soap operas that *Televisa* has done. ... The *Televisa* family planning soap operas have made the single most powerful contribution to the Mexican population success story."

Since the 1980s, Sabido's successful approach to "entertainment with proven social benefit" has been applied in over 200 health intervention programs in over 50 countries in Latin America, Africa, and Asia, dealing with such educational issues as HIV/AIDS prevention, family planning, environmental health, teenage pregnancy prevention, and gender equality.[1–2]

Twende na Wakati *(Let's Go with the Times):* *A Radio Serial*

Mkwaju is a truck driver along the national routes in Tanzania. Although Mkwaju is married, he has many girlfriends along his route—he is quite the sexual athlete. Tunu, Mkwaju's subservient wife, stays at home to care for their children. She is becoming more and more frustrated with her husband's antics, especially the way he squanders his earnings on women and alcohol. She finally decides to take things into her own hands, and starts her own small business, selling vegetables in the market. The business does well, thus giving Tunu the self-confidence to leave Mkwaju. Mkwaju contracts HIV as a result of his high-risk lifestyle, and eventually develops symptoms of AIDS. In an act of compassion, Tunu cares for him until he dies. But, his legacy lives on through his son Kibuyu who is beginning to follow in his father's footsteps. He regularly smokes marijuana with his friends on the outskirts of the city, and steals money from unsuspecting passers-by. Will Kibuyu suffer the same fate as his father? Or, will he learn from his mother how to succeed in life?[3]

This excerpt from *Twende na Wakati* (Let's Go with the Times), a radio serial drama broadcast twice weekly over Radio Tanzania, demonstrates the power of the Sabido methodology. The program was evaluated using an experimental design, pre- and post-intervention measurements of dependent variables, and measurement triangulation using an independent data source to provide more definitive evidence of the effects of the strategy on behavior change.[4] It was the first evaluation of an entertainment-education program to apply all three of these evaluation measures on a national level.

Results of Twende na Wakati

Beginning in July 1993, Radio Tanzania broadcast *Twende na Wakati* twice weekly during prime time (at 6:30 pm) for 30 minutes. The radio station at Dodoma, however, did not broadcast this program, and instead broadcast locally produced programs in this time slot, thus serving as the comparison area in the field experiment (see Figure 8–1). However, the Dodoma area received all other elements of the national family planning program, including several other radio programs. Then in September 1995, after two years of broadcasts, Radio Tanzania began broadcasting *Twende na Wakati* in the Dodoma area.

By the end of 1993, *Twende na Wakati* was the most popular radio program in Tanzania, with 57 percent of the radio population listening. Independent research by the University of New Mexico and the Population Family Life Education Programme of the Government of Tanzania measured the effects caused by the program with regard to such issues as AIDS prevention behavior, ideal age of marriage for women, and use of family planning.[5] Though the population of the Dodoma comparison area was more urban than the rest of the country, a multiple regression analysis eliminated the influence such differences might have accounted for (e.g., increased access to information and services, higher income, or level of education). Nationwide random sample surveys of 2,750 people were conducted before, during, and after the broadcast of the program. Data were also collected from the AIDS Control Programme of the government, the Ministry of Health,

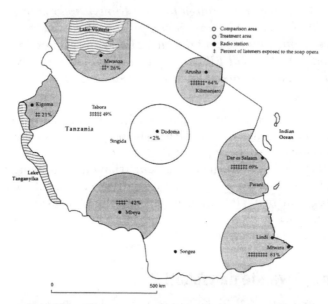

Figure 8–1. Map of Tanzania

Source: E. M. Rogers et al., "Effects of an Entertainment-Education Soap Opera on Family Planning in Tanzania," *Studies in Family Planning* 30(3) (1999): 193–211.

and the Demographic and Health Survey, all of which reinforced the findings of the significant impact on attitudes and behavior.[6–7]

Among the findings was a significant increase in the percentage of the population who perceive that they might be at risk of HIV infection; an increase in people's belief that they can take effective action to prevent HIV/AIDS; an increase in interpersonal communication about HIV/AIDS; an increase in the belief that individuals, rather than deities or fate, can determine how many children they will have; an increase in the belief that children in small families have better lives than children in large families; and an increase in the percentage of respondents who approve of family planning.

The study also provided evidence that the Tanzanian radio serial stimulated important behavioral changes. Of the listeners surveyed, 82 percent said the program caused them to change their behavior to avoid HIV infection by limiting the number of sexual partners and by using condoms. Independent data from the AIDS Control Programme of the government of Tanzania showed a 153 percent increase in condom distribution in the broadcast areas during the first year of the serial drama, while condom distribution in the Dodoma non-broadcast area increased only 16 percent in the same time period (See Figure 8–2.)

The program was also effective in the promotion of family planning. There was a strong positive relationship between listenership levels by district and the change in the percentage of men and women who were currently using any family planning method. The research also showed an increase in the percentage of Tanzanians in the areas of the broadcast who discussed family planning with their spouses. The program also had a significant effect in raising the ideal age of marriage for women and the ideal age of first pregnancy.

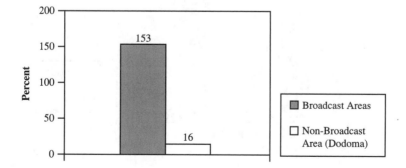

Figure 8–2. Increase in Condom Use

Source: E. M. Rogers et al., "Effects of an Entertainment-Education Soap Opera on Family Planning in Tanzania," *Studies in Family Planning* 30(3) (1999): 193–211.

Because of its experimental design, the evaluation results were able to disaggregate the effects of the radio serial drama from other family planning promotions and HIV/AIDS prevention programs being implemented throughout Tanzania. In regions where *Twende na Wakati* was broadcast, the percentage of married women who used a family planning method increased 10 percent in the first two years of the program, while the corresponding percentage stayed flat in Dodoma during the same period, when the program was not broadcast there. Then when the program was broadcast in Dodoma, the contraceptive prevalence rate increased 16 percent. In regions where the program was broadcast, the average number of new family planning adopters per clinic, in a sample of 21 clinics, increased by 32 percent from June 1993 (the month before the show began airing) to December 1994. Over the same period, the average number of new adopters at clinics in the Dodoma area remained essentially flat. (See Figure 8–3.)

Independent data from Ministry of Health clinics showed that 41 percent of new adopters of family planning methods were influenced by the serial drama to seek family planning. This percentage included 25 percent who cited the serial drama by name when asked why they had come to the clinic, and another 16 percent who cited "something on the radio" and then identified the serial drama when shown a list of programs currently on the air. Another family planning serial drama, using

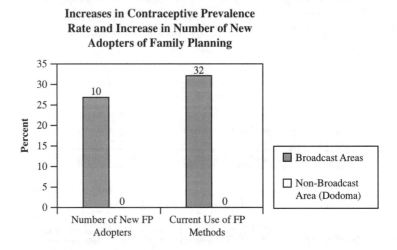

Figure 8–3. Family Planning Indicators

Source: P. W. Vaughan et al., "Entertainment-Education and HIV/AIDS Prevention: A Field Experiment in Tanzania," *Journal of Health Communication* (5) Supplement (2000): 81–100.

**Percent of New Adopters of FP and
Reasons Motivating Use**

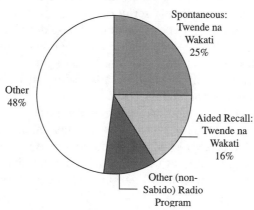

Figure 8–4. New Family Planning Adopters

Source: P. W. Vaughan et al., "Entertainment-Education and HIV/AIDS Prevention: A Field Experiment in Tanzania," *Journal of Health Communication* (5) Supplement (2000): 81–100.

a different methodology, was broadcast nationwide by Radio Tanzania at the same time and was cited by just 11 percent of new family planning adopters at the same Ministry of Health clinics. (See Figure 8–4.)

An Empirical and Reproducible Approach to Entertainment-Education

Twende na Wakati produced such impressive behavior change results because it was designed in the Sabido model, which uses elements of communication and behavioral theories in order to reinforce specific values, attitudes, and behaviors.[8] As mentioned, another radio serial drama that was developed using a different methodology was broadcast over the same period in Tanzania—with significantly less impact.

Thus, the results described demonstrate how important the design of the serial drama is to success in terms of behavior change. Sabido-style serial dramas achieve results because they are developed using an empirical and reproducible approach to behavior change communication via mass media. In fact, every detail of a Sabido-style serial drama is developed according to a theoretical and empirical research-based formula in order to reinforce a coherent set of interrelated values that is tied to specific prosocial behaviors. The Sabido methodology is also a replicable methodology that, although formularized, is adaptable to the individual values and cultures of each country where it is used.

The Sabido methodology is based on theoretical and social research that is used to develop mass media serial dramas that are based on the realities that people in the audience face daily. These dramas communicate at the emotional level as well as the cognitive level, and further establish the conditions for social learning to take place. Sabido-style serial dramas portray role models who realistically learn to live more fulfilling personal and interpersonal lives.

The Sabido methodology comprehensively reinforces prosocial attitudes and motivates behavior change using mass media channels. Sabido's approach comprises a theoretical dimension as well as methodologies for formative and summative evaluation research that are adaptable to varied commercial media and national infrastructures.

Entertainment as Education

The major tenet of the Sabido methodology is that education does not have to be boring—and that entertainment can be educational. Sabido originally termed his approach "entertainment with proven social benefit." Since then, many communication professionals and scholars have applied the term "entertainment-education" to the Sabido approach. However, the Sabido methodology is more than mere entertainment-education.

The following is a definition of the standard use of entertainment as education, but as will be shown later, the Sabido methodology takes a different approach.

> *Entertainment-education is defined as the process of purposely designing and implementing a media message to both entertain and educate, in order to increase audience members' knowledge about an educational issue, create favorable attitudes, shift social norms, and change overt behavior.*[9–10]

Singhal further defines entertainment-education as a "performance [that] captures the interest or attention of an individual, giving them pleasure, amusement, or gratification while simultaneously helping the individual to develop a skill or to achieve a particular end by boosting his/her mental, moral or physical powers."[11] A common goal of entertainment-education programs is to entertain and educate audiences in order to catalyze social change in a socially desirable manner.

Since the 1980s, the entertainment-education strategy has been used in over 200 health intervention programs in over 50 countries in Latin America, Africa, and Asia, dealing mainly with reproductive health issues such as HIV/AIDS prevention, family planning, environmental health, teenage pregnancy prevention, and gender equality.[12]

Entertainment-education comes in many different sizes and shapes:

- Individual films and videos are a good medium to use in Asia and Africa where they are shown from video vans as well as on national media.

- Variety shows are increasingly popular with youth in developing countries—many of these programs engage young people directly in content and production.[13]

- Television and radio spots often include entertainment-education through short narratives or through use of familiar characters.[14–15]

- Street theater, community radio, indigenous storytellers, drama contests, and community rallies with local performers incorporate and/or adapt national entertainment-education productions.[16]

Many of these entertainment-education programs attract very large audiences and bring about major audience effects in knowledge and attitude, with significant and valuable overt behavior changes. In fact, evaluation research indicates that if these entertainment-education media are implemented properly, relatively strong effects on knowledge gain, attitude change, and behavior change result.[17]

Although these entertainment-education programs certainly produce results, they do not have the same magnitude of effects achieved by Sabido-style programs, as seen in the example of *Twende na Wakati*.[18]

The Sabido Difference: Beyond Mere Entertainment-Education

Successful use of the Sabido methodology hinges on two key factors: (1) use of the serial drama format and (2) rigorous adherence to the theories underlying the methodology. As seen in the previous examples of other types of entertainment-education, results can be achieved even when these two factors are not strictly applied, but it has been repeatedly demonstrated that sustained behavior change is best achieved when the methodology is applied in its "purest" form.

Format: The Serial Drama

First and foremost, the Sabido methodology requires the use of serial drama. Serial dramas that span several months or years are an extremely powerful form of entertainment-education that influence both specific health behaviors and related social norms. Why?

- Serial dramas capture the attention and the emotions of the audience on a continuous basis
- Serial dramas provide repetition and continuity that allow audiences to identify more and more closely with the fictional characters, their problems, and their social environment
- Serial dramas have characters who develop a change in behavior slowly, the same hesitations and setbacks that occur in real life
- Serial dramas have various subplots that introduce different issues in a logical and credible way through different characters, a key characteristic of conventional soap operas
- Serial dramas build a realistic social context that mirrors society and creates multiple opportunities to present a social issue in various forms.[19]

Serial dramas present different perspectives and stimulate audience discussions that can lead to both individual health behavior change and to a change in social norms.[20–24] As Piotrow states, "Of all the formats for entertainment-education programs [that] have been adapted, developed, tested, or contributed to, serial drama—on television where possible, or on radio when access to television is limited—has proven to be a highly effective format to promote long-term changes in health behavior and to influence the social norms that can reinforce such changes."[25]

Theories Underlying the Sabido Methodology

Second, the Sabido methodology is based on various communication theories, each of which plays an essential role in the development of a Sabido-style serial drama. The application of these theories is critical to the success of the Sabido methodology in achieving behavior change.

The different theories that guide the development of Sabido-style serial dramas provide the methodology with a foundation for the structure and design of messages, characters, and plots—a foundation based on formative evaluation research. The theories also provide a frame-

Telenovelas vs. U.S. Soap Operas

Whereas the U.S. type of soap opera has its roots in domestic novels and film chapter plays, both directed to an almost exclusively female audience, the origins of the Latin American telenovela can be traced to the nineteenth century serialized stories and novels that appeared in European newspapers and magazines and were penned by the likes of Charles Dickens and Eugene Sue for male and female readers alike.[26]

The U.S. soap opera is an open-ended story that continues as long as advertisers and ratings are in sufficient abundance; each telenovela, on the other hand, consists of a finite number of episodes, in which a central story is told until its conclusion.[27]

The telenovela is the backbone of the Sabido methodology for several reasons:

1. The emotional tone of this format produces an identification that can be used to teach the audience a desired social behavior. Continued exposure to the basic message is important.

2. In contrast to the North American soap opera, the Latin American telenovela has a definite beginning, middle, and end and thus provides an opportunity to tie in information about health organizations, and expand the infrastructure services.

3. The telenovela format connects the audience with the infrastructure services in short epilogues that convey relevant information at the end of every episode.

4. Because the telenovela format is a reflection on what is good and bad in society, it is easy to add characters for identification by individuals and groups in the audience, so they can learn social behavior change without harming audience ratings.

work to articulate hypotheses for summative (evaluation) research on the impact of the program.

The Sabido methodology (Table 8–1) draws from five theories of communication and behavior change: (a) a circular adaptation of Shannon and Weaver's Communication Model,[28] (b) Bentley's Dramatic Theory,[29] (c) Jung's Theory of Archetypes and Stereotypes and the Collective Unconscious,[30] (d) the Social Learning Theory of Albert Bandura,[31] and (e) MacLean's Concept of the Triune Brain,[32]—all supplemented by Sabido's own Theory of the Tone.[33]

Table 8–1. Theories Underlying the Sabido Methodology

THEORY	FUNCTION IN SABIDO-STYLE SOAP OPERA
Communication Model (Shannon and Weaver)	Provides a model for the communication process through which distinct sources, messages, receivers, and responses are linked.
Dramatic Theory (Bentley)	Provides a model for characters, their interrelationships, and plot construction.
Archetypes and Stereotypes (Jung)	Provides a model for characters that embody universal human physiological and psychological energies.
Social Learning Theory (Bandura)	Provides a model in which learning from soap opera characters can take place.
Concept of the Triune Brain (MacLean)	Provides a model for sending complete messages that communicate with various centers of perception.
Theory of the Tone (Sabido)	

Source: H. Nariman, *Soap Operas for Social Change* (Westport, CT: Praeger, 1993).

Communication Model: Shannon and Weaver, 1949

Shannon and Weaver's Communication Model has five basic factors, arranged in a linear format.[34] The components in this model are:

1. The information source selects a desired message out of a set of possible messages.
2. The transmitter changes the message into a signal that is sent over the communication channel to the receiver.
3. The receiver is a sort of inverse transmitter, changing the transmitted signal back into a message, and interpreting this message.
4. This message is then sent to the destination. The destination can be another receiver (i.e., the message is passed on to someone else), or the message can rest with the initial receiver, and the transmission is achieved.
5. In the process of transmitting a message, certain information that was not intended by the information source is unavoidably added to the signal (or message). This "noise" can be internal (i.e., coming from the receiver's own knowledge, attitudes, or beliefs) or external (i.e., coming from other sources). Such internal or external noise can either strengthen the intended effect of a message (if the information confirms the message), or weaken the intended effect (if the information in the noise contradicts the original message).

Information

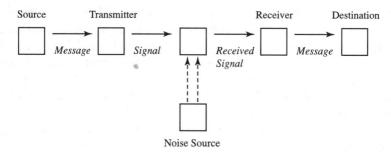

Figure 8–5. Shannon and Weaver's Model of Communication

Source: C. E. Shannon and W. Weaver, eds., *The Mathematical Theory of Communication* (Urbana, IL: University of Illinois, 1949). Cited in H. Naiman, *Soap Operas for Social Change* (Westport, CT: Praeger, 1993).

Sabido adapted Shannon and Weaver's linear diagram to form a communication circuit that depicts the circular nature of the communication process (Figure 8–6). He then applied this circuit to a serial drama. In the case of a commercial soap opera on television, the communicator is the manufacturer of a product, the message is "buy this product," the medium is the soap opera, the receiver is the consumer, and the response is the purchase of the product and television ratings.

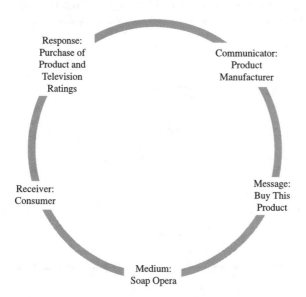

Figure 8–6. Sabido's Circular Model of Communication

Source: H. Naiman, *Soap Operas for Social Change* (Westport, CT: Praeger, 1993).

Sabido took this circular model one step further to represent two-step communication interactions. For this, he introduced the two-step flow theory of communication (Figure 8–7) described by the sociologist Paul F. Lazarsfeld,[35] which states that messages in mass media have the majority of their impact on a minority of receivers. These people will then communicate the message to others, hence a two-step flow. Although the direct effect of most mass media messages on behavior change are often modest,[36] the indirect effects of the media in encouraging peer communication can be substantial. This process of communication flow is substantiated by more recent communication theories, most notably Rogers's Diffusion of Innovations theory.[37]

These "water cooler" discussions are very important in explaining how Sabido-style serial dramas affect behavior change within a community. Audience members often conduct discussions with their peers regarding important social issues that are similar to those of the characters' "on the air." This is because the characters provide a model on how to discuss issues that are sensitive, or even taboo, and discussions between characters indicate a certain social acceptance of these issues.

In their discussion of the results of *Twende na Wakati*, Rogers and colleagues state that, "One of the main processes through which the serial drama changed Tanzanian listeners' family planning behavior was by stimulating interpersonal communication on the subject."[38] The authors continue, "When mass media messages stimulate peer communication about the program content, this interpersonal communication can change individuals' behavior."[39] Married women who listened to

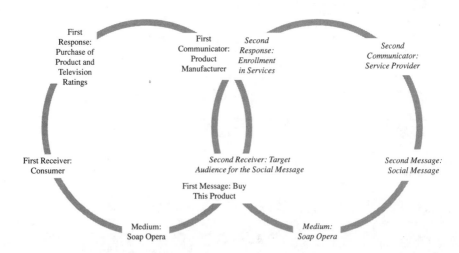

Figure 8–7. Two-Step Flow of Communication

Source: H. Naiman, *Soap Operas for Social Change* (Westport, CT: Praeger, 1993).

Twende na Wakati and who talked with their spouses, especially those who talked about the family planning content of the serial drama, were more likely than others (64 percent vs. 19 percent) to adopt family planning methods. Married women who talked with their spouses about family planning also had a more accurate perception of their spouse's attitude toward family planning than did those who did not. Spousal communication about family planning, which was stimulated by exposure to *Twende na Wakati,* therefore played an important role in adoption of a contraceptive method.

More recently, findings from a study of a Sabido-style radio serial drama in Ethiopia show that new family planning acceptors use this two-step model to confirm their intention to seek family planning services before they actually visit the clinic. Almost 60 percent of new adopters surveyed at selected family planning clinics throughout the country said they had talked with their spouse (17.4 percent) or friends/neighbors (42.2 percent) about their decision before finally coming to the clinic for services, mimicking the course followed by characters in the radio program.[40]

Dramatic Theory: Bentley, 1967

Dramatic Theory describes the structure and effects of five genres of theater (tragedy, comedy, tragicomedy, farce, and melodrama). Among these genres, melodrama presents reality in a slightly exaggerated sense in which the moral universes of good and evil are in discord. Sabido employed Bentley's structure of the melodrama genre as a basis from which to design characters and plots. "Good" characters in Sabido-style serial dramas accept the proposed social behavior, and "evil" characters reject it. Plots are then constructed around the relationships between good and evil characters as they move closer to or farther away from the proposed social behavior. Their actions encourage the audience to either champion or reject these characters accordingly.[41]

The tension between the good and evil characters evoked by the melodrama places the audience between the forces of good and evil. But, in a twist of the typical audience role in melodrama, where audience members simply watch or listen to the battle between good and evil, Sabido inserted the audience into the heart of the action—by representing audience members through a third group, one that is uncertain about the social behavior in question. These "uncertain" characters are intended to be those with which the target audience most closely identifies. As will be shown later, it is also these "transitional" characters who will guide the audience members through their own evolution toward adoption of desired behavior changes.

Although the three groups of characters in Sabido-style serial dramas are exaggerated as is the case in melodrama, they are modeled on real people within the target audience and the perceptions these people might have regarding the social value and behavior being presented.

Archetypes and Stereotypes—Theory of the Collective Unconscious: Jung, 1970

Jung's theory states that there are certain scripts or stories with familiar patterns and characters that people have played throughout history. These universal scripts or stories appear in myths, legends, and folktales around the world. Jung posited that these universal scripts or stories are the "archetypes of a collective unconscious" and share common characters such as "Prince Charming," "the mother," and "the warrior." Jung further suggests that these archetypes are expressions of a primordial, collective unconscious shared by diverse cultures.

Probably the most commonly known universal script is the "Cinderella" story. This story describes the rags to riches evolution of the archetypical "good" and "pure" Cinderella, abused at the hands of an "evil" stepmother and stepsisters, who, aided by her Fairy Godmother, finds her prince and ultimately lives "happily ever after."

Sabido used the archetypes described in Jung's theory as a basis for developing characters that embody universal psychological and physiological characteristics to address themes within the serial drama.[42] Through these characters, the viewer finds an archetypical essence of him- or herself that interacts with the social message. Sabido portrayed these archetypes as positive or negative stereotypes, representing the societal norms of the target audience.

Sabido-style serial dramas rely on extensive formative research to identify the culture- or country-specific versions of these archetypes and to identify local archetypes that represent the prosocial values (or the antithesis of these values) that will be addressed in the serial drama. If the formative research on which the serial drama is based is done properly, the scriptwriters will be able to develop archetypical characters with which audience members will be able to identify. The formative research is used to develop a grid of positive and negative social "values" that these positive and negative characters will embody. (The use of formative research in development of a Sabido-style serial drama will be explained later in this chapter.)

Social Learning Theory: Bandura, 1977 and Social Cognitive Theory: Bandura, 1986

Social Learning Theory, as articulated by the Stanford University psychologist Professor Albert Bandura, explains how people learn new behaviors from vicariously experiencing the actions of others. Bandura postulates that there are two basic modes of learning. People can either learn through the direct experience of trial and error and the rewarding and punishing effects of actions, or through the power of social modeling. Trial-and-error learning by direct experience is not only tedious but harmful when errors produce costly or injurious consequences. So, many people will short-cut this process by learning from the successes and mistakes of others. This short-cut, called vicarious learning, or modeling, is a key tenet of Bandura's Social Learning Theory.[43]

According to Social Learning Theory, people not only learn in formal situations such as classrooms, but also by observing models. In fact, the largest portion of learning to adapt to society takes place through such observational learning. The models used in this observational learning can be people in real life or characters in mass media (such as television or radio). Sabido-style serial dramas use Bandura's Social Learning Theory to guide the design of media role models through which viewers can learn social behaviors. A major advantage of modeling through the media is that it can reach a vast population simultaneously in widely dispersed locales.

A key to the use of Social Learning Theory in Sabido-style serial dramas is use of appropriate models that are visibly rewarded (or punished) in front of the audience, in order to convey the values that are being promoted by the serial drama into behavior. Social Learning Theory postulates that positive rewards have a vicarious effect on the observer (in this case, the audience) and can motivate audience members to practice similar behavior(s). Punishing a role model for practicing a socially undesirable behavior likewise provides a vicarious experience for the observer and can inhibit his or her practice of the same behavior. This adoption is called modeling because it is based on the role model's conduct. Through modeling it is possible to acquire new forms of behavior and to strengthen or weaken certain behaviors. In Sabido-style serial dramas, characters "teach" audience members via modeling so that they are able to make a recommended response.

Sabido determined that three types of characters are fundamental to successful modeling by audience members. The first two types of characters are positive and negative role models. They embody positive and negative behaviors concerning the social issues addressed in the serial drama (and are based on Jung's theory of archetypes and stereotypes, previously described). These characters will not change during the course of the serial drama, but are repeatedly rewarded or punished for their behaviors. The consequences of these positive or negative behaviors must be directly linked to the behavior in question: for example, a truck driver character that is practicing at-risk sexual behavior should suffer from a sexually transmitted infection or even contract HIV, but should not be the victim of a traffic accident.

The third type of character is the "transitional character." These characters are neither positive nor negative but somewhere in the middle. These transitional characters play the pivotal role in a Sabido-style serial drama and are designed to represent members of the target audience. The transitional characters' evolution toward the desired behavior is that which the audience members will use to model their own behavior change.

For example, in Sabido's first social content serial drama *Ven Conmigo* ("Come with Me"), which dealt with adult literacy, transitional characters were specifically chosen from specific sub-groups (e.g., the elderly, young adults, housewives) who represented the key target audiences for the national literacy campaign in Mexico. One of the main transitional characters was a grandfather who struggled to read the many letters he received from his favorite granddaughter. In a cathartic episode, he graduates from literacy training, and is finally able to read his granddaughter's letters, albeit with teary eyes. In the year preceding the broadcast of *Ven Conmigo*, the national literacy campaign had registered 99,000 students. Following the broadcast of this episode (and the epilogue that provided information about registration in the literacy campaign), 250,000 people registered for literacy training. By the end of the serial drama, 840,000 people had registered for the literacy program—an increase of almost 850 percent from the preceding year.

To motivate changes in behavior among the target audience, it is imperative that audience members not only identify with these transitional characters, but empathize with these characters as they first experience the suffering that compels them to change negative behaviors, and then struggle during the process of change. Thus, the grandfather in *Ven Conmigo* struggles against nay-sayers who disparage his efforts to learn to read by reasoning that the elderly cannot possibly learn to read—and that his efforts to become literate are futile. The grandfather eventually surmounts this wall of cynicism and proves that, in fact, "old dogs can learn new tricks." As was demonstrated by this example, the evolution of the transitional characters must be gradual, or the audience will reject the change process as being unrealistic. If the characters' evolution is not gradual and fret with obstacles, the audience will expect that their own progress toward positive change will be unrealistically rapid and facile.

But why do people identify with some models and not with others?[44]

- First, the model must attract the attention of the observer. Attention is increased when the models are perceived as attractive—and this is more likely when the model is perceived as having a high status as opposed to a low status in society.

- Next, the information must be retained by the audience members. The model's behavior is most likely to be retained by the observer when the model is perceived as close to familiar and significant things in his/her life.

- Motor reproduction also influences the degree of modeling. Motor reproduction is the translation of retained symbols (or ideas) into guides for behavior (action). Motor reproduction conveys how to get from an idea to concrete action. This is encouraged by having the role models in Sabido-style serial dramas demonstrate the prosocial behaviors in realistic circumstances that the viewer can easily relate to his/her own life.

- As previously mentioned, modeling is also dependent on motivational, or reinforcement, processes. It is through motivation and reinforcement that the viewer is actually encouraged to practice the behavior acquired through the preceding three subprocesses. According to the Social Learning Theory, the observer sees the consequences of the model's behavior and forms a series of expectations regarding rewards and punishments for his or her own practice of this behavior. If the conditions in which he or she observed the model practice the behavior can be generalized to the viewer's own circumstances, it is likely that the viewer will be motivated to practice the behavior also. Also, the model must be rewarded for positive (prosocial) behavior and punished for negative behavior. This motivates the members of the audience to practice the behaviors that are rewarded. In this way, the observer learns vicariously by watching the model being rewarded or punished.

Bandura also developed a related theory, Social Cognitive Theory, that explains behavior change can occur only when an individual feels sufficiently empowered to change. If an individual feels that the society, culture, religion, or his/her deity (or "Fate") dictates individual behavior and its consequences, there is little that communication can do to impact behavior change. For example, if a woman perceives that Fate determines the number of children she will ultimately bear, even a well-conceived family planning communication campaign will have little effect in motivating her to plan or space her pregnancies—she feels that this decision is not hers to make.

Bandura termed this perception of self-determination "self-efficacy." The more self-efficacy an individual perceives, the more likely he or she will be to feel empowered to make decisions that affect his/her life and circumstances.

Research has shown that Sabido-style serial dramas can increase self-efficacy among audience members. According to Rogers, the Sabido-style serial drama *Twende na Wakati* produced a marked increase in listeners' self-efficacy with regard to family size in Tanzania.[45] In fact, the series title, which means "Let's Go with the Times," was defined in several episodes as "taking charge of one's life." Positive and transitional role models in *Twende na Wakati* exemplified this self-efficacy and they were rewarded in the storyline for taking charge of their lives by adopting a family planning method, or by otherwise taking control of and responsibility for their reproductive health and that of their partner(s). Negative role models such as Mkwaju, who lacked such control, were punished by events.

The content of *Twende na Wakati* that dealt with self-efficacy had a marked effect on listeners' beliefs and, indirectly, on their family planning behavior. For example, married women in the 1995 survey who believed they could determine the size of their family were much more likely than others (51 percent vs. 16 percent) to use a family planning method.[46]

How can we increase audience members' perceptions of their own self-efficacy? Bandura states that people's beliefs in their efficacy are developed by four main sources of influence. These include mastery experiences, seeing people similar to themselves manage task demands successfully; social persuasion that one has the capabilities to succeed in given activities; and inferences from somatic and emotional states indicative of personal strengths and vulnerabilities. Because ordinary realities are strewn with impediments, adversities, setbacks, frustrations, and inequities, people must have a robust sense of efficacy to sustain the perseverant effort needed to succeed. As Bandura notes, for those who have a high sense of self-efficacy, failure is informative.[47]

Triune Brain Theory: MacLean, 1973 and Theory of the Tone: Sabido, 2002

The Sabido methodology is based on conveying a holistic message that is perceived by audience members on several levels of awareness. Sabido began his career as a theater director. In his work in the theater, Sabido discovered that actors can have different effects on the audience by channeling their acting energy through three different body zones. If actors focus their energy behind their eyes, the tone of the production is conceptual. If actors focus energy in the base of the neck, the tone of the production is emotive. If actors focus energy in the pubic area, the tone of the production is primal. Sabido instinctively understood that in order to motivate or persuade, it is necessary to provide a complete message that speaks to these three levels of perception.

However, Sabido lacked a theoretical explanation for what he was observing. He eventually discovered Paul MacLean's Concept of the Triune Brain, which presents a model of human brain structure with three levels of perception—cognitive, affective, and predispositional.

Sabido was particularly taken by MacLean's division of the brain into three zones. In his book, *A Triune Concept of the Brain and Behavior*, MacLean defines these three zones:

- The first zone is the reptilian zone of the brain and is common to all animal life—its purpose is self-preservation. It has four functions: feeding, fighting, fleeing, and fornicating.
- The second zone of the brain is the paleo-mammalian brain. This zone is common to all mammals and is the source of most of memory. It is also the seat of emotions. As such, it is the primary residence of human values.
- The third zone of the brain is the neo-mammalian brain. MacLean posits that this zone is exclusive to the human race and is the center of human cognition.[48]

Thus MacLean's theory gave him the scientific basis he needed to focus on the emotional (second zone) and human instinctive/impulse (first zone) as the basis for his serial dramas, with the third (cognitive zone) used primarily to reinforce the first and second zones messages in the drama.

In summary, the Sabido methodology for development of mass media entertainment-education serial dramas is unique in that it is designed according to elements of communication and behavioral theories. These confirm specific values, attitudes, and behaviors that viewers can use in their own personal advancement.

Key Steps in the Development of a Sabido-Style Serial Drama

The development of a Sabido-style serial drama is a collaborative process between technical advisers who have extensive experience with the methodology, and the radio and/or television broadcasters, appropriate government ministries, and nongovernmental organizations that will be trained in the use of the methodology.

Formative Research

In a Sabido-style serial drama, formative research is used to gather information about the characteristics, needs, and preferences of the target audience. This information is used to design the characters, settings, and storylines of the serial drama. Also, this information is used to determine the key values and issues that will be addressed by the serial drama.

The formative research studies the habits and lifestyles of members of the target audience to determine their needs, desires, behaviors, and media usage in order to develop understandable, high-quality, culturally appropriate characters and storylines.

Formative research uses both quantitative and qualitative methods; and employs methods such as surveys, focus group interviews, analyses of demographic/health data, collaborative workshops, field observation, and pilot testing of episodes with a sample of the target audience.

Sabido-style serial dramas differ from many other communication approaches that are largely "message driven." However, there is little evidence that "messages" deliver behavior change. The Sabido methodology is driven by social-science and audience research, which is one of the reasons why it is so effective.

Literature Review

The formative research begins with a review of published reports analyzing the effects of the culture on issues to be addressed by the program, and includes summaries of studies on behavior of the target audience related to these issues. This review of the existing literature assists the research team to determine what additional research studies will be necessary to complete the body of knowledge available on the topic(s) to be addressed by the serial's drama; the audience knowledge, attitudes, and practices with regard to these topics; and the infrastructure of information and services available concerning these topics.

Media Analysis

The formative research also includes an assessment of the reach of the radio and television systems throughout the country; the availability of proper equipment and power supply for broadcast during key times; attitudes among the key leaders of each broadcast station regarding the issues to be addressed in the program; the continuity of broadcast programs and personnel at the stations; and the openness of the media outlets to initiate new programs, such as serial dramas, as a means to promote health and social development in the country. The media analysis will also determine listenership or viewership habits of the target audience, so that an optimum time can be selected for broadcast of the program.

Social Services Infrastructure Analysis

The formative research also describes the current situation with regard to availability of services and infrastructure to assist target audience members to adopt new behaviors (e.g., accessibility of family planning clinics, or HIV counseling and testing services). This is critical to ensure that the serial drama does not create demand for services that do not exist—or that demand does not outstrip available supply of services related to the topic(s) addressed by the serial drama.

The importance of formative research to help shape the content of the serial drama cannot be overemphasized. Such formative research can identify, for example, whether the primary need is for correct information on measures to prevent HIV/AIDS; changing the image of condom usage in the culture; helping people understand relative risk of protected vs. unprotected sex; showing girls and women how to avoid unwanted sexual experiences; or showing people how to deal with emotional tensions attached to condom use within long-term relationships. This research helps to determine the validity of common assumptions about sexual behavior in any culture in order to ascertain the most effective strategies to reduce sexual risk.[49]

Development of the Moral Framework and Values Grid

The formative research is used to develop a moral framework, which is in turn used to develop a values grid on which the messages in the serial drama will be based.

The moral framework for a Sabido-style serial drama is a document that summarizes the existing legal and policy framework underlying the topics to be addressed in the serial drama. The moral framework includes an analysis of the country's ideology, constitution of the country, and any relevant legislation regarding the subject in question (e.g., family planning, HIV/AIDS, gender equality). The moral framework also examines fundamental principles laid down in United Nations covenants and declarations, such as the Cairo Programme of Action, to which the country is a signatory.

The moral framework ensures that the social message corresponds to issues that are officially sanctioned within the country and that it is relevant to an agenda articulated by national policymakers—the serial drama should not create values, but should reinforce pre-existing prosocial values, attitudes, and behaviors.

Moral frameworks have been developed for many countries, each based on that nation's religious, cultural, political, or other relevant positions. Therefore, a moral framework that has been developed for one country cannot be applied to another country, because the policies and values could be incompatible. For example, Islamic Sudanese women would likely not emulate or even identify with characters based on a moral framework for Catholic Brazil.

The Moral Framework

Sabido-style serial dramas are based on the findings of extensive formative research that helps the scriptwriters and producers to develop the characters, storylines, settings, and dialogue. The positive (pro-social) values that are promoted by the serial drama are based on a Moral Framework (or a moral statement) that formulates the moral positions on the issues to be addressed by the serial drama. This moral framework is signed by representatives of governmental, social, religious, cultural, and community organizations to demonstrate their acceptance of the values presented in the document.

Moral Frameworks have been developed for many countries, each based on that nation's religious, cultural, political, or other national moral positions. While the frameworks have enabled researchers, writers, and producers to create programs that are effective for that particular country, the programs cannot be run in other countries because they are often morally incompatible. For example, Islamic Iranian women would not be likely to emulate or even identify with television characters based on a Moral Framework for Catholic Brazil. Thus, in order to spread the benefits of family planning programming, there is a need for a framework that is universally acceptable to the world's nations and on which universally acceptable storylines and characters can be developed.

The Moral Framework includes summaries of U.N. documents such as the Cairo Program of Action, the United Nations Declaration of Human Rights, the Rio Environmental Summit, and other internationally agreed upon documents as a universally acceptable moral framework for use in the production of education-entertainment family planning programs.

The position statements set forth in the Moral Framework for specific countries are based on agreements from a number of international conventions, conferences, and declarations coordinated through the United Nations. Each statement is derived from one of those agreements. An abbreviation of the conference title indicates which statements are based on which agreements.

The final section of the Moral Framework includes a grid that displays the countries of the world and which agreements each country has ratified. It is important to note that while agreements of U.N. conventions are legally binding, declarations and those documents resulting from conferences are not. Consequently, the grid shows which countries have ratified the U.N. conventions, as well as which countries were represented at U.N. International Conferences such as the International Conference on Population and Development in Cairo and the World Conference on Women in Beijing.

The moral framework forms the basis for the values grid, which is a listing of the positive and negative values that will be promoted (or negated) in the serial drama. The values grid, a compilation of positive and negative values that will be promoted (or negated) in the serial drama, is then created out of the moral framework. The values grid consists of statements such as: "It is good that parents send their daughters to school," or "It is bad that husbands beat their wives."

The values grid, depicted in Table 8–2, is used to develop the positive and negative characters, who embody the positive and negative values in the values grid. During the course of the serial drama, the transitional characters evolve to adopt the positive values and behaviors promoted by the program. Transitional characters start out as being neutral toward the positive and negative values in the values grid, but evolve to adopt the positive values and behaviors promoted by the program.

Table 8–2. Sudan Values Grid (February 2004)

A. HEALTH

Maternal Mortality

IT IS GOOD THAT...	IT IS BAD THAT...
1 It is good that individuals in the community strive to reduce maternal mortality during pregnancy and delivery.	It is bad that individuals in the community do not strive to reduce maternal mortality during pregnancy and delivery.
2 It is good that individuals strive to improve the quality of services provided that will increase awareness of the high prevalence of maternal mortality rate in the society.	It is bad that individuals do not strive to improve the quality of services provided that would increase awareness of the high prevalence of maternal mortality rate in the society.
3 It is good that service providers take measures to improve the general health status of the people.	It is bad that service providers do not take measures to improve the general health status of the people.
4 It is good that individual members of the community know and understand the best practices in nutrition that include a balanced diet.	It is bad that individual members of the community do not understand the best practices in nutrition that include a balanced diet.

continues

Table 8–2. *continued*

IT IS GOOD THAT...	IT IS BAD THAT...
HIV/AIDS	
1 It is good that individuals within the community recognize that HIV/AIDS exists and is a threat to society.	It is bad that individuals within the community do not recognize that HIV/AIDS exists and is a threat to society.
2 It is good that individuals within society know that everyone who is sexually active stands a risk of contracting HIV/AIDS.	It is bad that individuals within society do not know that everyone who is sexually active stands a risk of contracting HIV/AIDS.
3 It is good that individuals know the various modes of HIV/AIDS transmission.	It is bad that individuals do not know the various modes of HIV/AIDS transmission.
4 It is good that individuals go for counseling and testing in order that they know their HIV/AIDS status.	It is bad that individuals do not go for counseling and testing in order that they know their HIV/AIDS status.
5 It is good that people practice safe sex.	It is bad that people do not practice safe sex.
6 It is good that people are aware of the link between STI and HIV/AIDS.	It is bad that people are not aware of the link between STI and HIV/AIDS.
7 It is good that people go for treatment as soon as they get infected with STIs.	It is bad that people do not go for treatment as soon as they get infected with STIs.
8 It is good that people accept and give care to victims of HIV/AIDS.	It is bad that people do not accept and do not give care to victims of HIV/AIDS.
9 It is good that society accepts and takes care of AIDS orphans.	It is bad that society does not accept and does not take care of AIDS orphans.
10 It is good that HIV positive people do not lose their jobs because of their status.	It is bad that HIV positive people lose their jobs because of their health status.
11 It is good that society understands the basic needs of HIV/AIDS sufferers.	It is bad that society does not understand the basic needs of HIV/AIDS sufferers.
12 It is good that HIV positive pregnant women are provided with anti-retroviral therapy.	It is bad that HIV-positive pregnant women are not provided with anti-retroviral therapy.
13 It is good that people know that HIV-positive mothers can transmit HIV to their children during pregnancy, delivery, and breastfeeding.	It is bad that people do not know that HIV-positive mothers can transmit HIV to their children during pregnancy, delivery, and breastfeeding.

continues

Table 8–2. *continued*

IT IS GOOD THAT...	IT IS BAD THAT...

FAMILY PLANNING

	IT IS GOOD THAT...	IT IS BAD THAT...
1	It is good that individuals in society have enough correct information about family planning.	It is bad that individuals in society do not have enough correct information about family planning.
2	It is good that individuals know the different modern methods of family planning.	It is bad that individuals do not know the different modern methods of family planning.
3	It is good that people are informed that they should bear children they can afford to provide with basic necessities including food, clothing, shelter, and education.	It is bad that people are not informed that they should bear children they can afford to provide with basic necessities including food, clothing, shelter, and education.
4	It is good that parents understand that a good parent is one who, besides providing basic necessities, will treat his/her children equally.	It is bad that parents do not understand that a good parent is one who, besides providing basic necessities, will treat his/her children equally.
5	It is good that pregnant women attend ante- and pre-natal clinics.	It is bad that pregnant women do not attend ante- and pre-natal clinics.
6	It is good that HIV negative mothers breastfeed their babies for at least two years.	It is bad that HIV negative mothers do not breastfeed their babies for at least two years.
7	It is good that children are immunized against childhood diseases such as tetanus, whooping cough, measles, diphtheria, polio, etc.	It is bad that children are not immunized against childhood diseases such as tetanus, whooping cough, measles, diphtheria, polio, etc.
8	It is good that couples who cannot have children are examined and given appropriate treatment.	It is bad that couples who cannot have children are not examined and are not given appropriate treatment.
9	It is good that pregnant women understand that malaria can affect their unborn babies.	It is bad that pregnant women do not understand that malaria can affect their unborn babies.
10	It is good that women who are planning to get married get immunized against tetanus before marriage and pregnancy.	It is not good that women who are planning to get married do not get immunized against tetanus before marriage and pregnancy.
11	It is good that traditional birth attendants (TBAs) refer complicated maternal cases to maternal and child health (MCH) clinics.	It is bad that traditional birth attendants (TBAs) do not refer complicated maternal cases to maternal and child health (MCH) clinics.

continues

Table 8–2. *continued*

IT IS GOOD THAT...	IT IS BAD THAT...
B. SOCIOCULTURAL ISSUES/RELIGION	
1 It is good that parents take their children to school instead of encouraging them to go out to work.	It is bad that parents do not take their children to school and encourage them to go out to work.
2 It is good that parents and individuals create an enabling environment at home in order to discourage children from seeking employment.	It is bad that parents do not create an enabling environment at home in order to discourage children from seeking employment.
3 It is good that parents understand the hazards of child labor.	It is bad that parents do not understand the hazards of child labor.
4 It is good that people understand the importance of hard work.	It is bad that people do not understand the importance of hard work.
5 It is good that parents recognize the importance that their children stay in school until the child reaches the highest level instead of dropping out midway.	It is bad that parents do not recognize the importance that their children stay in school until they have reached the highest level instead of dropping out midway.
6 It is good that parents and guardians understand the negative effects of early marriage by children.	It is bad that parents and guardians do not understand the negative effects of early marriage by children.
7 It is good that men respect women and vice versa.	It is bad that men do not respect women and vice versa.
8 It is good that men and women are allowed (responsibly) to marry spouses of their own choice.	It is bad that men and women are not allowed (responsibly) to marry spouses of their own choice.
9 It is good that individuals understand the negative consequences of early marriage.	It is bad that individuals do not understand the negative consequences of early marriage.
10 It is good that parents realize that poor social upbringing of children results in negative consequences.	It is bad that parents do not realize that poor social upbringing of children results in negative consequences.
11 It is good that parents understand that marrying off young girls to older men brings about social problems to the girls.	It is bad that parents do not understand that marrying off young girls to older men brings about social problems to the girls.

continues

Table 8–2. *continued*	

IT IS GOOD THAT...	IT IS BAD THAT...
VIOLENCE	
1 It is good that husbands refrain from physical and psychological violence against their wives.	It is bad that husbands engage in physical and psychological violence against their wives.
2 It is good that spouses create a harmonious environment in the home.	It is bad that spouses do not create a harmonious environment in the home.
GENDER	
1 It is good that individuals are aware of important gender issues.	It is bad that individuals are not aware of important gender issues.
2 It is good that parents provide education equally to both girls and boys.	It is bad that parents do not provide education equally to both girls and boys.
3 It is good a parent values a son and a daughter equally.	It is bad a parent does not value a son and a daughter equally.
4 It is good that men understand that women deserve equal job opportunities and equal pay.	It is bad that men do not understand that women deserve equal job opportunities and equal pay.
5 It is good that women have a bigger role in all aspects of life.	It is bad that women do not have a bigger role in all aspects of life.
MISCONCEPTIONS/RUMORS	
1 It is good that individuals understand that mosquitoes do not spread HIV/AIDS.	It is bad that individuals do not understand that mosquitoes do not spread HIV/AIDS.
2 It is good that individuals understand that getting infected with HIV/AIDS is not a curse from God—it is a disease like any other.	It is bad that individuals do not understand that getting infected with HIV/AIDS is not a curse from God—it is a disease like any other.
3 It is good that men understand that female human beings are as intelligent as their male counterparts.	It is bad that men do not understand that female human beings are as intelligent as their male counterparts.
HARMFUL TRADITIONAL PRACTICES	
1 It is good that individuals understand the harmful effects of female genital mutilation (FGM).	It is bad that individuals do not understand the harmful effects of female genital mutilation (FGM).
2 It is good that people understand the medical complications brought about by FGM.	It is bad that people do not understand the medical complications brought about by FGM.

continues

Table 8–2. *continued*

IT IS GOOD THAT...	IT IS BAD THAT...
3 It is good that men understand the physical pain, agony, and mental anguish women undergo during and after circumcision.	It is bad that men do not understand the physical pain, agony, and mental anguish women undergo during and after circumcision.
4 It is good that men understand the lifelong complications that accompany female circumcision.	It is bad that men do not understand the lifelong complications that accompany female circumcision.

C. ECONOMIC ISSUES

1 It is good that every citizen plays a role in development of the national economy.	It is bad that some citizens do not play a role in development of the national economy.
2 It is good that women have an opportunity to engage in viable income-generating activities.	It is bad that women do not have an opportunity to engage in viable income-generating activities.
3 It is good that men realize that if you can educate a man you educate an individual, but if you educate a woman you educate the entire nation.	It is bad that men do not realize that if you can educate a man you educate an individual, but if you educate a woman you educate the entire nation.
4 It is good that individuals understand the root causes of poverty.	It is bad that individuals do not understand the root causes of poverty.

D. PEOPLE WITH SPECIAL NEEDS

YOUTH

1 It is good that society understands that the future of any nation lies in its youth.	It is bad that society does not understand that the future of any nation lies in its youth.
2 It is good that individuals understand the importance of youth participation in sporting activities during their leisure time.	It is bad that individuals do not understand the importance of youth participation in sporting activities during their leisure time.

PEOPLE/CHILDREN WITH DISABILITIES

1 It is good that guardians of orphaned children encourage them to make use of their exemption from paying school fees.	It is bad that guardians of orphaned children do not encourage them to make use of their exemption from paying school fees.
2 It is good that disabled people are given an opportunity in economic activities in the country.	It is bad that disabled people are not given an opportunity in economic activities in the country.

continues

Table 8–2. *continued*

IT IS GOOD THAT...	IT IS BAD THAT...
3 It is good that children with disabilities are given an opportunity to acquire education.	It is bad that children with disabilities are not given an opportunity to acquire education.

E. DIALOGUE	
1 It is good that there is a quality dialogue between wives and husbands.	It is bad that there is no quality dialogue between wives and husbands.
2 It is good that parents open channels of communication between themselves and their children.	It is bad that parents do not open channels of communication between themselves and their children.
3 It is good that siblings learn how to communicate among themselves.	It is bad that siblings do not learn how to communicate among themselves.
4 It is good that parents communicate with teachers about their children.	It is bad that parents do not communicate with teachers about their children.

Advisory Committee

During the formative research, an advisory committee, composed of representatives of relevant ministries, nongovernmental organizations, and other institutions is formed. This committee ensures that producers and scriptwriters have appropriate factual information regarding the issues and helps bring about coordination of the infrastructure with the media campaign. If the drama is effective, it will undoubtedly stimulate a demand for information and services related to the social issue(s) promoted by the program, and so it is critical to ensure that these services exist. Thus, representatives of service organizations are invited to join the advisory committee, so that these organizations can receive "advance warning" of episodes that should motivate members of the target audience to seek these services. In this way, these organizations can ensure that the service infrastructure is ready to meet the increased demand. Advisory committee members also review scripts to ensure technical accuracy.

In-Depth Workshop (Training of Producers and Scriptwriters)

When the formative research is completed, producers and scriptwriters are trained in the Sabido methodology during a month-long, in-depth training workshop. During the first several days of the workshop, the findings of the formative research are presented to provide scriptwriters a basis for the development of characters and storylines of the serial drama.

The rest of the training workshop consists of the actual design of the theme, characters, and storyline of the serial drama by the production and writing team. Four pilot episodes are produced and recorded at the end of the workshop.

Pre-Testing of Pilot Episodes

These pilot episodes are pre-tested in the field with selected members of the target audience. The scriptwriters then make appropriate revisions (if necessary) to these pilot episodes, based on the reactions of this focus group.

Production[50]

In development of any drama, the writer typically first conceives a plot. As the plot is developed, characters are created, and the scriptwriter writes scenes that depict the interactions between and among the characters. Miguel Sabido's approach to pro-social drama is the reverse of this—it proceeds from research to values to characters to interactions to plot.

Sabido-style serial dramas are written and produced by qualified indigenous scriptwriters and producers, who receive in-depth training in the Sabido methodology. Scriptwriters and producers who are nationals of the country in question are used not only to build the capacity of local personnel, but because culturally relevant, true-to-life drama can only be written by those who are native to that culture. These scriptwriters and producers are then trained in the specific elements of development of a Sabido-style serial drama, outlined as follows.

Plot Construction

The objective of a Sabido-style serial drama is to transmit a specific pro-social message. In addition, the serial drama is designed to reinforce the values described in the values grid, and to show their relationship to specific pro-social attitudes and behaviors. The values grid provides the scriptwriters and producers with positive and negative values to use in the development of characters, settings, and storylines for the serial drama. As mentioned previously, the issues described in the values grid are based on extensive formative research, including a study of the country's ideology, constitution, laws, and policies, and any UN documents to which the country is signatory.

Characters

Characters are divided into three groups: (1) positive characters who support the prosocial behavior; (2) negative characters who reject the prosocial behavior; and (3) transitional characters who are uncertain about the pro-social behavior. A psychological, demographic, and socioeconomic profile is created for each character. The names of the characters are also carefully chosen to embody the values that the character represents. The names of characters are extremely important in defining the character's role within the serial drama. For example a positive character should have a name, such as Angel Goodfellow or an equivalent name in another language, that reinforces his or her positive characteristics; and a negative character should be given a name, such as Noah Stealing or the equivalent, that reflects a negative value in the society. If well chosen, audience members will react to and reinforce the use of these names to define values and traits, for example, a mountain in the Bale region of southern Ethiopia has been renamed "Ababullo" mountain, after a strong negative male character in the Sabido-style radio serial drama being broadcast over Radio Ethiopia.

Characters that support the pro-social behavior should hold a societal status that the target audience looks up to, thereby reinforcing the positive aspects of the behavior change. Those characters who reject the pro-social behavior should embody stereotypes that the target audience recognizes as social outcasts, for example, gang members or thieves. This association will deter the audience from rejecting the pro-social behavior. The uncertain (transitional) characters should be recognizable to the target audience, as being caught between the other two groups of characters. This could be, for example, a confused teenager subject to peer pressure in school. It is with this third group that the audience should most closely identify, as a conscious choice is required to sustain a behavior change.

During the course of the serial drama, each of these three characters moves toward or away from the pro-social behavior and is appropriately rewarded or punished. These movements, rewards, and punishments are carefully plotted according to the number of episodes in the serial drama in order to sustain the drama and to tell the story.

Episodes and Scripts

Episodes of the serial drama are developed and written based on the paths that the transitional characters follow in their evolution toward adoption of the pro-social behavior being promoted by the serial drama. During the course of this evolution, the negative characters will try to impede the progress of the transitional characters in their attempts to adopt pro-social behavior, while the positive characters will tirelessly motivate and assist the transitional characters toward the desired behavior change. Drama is created through the conflicts between the positive and negative characters, and perhaps even within the transitional characters themselves as they battle their own doubts and the situations they find themselves in during the course of this behavior change. Each standard 15-minute episode contains approximately three scenes, which take place in different settings and involve interactions between different characters. They all move between the settings, and interact in various ways, to show changing and evolving relationships during the course of the story.

Each scene is written to build to an emotional peak and should end with a cliffhanger to create suspense, and to ensure that audience members tune in for the next episode.

Epilogues

One-minute epilogues follow each episode. The epilogue is narrated by a popular opinion leader or entertainment figure who is not a character in the serial drama. Epilogues are designed to be conversational and to call attention to key movements in the episode. They also provide specific details about the available infrastructure in the community where viewers can receive additional information about the pro-social behaviors being presented. Epilogues can be used to create a source of feedback by soliciting viewers to send in cards and letters with their opinions of the serial drama.

Monitoring

The monitoring process gives the producers and writers valuable information about the public's receptivity to the program and its characters. The feedback shows how members of the target audience are interpreting characters and content of the program, and helps gauge audience reaction to key messages and issues in the serial drama. Monitoring also provides measures of parasocial interaction and audience involvement, which help to determine specific effects of the characters on behavior change.

A variety of qualitative and quantitative research methodologies can be used to monitor the impact of a Sabido-style serial drama during broadcast. Monitoring can include analysis of audience letters; checking clinic data, for example, to track adoption of family planning behaviors; for example; and continuous content analysis of the entertainment-education messages to determine if the scripts are consistent with desired educational goals.

Monitoring effectiveness of the drama can also include data gleaned from interviews with listening groups, and surveys on how to persuade family members to listen to the programs. Feedback from this research is given to writers so that appropriate adjustments can be made to story-lines if the audience is not interpreting characters or messages the way the producers intend. This kind of feedback allows entertainment-education media producers to make appropriate mid-course corrections.

Audience letters are another useful means of gathering useful monitoring data. Audience letters are usually unsolicited, unprompted (and

Radio Is Changing Lives in Ethiopia

Two social content radio serial dramas, Yeken Kignit (Looking Over One's Daily Life) and Dhimbiba (Getting the Best out of Life), are changing behavior in Ethiopia.

Results of a study in 48 selected health facilities around the country show that more than a third (35 percent) of new family planning clients in Ethiopia have heard one of the radio soap operas. Nearly 6 percent of the new clients said they visited the clinic as a result of listening to one of the dramas. Of the total number of new clients interviewed, about 8 percent cited radio as their main source of information on reproductive health; family planning; HIV/AIDS; and other related reproductive health services they sought at the clinics. Among clients who cited radio as the main source of information on reproductive health services, 70 percent cited one of the two radio serial dramas.

Since the programs began broadcasting in June 2002, over 10,000 letters from enthusiastic listeners have arrived at Population Media Center's (PMC) Ethiopia office, the U.S.-based organization behind the dramas. PMC continues to receive approximately 250 letters each day from listeners.

The steady stream of letters indicates that listeners are developing strong emotional bonds to the characters in the dramas. "I admire your drama. I appreciate its educational role. Its messages are very valuable...I have learned many things from it and have changed my attitude," says Yenegata Alehegne, a listener from Wukro, Ethiopia.

Lema Tesfaye, another listener from Arssi, Ethiopia writes, "As for HIV/AIDS, the people here believe that it is a problem limited to urban centers and that it has no relevance to rural areas. Your drama is telling them that this is wrong. I have undergone a change of behavior due to the drama...I encourage you to keep up the good work."

The dramas are tackling issues such as marriage by abduction, education of daughters, and spousal communication. The programs are supported by funding from the Packard Foundation, the HIV/AIDS Prevention and Control Office of the Government of Ethiopia (HAPCO), the Charles Evans Hughes Memorial Foundation, Save the Children USA, CARE-Ethiopia, and individual donors.

hence, free of possible researchers' biases), and provide rich insights about how a Sabido-style serial drama affects the audience.[51–52]

Another important measure of how a Sabido-style serial drama motivates behavior change is the degree to which the program stimulates interpersonal communication between audience members and those who do not listen to the drama. This is a proxy measure of the indirect effects of the serial drama, as derived from the two-step communication flow process described earlier in this chapter. Singhal and Rogers suggest that producers incorporate "markers" into the design of serial dramas to measure this effect. "Markers" are distinct elements of a message that are uniquely identifiable.[53]

In a Sabido-style serial drama broadcast on the Caribbean island of St. Lucia, a new condom named *Catapult* was introduced. This new name was identified by 28 percent of the radio program's listeners, validating their direct exposure to the radio program, and by 13 percent of the non-listeners, which suggests that the message diffused via interpersonal channels (thus providing a test of diffusion of interventions theory).[54] Alternatively, a marker or trace might consist of creatively naming characters or settings in an entertainment-education drama. In Population Media Center's radio serial in Sudan, settings were given name markers to assist researchers to measure the degree of interpersonal communication stimulated by the program.

Summative (Evaluation) Research

Summative research is defined as that which takes place after broadcast and is used to quantify the effects on the audience and to assess the validity of the original design and hypotheses. It is primarily based on quantitative as opposed to qualitative research.[55]

Evaluation research usually employs a quantitative survey of audience members and non-audience members during and after the broadcasts, and compares differences in knowledge, attitudes, and behavior between these two groups. Evaluation research thus seeks to measure the effects of the serial drama on audience behavior.

Quantitative data should be gathered on the knowledge, attitudes, and behaviors of members of the target audience before broadcast begins, to provide baseline measures. This baseline allows researchers to document subsequent changes.

A Call to Action:
Future Directions, Ideas for Future Progress

Often, the main question posed about communication interventions is: "Did the intervention change behavior?" The Sabido methodology has proven time and again that this approach does, in fact, achieve behavior-change results. The cost-effectiveness of the intervention has also been proven—Sabido-style serial dramas over the mass media have demonstrated a cost-effectiveness unmatched by any other communication approach in changing individual behavior.

Now the question emerges: "Can the Sabido methodology be used to stimulate behavior change at the community level?"

Recent studies are beginning to investigate how mass media serial dramas can lead to changes at the system or community level. For example, in India, the radio serial drama *Taru* is accompanied by such ground-based activities as folk performances, group listening, and the availability of local health services. An evaluation of this program shows that it leads over time to changes in group, community, and organizational norms—and is leading people to enhanced levels of collective activism, defined as the degree to which people in a system believe they can organize and execute a course of action required to achieve collective goals. Additional studies are needed to explore how serial drama can be used to effect community-level change.

Another question is: "How can the use of serial drama be used to maximum effect within a comprehensive communication intervention?"

Although many communication programs have explored use of multiple channels to communicate about a specific issue, the question of how to maximize the synergistic effects of these multiple communication channels is still unanswered. Also, remains unknown how to most effectively employ various communication channels to provide optimal results. This question of "media mix" will certainly vary for each different target audience, and for different issues or messages.

Several communication programs are beginning to explore how mass media serial dramas can be used in concert with other, more "on the ground" approaches, such as interpersonal communication. For example, in India, Population Media Center is working in partnership with the Program for Appropriate Technology for Health (PATH) to develop a comprehensive behavior change communication program about HIV/AIDS prevention. The program includes a radio serial drama, audio cassettes of the program for high-risk groups such as commercial sex workers and truckers (who might not be available to listen to the radio drama when it is broadcast), and a series of innovative community-level interventions such as magnet theater, "talk-back" interactive programs, and training of service providers in interpersonal communication. For example, "magnet theater" is a unique and powerful BCC method for fostering community dialogue about the behaviors and social norms that contribute to the spread of HIV/AIDS. It is so named because audiences are "pulled" to weekly performances at fixed locations, with the intention of communicating behavioral change (adapted from "PATH Today").

Finally, it should be noted that the Sabido methodology can (and has) been used to address issues other than reproductive health or even health in general. For example, in a project funded by the United States Agency for International Development (USAID), Population Media Center (PMC) is developing a radio serial drama to address exploitative child labor and child trafficking in three West African countries—Mali, Burkina Faso, and the Ivory Coast.

PMC is also working on a program in Rwanda that will deal with preservation of the habitat of endangered mountain gorillas. This program will undoubtedly also deal with issues such as conflict mediation and peaceful relations between ethnic groups.

Entertainment programs have an influence on our behavior, whether we realize it or not. Many of you may be familiar with the popular television comedy series *Friends*. If millions of teenage girls cut their hair to look like Rachel, imagine the potential of such characters to promote to safer sex behaviors? Imagine if shows like *Friends* employed the Sabido methodology. How many of the millions who were glued to the exploits of Rachel and Ross would also have learned something in the process? This is the reason why audiences from the Philippines to India, from Tanzania to Ethiopia, and from Mexico to Bolivia find Sabido-style serial dramas irresistible—and more than merely educational in an entertaining way.

Notes

1. A. Singhal and E. M. Rogers, *Entertainment-Education: A Communication Strategy for Social Change* (Mahwah, NJ: Lawrence Erlbaum Associates, 1999).

2. P. T. Piotrow et al., *Health Communication: Lessons from Family Planning and Reproductive Health* (Westport, CT: Praeger, 1997).

3. R. Haji. Personal Communication, March 1, 2004.

4. E. M. Rogers et al., "Effects of an Entertainment-Education Soap Opera on Family Planning in Tanzania," *Studies in Family Planning* 30(3) (1999): 193–211.

5. P. W. Vaughan et al., "Entertainment-Education and HIV/AIDS Prevention: A Field Experiment in Tanzania," *Journal of Health Communication* 5 (Supplement) (2000): 81–100.

6. P. W. Vaughan and E. M. Rogers, "A Staged Model of Communication Effects: Evidence from an Entertainment-Education Radio Soap Opera in Tanzania," *Journal of Health Communication* 5(2) (2000): 203–227.

7. Singhal and Rogers, *Entertainment-Education: A Communication Strategy for Social Change*.

8. H. Nariman, *Soap Operas for Social Change* (Westport, CT: Praeger, 1993).

9. A. Singhal and E. M. Rogers, "A Theoretical Agenda for Entertainment-Education," *Communication Theory* 12(2) (2002): 117–135.

10. A. Singhal et al., *Entertainment-Education and Social Change: History, Research and Practice* (Mahwah, NJ: Lawrence Erlbaum Associates, 2004).

11. Singhal and Rogers, *Entertainment-Education: A Communication Strategy for Social Change*.

12. Singhal and Rogers, *Entertainment-Education: A Communication Strategy for Social Change*.

13. K. Kiragu et al., *Adolescent Reproductive Health Needs in Kenya: A Communication Response æEvaluation of the Kenya Youth Initiative Project* (Baltimore, MD: Johns Hopkins School of Public Health, Center for Communication Programs, 1998). Cited in A. Singhal et al., *Entertainment-Education and Social Change: History, Research, and Practice* (Mahwah, NJ: Lawrence Erlbaum Associates, 2004).

14. D. L. Kincaid et al., "Impact of a Mass Media Vasectomy Promotion Campaign in Brazil," *International Family Planning Perspectives* 12(4) (1996): 169–175.

15. C. Underwood, *Impact of the HEART Campaign: Findings from the Youth Surveys in Zambia 1999 & 2000* (Baltimore, MD: Johns Hopkins School of Public Health, Center for Communication Programs, 2001).

16. T. W. Valente, P. R. Poppe, and A. P. Merritt, "Mass-Media Generated Interpersonal Communication as Sources of Information about Family Planning," *Journal of Health Communication*. 1 (1995): 247–265.

17. Piotrow et al., *Health Communication: Lessons from Family Planning and Reproductive Health*.

18. A. Singhal, E. M. Rogers, and W. J. Brown, "Harnessing the Potential of Entertainment-Education *Telenovelas*," *Gazette* 51 (1993): 1–18.

19. P. L. Coleman and R. C. Meyer (eds.), *Proceedings from the Enter-Educate Conference: Entertainment for Social Change* (Baltimore, MD: Johns Hopkins University, Population Communication Services, 1990).

20. Johns Hopkins University, Center for Communication Programs. *Reaching Men Worldwide: Lessons Learned from Family Planning and Communication Project, 1986-1996*. Working Paper No. 3, Baltimore, MD, 1997.

21. M. E. Figueroa et al., *Communication for Social Change: A Framework for Measuring the Process and Its Outcomes* (New York: Rockefeller Foundation and Johns Hopkins University, Center for Communication Programs, 2002).

22. D. L. Kincaid, *Using Television Dramas to Accelerate Social Change: The Enter-Educate Approach to Family Planning Promotion in Turkey, Pakistan, and Egypt*. Paper presented at the International Communication Association, Washington, DC, 1993.

23. D. L. Kincaid, "Drama, Emotion and Cultural Convergence," *Communication Theory* 12(2) (2002): 136–152.

24. NEEF and Johns Hopkins University, Center for Communication Programs, "Think Big, Start Small, Act Now," in *Proceedings of the Third International Entertainment-Education Conference for Social Change*, Amsterdam, The Netherlands, September 17–22, 2000.

25. P. T. Piotrow and E. de Fossard. Cited in A. Singhal et al., *Entertainment-Education and Social Change: History, Research and Practice* (Mahwah, NJ: Lawrence Erlbaum Associates, 2004).

26. G. Frey-Vor, "Soap Opera," *Communication Research Trends* 10(2) (1990): 1–12.

27. Nariman, *Soap Operas for Social Change*.

28. S. T. Rovigatti. Cited in Televisa's Institute of Communication Research, *Toward the Social Use of Soap Operas*. Paper presented at the International Institute of Communication, Strassburg, France. 1981.

29. E. Bentley, *The Life of Drama* (New York: Atheneum, 1967).

30. C. G. Jung, *Archetypes and the Collective Unconscious* (Buenos Aires: Editorial Paidos, 1970).

31. A. Bandura, *Social Learning Theory* (Englewood Cliffs, NJ: Prentice-Hall, 1977).

32. P. D. MacLean, "A Triune Concept of the Brain and Behavior, including Psychology of Memory, Sleep and Dreaming," in ed. V. A. Kral, *Proceedings of the Ontario Mental Health Foundation Meeting at Queen's University* (Toronto: University of Toronto Press, 1973).

33. M. Sabido, *The Tone, Theoretical Occurrences, and Potential Adventures and Entertainment with Social Benefit* (Mexico City: National Autonomous University of Mexico Press, 2002).

34. C. E. Shannon and W. Weaver, *The Mathematical Theory of Communication* (Urbana, IL: University of Illinois Press, 1949).

35. P. F. Lazarfeld, B. Berelson, and H. Gaudet, *The People's Choice* (New York: Columbia University Press, 1944).

36. J. T. Klapper, *The Effects of Mass Communication* (Glenco, IL: The Free Press, 1960).

37. E. M. Rogers, *Diffusion of Innovations* (New York, NY: The Free Press, 1962).

38. Rogers et al., "Effects of an Entertainment-Education Soap Opera on Family Planning in Tanzania."

39. Rogers et al., "Effects of an Entertainment-Education Soap Opera on Family Planning in Tanzania."

40. Population Media Center, *Ethiopia, Facility Assessment Report* (Addis Ababa, Ethiopia, February 2004).

41. Nariman, *Soap Operas for Social Change*.

42. P. Svenkerud, R. Rahoi, and A. Singhal, "Incorporating Ambiguity and Archetypes and Change in Entertainment-Education Programming. Lessons Learned from *Oshin*," *Gazette* 55 (1995): 147–168.

43. A. Bandura, "Growing Primacy of Human Agency in Adaptation and Change in the Electronic Era," *European Psychologist* 7 (2002): 2–16.

44. Televisa's Institute of Communication Research. *Toward the Social Use of Soap Operas*. Paper presented at the International Institute of Communication, Strassburg, France, 1981.

45. Rogers et al., "Effects of an Entertainment-Education Soap Opera on Family Planning in Tanzania."

46. Rogers et al., "Effects of an Entertainment-Education Soap Opera on Family Planning in Tanzania."

47. A. Bandura. Personal Communication, 2004.

48. D. O. Poindexter. Personal Communication, 2004.

49. W. N. Ryerson. *Background on the Work of Population Media Center* (Shelburne, VT: Population Media Center, 2002).

50. Nariman, *Soap Operas for Social Change*.

51. S. Law and A. Singhal, "Efficacy in Letter-Writing to an Entertainment-Education Radio Serial," *Gazette* 61(5) (1999): 355–372.

52. S. Sood and E. M. Rogers, "Dimensions of Intense Parasocial Interaction by Letter-Writers to a Popular Entertainment-Education Soap Opera in India," *Journal of Broadcasting and Electronic Media* 44 (2000): 386–414.

53. Singhal and Rogers, *Entertainment-Education: A Communication Strategy for Social Change*.

54. P. Vaughan, A. Regis, and E. St. Catherine, "Effects of an Entertainment-Education Radio Soap Opera on Family Planning and HIV Prevention in St. Lucia," *International Family Planning Perspectives* 26(4) (2000): 148–157.

55. H. Lopez Romo, Personal Interview, 1990. Cited in H. Nariman, *Soap Operas for Social Change* (Westport, CT: Praeger, 1993).

CHAPTER NINE

Pre-Crisis Relationships

Kurt Wise

Chapter Questions

1. How can a public relations approach to relationship management prepare organizations for dealing with crisis management?
2. What are some relationship-building strategies for maintaining and assessing good relationships before a crisis occurs?
3. Why is pre-crisis relationship-building especially important for public health organizations?

Introduction

Many of the authors contributing to this book approach their subjects from a public health perspective, having spent years as professionals or scholars in the field. I come from a different perspective—the perspective of a public relations counselor and educator. I believe modern public relations approaches to the management of communication have direct applicability to public health, including the handling of public health crises.

Crisis management and crisis communication have attracted much attention among those who practice and study public relations. Several books have been written about crisis management.[1–3] Journal articles and book chapters about crisis-related topics written from public relations viewpoints include such subjects as crisis planning,[4] image restoration,[5] legal matters,[6] response strategies,[7] and theoretical approaches to the study of crisis management and communication.[8]

One of the most exciting developments in recent years is the increased attention directed to *pre-crisis relationships* and their importance in helping organizations—including those involved in public health—effectively manage a crisis. It is the nature of these relationships that will be the focus of this chapter.

Why Worry about What Happens *Before* a Crisis?

There is no question those responsible for managing a public health crisis have important responsibilities. But far too often, public health bodies and other institutions that face public health crises become so focused on *planning* for a future crisis that they fail to see the importance of building and maintaining relationships with strategic constituencies (groups most able to help or harm an organization) *before* a crisis occurs. Crisis planning is, indeed, necessary. Leaders in public health must also remember, however, that the nature of pre-crisis relationships has a direct impact on an organization's ability to manage a crisis in the most effective manner.

There is a tendency to view crises as isolated events. A crisis begins, it runs its course, and it ends. Such thinking is flawed. As long-time crisis researcher W. Timothy Coombs put it, crises are better thought of as one episode in an ongoing relationship.[9]

Think about this perspective in personal terms using two slightly different scenarios. You're heading out the door one morning to go to work. You open the garage door and are about to get in the car when you realize you have a flat tire. Mechanical matters have never been your strong suit. But you have no choice but to change the tire.

In one scenario, just as you're about to begin work, your next-door neighbor happens by. You've known your neighbor for years and have a good relationship. Two years ago, you both put in a simple split-rail fence between your houses. Your neighbor has been to your house a few times a year and vice versa. You know your neighbor is easy to work with and doesn't seem to let little things get in the way of a job.

In the second scenario, another neighbor walks by. This neighbor lives about seven or eight houses down the street. You don't know this neighbor very well. You have waved when walking down the sidewalk, but that's about it. The neighbor seems like a nice person, but you have no relationship at all. This neighbor sees you are about to change a tire and offers to help.

If you had to choose one of the neighbors to help you change the tire, what choice would you make? In which scenario would you feel more *comfortable*, and thus less likely to be nervous and to do a better job? Of course, you would choose to work with the neighbor with whom you have the most positive relationship. The tire might get changed in either case, but in which case is it likely to get changed more efficiently and quickly?

This chapter is based on a simple contention: The better a pre-crisis relationship between organizational crisis managers and representatives of their strategic constituencies, the more likely it is a crisis will be managed as effectively as possible. This is especially true with public health organizations involved in crisis management because public health organizations must manage crises with the help of other institutions.

A Public Relations Perspective on the Anthrax Attacks of 2001

The importance of relationships in the public health field was demonstrated in the nation's response to the anthrax attacks of 2001. My purpose is not to review the attacks in detail here. It is clear, however, valuable lessons were learned during America's experience with bioterror in 2001.

Consider the following conclusions from the General Accounting Office (GAO) in its review of the anthrax attacks:

> Local and state public health officials reported that they had typically planned for coordination of the emergency response but had not fully anticipated the extent to which they would have to coordinate with a wide range of both public and private entities involved in the response to the anthrax incidents, both locally and in other jurisdictions. Among others, public health departments had to coordinate their responses with those of local and federal law enforcement, emergency responders, the postal community, environmental agencies, and clinicians. . . . In addition, *some plans had not anticipated the need to forge quick relationships between public health departments and local groups affected by the incidents but not expressly mentioned in the plans. . . . The relationships to support coordination had not been formed or tested* [italics added] (pp. 11–12, 14).[10]

Let's put the GAO's conclusions into more straightforward language: Crisis planning is important, but coordination works better when well-established, positive relationships are already in place. Building and maintaining such relationships is key to what modern public relations practitioners should be doing to maximize their contributions to their organizations, including public health organizations.

Public Relations and Relationship Management

Even though public relations has drawn considerable attention in the press over the last half century, much of the attention has been less than flattering. As noted by J. E. Grunig, this attention "has produced more suspicion, fear, and antipathy than respect. Most people seem to view public relations as a mysterious hidden persuader working for the rich and powerful to deceive and take advantage of the less powerful" (p. 23).[11] Negative connotations of the term "public relations" are common, for example, in print[12] as well as other media.

When I use the term "public relations," I do not mean "spin." Modern public relations has nothing to do with the "anything goes" philosophy that many associate with the field. Public relations, if practiced professionally, also goes far beyond the limited view that public relations is nothing more than media relations. Increasingly, public relations personnel are viewed as *relationship managers*. The relationship management perspective, Ledingham said, "holds that public relations balances the interests of the organization and the public through the management of organization-public relationships" (p. 181).[13]

Those in leadership positions in public health should ask their public relations practitioners—if the practitioners are qualified—to do more than just manage media relations. They should strive to become relationship managers, that is, to build and maintain positive relationships with strategic constituencies. These relationships need persistent attention, because as Ledingham noted, the nature of organization-public relationships changes over time.[14]

Successful public health management depends on partnerships. The wide range of responsibilities that fall to public health bodies makes partnerships a necessity. No public health body can meet its goals without partnerships involving other organizations. Because adequate staffing at many public health organizations is a constant challenge, such agencies depend on partnerships with other agencies, nonprofit organizations, and for-profit medical facilities, among others.

I agree with public relations scholar J. E. Grunig who argued that the most important *value* of the public relations profession should be *collaboration*: "I believe that public relations will have its greatest value to client organizations, to [the public] and to society if it views collaboration as the core of its philosophy. . . ." (p. 25).[15] Public relations practitioners should help public health organizations solve the collaboration and relationship difficulties that might hamper future public health crises.

What public health leaders must recognize is that in order for partnerships to function optimally during a crisis, it is necessary to manage relationships before a crisis. As Ledingham notes, "Successful organization-public relationships develop around common interests and shared solutions to common problems" (p. 188).[16] Although Ledingham was not writing about the field of public health, his basic idea speaks directly to the partnerships formed in the public health community. Public health bodies must work with a wide array of public and private organizations in the most effective manner if crises are to be managed effectively as organizations seek "shared solutions" to public health crises.

Relationship Maintenance

Relationships need attention—or maintenance—if they are to thrive. Public health bodies must begin to address their relationships by adopting relationship *maintenance strategies*. Public health agencies and their strategic constituencies must operate effectively during a crisis, and that likelihood is *increased* if the relationships have been developed and maintained in a thoughtful, deliberate manner. L. A. Grunig and colleagues suggested the following list of maintenance strategies[17] (building on the research of Hon and J. E. Grunig, 1999[18]): access, disclosure or openness, assurances of legitimacy, networking, sharing of tasks, and integrative strategies of conflict resolution. Each is addressed, as follows, in the context of public health.

- *Access*. Those employed by public health organizations must provide representatives of strategic constituencies with access to organizational leaders and a voice in the organization's decision-making process.
- *Disclosure or openness*. Both employees of the public health body and strategic constituency representatives must be willing to convey their ideas and concerns about issues as well as the nature of the organization-public relationship.
- *Assurances of legitimacy*. Each party in the relationship must be assured that its concerns are legitimate and demonstrate that it is committed to maintaining the relationship.
- *Networking*. The public health organization must build networks with the same organizations as their strategic constituencies (when possible).
- *Sharing of tasks*. The public health body must share its problem-solving efforts with strategic constituencies.
- *Integrative strategies of conflict resolution*. Both parties should seek common or complementary interests in solving problems together.

If leaders of public health organizations make a consistent, concerted effort to manage organization-public relationships by paying attention to the maintenance strategies mentioned here, it is more likely the organization will be able to manage a crisis effectively. Organizations that ignore relationship maintenance strategies take a risk—a risk that relationship difficulties will make managing crises more difficult.

Many leaders in public health might react negatively to the point made about access. Access, as described here, means more than just listening to strategic constituencies. Access means giving strategic constituencies a real voice in an organization's decision-making process. To some in public health, this can seem an unrealistic expectation. Why should "outsiders" have a say in how *our* organization is run?

The answer is that by giving strategic constituency representatives input into "your" organization's decision-making process, you help to maintain your relationship with outside organizations that are key to the ability of public health organizations to achieve their goals, including the ability to effectively manage a crisis.

But how does an organization go about evaluating its relationships? How do public health leaders know if their organization's relationships with strategic constituencies are positive, negative, or somewhere in the middle? This issue is addressed in the next section.

Assessing Relationships

Relationship assessment should be instituted in public health organizations. The idea that relationships can—and should—be measured might strike some as odd. But interpersonal communication researchers have been assessing relationships for years. Public relations scholars have recently used interpersonal concepts in relationship assessment and applied those concepts to relationships between organizations and their strategic constituencies. Hon and J. E. Grunig[19] said relationships involving an organization and its key constituencies can be measured by focusing on its key elements. Four of the elements are listed here:

- Control Mutuality—The degree to which parties agree on who has the rightful power to influence the another. Stable relationships require that organizations and strategic constituencies have some control over the other.

- Trust—One party's level of confidence and willingness to open up to the other party. The dimensions of trust are integrity, the belief that an organization is fair and just; dependability, the belief that an organization will do what it says it will do; and competence, the belief that an organization has the ability to do what it says it will do.

- Satisfaction—The extent to which each party feels favorably toward the other because positive expectations about the relationship are enforced. A satisfying relationship is one in which the benefits outweigh the costs.

- Commitment—The extent to which each party believes and feels that the relationship is worth spending energy to maintain and promote. The dimensions of commitment are continuance commitment, which refers to a certain line of action; and affective commitment, which is an emotional orientation.

Both quantitative and qualitative methods can be used to measure the perceptions of a relationship between an organization and its strategic constituencies. Formal questionnaires can be used if quantitative data are desired.[20] If more in-depth information is deemed necessary, qualitative methods can also be used, including interviews and focus groups.[21]

Of the elements listed in the previous bullet list, perhaps trust is the most important. The concept has been thoroughly researched by scholars in the interpersonal field.[22] In reviewing the public health system's response to the anthrax attacks of 2001, Shore concludes, "Indeed, it could be argued that we are not in the health care business—we are in the trust business" (p. 14).[23] If organizations that collaborate to address a public health crisis in the future are indeed in the trust business—as Shore suggests—then adopting relationship maintenance strategies will help organizations prepare for effective management of those crises by helping to build trust.

Managing organization-public relationships is not a simple task, especially given today's public health environment. As Turnock notes, "In the twenty-first century, public health is a complex partnership among federal agencies, state and local governments, nongovernmental organizations, academia, and community members" (p. 247).[24] If public relations practitioners have been adequately trained, they are ideal professionals to manage this difficult and necessary task.

Who Will Be Responsible for These Tasks at My Organization?

Suppose you read this chapter and thought to yourself, "That's all well and good, but how do I actually do this at my organization? We're understaffed as it is."

I suggest the oversight of relationship management should be the job of an organization's public relations director. Public relations professionals who occupy prominent positions in organizations must be more than *technicians*—individuals who specialize in such tasks as writing news releases or speaking to the media. They must be *managers*—responsible for conceptualizing and directing public relations programs. They must be more than former reporters who have never studied public relations at an institution of higher learning and/or know little or nothing about the state of the field today.

I do not suggest one individual can possibly maintain relationships with the literally dozens of people and organizations necessary for public health organizations to carry out their tasks. I do suggest properly trained public relations professionals can oversee a relationship management program, gathering information from organization employees and strategic constituency representatives about the status of relationships. Perhaps organizations do not have the budget necessary to conduct formal relationship research as outlined in a previous section, but at the very least, public relations managers can institute informal relationship assessment methods in an effort to gain a greater understanding of the state of the organization's relationships with its strategic constituencies.

A Word about Culture

Although organizational culture in public health organizations is not the focus of this chapter, it bears mentioning with respect to an organization's ability to manage crisis situations effectively. Organizational culture means different things to different people, but perhaps L. A. Grunig, J. E. Grunig, and D. Dozier captured the essence best when they defined culture as, "the sum total of shared values, symbols, meanings, beliefs, assumptions, and expectations that organize and integrate a group of people who work together" (p. 482).[25]

Culture, in my view, has more to do with an organization's ability to manage a crisis than the presence of a crisis plan. Marra[26] noted the importance of culture in the ability of AT&T to manage a crisis, and my own research[27] found culture was the most important factor in helping a small Connecticut hospital effectively manage a crisis when it was responsible for treating one of the nation's first victims of the 2001 anthrax attacks.

Public relations practitioners can help an organization foster the kind of organizational culture that responds effectively to a crisis, and such a culture includes the building and maintenance of positive, mutually beneficial relationships with an organization's strategic constituencies.

Conclusion

Crisis planning is essential to any organization's handling of a crisis, including a public health organization. But one of the key lessons of the nation's experience with the anthrax attacks of 2001 demonstrates that plans are not enough. Even with a quality crisis plan, the nature of pre-crisis relationships has a direct impact on an organization's ability to manage the tasks of coordination and communication that accompany any crisis. Public health leaders can better prepare their organizations for the next crisis if the leaders institute a relationship management program at their institutions. Positive relationships do not just "happen." They are the result of effort and management. Like many of the activities in public health, adopting a relationship management perspective might not pay immediate dividends visible to the general public. When a crisis occurs, however, the benefits of more effective crisis management will be seen.

Notes

1. W. T. Coombs, *Ongoing Crisis Communication: Planning, Managing, and Responding* (Thousand Oaks, CA: Sage Publications, 1999).

2. K. Fearn-Banks, *Crisis Communications: A Casebook Approach*, 2d ed. (Mahwah, NJ: Lawrence Erlbaum Associates, 2002).

3. O. Lerbinger, *The Crisis Manager: Facing Risk and Responsibility* (Mahwah, NJ: Lawrence Erlbaum Associates, 1997).

4. C. Caywood and K. P. Stocker, "The Ultimate Crisis Plan," in *Crisis Response: Inside Stories on Managing Image under Siege*, ed. J. A. Gottschalk (Detroit: Visible Ink Press, 1993), 409–427.

5. J. R. Blaney, W. L. Benoit, and L. M. Brazeal, "Blowout! Firestone's Image Restoration Campaign," *Public Relations Review* 28 (2002): 379–392.

6. K. Fitzpatrick and M. S. Rubin, "Public Relations vs. Legal Strategies in Organizational Crisis Decisions," *Public Relations Review* 21 (1999): 21–33.

7. W. T. Coombs, "Choosing the Right Words: The Development of Guidelines for the Selection of the 'Appropriate' Crisis Response Strategies," *Management Communication Quarterly* 8 (1995): 447–476.

8. W. T. Coombs and S. J. Holladay, "Helping Crisis Managers Protect Reputational Assets: Initial Tests of the Situational Crisis Communication Theory," *Management Communication Quarterly* 16 (2002): 165–186.

9. W. T. Coombs, "Crisis Management: Advantages of a Relational Perspective," in *Public Relations as Relationship Management: A Relational Approach to the Study and Practice of Public Relations*, eds. J. A. Ledingham and S. D. Bruning (Mahwah, NJ: Lawrence Erlbaum Associates, 2000), pp. 73–93.

10. *Bioterrorism: Public Health Response to Anthrax Incidents of 2001* (Washington, DC: General Accounting Office, 2003) (GAO Publication No. 04-152).

11. J. E. Grunig, "Collectivism, Collaboration, and Societal Corporatism as Core Professional Values in Public Relations," *Journal of Public Relations Research* 12 (2000): 23–48.

12. J. K. Henderson, "Negative Connotations in the Use of the Term 'Public Relations' in the Print Media," *Public Relations* Review 24 (1998): 45–54.

13. J. Ledingham, "Explicating Relationship Management as a General Theory of Public Relations," *Journal of Public Relations Research* 15 (2003): 181–198.

14. Ledingham, "Explicating Relationship Management as a General Theory of Public Relations."

15. Grunig, "Collectivism, Collaboration, and Societal Corporatism as Core Professional Values in Public Relations."

16. Ledingham, "Explicating Relationship Management as a General Theory of Public Relations."

17. L. A. Grunig, J. E. Grunig, and D. A. Dozier, *Excellent Public Relations and Effective Organizations: A Study of Communication Management in Three Countries* (Mahwah, NJ: Lawrence Erlbaum Associates, 2002).

18. L. C. Hon and J. E. Grunig, *Guidelines for Measuring Relationships in Public Relations* (Gainesville, FL: The Institute for Public Relations, Commission on PR Measurement and Evaluation, 1999).

19. Hon and Grunig, *Guidelines for Measuring Relationships in Public Relations.*

20. Hon and Grunig, *Guidelines for Measuring Relationships in Public Relations.*

21. J. E. Grunig, *Qualitative Methods for Assessing Relationships between Organizations and Publics* (Gainesville, FL: The Institute for Public Relations, Commission on PR Measurement and Evaluation, 2002).

22. D. J. Canary and W. R. Cupach, "Relational and Episodic Characteristics Associated with Conflict Tactics," *Journal of Social and Personal Relationships* 5 (1988): 305–325.

23. D. A. Shore, "Communicating in Times of Uncertainty: The Need for Trust," *Journal of Health Communication* 8 (2003): 13–14.

24. B. J. Turnock, *Public Health: What It Is and How It Works* (Gaithersburg, MD: Aspen Publishers, 2001).

25. Grunig, Grunig, and Dozier, *Excellent Public Relations and Effective Organizations: A Study of Communication Management in Three Countries.*

26. F. J. Marra, "Crisis Communication Plans: Poor Predictors of Excellent Crisis Public Relations," *Public Relations Review* 24 (1998): 461–474.

27. K. Wise, "The Oxford Incident: Organizational Culture's Role in an Anthrax Crisis," *Public Relations Review* 29 (2003): 461–472.

CHAPTER TEN

Community-Assisted Marketing Strategies

Muhiuddin Haider, Gillian Lyon-Powers, and Sarah Al-Shoura

Chapter Questions

1. How do Community-Assisted Marketing Strategies (CAMS) achieve the maximum level of participation from the community?
2. How is CAMS used to determine what level or degree of community participation should be achieved?
3. How is community involvement in health marketing campaigns used to achieve sustainable behavior change in the examples given?

Introduction

Community-Assisted Marketing Strategies (CAMS) is an approach that seeks to expand the role communities play in health behavior change marketing interventions. The CAMS approach is rooted in the idea that behavior change campaigns are more effective when communities participate actively in the design, implementation, and evaluation of programs.

Community participation has been defined as "an active process by which the beneficiary or client groups influence the direction and execution of development projects with the view to enhancing their well-being in terms of income, personal growth, self-reliance, or other values that they cherish."[1] Participation is a horizontal exchange, whereby the emphasis is placed on the process of developing, executing, and monitoring an intervention. Paul Freire's ideas of community development followed this line of thought.[2] He asserts that community participation empowers beneficiaries to initiate action and influence the processes and outcomes of development interventions. Typically, community participation culminates in the ownership of the activities and thus stands a greater chance of sustainability.

Community Participation

Levels of community participation vary from one development intervention to another. The models of Samuel Paul and Susan Rifkin offer examples of the degrees or levels of community participation.[3-4] According to Paul, community participation can be measured by the degree of intensity and is divided into four distinct categories. The most basic level is information sharing, progressing to consultation, decision making, and finally the greatest level of participation is initiating action.[5]

Information sharing refers to when the organization sponsoring the intervention shares vital information and knowledge with the beneficiaries in order to "facilitate individual or collective action."[6] This level occurs frequently in health projects when the shared information is intended to stimulate a desired behavior change such as promoting contraceptive use. This level, however, is often a one-way form of communication. It is only at the second level, *consultation,* where there is more of an exchange. At this level of community participation, beneficiaries are consulted on the health concern at some or all stages of the intervention, and feedback from the community is then incorporated in the design and implementation stages of the project. Community participation intensifies further during the *decision-making* level, as beneficiaries have either a joint or an exclusive role in the actual design and implementation of the activity. Lastly, community participation is at its most intense form during the *initiating action* stage because it is the beneficiaries who identify a problem, design the solutions and projects, and utilize local resources and/or seek external assistance to help address the community-identified needs.

Similarly, Rifkin identifies five levels of community participation in the context of family planning interventions.[7] Communities can participate during the following program stages: benefits, activities, implementation, monitoring and evaluation, and planning. The level of program benefits is the most passive form of participation, as communities have little input or involvement in the project except as a receptor. Conversely, the maximum level of participation occurs when communities participate in the actual planning of programs. Communities initiate and decide themselves what programs they deem important and seek additional technical assistance and expertise from agencies and/or the government if necessary. The three other levels fall somewhere between these two extremes.

How the CAMS Model Works

CAMS is an approach to maximize community participation in marketing health campaigns to engender sustained behavior change. CAMS strives to involve communities at all levels of the marketing mix (product, price, place, and promotion) by incorporating elements of Paul's model. The marketing mix model is utilized to design audience-focused, marketing interventions that incorporate the elements of product, price, place, and promotion, commonly referred to as the Four Ps. This model is typically used in both social and commercial marketing interventions. Depending on the current level of community participation, the intensity of community involvement can vary from one P to the next and/or comprise more than one level of intensity.

Some common combinations of degrees of community participation within the marketing mix are outlined as follows.

- **Product**—During product design, degrees of community participation can run the gamut. For example, in a condom promotion campaign, communities can be *consulted* to provide feedback to the project concerning attitudes, practices, and knowledge around the product's quality, styling, and packaging. The community could also play a role in the *decision-making* process in regard to the product's branding—name, sign, symbol, or a combination thereof—to enhance its acceptance and appeal. An example of *initiating action* is when a community approaches a project or distributor and asks for condoms for use in the community.

- **Price**—Community-led surveys can help determine the range of prices both monetary and nonmonetary such as time, effort, social, and behavioral costs that persuade target populations to adopt the product. Community *consultation* and involvement in *decision making* to develop incentive strategies (e.g., free product samples, coupons, premium offers, and contests and sweepstakes) help to stimulate behavior change in the community.

- **Place (Distribution)**—Communities can be *consulted* and/or included in the *decision-making* process to identify pre-existing distribution points (e.g., kiosks, vendors, local markets, health centers, health extension services/workers, and community centers) for the product. Community members such as shop and kiosk owners can be encouraged to *initiate action* by organizing themselves into marketing committees and recruit others to become distribution points. Greater community involvement will lead to increased availability and accessibility of the product as well as the likelihood of being utilized. Maximum community participation can foster this process.

- **Promotion**—National or regional mass media campaigns are more effective if community members are involved in all stages of message development and channel selection. For this to occur, communities must be more than just informed. *Consulting* with the community and involving the community in *deciding* on appropriate media channels and other vehicles for transmitting messages, for example, through song, dance, and theater groups, can further encourage adoption of a behavior change/marketing product. Important interpersonal channels can be used at each level of participation but are particularly instrumental in *initiating action* when formal and informal opinion leaders, community health volunteers, and traditional birth attendants are the ones who promote health activities.

CAMS as an Assessment Tool

The other component to the CAMS approach is assessing current level of community participation to determine the technical, organizational, and human capacity levels of each individual community. Only then can it be ascertained what level or degree of community participation should be achieved. The assessment should include the community's readiness to participate in a particular activity.

Human resources and organizational capabilities are critical determinants of community participation. Identification of existing and/or under-exploited organizational structures within the community can initiate, support, and maintain health marketing activities and the integration of behavior change into existing programs.[8] Different qualitative methods can be applied such as community mapping, in-depth and informant interviews, and focus groups to collect this information. For example, community mapping and conducting interviews with community members both help to identify and capitalize on women in the market as distributors for contraceptive products.

Identification of key groups and persons with complementary expertise and resources will also add value to the health marketing campaign. For example, community health workers or community members with prior experience in health activities management are excellent resources. Similarly, inclusion of influential groups or persons should be assessed and utilized such as religious and community leaders as well as other respected community individuals. They can have a positive impact on the acceptance of behavior within the community in addition to mobilizing others.

Examples

The examples highlighted as follows illustrate the participatory community elements that are the underpinnings to the CAMS approach. Although these activities were not developed with the CAMS models in mind, they embody the principles of CAMS that illustrate the power of community involvement in marketing interventions to adopt healthy behaviors.

The Safe Water System (SWS) project provides the first example of how community participation in certain aspects of the marketing mix can help to successfully market products for behavior change at the community level. Led by the Pan American Health Organization, the World Health Organization, and the Centers for Disease Control and Prevention, and implemented by instrumental organizations such as CARE and Population Services International, the SWS project is a large effort to decrease diarrheal diseases.[9] The SWS project is a comprehensive program that combines a low-cost, safe, easy-to-use, and locally produced water purifying solution, sodium hypochlorite, with specific hygiene practices, all of which help to protect drinking water in the home.[10] When community volunteers are utilized, they play a decisive role to promote and demonstrate the benefits of the water purifying solution in their communities. Existing establishments such as village kiosks, pharmacies, local markets, and health facilities are also used to sell the product at a price commensurate to what community members can afford. For example in the New Delhi slums, trained volunteers provide individual door-to-door and lively group demonstrations on how to properly use the solution, store drinking water once treated, and discuss other salient hygiene practices for safe water in the home. These SWS volunteers also participate in developing locally appropriate educational materials to raise awareness of how to prevent diarrheal diseases.[11]

Another example of the CAMS principles in health marketing campaigns is through utilizing men as community-based distributors (CBDs) of condoms in the promotion of dual protection—protection against pregnancy and HIV/AIDS/STIs.[12] The idea is that by having respected men taking on the role as CBDs, male clients might be more responsive to adopt family planning and HIV/AIDS/STIs prevention practices, particularly in conservative societies. For example in Cameroon, the Ministry of Health utilized existing and respected male community leaders and trained them as CBDs to sensitize couples about family planning, provide referrals to family planning clinics, and sell condoms. Similarly, male CBDs in Ghana were also effective in discussing family planning with village elders in traditional societies, where discussing sexuality with the opposite sex is taboo.[13] In Peru and Kenya, village men proved to be receptive to male CBDs and as a result sold more condoms per month as compared to their female counterparts.[14]

Community participation can also play a vital role in programs for the prevention or treatment of tuberculosis (TB).[15] A TB program in Ethiopia provides an innovative illustration of how CAMS elements can help to change behaviors. In a rural district of Estie, clubs were formed by TB clients living in the same neighborhood. They meet during outpatient appointments. Each club elects a leader who ensures that all members attend the TB clinic and arranges weekly supportive meetings to promote compliance with treatment or preventive regimens. For example, if a club member is not making progress or experiences drug side effects, the club leader refers the client to the local facility for help. These clubs work with community and religious leaders and health workers to identify potential people in the community to seek diagnosis and treatment as well as provide awareness activities to members in the community. The major notable outcome is that those communities with TB clubs have higher clinic attendance and treatment success rates than in other parts of Ethiopia.[16]

Lastly, the World Bank-supported Family Welfare Urban Slums Project (IPP VII) in Hyderabad, India is maximizing participation from community women to work with nongovernmental organizations (NGOs). One of the many examples of community participation in the IPP VII project is women's health groups that act as forums to discuss health concerns and for NGOs to learn about the health status and needs of community members.[17] This forum enables women to lead discussions about their most pressing issues with a designated NGO representative; together, they arrive at potential solutions. Some of the women's groups also provide revolving funds to their members, whereby women members take the deciding role as to how the funds should be used. Funds are often used to establish a library for girls, repair community wells, and construct latrines.

Next Steps

Data, evidence, insights, and examples provided in this chapter reinforce the interplay of community participation in all stages of the marketing mix. Further analysis will be required to develop strategies for community participation as an effective means to institutionalize private sector operations in health and family planning environments. Secondly, the CAMS approach needs to be implemented and evaluated to provide proven evidence-based interventions and strategies. There is a need to garner demonstrated results and experiments to determine the "real" value community participation can contribute to the health marketing programs for sustained behavior change. In particular, we need to explore the linkages between strategic communication and CAMS and demonstrate how CAMS can play a role in scaling up marketing products and strengthening the role of partnerships among government, NGOs, and the private sector.

Acknowledgment: Dr. Haider would like to acknowledge the contribution of Aritjit Ghosh for his initial research.

Notes

1. P. Kotler, N. Roberto, and N. Lee, *Social Marketing: Improving the Quality of Life* (Thousand Oaks, CA: Sage Publications, 2002).
2. P. Freire, *The Pedagogy of the Oppressed* (NY: Seabury, 1970).
3. S. Paul, "Community Participation in Development Projects," *Finance and Development* 24(4) (1987).
4. S. Rifkin, *Community Participation in Maternal and Child Health/Family Planning Programmes: An Analysis Based on Case Studies* (Geneva: World Health Organization, 1990).
5. Paul, "Community Participation in Development Projects."
6. Paul, "Community Participation in Development Projects."
7. Rifkin, *Community Participation in Maternal and Child Health/Family Planning Programmes: An Analysis Based on Case Studies*.
8. B. Jacobs and N. Price, "Community Participation in Externally Funded Health Projects: Lessons from Cambodia," *Health Policy and Planning* 18(4) (2003): 399–410.
9. Centers for Disease Control and Prevention, *Safe Water System*. Retrieved on October 28, 2003, from http://www.cdc.gov/safewater.
10. U.S. Agency for International Development and U.S. Department of Health and Human Services, *Fact Sheet: Safe Water System*, April 2003. Retrieved on October 28, 2003, from http://www.state.gov/g/oes/rls/fs/2003.
11. Centers for Disease Control and Prevention, *Safe Water System*.
12. Population Council, "Using Men as Community-based Distributors of Condoms," *Frontiers in Reproductive Health Program Brief*, No. 2, January 2002.

13. Population Council, "Using Men as Community-based Distributors of Condoms."

14. Population Council, "Using Men as Community-based Distributors of Condoms."

15. H. Getahun and D. Maher, "Contribution of 'TB Clubs' to Tuberculosis Control in a Rural District in Ethiopia," *International Journal of Tuberculosis and Lung Disease* 4(2) (February 2000): 174–178.

16. Getahun and Maher, "Contribution of 'TB Clubs' to Tuberculosis Control in a Rural District in Ethiopia."

17. K. Gill, *If We Walk Together: Communities, NGOs, and Government in Partnership for Health—The IPP VII Hyderabad Experience* (Washington, DC: The International Bank for Reconstruction and Development/The World Bank, 1999).

CHAPTER ELEVEN

Reproductive Health: A Communication Challenge in the Twenty-first Century

Fariyal F. Fikree

Chapter Questions

1. What are the most important factors to consider in order to develop an effective and sustainable communication strategy?
2. How are communication channels chosen in the three case studies presented here? How are they evaluated?
3. What lessons concerning communications for reproductive health can be taken from these case studies?

Introduction

In today's world, men, women, and adolescents aspire to a healthy reproductive life, even when they are confronted with the enormous challenges to maintain a productive and economically viable lifestyle. In addition, they face obstacles to their reproductive and sexual health, including the increasing rates of maternal mortality; the incidence of sexually transmitted diseases, particularly HIV/AIDS; accessibility to contraceptives and family planning services; and the burden of domestic violence. Alleviating these problems are the significant health goals in the new millennium. The focus of this chapter is on the process of communication to achieve good reproductive health that depends as much on availability, accessibility, and affordability of health care as on dispelling misperceptions and inappropriate knowledge regarding prevention, treatment, and care-seeking, as well as the use of technology among providers and clients of reproductive health services.

Communication is a key process underlying changes in knowledge, attitude, and health behavior (preventive and curative). The channels for this communication can occur at all levels—personal, family, community, the health sector, and mass media. Furthermore, this communication can be spontaneous at the personal, family, and community level, or be planned as part of an information, education, or behavior change communication strategy implemented by government or nongovernmental organizations. The expected outcome of these spontaneous or deliberate information strategies is improved health behavior by initiating, accelerating, or reinforcing changes in knowledge, attitude, and behavior so as to eliminate misperceptions or inappropriate knowledge regarding reproductive health and reproductive health services. Communication strategies employ multiple channels—interpersonal communication, mass media, and traditional modes—to promote appropriate and correct health knowledge and thereby modify behavior.

Presented here are three case studies that demonstrate the potential roles that diverse communication channels play in achieving behavior change for a safer and healthier reproductive life. The first case study focuses on the impact of interpersonal communication on birth preparedness in a low socioeconomic settlement of Karachi, Pakistan. The second case study describes an intervention project that aims to change health care providers' knowledge regarding emergency contraceptives in Kakuma refugee camps in Kenya. The last case study from Karachi, Pakistan documents appropriate uses of technology by describing the knowledge necessary for appropriate use and efficacy of five nonpermanent contraceptive methods among men and women living in urban slums.

Case Study One: Safe Motherhood

Timely referrals for obstetric emergencies to the nearest health facility that offers comprehensive obstetric care was the aim of the Safe Motherhood Project implemented in a low socioeconomic settlement of Karachi with a population of nearly 60,000. The design of the study was based on prior evidence[1] that highlighted delayed referrals due to client-related factors (family hesitancy, husband not present, and lack of awareness of the severity of the problem) and inappropriate services (improper and delayed referrals).

An essential component of the intervention strategy was to facilitate behavior change and health promotion at the community level with a deliberate information, education, and communication (IEC) strategy that focused on major obstetric complications while simultaneously improving quality of health care services at the community level.

The design and implementation methodology of the community-based IEC campaign was based on formative research that assessed community perspectives regarding obstetric complications, knowledge of danger signs during pregnancy, delivery and the postpartum period, familial decision making, quality and accessibility of health care services for a perceived obstetric complication, and forecasting for appropriate mode/s of communication. The evidence gleaned from the formative research[2] facilitated the development of messages and materials for the counseling campaign targeting pregnant women, their husbands, and other family members. Strategies to build awareness emphasized: (1) the necessity of attending at least three antenatal care clinics, (2) understanding the severity of major obstetric complications and timely recognition at the household level, and (3) birth preparedness and necessity of referral to a tertiary health care facility. These were the key components of the IEC materials and counseling messages. The counseling strategy was direct counseling at the household level with couples and other male/female adult family members. Several direct counseling sessions were held at the household level with the couple and other sessions for adult family members either as a group or individually.

Evaluation of the counseling sessions[3] revealed substantial knowledge improvement regarding preventive obstetrics and serious, life-threatening obstetric complications. Specifically, knowledge regarding how to conduct discussions to receive permission from family elders/husband for referrals to a hospital in the advent of an obstetric emergency; referral to the identified health facility; and taking along a blood donor were significantly improved. Change in knowledge is the initial step in a multifaceted domain culminating in behavior change. Evidence from several case notes documented that couples/families who received counseling began to change their behavior patterns by demanding tetanus toxoid immunizations during antenatal care visits, or recognizing and promptly receiving referrals in the event of severe obstetric complications such as prolonged labor and high blood pressure with severe headache.

Case Study Two: Emergency Contraception

Constructing an effective training and communication strategy to improve the knowledge, skills, and outreach for emergency contraceptives in a refugee settlement in northern Kenya was the objective of an operations research project in the refugee camps in Kakuma District, Kenya. Sexual violence including rape was previously identified as a major concern to community and tribal leaders. However, identifying the broad paradigms of introducing emergency contraceptives in this conservative community for universal acceptance was challenging.

Evidence[4] gained from qualitative and quantitative research conducted among health care providers, women, and community leaders including youth groups illustrated the magnitude of inappropriate knowledge regarding emergency contraceptives. Recognizing the sensitive issues pertaining to sexual violence, women support groups and youth groups were identified as appropriate avenues for dissemination of emergency contraceptive information at the community level. A two-day intensive training session was held for professional health service providers, outreach workers, and leaders of the support groups to disseminate information regarding emergency contraceptives, including appropriate regimen knowledge.

Program evaluation[5] revealed improvement in the knowledge levels among health care providers regarding regimen protocols, though the felt need for a concerted effort to translate this awareness into practice was expressed especially by the outreach workers. On the other hand, knowledge levels among youth groups and women improved only marginally. Sexual violence, especially rape, and emergency contraceptives to prevent unwanted pregnancy are sensitive topics in any community and particularly so in refugee camps. Tribal leaders, youth groups, and women support groups advocate raising awareness of emergency contraceptives, but as part of an integrated reproductive health and safe motherhood program that addresses a broader spectrum of health issues rather than as a vertical program.

Case Study Three: Nonpermanent Contraceptives

A significant increase in contraceptive prevalence rate from just under 20 percent in 1989[6] to a little over 50 percent in 2001[7] among the urban poor in Karachi, Pakistan augurs well for the family planning program that incorporates mass media, social marketing, and counseling implemented in these locales. Do increased rates of, and the perceptible shift to, the use of non-permanent methods point to the quality of care (informed choice and counseling) offered to clients in the public/private clinics?

This case examines the quality and efficacy of information-sharing methods, either face-to-face counseling, group counseling, or via media outlets, and the impact the method has on a population's knowledge and appropriate use of contraceptive technologies, to include condoms, oral pills, and IUDs.

Nearly all men and women interviewed knew where to obtain any one of these methods—a result of the massive mass media campaign. One of the key components of a service provider inter-action, is to provide clients with accurate information about the contraceptive method chosen (e.g., how to use it, and its effectiveness). Method efficacy was assessed by the client's level of awareness regarding the effectiveness of a method, whereas the gold standard to assess appropriate use was defined as the correct usage of the chosen contraceptive method.

Most male respondents (78%) knew the appropriate use of condoms, but this was not the case for oral pills (13%), injectables (13%), or intrauterine devices (IUDs) (8%). Female respondents scored best for oral pills (39%) but not for IUDs (19%), injectables (17%), or condoms (5%). Efficacy knowledge levels were also disappointing though comparatively better than knowledge of appropriate use. Efficacy knowledge was highest for IUDs (male 36%; female 43%) and lowest for condoms (male 11%; female 16%). The mismatch between appropriate use and efficacy knowledge for condoms correlates to men's practical experiences with condom rupture, unwanted pregnancy, and ineffective counseling. The results of this study call for concerted efforts to improve interpersonal communication regarding appropriate use of contraceptive technology to prevent unwanted pregnancy.

Lessons Learned and Work to Be Done

These case studies describe the process and outcome of implementing various behavior change communication strategies. The Safe Motherhood Project's approach was limited to one-on-one communication with the identified key stakeholders at the family/community level. The process of defining the appropriate strategy, based on the information gathered during the formative research phase of the project, was the driving force for its palatability and acceptance in these conservative communities. Improvements in the level of knowledge and health-seeking behavior pattern illustrated that the knowledge acquired was assimilated and translated into action. Alternatively, though the same formative research approach was applied in the communication strategy to raise awareness regarding emergency contraceptives, the evaluation identified the vertical approach as a major hindrance to program acceptability. The level of community awareness improved, but the key stakeholders were disappointed that the improvement was not as high as anticipated. The formative research identified the approach in terms of one-on-one communication and involvement of women's and support groups, and so on. However, what the research failed to identify was that the key messages should be contained within a comprehensive set of reproductive health messages that address a number of issues, rather than independent messages to offset the sensitivity of the topic. The challenge that communication strategists face is to understand the full range of complexities that reproductive health messages, especially sensitive sexual health messages, have to confront to be acceptable to the community—the first step in developing an effective and sustainable communication strategy.

The third case study highlights a major lacuna in client-provider communication regarding exchange of accurate information that sustains behavior change—the end-target of communication strategies. Contraceptive users were generally unable to correctly identify efficacy or appropriate use for condoms, oral pills, and IUDs, which suggests a breakdown in client-provider interaction. Providers, whether specialists or outreach workers, are trained, competent, and caring community members whose aim is to provide the best health care to their clients. On the other hand, clients are concerned about their reproductive choices or health problems and seek preventive or curative care to improve their health. The results of the case study do not identify whether the problem lies with the provider (lack of technical knowledge or skills, lack of time, or lack of respect for the client); or with the client (inability to ask questions, passive participation in the dialogue, unable to insist on good care).

However, the case study strategically identifies the outcome of inadequate client-provider dialogue and provides solid evidence for further investigation. The next step, assessing where the problem lies, therefore must be an integral component of any communication strategy.

In summary, the case studies highlight that an evidence-based framework is essential for communication strategies to effectively confront the reproductive and sexual health challenges of the twenty-first century and to improve the health and well-being of men, women, and adolescents.

Conclusion

Consistent and effective communication contributes to improving reproductive and other health behaviors by creating more satisfied and empowered clients, which then results in better health outcomes. The case studies described here demonstrate that strengths and weaknesses of a single or multiple channel(s) of communication must be identified through rigorous research and comprise an integral component of any communication program of activities.

The evidence that knowledge of contraceptive use is poor must be integrated into a holistic reproductive health program that targets the next level of programmatic and policy level activities. For an effective and sustainable communication strategy that meets the demands of and is sensitive to the needs of all stakeholders, a comprehensive approach must be adopted. This approach would link the population and community influentials with program managers and policy makers. Hence, the underlying premise of a communication strategy that effectively tackles the communication challenges of the new millennium must embody a cyclical "evidence" framework that revolves around the following steps:

1. Conduct a formative assessment regarding the knowledge and behavior of the target audience (clients and/or providers), technical competency (providers), and appropriate modes of communication (clients/community influentials and/or providers).

2. Design the communication strategy (e.g., message development, mode of communication) and monitor/evaluate the design in collaboration with stakeholders (community influentials, providers, program managers, and policy makers).

3. Implement the program with facilitative supervision to identify and correct problems.

4. Gather credible process, outcome, and impact evidence to justify conclusions.

5. Share lessons learned with stakeholders (community influentials, providers, program managers, and policy makers).

To achieve the millennium development goals targeted to reproductive health, communication strategies for appropriate behavior change should be a key commitment of policy makers and program managers. However, it is essential that they be key stakeholders in the steps outlined to enable the translation of evidence-based findings to policy formulation and programmatic implementation. The challenge for the new millennium is the shift to an evidence-based paradigm.

Notes

1. S. N. Jafarey and R. Korejo, "Mothers Brought Dead: An Inquiry into Causes of Delay," *Social Science and Medicine* 36(3) (1993): 371–372.

2. N. Kureshy, *Safe Mother Project, Korangi 8, Karachi: Formative Research Report*, 1998.

3. F. F. Fikree, S. N. Jafarey, and N. Kureshy, *Assessing the Effectiveness of a Safe Motherhood IEC Counseling Strategy in Korangi 8, Karachi*, 1998.

4. E. Muia, F. F. Fikree, and J. Olenja, *Enhancing the Use of Emergency Contraception in a Refugee Setting: Findings from a Baseline Survey in Kakuma Refugee Camps, Kenya*, 2000.

5. E. Muia et al., *Emergency Contraception Operations Research Project, Kakuma Refugee Camp, Kenya. Final Report*, 2002.

6. F. F. Fikree, *Determinants of Perinatal and Maternal Mortality in Karachi, Pakistan*. Doctorate of Public Health dissertation, School of Hygiene and Public Health, Johns Hopkins University, 1993.

7. F. F. Fikree, S. Saleem, and N. Sami, *Gender Perspectives on Induced Abortion: Knowledge and Attitude*. A community-based study in Karachi, Pakistan, 2002.

CHAPTER TWELVE

The Case of "Friends of the Pill": Expanding the Market for Low-Dose Oral Contraceptives in India

Rita Leavell and Anand Verdhan Sinha

Chapter Questions

1. What were the challenges to promoting oral contraceptives in India? How were these challenges addressed through the "Goli ke Hamjoli" campaign?
2. What can be learned from some of the outreach approaches that did not work in the campaign?
3. What are the benefits of a category campaign? What are key elements to consider when developing and implementing a category campaign?

Introduction

In the study of oral contraceptives (OCs) in India in 1998, there was no immediately apparent reason for such low use of OCs. Only 2.1 percent of married women of reproductive age used OCs,[1] as opposed to the average 15 percent to 20 percent in other countries.[2] (See Figure 12–1.) The Government of India had made the method easy to obtain by allowing nonprescription formulations and by providing free products through public clinics. It had also launched the subsidized brand *Mala-D* in 1989, advertised it on television, and distributed it through a pharmaceutical firm in a social marketing program. When the commercial pharmaceutical firm pulled out of the program in 1995, the government provided the formulation for *Mala-D* to multiple social marketing agencies and subsidized its rate for them to launch their own brands of the same prescription.

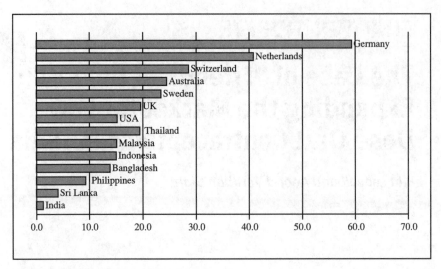

Figure 12–1. Use of OCs in Various Countries

Commercial pharmaceutical manufacturers launched their own OC brands on the market as early as 1972. There was wide availability of both subsidized and commercial brands of OCs, at affordable prices ranging from $0.04 to $1.50 per cycle. Yet even in urban India, use of OCs was only 2.7 percent and total sales of OCs on the market, as tracked by retail audits,[3] had been stagnant for four years.

A rapid assessment of the situation included discussions with government officials and pharmaceutical firms, review of market trends and family planning method use, and primary and secondary research among physicians and potential consumers. A picture began to emerge of a much maligned and underappreciated method. Studies showed over 95 percent awareness among the adult population of OCs, but low levels of correct knowledge about it. There appeared to be major concerns about side effects and plenty of myths about its use and potential dangers.

Sterilization was strongly promoted by the government in its Family Welfare program, accounting for 80 percent of all modern methods used by married women of reproductive age, and allowing space between pregnancies was not a strongly perceived need. OCs were also distributed in the public sector, but health workers were reluctant to advise their use and had their own concerns regarding potential side effects. Physicians were hesitant to prescribe the method, arguing that there might be adverse consequences from long-term use of hormones and that the idea of taking daily allopathic medicines did not fit the Indian mindset. After initial enthusiasm in the 1970s, commercial firms made limited investments in OCs due to physicians' negative reactions and the low demand. The key words were "low demand"—among consumers, physicians, public sector providers, and the general public.

As over two-thirds of users acquired OCs from pharmacies (referred to as "chemists" in India), trends in sales through the market most strongly reflected actual use. After an initial surge in sales with the launch of the government brand *Mala-D,* the OC market grew very slowly. Commercial firms spent their energy encouraging physicians to switch brands. Social marketing firms also focused primarily on brand promotion and expanded distribution. With such a small overall market, no commercial company had the resources to invest in generating consumer demand and, even less, the willingness to invest in expanding everyone's market at the possible expense of their own.

"Goli Ke Hamjoli" Is Born

The situation called for a different paradigm—an *OC category or "generic" approach* to build consumer demand, change health provider attitudes, and lead to a growth in the *total* market of OCs. The United States Agency for International Development (USAID) agreed to fund the development of the OC market through its Program for Advancement of Commercial Technology—Child and Reproductive Health (PACT-CRH) with ICICI Bank Ltd. This program uses the commercial stature of India's largest private bank to work with the health and pharmaceutical industry to develop and market products that can meet India's health objectives.

And so "Goli ke Hamjoli"—Hindi for "Friends of the Pill"—was born. Its explicit goal was to increase the use of commercially available low dose OCs in urban areas of North India.

Commercially available—because it would include all brands of OCs, full priced and subsidized, available in the market.

Low dose (i.e., ≤ 30 mcg estrogen)—because these formulations were nonprescription, recommended for first-time users, and caused fewer side effects than older higher dose formulations still popular with many Indian physicians.

Urban areas—because urban areas had wide product availability through pharmacies, a large population of physicians, good access to mass media, and high consumer purchasing power.

North India—because the "Hindi belt" states had a common language for media purposes, contained 42 percent of India's population of one billion,[4] and was the focus of government attention with higher fertility and infant mortality rates than the rest of India (see Figure 12–2).

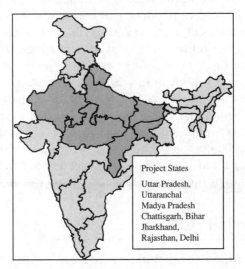

Figure 12–2. Map of India and the Project States

Market expansion and demand creation represented a new venture for the PACT-CRH program, as its prime focus had been to support product development, new technology, and improvements in quality. ICICI Bank's role would be to provide financial oversight for the project and use its influence with industry to negotiate Memoranda of Understanding with commercial OC pharmaceutical partners. It would also contract an advertising agency to provide communication services for demand creation for OCs. However, to provide strategic direction for the campaign and oversight of advertising and other marketing elements, USAID provided technical assistance for marketing through its globally funded Social Marketing for Change and later Commercial Marketing Strategies (CMS) projects.

The project components included advertising; public relations; consumer outreach; extensive training and promotion to chemists and physicians to address barriers to OC use; and market research for program planning and feedback. The project would improve the environment for acceptance of OCs and give women information on correct use and benefits of OCs. It would also address the many myths about side effects and long-term effects on health and fertility.

As a "category" campaign, however, the project would not promote any particular OC brand, but use a generic strategy to promote use of all low dose OCs. The only exception to this strategy in terms of expanded brand visibility would be commercial partners.

Goli ke Hamjoli Product Partners

Under the terms of the PACT-CRH program, only commercial pharmaceutical partners could be considered, and there remained only three firms widely distributing OCs in India (down from ten in the 1970s). OC product availability was not a major issue in urban North India, as *Mala-D* was available in over 90 percent of pharmacies. However, the leading commercial brand, Wyeth's *Ovral-L,* was available in only 55 percent of pharmacies and the others were much lower. All three commercial firms considered OCs to be low on their list of investment priorities and limited their product marketing to select obstetricians and gynecologists as prescription only drugs. Despite advances elsewhere, no new formulations had been introduced in India in 10 years.

Initial discussions with the pharmaceutical firms were not promising. Organon (until recently known in India as Infar) granted a brief but disappointing interview, and German Remedies (Indian affiliate of Schering) did not respond. Wyeth was willing to consider a partnership if it did not involve major costs for them. They argued that OCs were not an important product for Wyeth in India and the thin profit margins did not justify a major investment. Their brand *Ovral L* was the market leader (among commercial brands) and although it was the same formulation as *Mala-D*, it was still registered as a prescription product. Wyeth did however agree to a two-year partnership where they would expand the distribution of *Ovral L*, change the product to nonprescription status, and promote the brand through Goli ke Hamjoli and *Ovral L* promotional materials to more physicians.

Two years later, watching the sales of *Ovral L* climb rapidly, both Organon and German Remedies were eager to join the project. Organon obtained special permission for its product *Novelon* to become nonprescription, while German Remedies launched a new mid-priced product for North India, *Bandhan*.

Understanding the Potential Consumer

To conduct the communications campaign, ICICI selected one of India's most creative agencies, Ogilvy and Mather, for both advertising and public relations. However, before arriving at a strategy to "create demand" among potential OC users, some basic consumer insight was required.

So who was this woman of urban North India who might want to use an OC? A round of qualitative research through focus groups revealed her situation.[5] Most Indian women were expected to have their first child right after marriage. No spacing method was used to delay this first birth, and she had very little knowledge about reproductive health and fertility control when she married. She expected her husband to handle the situation if necessary, and little discussion took place between them on the subject. However, after the first child, especially if a boy was born, she suddenly had a better position in the family and some time and space before the pressure from mother-in-law or family for another child. This young woman wanted to delay the pregnancy of her next child and was searching for options; however, OC was seldom one of them.

First of all, there were concerns about the side effects, heard in whispers from friends; it made women "giddy" or had unknown, serious physical reactions. Rumors were spread that these Western-made pills, if taken every day, would pile up in the stomach and so should be taken for only a limited time. OCs might render a woman infertile or cause her to give birth to only girls, so it was better to take OCs after producing sons, if at all. There was also little understanding of how to use OCs and, anyway, natural methods were considered to be the safest and fairly reliable.

How could a communication campaign reach such a woman and change her attitudes, her decision-making environment, and eventually her acceptance of OC use? A creative solution appeared after arriving at an understanding of the woman's needs. When a girl married, she left her family where she was a beloved daughter and entered a new home as the lowest ranking member with many expectations placed upon her. In this new life with many responsibilities, she needed to know that there were some things in life that were in her control—such as the timing of the next birth. If she could be convinced that OCs were not only effective but also safe, and even had health benefits, then she might be willing to use them.

Her primary sources of information on fertility control were friends and perhaps her husband. Her husband usually agreed to the idea of spacing pregnancies and birth control, but left the method selection up to her, as long as it was considered safe. Mothers-in-law were more influential in deciding the number of children than advising about choice of methods. If a physician told her it was acceptable to use OCs, she might consider it, or alternatively, if a friend visited a physician and received such information, she would be more willing to try OCs.

However, her other potential sources of information included mass media-television and print. A review of national readership surveys showed that television use was growing rapidly in urban North India. The focus groups confirmed this trend and that for women in the household, primetime viewing was early afternoon, when housework was done and children were still away at school. Unfortunately, newspapers were not a major source of information (except for men), and magazines were not really popular except for cinema rags.

Through a combination of market analysis and qualitative research, a picture of the target audience evolved. There were approximately 5.4 million potential OC users. Their profile included: urban, married middle to low income women aged 18 to 29; with one or two children; interest in spacing their next pregnancy; no interest in sterilization; dissatisfaction with their current method; or not using any method. The most cost-efficient way to reach them would be through television, with more in-depth information provided through print, discussion with their physicians, or outreach efforts.

The Communications Campaign— Reaching the Consumer

Armed with this information on our potential consumer's needs, desires, fears, and influencers in regard to family planning, a communications campaign strategy and plan were developed. In the first year, these included the use of TV commercials, print articles, and point of sale (POS) materials at pharmacists. A campaign logo (see Figure 12–3) of "Goli ke Hamjoli" was developed as a unifying symbol of all low dose OCs and was placed on all campaign materials.

The first TV commercial was based directly on research findings—a young woman reminisces about her first days after marriage, when she entered a new household as a wife, a daughter-in-law, and then a mother. The protagonist explained how one tiny thing helped her to plan her life and her family—the pill. This was followed by a scene of a caring physician, explaining that today's OCs were different, very effective, had fewer side effects, and that any side effects, if experienced,

Figure 12–3. The Goli ke Hamjoli Campaign Logo

would soon disappear. Viewers were encouraged to visit their physicians or pharmacists for more information.

Although this ad was a "clutter breaker," a tracking study two months post-launch showed relatively low awareness of the Goli ke Hamjoli concept and logo.[6] Interest was generated among women to try OCs, and there was a sense of excitement that it might be a new brand. However, no one knew anyone else who had tried OCs—it was not a topic widely discussed. The ad agency then convinced four popular female television stars to provide pro bono support to the campaign by endorsing the pill. By the end of the first year, the first tracking study among the target audience showed that Goli ke Hamjoli had an outstanding 78 percent awareness and excellent recall of messages. Sales of OCs went up sharply.

However, behavior change is never that easy. In tracking studies over the next few years, it was shown that there were still many barriers to OC use. And although intention to use OCs remained high, trial and continuation did not grow as rapidly after the first two years of early adopters. New reasons and justifications for non-use regularly emerged. An iterative process of creative development informed by qualitative research focused on the profile of OC women who intended to use OCs, and their changing barriers to adoption.[7]

Over the five-year period of Goli ke Hamjoli, 19 theme and informational advertisements were developed, adapted to address new barriers, and aired as old ones disappeared. The advertising concepts had high emotional appeal and empathy, showing a deep understanding of the woman's situation in life. Each ad had a specific call to action—from directing women to their physicians or pharmacists for more information, to telling them there were many brands available in the market, one of which would suit them.

The media placement strategy was to maintain continuous presence on the air, dominate high-rated programs, and leverage pro bono airtime from channels as a public service awareness campaign. Advertisements were primarily aired in the afternoon and primetime evening slots, especially during soap operas, on the terrestrial channel (Doordarshan), as well as the leading satellite channels (STAR, ZEE, and Sony). STAR and Sony contributed major support by providing free time for commercials, and eventually broadcast short public service announcements.

Support materials and collaterals based on the theme ads, but providing more in-depth information, were designed and distributed at pharmacies, clinics, beauty salons, and at neighborhood events to increase visibility of the campaign. The Goli ke Hamjoli consumer brochures and informational materials always listed all the low-dose OC brands on the market. However, POS promotional materials tied into the commercial brand partners.

Public relations supported the program by conducting workshops for journalists and others from the media to provide them with correct information about OCs. A set of key messages was developed, intending to place the OC in a woman's life in every possible context—from an ideal family planning method to beauty benefits to harmony in relationships with husbands. A battery of scientific articles with information about OC use, the benefits other than contraception, research updates, and user testimonials was developed. Regular interaction with editors and health journalists ensured placement of over 450 articles in relevant and widely read national and local dailies and magazines.

Inreach—Outreach Efforts

From the beginning, it was clear that some form of interpersonal communication was needed to convince many women to close the loop on the decision to use an OC. However, what would be a cost-effective way to reach such a large target audience spread widely across North India, a population that did not regularly leave their homes?

Ogilvy Public Relations first proposed to use local civic groups such as Rotary, Inner Wheel, and Lions Clubs to promote the pill through local volunteer activities. Small campaign launches were conducted with influential community leaders in 12 key cities, explaining the purpose of Goli ke Hamjoli and correcting negative perceptions about OCs. Although willing to assist in such an important endeavor as "population control," these groups saw their role as reaching "the masses"—in villages and urban slums, through volunteer activities, and free medical care. This, however, was not the target audience for Goli ke Hamjoli.

Ogilvy and Mather Direct Marketing then had an idea—Why not get interested potential users to identify themselves by answering an ad, so that individuals could be contacted, provided with information, and encouraged to try OCs? A project was piloted in two cities. Ads and survey forms were distributed, and women responded, indicating their family planning status and whether they wished to receive information on OCs. One group would be called on by counselors in person and the other contacted through mail. Wyeth provided special *Ovral L* discount coupons for prospective users. There was an excellent response to the ad mainly because a device was used to give respondents a chance to enter a lottery! Interpersonal contact with intenders delivered a better response rate in use of coupons than mail, but a follow-up survey showed that continued use was quite low.[8] Further analysis showed that this would be a slow, logistically difficult and expensive way to reach potential consumers, and the idea of soliciting individual interest was shelved.

The next step was to concede that women probably wanted reassurance from a physician about the method. Public relations contacted over 350 leading physicians in 19 cities and convinced them to form a network to provide free counseling to women on reproductive health and low-dose OCs. In addition, they also acted as media spokespersons in their cities and provided on-ground support for later Goli ke Hamjoli community outreach programs. This activity was quite successful in that it gained visibility for the program and also the active support of the medical community in these towns.

However, the program still needed more outreach efforts to extend access to women even if they didn't come to a clinic. Ogilvy Outreach worked with local nongovernmental organizations (NGOs) in four cities to encourage their volunteers to reach out to women in groups and at home, while also selling various brands of OCs. The reported contact and use rates were encouraging. However, impact analysis showed that in keeping with the NGO approach, most of the contacts had been from the lowest socioeconomic levels, with users who preferred the much lower priced subsidized products. The only acceptable commercial brand was *Bandhan*, a mid-priced brand made by German Remedies. Unfortunately, supply problems with *Bandhan* led to discontinuation of the product and the NGO tie-in. Goli ke Hamjoli decided to turn over the contacts and networks to social marketing agencies, as it was good for overall OC use but did not match with the program's commercial sector focus.

In the fifth and final year of the program, a more effective approach evolved. Ogilvy Outreach recruited "Hamjolis" (Friends), women who were happy OC users to share their experience with middle to lower income women through small group meetings organized in their neighborhoods in the "Hamjoli Baatcheet" (Talk with Friends) program. The objectives were to promote correct information about OCs and generate positive word-of-mouth information flow. In eight pilot cities, Hamjolis met with 15,550 women of whom 9 percent were already using OCs, 2 percent had started OCs, and 10 percent said they intended to start.[9]

Outreach programs that year also included a pilot in eight cities conducted in association with the Federation of Obstetric and Gynecological Society of India (FOGSI) to reach over 4,000 college women with information about OCs and reproductive health. FOGSI as an organization had finally decided that OCs were a good method and it was time to reach out with important reproductive health information to the younger generation.

Although outreach continues to be effective in converting new users and supporting continuous use, it is an expensive way to reach such a large target group.

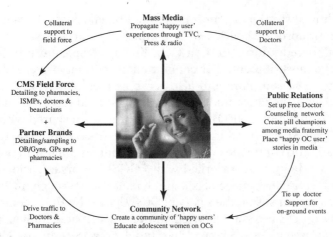

Figure 12–4. Diagram of Goli ke Hamjoli Campaign Elements and Design

Reaching Out to the Influencers

Gaining the medical community's support was critical for the successful promotion of the method and to encourage correct and consistent use by new adopters. Even though most OC brands do not require a prescription, women still relied on advice from friends and relatives, and most importantly from their physician, before deciding to use the method. Goli ke Hamjoli therefore also focused on interventions that would promote positive attitudinal and behavior change among health providers or, at a minimum, neutralize any negative bias.

Research played a key role in identifying health providers' concerns and barriers about promoting OCs. Many physicians had apprehensions about OCs causing cancer and had low levels of knowledge about correct use and the management of side effects.[10] As they were the primary influencers in the woman's decision-making process in adopting the pill, it was necessary to provide them with technical updates, and guidelines on OC counseling and use.

Brochures introducing the Goli ke Hamjoli program were sent out to over 5,000 physicians in the first year, with a list of all brands of low dose OCs, and common myths and facts. Mailers with important updates on the program, offers of consumer brochures, and technical guidelines on OC management continued to be sent out during the five years of the program. Incidentally, the database generated for this exercise also proved to be of great value later to the pharmaceutical partners in identifying potential new client physicians to target.

Leading obstetrician/gynecologists and female general practitioners (GPs) from across 21 cities were contacted to attend seminars and receive updated information on OCs. Key spokesperson physicians—usually the most influential or committed in their city—were identified to conduct the seminars and also serve as local experts. They were equipped with the latest findings of evidence-based research and World Health Organization (WHO) guidelines. These were shared with physicians at each seminar, addressing their concerns on low-dose OCs and giving them the confidence to prescribe the pill for long-term use.

Goli ke Hamjoli also worked with FOGSI, an organization of over 18,000 obstetrician/gynecologists and female GPs throughout India, to generate a consensus on the safety of OCs. Updated WHO recommended guidelines on OC use and management were distributed to members.

Research had also shown that Indigenous System of Medicine Practitioners (ISMPs) did not generally recommend OCs. In fact, they exerted considerable influence among women against OCs and urged them to discontinue the pill at the slightest sign of a potential side effect. Pharmacists also did not recommend OCs due to lack of knowledge and misconceptions about side effects.[11] Pharmacists often served as the primary source of medical advice on common illnesses, but for any questions on OCs or family planning, they would refer customers to a physician.

To address these two groups of providers not covered by pharmaceutical representatives or other health advocates, CMS deployed a field

Figure 12–5. Hamjoli Field Team with a Pharmacist

team of 100 Hamjoli field representatives to conduct workshops and train over 28,000 ISMPs and over 34,000 pharmacists (see Figure 12–5) in 34 major cities and 465 smaller towns of North India. On a regular two-month cycle, the Hamjoli field teams supported the program by informing, updating, interacting, and building a rapport with these ISMPs and pharmacists, and ensuring widespread on-ground visibility of POS materials and Goli ke Hamjoli signs. They also met with stock suppliers for local partner sales and reported on OC brand availability.

The Hamjoli Field Teams also regularly called on over 1,500 beauticians to enlist their support in promoting OCs to their clients. When outreach activities began, the Hamjoli field teams developed training and counseling skills among the the 'Hamjoli Baatcheet' satisfied pill users in the field and monitored on-ground activities in their respective cities. The Hamjoli field teams achieved a level of credibility and a reputation as an unbiased source of information that commercial and social marketing brand representatives could never hope to achieve.

Working with Pharmaceutical Firms

The Goli ke Hamjoli Program was initiated as a commercial partnership program to achieve social objectives. The goal was to expand the OC market through a synergy of demand creation for OC use and expanded brand promotion and distribution through commercial partners. An effort was also made to include the Goli ke Hamjoli logo on the OC partner packs or all low-dose OC packs. Because each commercial partner wanted exclusive rights to the logo, this idea was abandoned.

Wyeth, the first manufacturer to join the program with its brand *Ovral L,* also introduced a second, lower dose brand, *Loette,* during the course of the Goli ke Hamjoli campaign. To support the campaign Wyeth increased product distribution to cover 75 percent of pharmacy outlets in the program areas, linked its brands to the Goli ke Hamjoli campaign, and intensified the level of informing obstetrician/gynecologists and female GPs. Wyeth agreed to stop production of, and slowly withdraw, its older, high-dose brand *Ovral.* Encouraged by the market growth, it shared costs for training of senior sales and marketing staff in evidence-based detailing departments. Wyeth made its first forays into direct-to-consumer marketing through brand dispensers in pharmacies. In the course of the five years, Wyeth restructured its sales force for a special team on women's reproductive health and also set up a new manufacturing facility in India. OCs had become their second major profit category.

Organon, after successfully negotiating with the drug authorities to make *Novelon* a nonprescription brand, also chose to join the Goli ke

Hamjoli campaign. It incorporated the campaign logo on promotional materials for OCs and, over a four-year partnership, showed substantial sales increases from a small pre-campaign base. Organon also introduced a new lower dose OC brand and began the process of introducing other hormonal methods.

German Remedies, in order to join the campaign, introduced a mid-priced brand called *Bandhan*, specifically made for the North India project areas. Unfortunately, internal changes in the company resulted in problems with production and distribution of the brand, and the Memorandum of Understanding was discontinued in 2002.

Subsidized social marketing brands also wished to join the program and use the Goli ke Hamjoli logo (and some of their sales force promoted themselves as Goli ke Hamjoli), but USAID and ICICI did not agree to full partnership because the social marketing projects already received donor funding for brand promotion. However, Goli ke Hamjoli coordinated with the social marketing agencies by sharing information, encouraging partnerships with commercial firms, and identifying potential providers for subsidized products promotion. Their brands were also listed in all campaign informational materials.

Measuring Results

The Goli ke Hamjoli campaign's objectives were behavior changes among key potential users and providers; increased sales as an indicator of market growth, and supportive policy and regulatory changes for low-dose OCs. The impact of the campaign was assessed, based on changes in knowledge, attitudes, and behavior among women and providers, as shown in periodic quantitative surveys. Tracking surveys also provided OC-use data. However, the major indicator of market growth and increased OC use was sales trends.

The advertising campaign was tracked through a series of annual large-scale household surveys among the target audience: 18- to 29-year-old married women in urban areas who were not sterilized. Campaign impact was assessed in terms of awareness of ads; recall of key messages; and changes in attitudes over time about OCs. Information on changes in OC use, intention to use, and discontinuation or a switch to other methods was also gathered. The key findings from each track were used to guide the development of each subsequent phase of the campaign.

The track studies showed significant shifts in attitudes and practices. Women increasingly considered OCs to be an effective and safe method, and there was a significant increase over time in trial and adoption of the method.

Among other results, the most recent tracking survey[12] showed:

- OC use had increased significantly from 4 percent in 1998 to 11 percent in 2003.
- In 2003, only 14 percent of non-users mentioned fear of side effects as a reason for not using OCs, versus a previous 28 percent.
- Attitudes about long-term use had also changed. In 2003, 62 percent of women believed that OCs were safe for long-term use, compared to a previous 47 percent.

Structured surveys and mystery client studies among physicians were used to assess changes in their attitudes and levels of knowledge about OCs. The mystery client studies also revealed their actual practices and behavior in terms of handling of queries about side effects and recommending OCs to potential users.

Among physicians, attitudes toward OCs as a safe and effective method of birth control improved significantly. Studies showed that 73 percent of physicians mentioned OCs as the recommended method for first-time contraceptive intenders. This was a significant change from 1998, when physicians primarily recommended intrauterine devices and prescribed OCs only to married women with two or three children.

Shifts in attitudes and knowledge among pharmacists were assessed by comparing results of a baseline survey conducted in 1998 with a follow-up survey in 2000. The survey showed positive changes in attitudes, especially about side effects, and improvements in levels of knowledge about how to use OCs and noncontraceptive benefits. (See Table 12–1.)

Table 12–1. Attitudes and Knowledge Change among Chemists

STATEMENTS	1998	2000
Percentage who gave the correct response to the question, "If a woman forgets to take the pill for one day, what should she do?"	46%	86%
Percentage who agreed that side effects caused by OCs would disappear after a few months	54%	79%
Percentage who agreed that OCs lessen the risk of some types of cancer	16%	54%
Percentage who agreed that OCs can help regulate a woman's menstrual cycles	49%	73%

Sales of OCs, which reflect change in use levels, were measured over the five years using monthly retail store audits in urban areas of North India. These trends were further corroborated by confidential internal sales information provided by partner pharmaceutical firms and social marketing organizations.

Sales results showed that total OC sales volumes in urban areas of North India increased by 48 percent, compared to the rest of India where sales declined by 2 percent (see Figure 12–6).

Sales of commercial manufacturers' low-dose brands had increased by 22 percent in terms of volumes (while the market share of older high-dose OCs declined from 20 percent in 1998 to 12 percent). The market in the Goli ke Hamjoli project states now accounted for 32 percent of all India commercial brand sales versus 24 percent in 1998. Sales in terms of value for commercial brands had increased by 175 percent. For commercial manufacturers these were the most important criteria of evaluation and justification for further investment in the OC market.

Sales of subsidized brands, which represented two-thirds of the market volume, increased by 71 percent during the period of the campaign. Thus the original objectives of increase in total market volume and value were met, resulting in both increased use and market sustainability through commercial investment.

From a policy and enabling environment perspective, the OC market has been revitalized. The conservative commercial pharmaceutical firms have launched new OC brands and have begun to invest in other hormonal contraceptive methods. They have also started to use new physician informational approaches, evidence-based information, and direct-to-consumer marketing. Competing subsidized brands have expanded sales and can focus on lower income populations and accessibility in new areas such as rural markets.

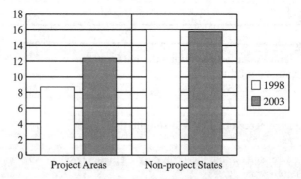

Figure 12–6. Annual OC Sales Volumes in Project States and Non-project States

Physician acceptance of hormonal methods is improving, especially among the younger generation. FOGSI issued a consensus statement on the safety and efficacy of low-dose OCs that was later co-signed by the government. At the urging of the United Nations Population Fund (UNFPA), the government also revised the formulation of its free and subsidized OCs. And finally, the Indian woman is finding that using an OC to plan her family is now a viable and socially acceptable option.

Lessons Learned

One of the principles of communications and marketing for public health should be that there is no "one size fits all" design—each situation requires careful analysis and strategic thinking before the right approach can be determined. Then, there must be willingness and flexibility to revise and innovate as research and monitoring indicate which activities have impact.

The Goli ke Hamjoli program has been a successful demonstration of an integrated communications approach linked to category product marketing on a major scale. Most of the 10 key strategic elements identified by Piotrow and Kincaid[13] in successful behavior change campaigns (for example, research-based, client-centered, service-linked, and professionally developed) were planned and effectively implemented. Modifications to the original design were based on campaign feedback and pilot activities used to identify workable and cost-effective approaches.

Behavior change requires a comprehensive strategy using all communication channels. Advertising can only bring about consideration and intention for trial. Unlike a new product category where there is simply a lack of knowledge, for OCs there was a need to first correct negative impressions. Health care providers can be a barrier or a channel and it was important, even in a nonprescription market, to win their acceptance to promote long-term use. Evidence-based research played a crucial role in this regard. Finally, happy users are the best word-of-mouth communication channel, but outreach can be a expensive way to find and reach such a large target audience.

Generic "category" campaigns can be especially effective when there are a range of affordable products already available. In that case, market expansion must focus on behavior change for acceptance of product use, not only brand promotion. When the total market expands, then all brands have the potential to grow. However, in a market where commercial full-priced, subsidized, and free products coexist, market segmentation is key to ensuring that different brands reach their intended consumer. This means brand positioning and differentiation by more than just price, a task that ideally would have been in the original program design and now has to evolve in the growing market.

The Goli ke Hamjoli program generated demand, created a supportive environment, and caused industry to enthusiastically participate in promoting OCs. However, bringing about behavior change for OC adoption requires a long-term, sustained effort to reach a critical mass of positive attitudes and acceptance of use. Was the campaign sufficient to cross the tipping point to make this method successful in India? Only time and future use patterns will tell. As newer contraceptive products enter the Indian market, OC use may not continue to increase substantially. However, in changing attitudes toward hormonal methods and in demonstrating the value of the private sector in meeting sustainable social goals, the Goli ke Hamjoli campaign has led the way to the future.

Notes

1. *National Family Health Survey 1998-99* (Mumbai, India: International Institute of Population Sciences, 2000).

2. *MEASURE DHS+ STATcompiler.* Online database. Calverton, MD. ORC Macro. Available at: http://www.measuredhs.com. Accessed December 12, 1999.

3. *Retail Store Audit Reports* (Mumbai, Vadodra, India: A C Nielsen, 1994–2003).

4. *Provisional Population Total: Census of India 2001* (New Delhi, India: Registrar General and Census Commissioner of India, 2002).

5. *Understanding Potential OC Users in North IndiaæA Qualitative Study* (New Delhi, India: ORG_MARG, 1998).

6. *Report on Goli ke Hamjoli Tracking Surveys 1998–2002* (New Delhi, India: IMRB International, 2003).

7. *Goli ke Hamjoli Communication Development and Testing 1999–2003* (New Delhi, India: Synovate India, 2003).

8. *Evaluation of the Goli ke Hamjoli Pilot Direct Contact Program* (New Delhi, India: ORG_MARG, 1999).

9. *Post Contact Evaluation of the Hamjoli Baatcheet Program* (New Delhi, India: Research International, 2003).

10. *Goli ke Hamjoli Mystery Client Survey among Doctors* (New Delhi, India: Synovate India, 2003).

11. *Report on Baseline and Follow-up Surveys among ChemistsæGoli ke Hamjoli* (New Delhi, India: IMRB International, 2001).

12. *Goli ke Hamjoli Tracking Surveys 2003* (New Delhi, India. Synovate India, 2004).

13. P. T. Piotrow and D. L. Kincaid, "Strategic Communication for International Health Programs," in *Public Communications Campaigns*, eds. R. Rice and C. Atkin, 3d ed. (Thousand Oaks, CA: Sage Publications, 2001).

CHAPTER THIRTEEN

The Importance of Client-Provider Interactions: Evidence from Family Planning Programs

Elaine Murphy and Kristina Gryboski

Chapter Questions

1. According to the evidence presented in this chapter, what are the results of high quality client and provider interactions in family planning programs?
2. What characterizes high quality provider interactions? How can these elements be implemented into program planning?
3. What types of goals and policies can encourage informed choice? What goals and policies hinder informed choice?

Introduction

Client-provider interactions (CPI) are the exchanges, both verbal and nonverbal, between health care providers and clients who seek health information or services. The client-provider encounter is a pivotal part of the ongoing process of health communication, and it can influence whether there is continuity of care and adherence to treatment. A landmark in the field of reproductive health (RH), the 1994 United Nations International Conference on Population and Development called for significant improvements in family planning (FP) programs and emphasized the importance of approaches that focus on meeting the needs of the individual—rather than promoting FP as a means of population control. The

Conference's emphasis on human rights and the importance of human-centered approaches is validated by a growing body of research and program experience in developing countries. This evidence suggests a strong relationship between the quality of CPI, including paying attention to contextual factors of clients' lives, and the adoption, correct use, and continuation of modern FP methods. While the guidance that follows focuses on FP services, the key processes of interacting with clients are relevant to other RH care, and to many other health services as well. To emphasize the importance of both the *process* of interacting with clients and the *information* essential for informed choice of contraceptive methods, the two are dealt with separately. In reality, they intertwine inseparably.

Key Processes in Client-Provider Interactions (CPI)

1. **Interpersonal Communications.** Clients are more likely to be satisfied with services if all staff, not only the counselor, treat them with respect and friendliness. In turn, client satisfaction is likely to lead to more effective use, higher rates of continuation of the same or other FP method, and positive word-of-mouth reports.[1-3] Conversely, poor CPI is associated with discontinuation and method failure. For example, research in Egypt found that client-centered (vs. physician-centered) consultations were associated with a threefold higher level of both client satisfaction and method continuation, even though the client-centered sessions lasted only one minute longer on average.[4] A study in Bangladesh found that, according to a quality-of-care index based on responses from survey respondents, clients value outreach workers who are usually or always responsive to questions, appreciative of the need for privacy, can be depended on to help with problems, are sympathetic to client needs, and provide enough information. This index was positively and significantly correlated with clients' contraceptive continuation.[5]

   Providers should encourage clients to ask follow-up questions about side effects or to clarify instructions; such encouragement is associated with positive outcomes. Disparities in social and economic class or ethnicity between the provider and client can inhibit the client from expressing concerns or asking questions.[6-7] Both verbal and nonverbal communication skills are important; counselors should "actively" listen and observe, and seek to understand clients' feelings as well as their medical and personal history. Body language that transmits warmth and interest (e.g., giving full attention, smiling and nodding when the client speaks) and a friendly tone of voice all enhance positive CPI.[8]

2. **Confidentiality and Privacy.** Clients feel more comfortable if assured that all information will be kept confidential and if visual and auditory privacy is maintained during counseling and FP procedures. This contributes to an atmosphere of trust in which the client and provider can explore emotions, sexuality, or gender-related aspects of method choice. The privacy and confidentiality of the client should be protected by all workers throughout the health services, including recordkeepers and receptionists. Post-Cairo FP services have expanded almost everywhere to include other RH services. Clients of RH services have many sensitive and diverse needs, for example, their reasons for contraception, tests, or treatment for HIV or other sexually transmitted infections (STIs); anti-retroviral drugs to prevent transmission of HIV from mother to child; counseling on intimate-partner violence; or treatment for complications due to unsafe abortion. While there has always been a need to protect the privacy and confidentiality of clients in health care settings, the HIV/AIDS epidemic has brought this need into greater focus. Research shows that clients' rights to privacy and confidentiality are so routinely violated that many clients either do not seek services at all or drop out of service or treatment programs.[9-10]

There is greater recognition today that failure to observe the client's rights to privacy and confidentiality can lead to severe consequences for the client. If someone who has power over the client (e.g., a husband) becomes aware of tests, treatment, or even advice given to the client and the person in power disapproves, the client can be subject to emotional and physical abuse. These repercussions can be especially severe with diseases and conditions that are stigmatized such as with HIV/AIDS, which can also threaten employment and community acceptance.

In order to avoid this problem, service providers of all types need practical guidance to develop and implement privacy and confidentiality policies and practices. It is critical that procedures to ensure confidentiality and privacy are made *explicit* to all who interact with clients, including those at the reception desk, drivers, and clerical staff who overhear private conversations or deal with confidential information about the client. This confidential information includes the client's identity and even the fact that the client has used the facility. Supervisors who monitor the observance of these practices need guidance on how to deal with breaches of confidentiality and privacy committed by the staff, and co-workers must be trained to do likewise with their colleagues. A new curriculum provides practical guidance on how to ensure privacy and confidentiality in RH services.[11] It also provides user-friendly job aids to help in this effort.

3. **Informed Choice.** Informed choice remains the guiding principle: Clients who already have a method preference should be given that method after screening and counseling, unless it is inappropriate for medical or personal reasons. Research shows that clients who receive the method they came for—and a large number have a preference before they interact with the provider—are significantly more likely to continue using the same method than are those who do not receive the method that they prefer.[12–13] However, even those clients who state a preference should be told about the availability of other methods that work in various ways, and asked if they would like to hear more about any or all of these methods. This is important in case the client asks for a method because it is the only one known to her, if she has been pressured to get that method, or if there has been a campaign to promote a specific method.

Programs that respond to a client's informed choice (unless medically inappropriate) recognize that there is no single method good for all clients. There is great variation in what clients and their partners find essential, attractive, inconvenient, or intolerable about contraceptive methods. Some want the convenience of a long-lasting, coitus-independent contraceptive like the intrauterine device (IUD) while others would see this as an undesirable foreign object in their bodies. Some clients place highest value on effectiveness in preventing pregnancy, while others weigh effectiveness against a method's potential impact on their sexual relations, personal feelings, or health.[14–15] Not surprisingly, continuation is also significantly increased if there is prior agreement by the couple on which method they prefer; couples counseling has been shown to be more effective in general than dealing with the woman or man alone.[16–17]

4. **Individualized Care.** Given that clients' lives and personalities (their intentions, preferences, knowledge, beliefs, skills, needs, and concerns about contraception) vary greatly, the most effective counseling is tailored to each individual.[18] Discovering individual characteristics, such as a client's difficulty with sticking to a routine, permits the provider to give special help when indi-

cated. For example, one U.S. study that examined dropouts and pregnancies among oral contraceptive (OC) users found that one-fourth to one-third of the users would have benefited from more counseling on actual *use behaviors,* such as helping clients develop practical strategies on how to remember to take the OC pill each day.[19] An analysis of data from Demographic and Health Surveys (DHS) found that first-time FP users and those under age 24 have the highest dropout rates; these clients are likely to need extra support.[20] Some clients need more information and greater reassurance about the overall safety risks, side effects, and the personal health impacts of FP methods; perhaps they have deeply held beliefs and perceptions reinforced by family and community attitudes and rumors. Clarification must be respectful; otherwise clients might not trust the provider's corrections of misinformation—or return for repeat visits.

In addition to individual factors, an FP client can fall into a certain lifecycle stage or life situation that requires special attention from the provider. A provider should "locate" a woman and her fertility intentions on her reproductive life course. The client can be a young, sexually active single woman who wants to avoid pregnancy, a breastfeeding married mother who wants to space the next birth, or an older woman who wants no more children. The counselor must also recognize that intentions can change over time and are often accompanied by ambivalence. In addition, the degree to which a woman has control over her sexual encounters has an impact on the selection of an FP method. For example, if a woman has a controlling or even violent partner, and/or if her partner opposes FP, she might prefer a nondetectable method, or might need to learn communication skills to discuss and negotiate reproductive matters with her partner. Furthermore, the nature of a woman's sexual activity is relevant. If her partner works elsewhere, she perhaps has only intermittent, infrequent sex. She can be in a mutually monogamous relationship or perhaps she has multiple sex partners and needs information on barrier methods or dual methods to protect her from both unwanted pregnancies and STIs. In sum, contraceptive counseling must be tailored to the needs of clients' different life-stages and lifestyles.[21–23]

5. **Dynamic Interaction.** Only counseling that is interactive and responsive can identify each client's needs, risks, concerns, and preferences within a life-stage and life-situation context. However, many FP providers tend to make counseling a one-way

process. This can be due in part to modeling the hierarchical behavior most health workers observe in their own schooling and workplace and in part to the social distance between providers and clients; this can make it more natural for the health worker to give "instructions to a patient" rather than "engaging with an individual." For example, in one videotaped study of counseling, providers talked at length about each available method and then asked the client to choose one. If there was hesitation, the provider recommended a method. There was rarely discussion of the reasons why a client should choose a particular method, or checking to see if the clients understood the information given. The study concluded that providers' skills could be strengthened in the areas of eliciting the needs of clients, prioritizing information to make it more relevant to the individual client, and empowering the client to make her own decision regarding FP.[24] This study and other research have given impetus to efforts to make counseling a more dynamic interaction, with much less "telling" and much more asking, assessing, listening, encouraging, establishing rapport, and clarifying—and explaining in advance to the client that such interaction is intended to help the client make the best choice.[25–26]

6. **Avoiding Information Overload.** There are limits to the amount of information people can understand and retain—another reason why counseling should not be dominated by a detailed recitation about every method offered in a program. Instead, providers should *focus on the client's selected method* and be brief, nontechnical, and clear. This approach enhances the client's understanding of the key information about that method (e.g., how to use it, what the side effects are) and also leaves time for questions, clarification, and checking for comprehension. Earlier in the session, however, all clients should be informed that there are a variety of methods available and that the counselor would be happy to describe any or all if the client so wishes. Information overload has negative consequences; one major study found that clients who received the most information were more likely to drop the method they received than those who received less information.[27] This could be due to an excess of information that reduced understanding of key points; or if the provider dominates the session with information-giving, there can be little time to help the client explore and choose the most suitable method. Affective factors can also be involved: a provider-dominated session can

lead to a lack of rapport or client dissatisfaction, factors inversely associated with remembering and adhering to a regimen. Studies by the United States have found that half or more of the information and instructions given during medical visits could not be recalled almost immediately after the visit. These studies also found that if the client was involved in making decisions, and if the counselor tailored the educational component to the individual's learning style, it engendered greater client satisfaction, adherence to therapies, and improved outcomes.[28–29] In addition, specific information that is organized logically is retained longer and more fully, especially if clients are encouraged to ask questions and repeat the instructions in their own words.[30]

7. **Using and Providing Memory Aids.** During the counseling session, use of posters, flipcharts, and illustrated take-home booklets— pre-tested for comprehension and cultural acceptability with client focus groups—helps the client understand key information and in addition reminds the provider to discuss important points. Letting clients see and handle contraceptive samples can also increase understanding as well as comfort level. Providing take-home educational materials during counseling helps clients recall instructions later when they review the materials, even if their literacy level is low. Take-home booklets on FP methods also help to disseminate accurate information to others, because clients often share the materials with their partners, relatives, and friends.[31–32]

Key Information for Clients Choosing a Contraceptive Method

1. **Effectiveness.** Effectiveness should be explained in easily understood terms. Providers must emphasize that client-controlled methods (e.g., OCs, barrier methods, natural FP, and the lactational amenenhorrea method can effectively prevent pregnancy but only if correctly and consistently used—unlike long-term and permanent methods (sterilization, implants, and IUDs) whose effectiveness is close to 100 percent once properly administered by the provider. For injectables, receiving the next injection at the time required is essential. Counseling can help each client weigh the trade-offs between effectiveness and other features of various methods. For clients who choose short-term methods,

providers should discuss how to plan for correct, consistent use and offer information on how to use OCs as emergency contraception (EC) and/or where pre-packaged EC can be obtained.

2. **Side effects.** Clients need information about common side effects and how to manage—or outlast—them. Providers should invite clients to return for advice if they encounter problems and reassure them that they can change methods if dissatisfied. DHS and other research identify side effects and perceived health problems as the major reasons clients give for dropping out of FP use; fear of these effects is also the major reason for not adopting modern methods in the first place.[33] One African study found that women who receive inadequate counseling about side effects are more likely to become FP dropouts when they experience side effects, while those who are fully counseled on side effects are likely to continue FP—with the same method or a different, more acceptable method.[34] In China, women who received pre-treatment counseling about DMPA (the injectable known as Depo-Provera) side effects and ongoing support were almost four times more likely to continue with that method than women who were not counseled.[35] Providers should discuss possible ways of dealing with the side effects, such as using a hot compress for cramping. Women who experience side effects for which they are not adequately prepared worry that their health is endangered or that the side effect, even if not dangerous in reality, can be permanent and debilitating.[36] They can even blame the method for unrelated ailments. Such worry, followed by discontinuation, is likely to discourage others from using the method, because of negative reports spread by word-of-mouth networks.[37] In addition, respectful clarification is called for if there are erroneous perceptions about the health and/or libido effects of male and female sterilization, for example, or the IUD traveling outside the uterus, or accumulation of pills in the body. Aside from rumors, in many countries the cultural beliefs about the health consequences of menstrual disruption, concerns about sexuality and menstruation, and religious and cultural restrictions on mobility placed on menstruating women pose concerns for women. Although from the biomedical perspective the lack of menstruation, occasional spotting, or irregular menstruation are not necessarily seen as a disadvantage, the social context has significance for women's lives and should not be dismissed as inconsequential. Providers should acknowledge this during counseling to help women weigh disadvantages and advantages of contraceptive options.[38–39]

3. **Advantages and Disadvantages.** In addition to side effects and health risks and benefits, providers and clients should discuss other important features of the method. These are often called "advantages and disadvantages," but it must be emphasized that such perceptions vary widely among individuals and couples. Some women want the highly effective, continual protection of the IUD or implant, while others might feel uncomfortable about a pelvic examination or want to have control over their method rather than depend on health workers to provide it. Some want methods with the fewest side effects and others want a method that does not require application at the time of having sex. Sexuality matters; many clients are concerned about the effect of various methods on extended bleeding or reduced libido. Clients also assess the mode of application differently: some favor injections while others shun them; some reject implants because they can be seen and recognized by others; some choose implants because they cannot remember to take pills; some want condoms because they offer dual protection.

4. **How to use.** Clients need brief, practical information on how to use their selected method and a basic explanation of how the method works, if it helps to clear up misperceptions or enhances correct usage (e.g., some clients think that OCs need be taken only when intercourse occurs). Clear, specific instructions are associated with better client adherence and outcomes, and are essential for counseling on user-dependent methods such as OCs and barrier methods. Clients need to develop strategies for using these methods consistently and correctly, and advice on what to do when a method fails or is used incorrectly (e.g., skipping OC pills). Programs that offer RH educational sessions or refer women to sources of instruction can help them use their methods correctly by increasing their understanding of how pregnancy occurs and how contraception works.

5. **When to return and what to do about complications.** Clients need advice on when to return for follow-up or re-supply. Clients should also be advised about the signs of rare complications and to seek immediate help should they occur. The follow-up counseling session is a good time to reinforce correct and consistent use of client-controlled methods and to ask whether the client is experiencing any unpleasant side effects that need management. The need to change methods can be discovered during follow-up if over time a client has developed medical contraindications to the method or if a change occurs in life-stage (e.g., a desire to get

pregnant in six months) or lifestyle (client now has multiple partners). In addition to scheduling return visits, providers should tell clients that they are welcome to return to the clinic any time they have concerns, or if they want to change or drop the method. Clients choosing implants should be helped to remember when it is time to have them removed—periodic follow-up visits can help—and that the effectiveness of the implants decreases rapidly after the expiration date. They should also be told that they can have the implants removed at any time before that date as well.

6. **STI prevention.** With the rising prevalence of STIs (including HIV), risk-assessment and STI/HIV prevention messages are becoming an integral part of FP counseling. Syndromic diagnosis of STIs followed by treatment or referral is also a growing trend, although its diagnostic accuracy has been called into question. At the very least, all clients should be informed whether their FP method protects them against STI/HIV and that abstinence, fidelity to an uninfected and faithful partner, or the consistent and correct use of condoms are the most effective means of protection available.[40]

Providers should be aware that those who use long-term and permanent methods might be less likely to use condoms for protection, possibly because contraception is a higher priority or because they erroneously believe that long-term and permanent methods provide protection against both unwanted pregnancies and STIs. Some—especially teens—can incorrectly believe that *all* contraceptives protect against STI/HIV. A study of adolescents in Jamaica found that only about 25 percent of them knew that OCs did not provide such protection.[41] Providers should help clients assess their level of STI/HIV risk and explain that the behavior of one's partner can also put a client at risk.[42] This can be done sensitively ("Many women are not aware . . ."). Counseling the couple together can be the most effective approach, if the woman is certain this will not lead to abuse and blame. It is difficult to assess an individual's risk of STI/HIV; for example, in many countries married women who are faithful to their husbands are among those at high risk (due to their husband's infidelity). Furthermore, singling out certain clients for STI/HIV counseling might stigmatize them.[43] Through standard clinic health talks, community education, and mass media campaigns, messages can help clients build skills in condom negotiation, and in communicating with partners about sex, as an effective addition to prevention messages. Providers should ensure during counseling sessions with clients that the client is aware which behaviors are risky and which methods protect against STI/HIV.[44]

Implications for Research, Training, Program Management and Policy

Research. Much of the research linking CPI and adoption, use-effectiveness, and continuation of FP is correlational and retrospective. More prospective research is needed—especially quasi-experimental operations research—to identify more precisely what good CPI "looks like" and how it can best be achieved. It would be useful to discover the relative significance of different components of CPI in bringing about desired outcomes—the amount and kind of information; the operationalized definition of respect and friendliness; the best ways to prepare clients for normal side effects without unduly alarming them; how to make sure that clients understand instructions for the method without patronizing them; and what might be the core "package" of individualized counseling when providers have little time to spend. Some recent studies in the Philippines and Senegal show that some interventions to improve CPI can lead to improved quality of care, but not lead to increased contraceptive continuation compared to the control group.[45] However, after combining providers from each group who practiced good CPI and comparing them with those who ranked lower in CPI, there was a positive correlation between good CPI and higher continuation. More research is needed to understand if there is a threshold effect beyond which even better CPI skills yield little or no additional positive outcomes. If so, it would be useful to identify which interventions are most effective at achieving this turning point.

There is also a need for more information on the relationship of certain client and provider characteristics (socioeconomic level, age, sex, personality) to outcomes. A study in Bangladesh found that the positive association of good CPI with contraceptive continuation was strongest among the poorest women.[46] This suggests that good CPI can have the biggest impact among clients who are disadvantaged and disempowered in society. An intervention in Indonesia that coached clients before their counseling sessions increased the clients' frequency of asking questions and expressing concerns to the provider. However, this increase did not apply to poorer and less educated women. Other research questions include: Will counseling take less time by omitting information for all methods or more time by exploring the client's special needs? Is there a relationship between the time invested in a new user and the effective use and continuation of FP? Can community-based organizations (e.g., women's and men's groups) effectively offer RH and FP information and counseling, reducing or reinforcing the work of hard-pressed service providers? This incomplete research agenda needs both sharpening and expansion. More research is needed on the effect of CPI on other RH behaviors, such as use of skilled care for childbirth. Some studies show that perception about quality of care and satisfaction can have a greater effect on whether a woman seeks maternal care than access or cost.[47] For example, in Bangladesh perceptions of "inattentive, discourteous staff behavior, lack of cooperation and lack of privacy" deter women from seeking maternity services.[48] In contrast, community-based traditional birth attendants in many developing countries are perceived as caring and sympathetic providers and sought for these skills, even though they are unequipped to handle obstetric emergencies.[49]

Training. While there is much more to know, "lessons learned" from the growing body of research on CPI have already been incorporated into some FP/RH training programs. There is nonetheless a need to develop, adapt, and disseminate curricula, both pre-service and in-service, that not only include elements of sound CPI but emphasize a client-centered, dynamic interaction as the central approach. Training in counseling yields positive results for provider and client; even radio-based distance education can improve providers' CPI performance.[50-52] Counseling training can recognize and reinforce providers' existing skills. At the same time, trainers can guide health workers to avoid giving too much or too little information in favor of helping each client make an informed choice through an interactive, participatory process. One pilot program in three sites in Latin America successfully trained FP providers to incorporate interactive counseling on sexuality, gender issues, and STI/HIV prevention in a three-day workshop, with follow-up and on-the-job support provided by on-site teams. Findings show a positive response to the new orientation by both providers and clients.

> By far the most noticeable change has been increased condom use. Although overall condom distribution increased dramatically in the first year of the project, many other factors related to condom availability and access limited the numbers distributed in subsequent years. Still, staff report that clients are increasingly requesting condoms. In Jamaica and Honduras, free samples are given to all new clients and counselors report that over 90 percent accept them. Some clients indicate that they are putting them in their partners' suitcases or drawers, or giving them to their adolescent children. In Brazil, 36 percent of clients adopting family planning for the first time now select condoms, and 5 percent elect to use dual methods. Women who participate in group discussions receive samples of condoms and many return for additional supplies."[53]

Effective training is based on adult learning principles and models the behaviors it recommends. It is therefore interactive and participatory; responsive to the knowledge-level, skills, values, and concerns of individual trainees; practice-oriented; and varied to allow for differing learning styles. In addition to training in counseling, periodic contraceptive technology and STI/HIV updates will increase provider confidence in communicating complete and accurate information to clients. Other learning and reinforcement approaches can be successful. Studies in Peru and Guatemala show that the use of job aids to improve CPI significantly increase quality-of-care scores as rated by simulated clients, from 18 points to 45 points out of a total 65 points in Guatemala, and from 28 points to 42 points in Peru.[54]

Program management. Effective management for CPI goes beyond training workshops for selected staff. It ideally involves all staff in a facility who interact with clients and includes clear guidelines, on-the-job training, training evaluation, course corrections, and ongoing management support for CPI. Job descriptions and performance evaluation indicators should be revised to reflect dynamic interaction counseling, informed choice, courtesy to clients by all staff, efficiency that reduces waiting time, and other aspects of the quality of care. Top managers must communicate clearly to staff that a client-centered program is a top priority and then show leadership and supportive supervision in implementing it. CPI also depends on a reliable supply of a wide range of methods, without which the client's informed choice is severely constrained. While all programs cannot offer auxiliary services, they can provide referrals for treatment of STIs.[55]

Policy. At an international meeting on counseling, participants stressed that policies established by governments, donors, and service facilities can either facilitate or hinder sound CPI and informed choice. Clear policies can establish informed choice as the client's right and high-quality counseling as the provider's reciprocal obligation. However, regulations such as those requiring that FP clients have spousal approval or have a certain number of children to receive some methods severely limit informed choice. Similarly, method-specific quotas, targets, or incentives are likely to put pressure on providers and interfere with counseling that maximizes informed choice.[56-57] Particularly within a donor-funded project, a program objective, "to increase the *use* of long-term and permanent methods" can easily be interpreted as a target independent of clients' needs and preferences. It would be more consistent with clients' rights to informed choice if the objective and corresponding evaluation indicators are phrased "to increase *availability* of long-term and permanent methods and accurate information about them." Similarly, programs should never

Strengthening Providers' Performance

- **Define clear expectations for good CPI** by disseminating and reinforcing policies, guidelines, job descriptions, and protocols that promote good CPI.
- **Give providers feedback on their performance** by focusing supervision on CPI and encouraging coworkers, clients, and the community to help.
- **Make CPI training more effective** by refining curricula, adopting proven training methods, and supporting trainees' efforts to apply new skills on the job.
- **Provide the space, supplies, and time** that providers need to counsel clients effectively.
- **Motivate providers** by recognizing and rewarding superior performance.
- **Match workers with jobs** to ensure that providers have the knowledge, attitudes, and skills essential for good CPI."

(Rudy, S. et al. Improving Client-provider Interaction. Population Reports, Series Q, No. 1 Baltimore, Johns Hopkins Bloomberg School of Public Health, 2003, www. populationreports.org)

reward staff for high monthly or yearly aggregate levels of sterilization procedures, IUD insertions, or distribution of other methods because such rewards conflict with the goal of helping each client to choose for herself the most appropriate method.

Conclusion

Research and program experience suggest that high-quality CPI—through courtesy and responsiveness to clients' needs—leads to increased adoption, effective use, and continuation of FP methods as well as to increased client satisfaction. Here we find a happy convergence of programmatic and demographic goals with principles of informed choice and human rights.

Notes

1. T. Delbanco and J. Daley, "Through the Patient's Eyes: Strategies toward More Successful Contraception," *Obstetrics & Gynecology* 88(3) (1996) (supplement).
2. P. Ley, "Satisfaction, Compliance and Communication," *British Journal of Clinical Psychology* 21 (1982): 241–254.

3. J. Bongaarts and S. Watkins, "Social Interactions and Contemporary Fertility Transitions," *Population and Development Review* 22(4) (1996): 639–682.

4. N. Abdel-Tawab and D. Roter, *Provider-Client Relations in Family Planning Clinics in Egypt*. Paper presented at the Annual Meeting of the Population Association of America, 1996.

5. M. Koenig, *The Impact of Quality of Care on Contraceptive Use: Evidence from Longitudinal Data from Rural Bangladesh*, Frontiers in Reproductive Health (Washington, DC: Population Council, 2003).

6. S. R. Schuler and Z. Hossain, "Family Planning Clinics through Women's Eyes and Voices: A Case Study from Rural Bangladesh," *International Family Planning Perspectives* 24(4) (1998).

7. Y. M. Kim et al., "Increasing Patient Participation in Reproductive Health Consultations: An Evaluation of 'Smart Patient' Coaching in Indonesia," *Patient Education and Counseling* 50 (2003).

8. E. Wells, "Family Planning Counseling: Meeting Individual Client Needs," *Outlook* 13(1) (1995).

9. *Ensuring Privacy and Confidentiality in Reproductive Health Services: A Training Module and Guide* (Washington, DC: PATH, 2003).

10. *Client-Provider Interactions in Family Planning Services: Guidance from Research and Program Experience*, USAID Office of Population's Maximizing Access and Quality Initiative, 2000.

11. *Ensuring Privacy and Confidentiality in Reproductive Health Services: A Training Module and Guide*.

12. C. Huezo and U. Mahorta, *Choice and User-Continuation of Methods of Contraception, a Multicentre Study* (London: IPPF, 1993).

13. S. Pariani et al., "Does Contraceptive Choice Make a Difference to Contraceptive Use? Evidence from East Java," *Studies in Family Planning* 22(6) (1991).

14. R. Dixon-Mueller, "The Sexuality Connection in Reproductive Health," in *Learning about Sexuality*, eds. S. Zeidenstein and K. Moore (Population Council and International Women's Health Coalition, 1995).

15. S. G. Garcia et al., *Documenting Preferences for Contraceptive Attributes*. Paper presented at Women's Health, Human Rights and Family Planning Programs in Mexico and Peru, Health & Development Policy Project and Population Council, 1996.

16. S. Becker, "Couples and Reproductive Health: Review of Couple Studies," *Studies in Family Planning* 27(6) (1996): 291–306.

17. Huezo and Mahorta, *Choice and User-Continuation of Methods of Contraception, a Multicentre Study*.

18. A. Jain and J. Bruce, *Implications of Reproductive Health for Objectives and Efficacy of Family Planning Programs*, Program Division Working Papers, No. 8 (New York: Population Council, 1993).

19. D. Oakley, "Rethinking Patient Counseling Techniques for Changing Contraceptive Use Behavior," *American Journal of Obstetrics & Gynecology* 170(5) (1994): 1585–1590.

20. M. M. Ali and J. Cleland, *Determinants of Contraceptive Discontinuation in Six Developing Countries*. Paper presented at the Annual Meeting of the Population Association of America, 1996.

21. M. Brady, personal communication, 1996.

22. R. Dixon-Mueller, *Population Policy and Women's Rights: Transforming Reproductive Choice* (Westport, CT: Praeger, 1993).

23. S. Edward, "The Role of Men in Contraceptive Decision-making: Current Knowledge and Future Implications," *Family Planning Perspectives* 26(2) (1994): 77–82.

24. Y. M. Kim et al., *Measuring the Quality of Family Planning Counseling: Integrating Observation, Interviews and Transcript Analysis in Ghana*, Ghana Ministry of Health and Johns Hopkins University, Center for Communications Programs, 1994.

25. L. D. Brown et al., *Improving Patient-Provider Communication: Implications for Quality of Care* (Bethesda, MD: University Research Corporation, 1995).

26. D. Roter and J. Hall, *Doctors Talking with Patients, Patients Talking with Doctors: Improving Communication in Medical Visits* (Westport, CT: Auburn House, 1992).

27. Huezo and Mahorta, *Choice and User-Continuation of Methods of Contraception, a Multicentre Study*.

28. Delbanco and Daley, "Through the Patient's Eyes: Strategies toward More Successful Contraception."

29. Ley, "Satisfaction, Compliance and Communication."

30. K. Bertakis, "The Communication of Information from Physician to Patient: A Method for Increasing Patient Retention and Satisfaction," *Journal of Family Practice* 32(2) (1977): 175–181.

31. S. Wittet et al., *Nepal: Evaluation of Family Planning Booklets. Report* (Baltimore, MD: Johns Hopkins University, Population Communication Services, 1985).

32. J. Haffey et al., "Communicating Contraception," *Populi* 11(2) (1984): 31–39.

33. Ali and Cleland, *Determinants of Contraceptive Discontinuation in Six Developing Countries*.

34. N. Cotten et al., "Early Discontinuation of Contraceptive Use in Niger and the Gambia," *International Family Planning Perspectives* 18(4) (1992): 145–149.

35. Z. Lei et al., "Effect of pretreatment counseling on discontinuation rates in Chinese women given depot medroxyprogesterone acetate for contraception," *Contraception* 53(6) (1996): 357–361.

36. G. Mtawali et al., "Contraceptive Side Effects; Responding to Clients' Concerns," *Outlook* 12(3) (1994).

37. Bongaarts and Watkins, "Social Interactions and Contemporary Fertility Transitions."

38. R. Henry, *Contraceptive Practice in Quirino Province, Philippines: Experiences of Side Effects* (Calverton, MD: University of the Philippines

Population Institute, University of Salette, and Macro International, Inc., 2001).

39. E. Wells, K. Gryboski, and E. Murphy, *Counseling on the Side Effects of Contraceptives*. Paper presented at the Society for Advancement of Reproductive Care Conference in Bali, Indonesia, 2001.

40. S. Pachauri, "Relationship between AIDS and Family Planning Programmes: A Rationale for Integrated Reproductive Health Services," *Health Transition Review* 4 (supplement) (1994): 321–348.

41. E. Eggleston et al., *Sexual Activities and Family Planning: Behavior, Attitudes, and Knowledge among Young Adolescents in Jamaica.* Paper presented at the Population Association Meetings, New Orleans, May 8–11, 1996.

42. M. Carael et al., "Extramarital Sex: Implications of Survey Results for STI/HIV Transmission," *Health Transition Review* 4 (supplement) (1994): 153–174.

43. N. L. Sloan et al., "Screening and Syndromic Approaches to Identify Gonorrhea and Chlamydian Infection among Women," *Studies in Family Planning* 1 (2000).

44. C. Coggins and A. Heimburger, "Sexual Risk, Sexually Transmitted Infections, and Contraceptive Options: Empowering Women in Mexico with Information and Choice," in *Responding to Cairo: Case Studies of Changing Practice in Reproductive Health and Family Planning*, eds. N. Haberman and D. Measham (New York: Population Council, 2000).

45. M. Costello, D. Sanogo, and J. Townsend, *Documenting the Impact of Quality of Care on Women's Reproductive Health, Philippines and Senegal*, Final Project Report No. 33, Frontiers in Reproductive Health (Washington, DC: Population Council, 2002).

46. Koenig, *The Impact of Quality of Care on Contraceptive Use: Evidence from Longitudinal Data from Rural Bangladesh*.

47. S. Andaleeb, "Public and Private Hospitals in Bangladesh: Service Quality and Predictors of Hospital Choice," *Health Policy and Planning* 15(1) (2000).

48. B. K. Paul and D. Rumsey, "Utilization of Health Facilities and Trained Birth Attendants for Childbirth in Rural Bangladesh: An Empirical Study," *Social Science and Medicine* 54 (2002).

49. J. D. McDermott et al., "Two Models of In-service Training to Improve Midwifery Skills: How Well Do They Work?" *Journal of Midwifery and Women's Health* 46(4) (2001).

50. C. Steele, "Counseling: An Evolving Process," *International Family Planning Perspectives* 19(2) (1993): 67–61.

51. Y. M. Kim et al., "Improving the Quality of Service Delivery in Nigeria," *Studies in Family Planning* 23(2) (1992): 118–127.

52. K. Heckert, *The Distance Education and Interpersonal Communication and Counseling Projects in Nepal.* Paper presented at the APHA Annual Meeting, 1996.

53. J. Becker and E. Leitman, "Introducing Sexuality within Family Planning: The Experience of the HIV/STD Prevention Projects from Latin America and the Caribbean," *Quality/Calidad, Qualite*, no. 8 (1997).

54. F. R. Leon et al., *Enhancing Quality for Clients: The Balanced Counseling Strategy*. Frontiers Program Brief No. 3 (Washington, DC: Population Council, 2003).

55. V. Jennings et al., *Analyzing the Organizational Context for a Positive Client-Provider Interaction: A Leadership Challenge for Reproductive Health*. MAQ Papers 1, No. 1 (Washington, DC: U.S. Agency for International Development) (2000).

56. *Family Planning Counseling: The International Experience* (New York: AVSC, 1982).

57. A. Fort, "More Evils of CYP," *Studies in Family Planning* 27(4) (1996): 228–231.

CHAPTER FOURTEEN

Monitoring Reproductive Health Social Marketing Programs in Developing Countries: Toward a More Strategic Approach

Ruth Berg and Dominique Meekers

Chapter Questions

1. Why are sales data misleading indicators of reproductive health (RH) social marketing program performance?
2. What is the main reason for over-reliance on sales data to measure RH social marketing programs?
3. What are other indicators that can be used for monitoring and evaluating RH social marketing programs more effectively?
4. What are the different options for obtaining data to measure program performance? What are the advantages or disadvantages for each method?

Abstract

The sophistication of reproductive health (RH) social marketing programs has increased substantially since the launch of the first contraceptive social marketing program in India over 30 years ago. Initially, condoms dominated the product mix of most RH social marketing programs, and marketing strategies were largely untargeted and supply-driven. Nowadays, these programs typically include a broad range of health products and services. Furthermore, most programs now incorporate behavior change communication, market segmentation, and services marketing approaches into their marketing strategies.

Unfortunately, RH social marketing monitoring practices have, for the most part, not kept pace with these developments. For various reasons, both international donors and social marketing organizations continue to place great emphasis on contraceptive sales as a key indicator of social marketing program performance.

This chapter provides several empirical examples that demonstrate how sales data can be a misleading measure of social marketing program success. We then propose some simple analyses of survey data that can be used to answer crucial questions about the impact of RH social marketing programs. The chapter closes with a list of key indicators for RH social marketing monitoring, a review of important sources of secondary data, and cost-effective ways to conduct primary data collection for program monitoring purposes.

Introduction

The sophistication of RH social marketing programs has increased substantially since the launch of the first contraceptive social marketing program in India over 30 years ago. Initially, condoms dominated the product mix of most RH social marketing programs, and marketing strategies were largely untargeted and supply-driven. Nowadays, these programs typically include a broad range of health products and services. Furthermore, most programs now incorporate behavior change communication, market segmentation, and services marketing approaches into their marketing strategies.[1–6]

Most social marketing programs strive for similar outcomes, although they may place emphasis on different aspects. In general, the goal of social marketing programs is to improve health, especially among needy populations, by expanding access to health products and services and promoting their use through mass media and interpersonal advertising and communication campaigns. However, these objectives must be accomplished without undermining the commercial sector. And it is against these goals that social marketing programs must be monitored and evaluated.

Unfortunately, RH social marketing monitoring practices have, for the most part, not kept pace with the increased sophistication of social marketing programs. For various reasons, both international donors and social marketing organizations continue to place great emphasis on product sales as a key indicator of social marketing program performance.[7–9]

One reason for this reliance on sales data is that they can easily be collected on a regular basis (sales data are usually available on a quarterly basis). Although social marketing programs are also increasingly collecting data to measure access (e.g., with data on distribution coverage and penetration) and behavior change (e.g., through indicators of self efficacy, perceived risk or contracting HIV/AIDS, intention to use family planning, etc.), this type of data collection is much more expensive to collect and requires greater technical expertise to collect correctly. Therefore, for most social marketing programs these data are not available on a regular basis.

Similarly, most social marketing programs only irregularly, if ever, assess whether they are meeting the health needs of their intended target group (i.e., needy populations) or whether they are segmenting the market effectively so as not to undermine the commercial sector. Again, the reason for less frequent measurement of success against these goals is that sales data cannot answer these questions, the relevant surveys are usually not readily available, and it is perceived expensive for cooperating agencies to collect the data themselves.[10]

Therefore, due largely to the time and perceived high expense associated with collecting needed data to better assess social marketing programs, there remains an over-reliance on sales data as the key indicator of social marketing program success. Yet, an increase in sales does not necessarily mean there has been a health impact, as increased project sales may have resulted from brand-switching, rather than from increased user-prevalence.

This chapter discusses why sales data can give misleading information about social marketing program success. We then show how simple analyses of survey data can be used to improve our understanding of the RH impact of social marketing programs. The chapter closes with a list of key indicators for RH social marketing monitoring, a review of important sources of secondary data, and cost-effective ways to conduct primary data collection for program monitoring purposes.

The Limitations of Using Sales Data for Program Monitoring

While using product sales to monitor the effectiveness of RH social marketing programs has the advantage that data can easily be collected on a regular basis, the disadvantage of sales data is that they cannot provide information about several crucial issues. Specifically, product sales data cannot provide information about brand switching, the extent to which the project target has been reached, and the efficiency of market segmentation. Moreover, sales data are not always a good indicator of health impact. Indicators directly derived from sales data, such as Couple-Years of Protection (CYP), suffer from similar limitations.[11–12]

Sales Data Do Not Provide Information on Brand Switching

The importance of considering brand-switching in evaluations of the impact of social marketing programs has been well documented.[13-15] Such analyses require having sales data for social marketing, public sector, and commercial brands. In most cases, however, sales data are available only for the socially marketed brands, as accurate data on public sector distribution and commercial sales are both difficult to obtain. Unfortunately, project sales data alone are insufficient to capture brand-switching.

Figure 14–1 shows an example using data on social marketing condom sales in Uganda. The results show that sales of the social marketing brand *Protector* began to decline when a new social marketing brand, *Lifeguard*, came on the market. Data on *Protector* sales from 1997 to 1999 could lead one to believe that there was a decline in overall levels of condom use, while data on *Lifeguard* sales would suggest—incorrectly—that levels of condom use were increasing. In fact, during that period from 1997 through 1999, there was very little change in the total use of social marketing condoms. Instead, the combined sales data shown in Figure 14–1 suggest that existing condom users were simply switching brands.

Data on sales of social marketed brands also do not allow one to monitor growth in the total condom market. Monitoring the total condom market, which could be used as a rough proxy for condom use, would require data on social marketing, as well as commercial and public sector sales.

Such data may also help clarify whether an increase in sales of social marketing condoms contributes to an increase in overall condom

Uganda Condom Sales (Millions)

Figure 14–1.   Trends in Sales of Social Marketed Condoms, Uganda 1995–2001

use, or whether it merely shows that existing users of public or commercial sector brands switched to the social marketing brand. Unfortunately, obtaining sales for the entire market for all social marketing products is difficult. Reliable data on public sector sales are rarely available,[16] as recordkeeping is not sufficiently detailed to distinguish between condoms that have been distributed to clinics and health centers, and those that actually reached the consumers. Reliable data on commercial condom sales are difficult to obtain because this is considered proprietary information.[17] Consequently, cases where sales data for the total condom market are available are few and far between. Fortunately, as we will show in subsequent sections of this chapter, information about brand-switching can be obtained easily through population-based surveys.[18]

Sales Data Do Not Show Whether the Intended Target Has Been Reached

Since social marketing projects predominantly distribute products through commercial wholesalers and distributors, project sales data typically only measure sales to the trade. When distributors and wholesalers have computerized recordkeeping, which is rare, it may be possible to obtain data on sales to individual retail outlets. However, data on sales to consumers never exist. Sales to consumers are sometimes tracked through audits at a sample of retail outlets. The results from this sample could potentially be used to estimate total sales to consumers.[19] Consequently, project sales data cannot be used to assess whether the social marketing project is reaching the intended target.[20] The majority of social marketing programs target low-income consumers (C and D socio-economic classes), although programs with an HIV prevention focus often also target high-risk groups.

Sales Data Do Not Reveal Whether the Market Is Efficiently Segmented

Project sales data do not allow one to determine whether the market is efficiently segmented across the commercial, social marketing, and public sectors. A recent review of social marketing projects concluded that there is a need to use a "Total Market Approach" (TMA) that integrates the interests and activities of all parties that operate in the market.[23] Ideally, public sector resources should be used to help the needy. For this to happen, the public sector should serve those segments that are unable to pay even for low-cost RH products. Social marketing programs should target those segments of the population that have some disposable income, but who cannot afford products distributed through the commercial sector. And finally, the commercial sector should provide products to those who do not fall in either of the first two categories, as these people are able to afford commercial products. The use of social marketed products, or even public sector products, by middle-class or wealthy persons would imply an inefficient use of tax dollars.

Sales Data Are Not Always a Good Indicator of Health Impact

Intuitively, one would expect sales patterns to correspond with patterns of use, which in turn should be reflected in health impact. For example, it stands to reason that if social marketing condom sales increase over time, a corresponding decrease in HIV prevalence can be expected. However, reality is much more complex, and increasing project sales do not always lead to improved health. For example, Figure 14–2 shows trends in urban HIV prevalence and social marketed condom sales in Botswana for the period from 1990 through 2001. The results clearly show that although sales of socially marketed condoms have increased fairly steadily through the study period, this has not been accompanied by a decrease in HIV prevalence.

There are several reasons why increasing sales of socially marketed products do not necessarily lead to health impact. One problem is that data on social marketing sales refer to sales to the trade, rather than to sales to consumers. Consequently, increased sales may reflect that distributors and wholesalers are filling the pipeline. This is particularly likely when the social marketing program is new, or when price increases are anticipated in a more mature program. In the latter case, retailers may try to stock up on products in order to increase their profit margin after the price increase.

In the case of condoms, another possible explanation is that while people may use them, they do not necessarily use them consistently. A

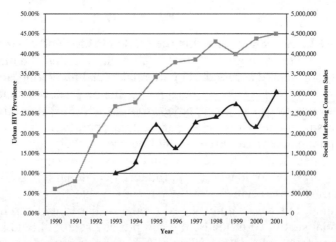

Figure 14–2. Trends in Social Marketing Condom Sales and HIV Prevalence in Pregnant Women in Botswana, 1990–2001

large body of literature documents that consistency of condom use has remained low in many countries served by social marketing programs, particularly with steady partners.[24–27] Also, although the products may be used, they are not necessarily used by those groups who have the largest need for them. Wastage and smuggling are other factors that may explain why increasing sales do not necessarily lead to improved health. However, there are no known cases of major problems with either smuggling or wastage.

For example, if condoms are predominantly used by HIV negative persons who are in a monogamous relationship, then increasing condoms sales is unlikely to reduce HIV incidence. Likewise, if most new condom users are shifting from another effective contraceptive method, then increasing condom sales is unlikely to reduce unwanted pregnancies or family size. For example, research on Zambia and Zimbabwe has shown that most users of the female condom were previously using male condoms.[28–29] Consequently, the health impact of rising sales of the female condom is expected to be small.

Finally, in some cases sales of socially marketed products comprise only a small fraction of the total market. Hence, rapidly increasing sales of socially marketed products (even when used by the intended target group) do not necessarily lead to observable changes in health indicators in the total target population.

Therefore, project sales data are an inaccurate indicator, if not an unreliable one, of health impact. Indicators that are derived directly from sales data, such as CYP suffer from similar weaknesses, and their limitations have been well documented elsewhere.[30–32]

Using Population-Based Surveys to Monitor Social Marketing Programs

Having established that product sales data are insufficient to monitor social marketing programs, we now illustrate how simple analyses of survey data can provide answers to crucial questions about the performance of RH social marketing programs. A recent review of Department for International Development funded social marketing programs identified, among others, the following priority topics:[33]

Assessing Whether the Intended Target Has Been Reached
Since survey data contain information about the background characteristics of the respondents, it is easy to verify whether users of social marketing products have characteristics that correspond with the intended target. Returning to the example of Uganda, we use data from a nationally representative population-based survey to examine to what extent the

socio-economic profile of condom users varies by condom brand (see Figure 14–3). Specifically, we show the profile of users of the two socially marketed brands (*Protector* and *Lifeguard*) and the public sector condom brand *Engabu*. The number of users of commercial brands (2.3% of all users) is too small to permit identification of their profile. As shown in Figure 14–3, the socio-economic profiles of all three brands are similar, with *Protector* doing a slightly better job than *Lifeguard* of meeting the C and D low-income target group. These findings have important program implications. First, the fact that the users of public sector condoms (*Engabu*) have a socio-economic profile that is similar to that of users of socially marketed brands suggests that most public users would be able to afford socially marketed condoms. Consequently, there is a need to increase efforts to switch condom users from public sector brands to social marketing brands.

The finding that users of the two social marketed brands also have a similar socio-economic profile raises the question whether it is an effective use of donor funds to support both brands. This is particularly a concern in cases where they are being marketed by two different social marketing organizations. In cases where donors do support two condom social marketing organizations in the same market, it may be more advantageous for the two organizations to segment the market, rather than duplicating effort as appears to be the case in Uganda.

Assessing Whether the Market Is Efficiently Segmented

Because surveys can identify users of social marketing, public sector, as well as commercial products, it is possible to assess whether the market is

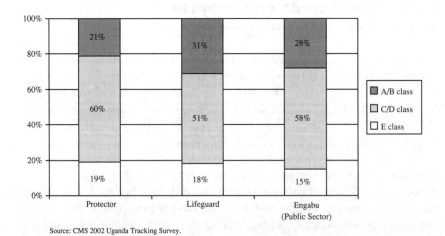

Source: CMS 2002 Uganda Tracking Survey.

Figure 14–3. Percentage Distribution of Condom Users in Uganda, by Socio-Economic Status and Condom Brand

segmented efficiently. Figure 14–4 shows the distribution of oral contraceptive (OC) users in urban India, by source and living standard (based on a standard of living index developed by Macro International. The results show that the share of OC users who are using social marketing and public sector brands increases with level of living standard. This pattern is indicative of a market that is segmented well. Nevertheless, the results also show that a fairly large share (45%) of high-income women are using subsidized social marketed or free public sector OC brands.

Project sales data also fail to reveal important shifts in market share. Survey data from urban North India indicate that while social marketing sales of OCs have increased, the commercial sector's share of all private sector OCs has decreased from 36 percent to 25 percent. These calculations are based on data from the 2002 ORG Retail Audit, Urban North India. These findings have important implications for contraceptive security. Indeed, the survey data reveal that both the social marketing program and the public sector should strive to improve market segmentation.

Assessing the Extent of Brand-Switching

Although few existing surveys collect data on brand-switching, such is relatively easy to do. For example, a study on Côte d'Ivoire asked respondents to identify their regular brand of condoms. Respondents were also asked whether they had tried any other condom brands before settling on their regular brand. If yes, they were asked if they used one of these brands regularly. Those who confirmed that this was the case were asked to provide the brand name.[34] The study shows that among current users of the socially

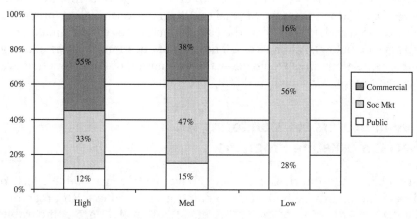

Source: All India, NFHS, 1998–99.

Figure 14–4. Percentage Distribution of OC Users in Urban India, by Source and Standard of Living

marketed *Prudence* condoms 83 percent were new users, 8 percent had switched from commercial brands, and 1 percent had switched from public sector condoms. The remaining 8 percent had used other condom brands before making *Prudence* their regular brand, but had no brand preference. A similar exercise for users of commercial condom brands indicated that only 23 percent were new users, while 46 percent had switched from the social marketing brand, and 0 percent from the public sector. An additional 17 percent had switched from a different commercial brand, and 14 percent previously did not have any brand preference.

Having documented that some users of social marketed brands switch to commercial brands, while others make the opposite switch, it is important to estimate the net effect of the condom social marketing program on the public and commercial sectors. This can be done easily by looking at the absolute number of respondents who switched in each direction. For example, the Côte d'Ivoire study included 124 regular users of commercial brands, of whom 57 had switched from the social marketing brand. This gain of 57 users was counteracted by a loss of 70 users who switched from commercial brands to the social marketing brand. Therefore, the commercial sector had a net loss of 13 users to the social marketing program. Thus, in absence of the social marketing program, it is estimated that there would have been 137 commercial sector brand users. Hence, the commercial sector lost 9.5 percent of users (13 out of 137) to the social marketing program. Doing the same exercise for the public sector shows that the public sector lost 59 percent of public sector condom users, which shows that the social marketing program helped reduce the burden on the public sector.

The preceding sections have illustrated that data from population-based sample surveys can be used to conduct rigorous monitoring of social marketing programs. Several existing large-scale survey programs already collect data that allow the calculation of the recommended indicators (see below). Adding a small number of questions to these existing survey questionnaires would allow the calculation of indicators that are needed to monitor social marketing programs.

Key Indicators for Monitoring RH Social Marketing Programs

In recent years, international donors have made considerable effort to develop standardized indicators to monitor and evaluate RH programs. The standardization of indicators ensures that data are comparable across countries, as well as across survey waves. More importantly, it ensures that different data collection agencies will collect comparable data, which increases the number of points of observation and facilitates triangulation of findings. Special efforts have also been made to move toward consistency in measurement across donor agencies. Therefore, indicator development working groups typically include representatives from several organizations. A compendium of recommended indicators for monitoring and evaluating RH programs, which describes their purpose and calculation, has been published by the MEASURE *Evaluation* program.[35] Similarly, reports describing the recommended indicators for monitoring and evaluating HIV/AIDS prevention programs are also available.[36-38]

Many of the recommended indicators are now being tracked through standardized population-based surveys. While the value of these indicators is undeniable, it must be recognized that they were designed for use by a wide range of RH and HIV prevention programs, rather than for social marketing programs per se. Consequently, there is a need to track additional indicators that focus on the unique aspects of social marketing programs.

While the required indicators may vary somewhat depending on the objectives of the program, Table 14–1 shows examples of illustrative indicators that are likely to be useful for a wide range of RH social marketing programs. At present, few social marketing programs collect data on health outcomes, as these tend to be difficult to measure in surveys. Nevertheless, indicators of self-reported levels of unwanted and mistimed pregnancies, and self-reported sexually transmitted infection (STI) symptoms can be collected in surveys. As collecting biomarker data in surveys becomes more commonplace, getting clinical data on health outcomes may also become feasible. As most social marketing programs aim to increase healthy behaviors, indicators of user-prevalence are often used for assessing program impact. However, as discussed previously, a TMA is needed to fully understand the net impact of the social marketing program, as well as its impact on the public and commercial sectors. Therefore, it is essential to also track indicators that measure use of products from each of the three sectors. This information should be supplemented with indicators on brand-switching, such as the percentage of users of socially marketed condoms who report having switched from public sector or commercial condoms.

Because social marketing programs aim to increase user-prevalence by increasing access to affordable products and by implementing advertising and behavior change communication campaigns to generate demand, indicators of the success of these specific activities are also needed. Specifically, there is a need to track indicators of method knowledge, access, self-efficacy, risk perception, social support, and the perceived quality of the products or services. And finally, there is a need

Table 14–1. Illustrative Indicators for Monitoring and Evaluating Reproductive Health Social Marketing Programs

	PROGRAM FOCUS	
	FAMILY PLANNING	STI/HIV PREVENTION
Health Outcomes		
	• Percentage of women in the target group who reported having a mistimed or unwanted pregnancy in the past two years	• Percentage of women/men in the target group who report having STI symptoms in the past year
Behavioral Outcomes		
	• Percentage of women/men in the target group who use modern contraception	• Percentage of women/men in the target group who report using a condom in last intercourse, by partner type
Total Market Approach (TMA)		
	• Percentage of women/men in the target group who use a socially marketed brand of contraception	• Percentage of women/men in the target group who report using a socially marketed condom brand in last intercourse, by partner type
	• Percentage of women/men in the target group who use a public sector brand of contraception	• Percentage of women/men in the target group who report using a public sector condom brand in last intercourse, by partner type
	• Percentage of women/men in the target group who use a commercial brand of contraception	• Percentage of women/men in the target group who report using a commercial condom brand in last intercourse, by partner type
Brand Switching		
	• Percentage of users of socially marketed FP brands who report having switched from a public sector brand	• Percentage of users of socially marketed condoms who report having switched from a public sector brand
	• Percentage of users of socially marketed FP brands who report having switched from a commercial brand	• Percentage of users of socially marketed condoms who report having switched from a commercial brand
Knowledge/Awareness		
	• Percentage of women/men who know at least two modern methods of family planning	• Percentage of women/men who know that consistent condom use reduces the risk of HIV infection
Access		
	• Percentage of women/men of reproductive age in the target group who know a source for socially marketed RH/FP methods within 15 minutes travel time	• Percentage of women/men of reproductive age in the target group who know a source for socially marketed condoms within 15 minutes travel time
	• Percentage of women/men in the target group who report the price	• Percentage of women/men in the target group who report the price of

(continued)

Table 14–1. *(continued)*

PROGRAM FOCUS	
FAMILY PLANNING	**STI/HIV PREVENTION**

Access *(continued)*

of socially marketed products is reasonable or inexpensive	socially marketed condoms is reasonable or inexpensive
• Percentage of women/men in the target group who report the price of commercial products is reasonable or inexpensive	• Percentage of women/men in the target group who report the price of commercial condoms is reasonable or inexpensive

Self-efficacy

• Percentage of sexually active women/men in the target group who feel confident that they could use modern family planning	• Percentage of sexually active women/men in the target group who feel confident that they could use condoms

Risk Perception

• Percentage of sexually active women/men in the target group who perceive themselves at risk of an unwanted or mistimed pregnancy	• Percentage of sexually active women/men in the target group who perceive themselves at risk of HIV/AIDS

Social Support

• Percentage of women/men in the target group who believe that their peers support family planning	• Percentage of women/men in the target group who believe that their peers support condom use

Quality of Care/Products

• Percentage of users of socially marketed RH/FP products that perceive them to be of good or high quality	• Percentage of users of socially marketed condoms that perceive them to be of good or high quality
• Percentage of users of public sector RH/FP products that perceive them to be of good or high quality	• Percentage of users of public sector condoms that perceive them to be of good or high quality
• Percentage of users of commercial RH/FP products that perceive them to be of good or high quality	• Percentage of users of commercial condoms that perceive them to be of good or high quality

Project Exposure

• Percentage of women/men in the target group exposed to the social marketing campaign	• Percentage of women/men in the target group exposed to the social marketing campaign
• Percentage of women/men in the target group who know the social marketing brand of modern contraceptives	• Percentage of women/men in the target group who know the social marketing condom brand
• Percentage of women/men in the target group who correctly recall social marketing messages about family planning	• Percentage of women/men in the target group who correctly recall social marketing messages about STI/HIV prevention

for indicators that measure the reach of the advertising and behavior change communication activities. Illustrative examples of indicators for each of these categories are provided in Table 14–1.

Data Sources

Most developing countries participate in one or more international survey programs. In many cases, these data can be used to monitor social marketing programs, although it may be necessary to negotiate adding questions to such surveys in order to obtain all the required information. When existing survey data are not available, or not appropriate, the social marketing program itself may need to commission a survey. The following sections discuss the most common options.

Large-scale National Surveys

The largest and most widely used survey program for developing countries is the Demographic and Health Surveys (DHS) program. DHS surveys provide data for a wide range of monitoring and evaluation indicators. The surveys are nationally representative household surveys, with sample sizes ranging from 5,000 to 30,000 households. Most surveys use a sample of women aged 15-49, but an increasing number of surveys also interview adult men. The questionnaires cover a wide variety of health topics, including reproductive behavior and intentions, contraception, antenatal, maternal and child health, and AIDS and other STIs.[39]

Typically, DHS surveys are conducted every five years, to allow measurement of trends in key indicators. However, a number of countries have supplemented the regular DHS surveys with interim DHS surveys. The interim surveys are conducted between rounds of regular DHS surveys, and tend to have shorter questionnaires and smaller sample sizes (approximately 2,000–3,000 households). Because the questionnaires are shorter, they tend to focus on key performance monitoring indicators, but may not include all data needed for a comprehensive impact evaluation.

The DHS survey program also offers an online tool, called STATcompiler, that enables Internet users to tabulate a large number of key RH indicators from the DHS surveys. STATcompiler allows users to compare indicators across countries, to tabulate trends in indicators, and to disaggregate the indicators by socio-economic background characteristics. The latter enables the user to examine trends in the indicators for specific program target groups. The STATcompiler program can be accessed free of charge at www.measuredhs.com/statcompiler.

Another important source of RH data are the International Reproductive Health Surveys by the Centers for Disease Control and Prevention (CDC). Like the DHS surveys, the CDC surveys typically collect information on family planning, fertility, maternal and child health, STI/HIV/AIDS, and other topics. Most of these surveys collect information on women in the reproductive ages, but in a few countries the surveys also include interviews with males. At the time of this writing, CDC International Reproductive Health Surveys had been conducted in 17 countries, mostly in Eastern Europe and Latin America.[40]

Targeted Surveys

The most widely known and used series of targeted surveys are the Behavioral Surveillance Surveys (BSS), which are implemented by Family Health International.[41–42] BSS aims to monitor behavior change among groups at high risk of HIV through repeated cross-sectional surveys, as part of a larger surveillance system to track the spread of the HIV epidemic. BSS surveys are particularly useful among populations that are difficult to reach through traditional population-based survey, such as sex workers and their clients, men who have sex with men, injecting drug users, long distance truck drivers, and youth. Although the frequency of data collection varies across countries, the general recommendation is to conduct surveys annually for groups among whom the HIV prevention program activities are concentrated.

The BSS questionnaires cover topics related to stigma and discrimination, knowledge and beliefs about HIV transmission, voluntary counseling and testing, high-risk sexual practices, and condom use. At present, repeat BSS surveys have been conducted in a large number of countries.[43]

Omnibus Surveys

In several countries, market research organizations regularly conduct *omnibus* surveys.[44] For example, RMS Media Services, an affiliate of Gallup International, offers omnibus surveys to Nigeria, Cameroon, Ghana, and Cote d'Ivoire.[45] Gallup affiliates in several other countries also offer such surveys. Omnibus surveys are syndicated surveys conducted at regular intervals. Typically, the implementing organization takes responsibility for the overall sampling frame and for collecting limited information about the respondents' background characteristics. Other organizations can then purchase additional questions to be added to the survey, which will be exclusive to them. Most market research organizations charge fixed fees for closed-ended and open-ended questions to an omnibus survey.

Although omnibus surveys are intended for commercial organizations, they can and have been used to monitor social marketing and other health programs.

Omnibus surveys tend to be conducted in very short intervals, sometimes as often as every two months or every four months. The high frequency at which omnibus surveys are conducted is one of their main advantages, as it allows closer monitoring than would be the case with the DHS surveys. The disadvantages of omnibus surveys include that they may not be nationally representative, but may cover only areas most salient for commercial sales. Another disadvantage is that these surveys do not always use rigorous sampling methods, which would limit the extent to which the results from omnibus surveys can be generalized. Before using omnibus surveys, it is therefore important to review their sampling procedures to assess whether the sample adequately covers the target population, and to ensure that the sampling is sufficiently rigorous to allow adequate monitoring.

Primary Data Collection by the Social Marketing Organization

In locations that have an existing survey program, such as a DHS or CDC reproductive health survey, there may be opportunities to "piggyback" questions that are specific to the social marketing program onto these surveys.[46] Piggybacking onto an existing survey is appealing, as it is likely to substantially reduce the cost of data collection to the social marketing organization. In fact, in many cases it will be possible to negotiate adding a small number of questions to such surveys free of charge. However, there are also important limitations to piggybacking. One common problem is that the existing questionnaire is already lengthy, and that it may not be possible to add all the required questions. It is also important to recognize that the survey population does not necessarily match the target population of the social marketing program. For example, many survey programs interview only women, while the social marketing program is likely to target both males and females. Even cases in where piggybacking is successful, the planned surveys may be too infrequent to allow rigorous monitoring. Consequently, it may be necessary for the social marketing organization to collect its own data during the interim period.

One possible low-cost alternative is for the social marketing organization to collect its own data by buying into an omnibus survey. However, since such surveys typically use different sampling procedures, it may not be possible to compare findings from omnibus surveys with those from a

DHS or CDC survey. This implies that using omnibus surveys will typically require that the social marketing organization buy into several rounds of the omnibus survey. This approach has been used very successfully by the Society for Family Health in Nigeria (see Box 14–1).

When neither piggybacking nor buying into an omnibus survey is feasible, the social marketing organization will need to conduct its own sample survey to obtain the required monitoring data. Because implementing a sample survey is a major endeavor, in-house primary data collection by the social marketing organization itself is generally not recommended. Rather, it is recommended that data collection be subcontracted to an experienced local survey research organization, with technical oversight from the social marketing organization's research department or an external organization (such as the USAID-funded MEASURE Evaluation project).

Conclusion

This chapter has illustrated that project sales data alone are insufficient to adequately monitor and assess the impact of RH social marketing programs. More strategic assessments of the performance of social marketing programs against their stated objectives can typically be obtained using population-based surveys.

Existing large-scale standardized population-based survey programs, such as the DHS and the CDC International Reproductive Health Surveys, are a valuable resource for monitoring social marketing programs. However, while such survey programs typically collect a lot of useful information, their standard questionnaire modules do not cover all the required information. Nevertheless, some social marketing programs have been able to negotiate the addition of a limited number of program-related questions.

Another limitation of the DHS and CDC surveys is that such surveys are typically conducted only once every five years, which is too infrequent for program monitoring. Recognizing this, an increasing number of countries are implementing interim DHS surveys, which reduces the interval between surveys to approximately two and a half years. While this increased frequency of survey waves substantially improves the ability to assess program impact, it still remains too infrequent for program monitoring, and to allow quick program adjustments.

It follows that rigorous monitoring of social marketing programs will often require that programs conduct their own population-based surveys, either to supplement existing survey programs, or in lieu of them. Such surveys allow a comprehensive examination of the market and the

Box 14-1. Using Omnibus Surveys for Monitoring Social Marketing Programs in Nigeria

A good example of the use of omnibus surveys for monitoring social marketing programs is the Society for Family Health (SFH) in Nigeria. SFH is the local affiliate of Population Services International, which distributes subsidized *Gold Circle* condoms and promotes their use through an intensive interpersonal and mass media advertising and communication campaign.[47] In the mid-1990s, SFH started monitoring its program by buying into an omnibus survey implemented by RMS Media Services, Ltd. RMS is a subsidiary of Research and Marketing Services, which is the Gallup International institute in both Nigeria and Ghana. The RMS Niger-bus survey is implemented bi-monthly and covers all 36 states in the country.[48] However, unlike the Nigeria Demographic and Health Survey, the Niger-bus survey is not fully representative of the total population. To remain cost-efficient, the Niger-bus survey covers only the capital of each state, and an area of approximately 100 miles around the capital. In addition, as most RMS clients are more interested in urban areas, which are more commercially developed, the Niger-bus survey over-samples urban areas (50% of the interviews are conducted in urban areas).

To meet its monitoring needs, SFH bought into the Niger-bus survey every six months. For this purpose, SFH developed a full-length sexual behavior and condom use survey questionnaire. This questionnaire covers detailed information about sexual behavior and condom use with different types of sexual partners, as well as about factors that may influence these behaviors, such as access of condoms, risk perception, self-efficacy, etc. The questionnaire also asks about exposure to specific aspects of the advertising and communication campaign. For example, one of the survey waves included questions about exposure to a public service announcement by soccer star Sunday Oliseh, which was broadcast during the African Cup of Nations. As the communication activities are implemented in relatively short bursts, the questions about campaign exposure typically vary across survey waves.

For each survey wave, SFH obtains the actual survey data set, which is then used to conduct further analyses. Having access to a series of surveys conducted at 6-month intervals has enabled SFH to conduct very rigorous program monitoring. For example, SFH uses the surveys to track progress in key project indicators among its main target groups, which include the poor, youth, and those with high-risk sexual behavior. When *Gold Circle* sales stagnated in the late 1990s, data from the Niger-bus surveys were used to inform the design of SFH's new behavior change strategy and to assess its impact.[49]

SFH has since stopped using the Niger-bus surveys to monitor program impact. Instead, the program is now being evaluated through a large-scale nationwide survey, which is being jointly funded by the British Department for International Development and the United States Agency for International Development (who also fund the SFH social marketing program). The new survey has a sample size of about 16,000 respondents, which will allow more detailed analyses than was the case with the Niger-bus surveys. However, due to the high cost of such a large-scale survey, it will be conducted only bi-annually.

role of social marketing in it. Collaborative efforts to fund, design, and evaluate social marketing programs using a common assessment tool has the potential to lead to better performance management, and consequently to stronger social marketing programs.

Acknowledgements: A preliminary version of this chapter, entitled "Towards a More Strategic Assessment of Social Marketing Programs" was presented at the end-of-project conference of the Commercial Market Strategies project, held in Washington, D.C., December 9, 2003.

Notes

1. F. Armand, *Social Marketing Models for Product-Based Reproductive Health Programs: A Comparative Analysis* (Washington, DC: Commercial Market Strategies Project, 2003).

2. Commercial Market Strategies, *Marketing Reproductive Health Services: Moving Beyond Traditional Social Marketing* (Washington, DC: Commercial Market Strategies, 2001).

3. P. Harvey, *Let Every Child Be Wanted: How Social Marketing Is Revolutionizing Contraceptive Use Around the World* (Westport, CT: Auburn House, 1999).

4. R. C. Israel and R. Nagano, *Promoting Reproductive Health for Young Adults through Social Marketing and Mass Media: A Review of Trends and Practices* (Washington, DC: FOCUS on Young Adults, 1997).

5. J. Meadley, R. Pollard, and M. Wheeler, *Review of DFID Approach to Social Marketing* (London: DFID Health Systems Resource Centre, British Department for International Development, 2003).

6. J. Neukom and L. Ashford, *Changing Youth Behavior through Social Marketing. Program Experiences and Research Findings from Cameroon, Madagascar, and Rwanda* (Washington, DC: Population Reference Bureau and Population Services International, 2003).

7. P. Harvey, "Measuring Results: Sales, CYPs, Contraceptive Prevalence," in *Let Every Child Be Wanted: How Social Marketing Is Revolutionizing Contraceptive Use Around the World* (Westport, CT: Auburn House, 1999), 147–166.

8. Meadley, Pollard, and Wheeler, *Review of DFID Approach to Social Marketing*.

9. N. Price, "Contraceptive Social Marketing: Pros and Cons," *Reproductive Health Matters* 3 (1994): 51–54.

10. Meadley, Pollard, and Wheeler, *Review of DFID Approach to Social Marketing*.

11. A. Fort, "More Evils of CYP," *Studies in Family Planning* 27 (1996): 228–231.

12. J. Shelton, "What's Wrong with CYP?" *Studies in Family Planning* 22(5) (1991): 332.

13. D. L. Altman and P. T. Piotrow, *Social Marketing: Does It Work?* Population Reports No. J-21 (Baltimore, MD: Population Information Program, Johns Hopkins University, 1980).

14. L. Liskin, C. Wharton, and R. Blackburn, *Condoms. Now More Than Ever.* Population Reports No. H-8 (Baltimore, MD: Population Information Program, Johns Hopkins University, 1990).

15. J. Sherris, B. B. Ravenholt, and R. H. Greenberg, *Contraceptive Social Marketing: Lessons from Experience.* Population Reports No. J-30 (Baltimore, MD: Population Information Program, Johns Hopkins University, 1985.

16. Meadley, Pollard, and Wheeler, *Review of DFID Approach to Social Marketing.*

17. J. Goodrich, K. Wellings, and D. McVey, "Using Condom Data to Assess the Impact of HIV/AIDS Preventive Interventions," *Health Education Research: Theory & Practice* 13(2) (1998): 267–274.

18. J. Bertrand, J. Stover, and R. Porter, "Methodologies for Evaluating the Impact of Contraceptive Social Marketing Programs," *Evaluation Review* 13(4) (1989): 323–354.

19. Bertrand, Stover, and Porter, "Methodologies for Evaluating the Impact of Contraceptive Social Marketing Programs."

20. N. Price, "The Performance of Social Marketing in Reaching the Poor and Vulnerable in AIDS Control Programmes," *Health and Policy Planning* 16(3) (2001): 231–239.

21. Price, "The Performance of Social Marketing in Reaching the Poor and Vulnerable in AIDS Control Programmes."

22. N. Price and R. Pollard, *Social Marketing: Issues for Appraisal, Monitoring and Evaluation* (London: Options, for the Health and Population Department, British Department for International Development, 1999).

23. Meadley, Pollard, and Wheeler, *Review of DFID Approach to Social Marketing.*

24. J. Adetunji and D. Meekers, "Consistency in Condom Use in the Context of HIV/AIDS in Zimbabwe," *Journal of Biosocial Science* 33 (2001): 121–138.

25. D. Meekers, "Patterns of Condom Use in Urban Males in Zimbabwe: Evidence from 4,600 Sexual Contacts," *AIDS Care* 15(3) (2003): 291–302.

26. D. Meekers and A.-E. Calvès, "Gender Differentials in Adolescent Sexual Activity and Reproductive Health Risks in Cameroon," *African Journal of Reproductive Health* 3(1) (1999): 51–67.

27. R. Van Rossem, D. Meekers, and Z. Akinyemi, "Consistent Condom Use with Different Types of Partners: Evidence from Two Nigerian Surveys," *AIDS Education and Prevention*, 13(3) (2001): 252–267.

28. S. Agha, "Intention to Use the Female Condom Following a Mass-Marketing Campaign in Lusaka, Zambia," *American Journal of Public Health* 91(2) (2001): 307–310.

29. D. Kerrigan et al., *The Female Condom: Dynamics of Use in Urban Zimbabwe* (Washington, DC: Horizons, The Population Council, 2000).

30. Fort, "More Evils of CYP."

31. Price, "Contraceptive Social Marketing: Pros and Cons."

32. Shelton, "What's Wrong with CYP?"

33. Meadley, Pollard, and Wheeler, *Review of DFID Approach to Social Marketing*.

34. D. Meekers, *Cote d'Ivoire Condom Consumer Profile Survey, 1998* (Washington, DC: Research Division, Population Services International, 1998).

35. J. T. Bertrand and G. Escudero, *Compendium of Indicators for Evaluating Reproductive Health Programs* (Chapel Hill, NC: MEASURE *Evaluation*, 2002).

36. *National AIDS Programmes: A Guide to Monitoring and Evaluation* (Geneva: Joint United Nations Programme on HIV/AIDS, 2000).

37. T. Mertens et al., "Prevention Indicators for Evaluating the Progress of National AIDS Programmes," *AIDS* 8 (1994): 1359–1369.

38. USAID, *USAID Handbook of Indicators for HIV/AIDS/STD Programs*, 2000. MEASURE/Evaluation, UNAIDS, WHO, FHI/IMPACT, Population Council/ HORIZONS, PSI/AIDSMARK, TvT/SYNERGY.

39. ORC Macro. *DHS Surveys*, 2004. www.measuredhs.com/aboutsurveys/ dhs_surveys.cfm. Accessed on July 10, 2004.

40. Centers for Disease Control and Prevention, *International Reproductive Health Surveys* , 2004. URL www.cdc.gov/reproductivehealth/logistics/ global_rhs.htm. Accessed on July 10, 2004.

41. Family Health International, *Surveillance*, 2003. Accessed on July 16, 2004.

42. Family Health International/Impact. *Behavioral Surveillance Surveys— Guidelines for Repeat Behavioral Surveys in Populations at Risk of HIV* (Arlington, VA: Family Health International/IMPACT, 2000).

43. Family Health International, *Surveillance*.

44. Bertrand, Stover, and Porter, "Methodologies for Evaluating the Impact of Contraceptive Social Marketing Programs."

45. RMS Media, *RMS Media Services*, 2004. http://www.internews.org/rmsmedia. Accessed on July 10, 2004.

46. Bertrand, Stover, and Porter, "Methodologies for Evaluating the Impact of Contraceptive Social Marketing Programs."

47. Population Services International, *Society for Family Health, PSI/Nigeria*, 2004. http://www.psi.org/where_we_work/nigeria.html. Accessed on July 10, 2004.

48. RMS Media, *RMS Media Services*.

49. D. Meekers, *Using Behavior Change Communications to Overcome Social Marketing Sales Plateaus: Case Studies of Nigeria and India* (Washington, DC: Commercial Market Strategies project, 2004).

CHAPTER FIFTEEN

Improving Program Effectiveness through Theory, Evaluation, and Results-Oriented Approaches: An STI/HIV/AIDS Prevention Program in the Philippines

Dallas Swendeman, Taigy Thomas, Chi Chiao, Kwa Sey, and Donald E. Morisky

Chapter Questions

1. How are communications theories incorporated into the overall intervention strategy in the example of the Philippines?
2. What is the value of targeting both individual and organizational behaviors?
3. What indicators were chosen to measure the impact of the program? Why?

Introduction

Health communication is at the core of all health promotion and disease prevention (HPDP) efforts. Communication raises awareness and influences attitudes, beliefs, and perceptions of disease risks. It also conveys the benefits of suggested action for behavior change.[1-2] These precursors to behavior change are based on a "rational-actor" model of human behavior, which has limited predictive ability in real-world settings because it is based on acting in one's own self-interest.[3] This runs counter to many observed behaviors, particularly in the health behavior domain. The accumulated evidence from HPDP evaluations indicates that health communications are necessary but often not sufficient to bring about an observable effect on behaviors or health outcomes.[4]

Individuals and communities can encounter significant barriers to changes motivated by shifts in risk-benefit perceptions. This suggests a broader conceptualization of health communications as a core element in a comprehensive process that essentially frames the implementation of HPDP programs. The purpose of this chapter is to highlight important tools for developing and evaluating health communication when viewed as a comprehensive process through an international example.

The theory and practice of HPDP programs have evolved to address barriers and bridge the gap between risk perceptions, intentions, and behaviors. Theories of health behavior change that are rooted in health communications, such as the Health Belief Model[5] and the Theory of Reasoned Action,[6] provide a conceptual framework for tailoring educational messages intended to influence individual and community health decisions.[7] Social Cognitive Theory[8] and Social Influence Theory[9] add a focus on learning new behaviors by watching and doing, building self-efficacy, and the importance of peer influences and social norms. Diffusion of Innovations[10] emphasizes the adoption process of new behaviors or technologies via social networks and communities, a process that essentially involves communication. Ecological models help widen program planners' perspectives on barriers and opportunities (i.e., enabling and predisposing factors) at not only the individual level but also at the organizational, community, and structural or policy levels.[11]

Health communication and HPDP practice has also increasingly recognized the importance of program planning, implementation, and evaluation. Improperly planned and implemented health communication and HPDP activities can have null or possibly negative effects, including the adoption and further dissemination of erroneous information or the rejection or denial of a threat entirely. In addition to the theories outlined here, communications-based program planning and implementation can be guided by theories or models of communication such as McGuire's Seven Steps Model[12] or the Centers for Disease Control and Prevention (CDC) Model.[13] Ongoing formative and process evaluation can also inform the development, quality, and adaptability of HPDP communications and programs.

Impact and outcome evaluation are integral to judging the effects of a program. *Impact evaluation* efforts consider the immediate programmatic effects on targeted cognitions (e.g., knowledge, risk factors, routes of transmission, attitudes, beliefs) and behavior (e.g., condom use, alcohol use, adherence to medication). *Outcomes evaluation* considers the programmatic effects on health status and the overall social benefit (e.g., incidence of sexually transmitted infections [STIs] and HIV prevalence). The ability to measure effectiveness depends heavily on specifying standards, measurement precision, effect size, and population or sample size.[14] Process evaluation also informs evaluation of program effectiveness by helping to identify the components of a program that contributed to its success or failure; to explain highly significant, moderate, and insignificant results; and to test and inform the theory and models that guide program planning and evaluation. The balance of the chapter will be dedicated to illustrating, through a case study, how evaluation, the specification of impacts and outcomes, and theory can inform the development and evaluation of a health communications based intervention program.

Empirical Example: An STI/HIV/AIDS Prevention Program in the Philippines

The AIDS epidemic continues to grow throughout the world with an estimated 1,650 new HIV infections per day and prevalence rates as high as 30 percent in some Sub-Saharan African countries.[15] The Philippines, a nation of some 75,000,000 people, has been relatively spared from the epidemic with UNAIDS (Joint United Nations Programme on HIV/AIDS) currently estimating only 10,000 HIV-infected individuals. Research conducted in the southern Philippines, funded by the U.S. National Institute of Allergy and Infectious Diseases, identified commercial sex workers (CSWs) and female bar workers as being at disproportionately high risk of HIV and STIs.[16] Female bar workers are employed in business establishments (bars, night clubs, karaoke TV centers, and massage parlors), which are sometimes referred to as the indirect sex establishment. Four metropolitan areas were selected for a four-group quasi-experimental study to test the relative effects of a nurse-delivered health education standard of care, trained peer educators, manager training, and the joint effects of peer educators and manager training.

CSWs and entertainment establishment managers were targeted by these four community-level interventions to increase HIV knowledge and reduce HIV risk behavior. All entertainment establishments within any given city were assigned to the same intervention. All establishment managers in each of the four participating study sites agreed to participate in the intervention program.

Results-Driven Community-Level Interventions

The interventions were designed to affect change at the community level by initiating and supporting the diffusion of HIV protective behaviors through peer networks or by encouraging the adoption of establishment educational policy that altered the commercial sex work environment to support and reinforce protected sex among their employees. Although at the onset of this study the structure and content of the interventions had already been determined, formative evaluation was conducted throughout the research study, and the results of this evaluation guided the content and objectives of subsequent intervention activities. Study impact and outcome indicators were not merely regarded as study endpoints but rather building blocks in an iterative process to develop increasingly more effective intervention activities. For example, the evaluation of intrapsychic impact indicators such as changes in HIV-related knowledge and attitudes during the first months of the intervention guided the conduct of future intervention activities designed to achieve extrapsychic outcomes such as condom use and negotiation skills. Booster intervention sessions were conducted whenever formative evaluation indicated that behavior relapse was occurring.

All the interventions were conducted for at least 24 months. At baseline, CSWs completed an informed consent form followed by an interviewer-administered quantitative questionnaire to assess their HIV-related knowledge, beliefs, attitudes, and behavior prior to participation in the intervention. Follow-up interviews were conducted at 24 months and 6 months after formal intervention activities ended at 30 months after baseline. Focus groups were also conducted to elicit qualitative data to supplement the structured interview data.

Intervention Communities

Standard Care (Ilo-Ilo). This community was exposed to the same standard care provided to all registered CSWs in the Philippines at their local Social Hygiene Clinic (SHC). The care includes free STI examination, prescription for treatment medicine if diagnosed, and educational counseling by the clinic nurses. Although prostitution is illegal in the Philippines, the national policy reflects a position of monitoring rather than attempting to eliminate commercial sex and thus driving the trade underground. All CSWs in the Philippines are required by law to register at the SHC and make weekly or bi-monthly visits for STI screening. The SHC nurse education program was conducted as a 10- to 20-minute group counseling session in the clinic while CSWs awaited results of their examination. The sessions were held on the day CSWs were scheduled to complete their STI screening appointments at the clinic and were typically attended by 30 to 50 CSWs. The sessions were primarily based on cognitive behavioral theories such as The Health Belief Model and The Theory of Reasoned Action, and were designed to effect individual-level behavior change or reinforce the maintenance of desirable behaviors. The SHC nurse outlined STI/HIV risk behaviors, the severity and undesirability of STI and HIV, and the efficacy of correct and consistent condom use to prevent infections. The study staff worked to enhance the prevention efforts of the SHC program by collaborating with the SHC nurses and CSWs to develop HIV educational posters, stickers, and brochures that were placed within the SHC and around the city and distributed among CSWs during their STI screening appointment. Research site coordinators held periodic meetings in the local SHC with SHC nurses, CSWs, and establishment managers, first to develop the education material and then to evaluate the appropriateness of the developed material.

Peer Counseling (Legaspi)

In this community peer counseling to promote HIV risk reduction behavior was implemented in addition to standard care. The intervention was grounded within a cognitive and sociostructural theoretical framework, employing elements of Social Cognitive Theory, Diffusion of Innovations Theory, and McGuire Inoculation Theory. These theories postulate that individuals are more likely to adopt new behaviors that have already been accepted by others who are similar to themselves and for whom they have respect. They have been successfully applied in numerous HIV prevention programs.[17] CSWs' "popular opinion leaders" (POLs) were recruited to participate in peer-leadership training. POLs were identified by asking each enrolled CSW to identify two peers she perceived as having substantial influence and whom she would consult for advice. Establishment managers were also asked to recommend CSWs with leadership qualities. The training sessions were composed of small group sessions that included sophisticated discussion of HIV epidemiology; misconceptions about transmission; high risk behaviors, and precautionary steps required to prevent HIV/STI; peer counseling techniques; how to build self-efficacy and influence others; how to budget finances; and how to enlist social support for personal changes. Educational videotapes with previously demonstrated high levels of efficacy in raising levels of consciousness about HIV and risk behavior and promoting discussion among similar populations in the Philippines were also utilized. A refresher training course was conducted one year following the initial training and was attended by both original and newly identified POLs.

Managerial Training (Cagayan de Oro de Oro)

This community was exposed to standard care plus managerial support in the form of enforced establishment based mandates requiring CSWs to use condoms within the establishment and complete monthly visits to the SHC. In a collaborative effort between City Health Officers and study researchers, an invitation was issued to all the managers of entertainment establishments to attend a seminar on STI/AIDS. At this seminar the global, national, and local profiles of HIV and STIs were discussed, including the modes of HIV transmission and prevention, as well as misconceptions about HIV/AIDS. The managers were also trained as to how they could play an essential role in the reinforcement, guidance, and support of safe sexual practices among their employees. With minimal encouragement by the study researchers and City Health Officers, the managers organized themselves into an association united by a goal to provide good and clean entertainment and follow agreed-upon rules and regulations regarding the conduct of entertainment services within their establishments.[18] Specifically they agreed to:

- Help the Department of Health/City Health Office to prevent HIV/AIDS and other STIs
- Train and educate entertainers within their establishments
- Provide protection for entertainers against violence and maltreatment from customers
- Monitor the CSWs within their establishments.

They also agreed to impose sanctions on violators of these rules. During the intervention period the association of managers met monthly to discuss technical aspects of HIV/AIDS prevention, the moral and legal aspects of the entertainment business, and how to organize cooperatives and social security within this context. The meetings were generally attended by representatives from the mayor's legal office, the Philippine National Police, the religious sector, the Cooperative Development Authority, and the social security system. A fine of 500 pesos was imposed on any manager who failed to attend a meeting.

Combined Intervention (Cebu)
In Cebu, CSWs and managers in entertainment establishments were exposed to the standard care, peer counseling, and managerial support as described for each of the other communities.

Socio-demographic Characteristics

At baseline 1,394 CSWs (98.6% female) participated in the study with 1,484 CSWs (100% female) at the 24-month assessment, and 1,586 CSWs (99.1% female) at the 30-month follow-up. Across assessment periods, CSWs' average age was about 23.5 years (SD = 5.5); their mean years of education was about nine years (SD = 2.3); and about 10 percent were married. They had worked as sex workers an average of 12.7 months (SD = 20.8) at baseline; 15.1 months (SD = 23.6) at post-intervention; and 17.6 months (SD = 27.7) at follow-up.

Formative Evaluation Results

Two major sexual health concerns were identified during the pre-intervention phase: (1) completion of STI medication regimens, and (2) access to condoms for safer sexual practices. Reports from the SHC identified high rates of STI recidivism among some CSWs. After testing positive and being prescribed a medication regimen by the physician, the CSWs returned to the SHC for reexamination after three days; if they tested negative, they received a physician authorization to return to work. However, at the next checkup approximately three weeks later, these same CSWs tested positive for the same STI. It was uncertain whether this was due to poor medication compliance or reinfection.

The clinic nurses conducted in-depth interviews with these individuals and determined that these CSWs did not purchase the entire medical regimen due to the prohibitive cost of the medication, typically equivalent to three days' wages. Because the law prohibits CSWs diagnosed with STIs from working, the medication costs were compounded by the additional lost wages the CSWs suffered. Faced with high costs and decreased income, CSWs purchased and completed only a fraction of the prescribed regimen, causing them to test negative at the three-day follow-up appointment. In response to this the managers' association, with some urging by the intervention staff, agreed to create a fund from which CSWs could borrow to pay for their entire medication regimen. The loans were paid back with interest, which gave employers an additional incentive to make the loans while also balancing the potential losses of a minority of unpaid loans.

During the needs assessment almost half (43.6%) of the CSWs reported that the price of condoms was too high to use them regularly. In addition, most establishments did not have clear policies and practices for condom use between CSWs and their clients, and such policies are influential in CSWs' safer sexual practice.[19–21] Given that a majority of women who become CSWs in the Philippines are driven to it by poverty,[22] the SHC provided free condoms to all CSWs. Furthermore, the interventions targeting managers (i.e., manager and combined conditions) encouraged the availability and promotion of condom use policies in the establishments.

Baseline Results

Two major needs were identified at the baseline assessment with regard to promoting protective sexual behaviors: (1) a great attitudinal discrepancy between CSWs and their employers, and (2) lack of establishment regulation to support condom use behaviors. For example, only

17.7 percent of CSWs disagreed that a CSW should have sex without a condom when customers offer extra money; 30.9 percent of employers agreed with practicing this risky sexual behavior (see Table 15–1). Only 46.7 percent of establishments at the baseline period had a condom use rule, despite the wide recognition that this rule is an influential determinant of condom use. Among CSWs who worked in establishments with mandatory condom use rules, 74.5 percent reported using condoms, compared to 58.5 percent of CSWs working in establishments without condom use rules (see Table 15–2).

Impact Evaluation Results

Condom use attitudes and establishment policy were examined as indicators of program impacts. CSWs' negative attitudes toward condom use declined substantively in all three intervention communities from baseline to post-intervention and follow-up (see Table 15–3). For example, in the combined intervention community, the proportion of CSWs who agreed or strongly agreed that condoms were too expensive to use regularly decreased from 50.1 percent, to 34.0 percent, to 15.0 percent, whereas the attitude of CSWs in the standard care community did not have a substantial change (33.1%, 43.2%, and 36.2% for each assessment respectively).

Table 15–1. Distribution of Low Expectations for Condom Use* among Commercial Sex Workers (CSWs) and Their Employers at Baseline Assessments

	AGREE	NEUTRAL	DISAGREE
CSWs	10.4%	66.9%	17.7%
Employers	30.9%	4.3%	64.8%

* Assessed by the item: "A CSW should have sex without a condom if customers offer her extra money."

Table 15–2. Distribution of Establishment Condom Use Rule and CSW Condom Use at Baseline Assessment

	CSWs CONDOM USE	
	Yes	No
Establishment has condom use rule		
Yes	74.5%	25.5%
No	58.5%	41.5%

Table 15–3. Distribution of Negative Condom Use Attitude* at Baseline, Post-test, and Follow-up Assessments by Intervention Communities

	LEGASPI (PEER COUNSELING)	CAGAYAN DE ORO (MANAGER TRAINING)	CEBU (COMBINED)	ILO-ILO (STANDARD CARE)
Baseline	25.7%	55.6%	50.1%	33.1%
Post-test	12.8%	36.4%	34.0%	43.2%
Follow-up	16.4%	30.2%	15.0%	36.2%

* Assessed by asking CSWs if the price of condoms is too high to use them regularly; responses range from strongly disagree to strongly agree. Reported percentages are CSWs who strongly agreed or agreed with the statement.

Establishment condom use policies also saw appreciable improvements at Cagayan de Oro (Manager Training) and Cebu (Combined) communities (see Table 15–4). In Cagayan de Oro, 39 percent of the establishments had a condom use rule at baseline, with this proportion increasing to 45 percent at the post-intervention and 60 percent at the follow-up periods. In Cebu, the proportion of establishments with the condom use rules also increased about 14 percent from baseline to follow-up.

Intervention impacts on behaviors related to STI/HIV were examined via two indicators: (1) condom use, and (2) SHC appointment-keeping. The proportion of CSWs that reported "always using condoms when having sex in order to lower the chance of getting AIDS" increased in the manager training (31% to 48.2%) and combined communities (45.1% to 49.1%) during the post-intervention and the follow-up period (see Table 15–5).

CSW appointment-keeping behaviors at the SHC also increased in the intervention communities compared to the standard care control. A total of 63 percent of CSWs in the intervention groups kept their appointments

Table 15–4. Distribution of Establishments Having a Condom Use Rule at Baseline, Post-test, and Follow-up Assessments, by Intervention Community

	LEGASPI (PEER COUNSELING)	CAGAYAN DE ORO (MANAGER TRAINING)	CEBU (COMBINED)	ILO-ILO (STANDARD CARE)
Baseline	39.0%	39.0%	52.0%	61.0%
Post-test	36.0%	45.0%	67.0%	56.0%
Follow-up	40.0%	60.0%	66.0%	57.0%

Table 15–5. Distribution of CSWs Reporting Always Using Condoms* at Post-test, and Follow-up Assessments by Intervention Community

	LEGASPI (PEER COUNSELING)	CAGAYAN DE ORO (MANAGER TRAINING)	CEBU (COMBINED)	ILO-ILO (STANDARD CARE)
Post-test	37.3%	31.0%	45.1%	27.5%
Follow-up	33.3%	48.2%	49.1%	17.7%

* Assessed by the question: "In the past six months, have you always used condoms when having sex to lower your chance of getting AIDS?"

at the SHC at baseline period, compared to 74 percent at the post-intervention period. On the other hand, 77 percent of CSWs in the standard care community kept their SHC appointments at baseline, declining to 67 percent at the post-intervention period.

Outcome Evaluation Results

STI rates were examined as the ultimate health outcome. There was a significant decrease in STIs among registered CSWs (required to attend SHCs) in the combined intervention community. STI rates per 1,000 clinic visits decreased from 36.4 at baseline to 14.6 at post-intervention (see Table 15–6). This represents a 60 percent reduction in STI rates. By contrast, there was no appreciable change in STI rates between the baseline and post-intervention periods for the manager training, peer counseling, or standard care communities. Thus, the evidence demonstrates that SHC-based education and treatment combined with peer education and manager training is the most effective STI/HIV prevention modality for CSWs in this case.

Table 15–6. STI Rates per 1,000 Clinic Visits for CSWs at Baseline and Post-test Assessments by Intervention Community

	LEGASPI (PEER COUNSELING)	CAGAYAN DE ORO (MANAGER TRAINING)	CEBU (COMBINED)	ILO-ILO (STANDARD CARE)
Baseline	54.8	33.7	36.4	44.6
Post-test	47.9	25.8	14.6	43.7
Difference	-6.9	-7.9	-21.8	-0.9
p-value	.461	.059	.001	ns.

Case Study Conclusions

This chapter highlights three broad strategies that can significantly improve the quality, impact, and outcomes of health communication and behavior change efforts: (1) the value of using theories of communication and behavior change to guide and inform program planning, implementation, and evaluation; (2) identifying and intervening with targets at multiple levels (e.g., individuals, organizations, communities), thus bringing to bear mutually reinforcing activities that modify both intrapsychic and extrapsychic factors related to the behaviors and outcomes of interest; and (3) the use of early and ongoing evaluation to inform adaptations of communication content and intervention activities to the changing context and needs of the targeted populations.

Theory-based Intervention Strategies

Theories of health-related communication and behavior change provide generalized schema that are useful to inform and structure the development of intervention programs across contexts, and to guide assessment of process, impacts, and outcomes. The case example presented in this chapter provides an illustration of these ideas in action. McGuire's Health Communication Persuasion Matrix provides a useful model to guide the implementation of communications-based interventions by drawing attention to source, message, channel, receivers, and destination of the communications. The Health Belief Model and the Theory of Reasoned Action/Planned Behavior are useful for informing the content or message of communications materials that essentially focus on modifying intrapsychic risk/benefit perceptions, for example, by raising awareness among CSWs of the risk of HIV/STIs and the effectiveness of condom use in preventing transmission. In this case study, the standard care nurse delivered health education, and information-based health promotion materials were guided by this level of communication and behavior change theory. As the results of this case indicate, and those of the research in this area more generally, interventions that focus solely on knowledge and risk perceptions often do not have measurable behavioral impacts or effects on health-related outcomes. However, shifts in knowledge and risk perceptions are important requisites for behavioral changes. Thus, the communications-based standard care was considered an integral component of the more comprehensive and strategic interventions implemented in the other communities in this case example.

Social Cognitive Theory informs intervention activities that attempt to bridge the gap between shifts in cognitions (e.g., knowledge, attitudes, beliefs) and behaviors. Tools such as role playing and behavioral practice help individuals learn how to act on their modified perceptions of risks and benefits of suggested actions, essentially building self-efficacy to be able to perform the desired behaviors. Social Cognitive Theory also highlights the importance of role modeling, social persuasion, and peer influences— concepts further emphasized by Social Influence Theory and Diffusion of Innovations Theory. In this case study these concepts were realized and implemented through the peer counseling interventions that identified POLs and trained them to disseminate communication messages and deliver behaviorally based intervention activities through their peer networks. The intervention acted as a "diffusion accelerator."[23] The evaluation results indicate measurable improvements in condom use attitudes, and a trend toward marginal improvement in STI outcomes.

A Multi-level Approach: Targeting Organizational Barriers

A large body of prevention research provides strong evidence that interventions designed for individuals based on social cognitive theories are efficacious. There is, however, growing concern about the limitations of models that focus solely on proximal individual-level determinants of behavior change.[24] Individual-level prevention efforts are efficacious, but interventions at the community or organizational level are important because they can remove barriers to individuals' behavior changes and therefore have an impact on a greater number of people. For example, there has been increasing recognition of the importance of community norms in preventing STIs and unplanned pregnancies. When community norms are changed, individual behaviors will be modified based on social influences within the person's network. Therefore, it is recommended that programs target multiple levels, as they can operate synergistically.

The results from the standard care and peer counseling condition do not make a convincing argument for the behavior change theories that guided those intervention components. However, these theories have informed many other effective health promotion programs.[25–26] Limitations in evaluative assessment or measurement, such as delay of impact or borrowing from the future, can explain the weak results from this case example. However, in the context of commercial sex work there are significant barriers related to the differential power dynamics between CSWs and their employers' and clients' expectations, aggregated in the form of workplace or work-environment norms. While the commercial sex work context provides easily imagined examples of such barriers as well as economic, organizational, and structural barriers, these categories of barriers are likely to occur in many other contexts and warrant attention in the planning of health promotion programs.

The manager training condition addressed these organizational barriers by intervening with establishment managers. The inclusion of the City Health Officers and representatives from local political, law enforcement, religious, and other authorities, as well as the implementation of a monetary fine on noncompliant managers represent structural-level interventions on organizational-level targets. The primary goal was to change the establishment norms and expectations for condom use among managers, clients, and workers, and STI screening and treatment compliance among workers. Notably, the managers organized into a professional association that facilitated the citywide adoption of these norms and standards. This very likely served to reduce incentives for competition between establishments based on drawing customers through low expectations for condom use; a potential barrier frequently cited in the commercial sex work context, most readily apparent for competition between individual workers[27] but also recognized between sex work establishments.[28] The results from the impact and outcome evaluations show greater effects for the standard care intervention targeting managers and organizational barriers compared to the peer counseling intervention. Negative condom use attitudes among sex workers decreased significantly, consistent condom use measures indicated sustained increases, and STI rate reductions showed more reliable trends.

These results indicate the substantial effect that targeting organizational and structural level factors can have when combined with health education campaigns. However, combining this organizational-level intervention with behaviorally oriented peer diffusion strategies shows the most striking effects. The results for the combined intervention show the greatest reductions in negative condom use attitudes, highest levels of condom use establishment rules, and most important, the highest reductions in STI rates among the four intervention conditions. These results also indicate the significant barrier that organizational factors might have played in stifling the standard care nurse education and health communications, and peer diffusion interventions.

Evidence-Driven Implementation and Adaptation

Aligning individual, organizational, and structural interests toward common goals while removing barriers and adding incentive systems at each level can have synergistic effects for health-related communications and interventions. However, identifying tractable barriers and appropriate incentive systems often comes only after an intervention has been implemented for some period of time and anecdotal evidence trickles in from the field. Strong formative evaluation and needs assessment during program design can mitigate this but unforeseen obstacles can easily arise or evolve in the changing context brought about by the intervention or from external factors. Ongoing monitoring of process, impacts, and outcomes—even if informal—can greatly enhance the chances for a successful intervention. In this case study, the condom and medication cost barriers illustrate the importance of this type of evaluation and the adaptation of the intervention that resulted.

Client attitudes and norms were also identified as significant barriers during intervention implementation. While interventions targeted at managers and establishments ultimately sought to shift client norms and expectations toward condom use, it is clear that further interventions targeted in other directions would be beneficial. In fact, it could be argued that, given the power dynamics in the commercial sex work context, intervening with clients could be more effective than targeting the sex workers. Subsequent to the intervention trial reported in this case example, a client-directed intervention was designed and implemented.

Notes

1. S. Kar, R. Alcalay, and S. Alex, *Health Communication: A Multicultural Perspective* (Thousand Oaks, CA: Sage Publications, 2001).
2. S. C. Ratzan, "Revolutionizing Health: Communication Can Make a Difference," *Journal of Health Communication* 4 (1999): 255–257.
3. A. Sen, "Rational Fools: A Critique of the Behavioral Assumptions of Economic Theory," *Philosophy and Public Affairs* 4 (1977): 318–344.
4. M. Barnes, B. Neiger, and R. Thackeray, "Health Communication," in eds. R. J. Bensley and J. Brookins-Fisher, *Community Health Education Methods: A Practical Guide*, 2d ed. (Sudbury, MA: Jones and Bartlett Publishers, 2003).
5. G. M. Hochbaum, *Public Participation in Medical Screening Programs: A Sociopsychological Study*, PHS publication no. 572 (Washington, DC: Government Printing Office, 1958).
6. I. Ajzen and M. Fishbein, "Belief, Attitude, Intention, and Behavior: An Introduction to Theory and Research," *International Journal of Gynecology & Obstetrics* 63 (1998): S175–S181.
7. C. Abraham, P. Sheeran, and S. Orbell, "Can Social Cognitive Models Contribute to the Effectiveness of HIV-Preventive Behavioural Interventions? A Brief Review of the Literature and a Reply to Joffe (1996; 1997) and Fife-Schaw (1997)," *British Journal of Medical Psychology* 71 (1998): 297–310.

8. A. Bandura, *Social Foundations of Thought and Action: A Social Cognitive Theory* (Englewood Cliffs, NJ: Prentice-Hall, 1986).

9. H. T. Reis, W. A. Collins, and E. Berscheid, "The Relationship Context of Human Behavior and Development," *Psychological Bulletin* 126 (2000): 844–872.

10. E. M. Rogers, "Diffusion of Preventive Innovations," *Addictive Behaviors* 27(6) (2002): 989–993.

11. C. Waldo and T. J. Coates, "Multiple Levels of Analysis and Intervention in HIV Prevention Science: Exemplars and Directions for New Research," *AIDS* 14 (Suppl. 2) (2000): S18–S26.

12. W. J. McGuire, "A Mediational Theory of Susceptibility to Social Influence," in eds. V. Gheorghiu et al., *Suggestibility: Theory and Research* (Heidelberg, Germany: Springer-Verlag, 1989), 305–322.

13. Centers for Disease Control and Prevention, *CDCynergy Content and Framework Workbook.* (Atlanta, GA: U.S. Department of Health and Human Services, Office of Communication, Office of the Director, 1999).

14. L. W. Green, "Evaluation and MeasurementæSome Dilemmas for Health Education," *American Journal of Public Health* 67(2) (1977): 155–161.

15. T. Barnett and A. Whiteside, *AIDS in the Twenty-first Century: Disease and Globalization* (Palgrave: Macmillan, 2002.

16. T. V. Tiglao et al., "Participatory Research Approach to HIV/AIDS Prevention among Sex Workers," *Promotion Education* 3 (1997): 25–28.

17. S. C. Kalichman, M. P. Carey, and B. T. Johnson, "Prevention of Sexually Transmitted HIV Infection: A Meta-analytic Review of the Behavioral Outcome Literature," *Annals of Behavioral Medicine* 18 (1996): 6–15.

18. D. E. Morisky et al., "The Impact of the Work Environment on Condom Use among Female Bar Workers in the Philippines," *Health Education & Behaviors* 29(4) (2002): 461–472.

19. Morisky et al., "The Impact of the Work Environment on Condom Use among Female Bar Workers in the Philippines."

20. D. E. Morisky et al., "Modeling Personal and Situational Influences on Condom Use among Establishment-based Commercial Sex Workers in the Philippines," *AIDS & Behavior* (2002): 163–172.

21. D. E. Morisky et al., "The Effects of Establishment Practices, Knowledge and Attitudes on Condom Use among Filipina Sex Workers," *AIDS Care* 10 (1998): 213–220.

22. L. S. Sobrevega and R. D. Sanchez, *Speaking Out: Hospitality Women in Davao City* (Talikala, Inc., 1996).

23. A. McAlister, "The Diffusion Accelerator: Combining Media and Interpersonal Communication in Community-Level Health Promotion Programs," in eds. N. H. Corby and R. J. Wolitski, *Community HIV Prevention: The Long Beach AIDS Community Demonstration Project* (Long Beach, CA: The University Press, 1997), 31–41.

24. W. Pequengnat and E. Stover, "Behavioral Prevention Is Today's AIDS Vaccine," *AIDS* 2000, 14 (Suppl. 2): S1–S7.

25. L. M. Coleman and N. J. Ford, "An Extensive Literature Review of the Evaluation of HIV Prevention Programmes," *Health Education Research* 1(3) (1996): 327–338.

26. C. Keller et al., "Predictive Ability of Social Cognitive Theory in Exercise Research: An Integrated Literature Review," *Online Journal of Knowledge Synthesis for Nursing* 6(2) (1999).

27. V. Rao et al., "Sex Workers and the Cost of Safe Sex: The Compensating Differential for Condom Use among Calcutta Prostitutes," *Journal of Development Economics* 71(2) (2003): 585–603.

28. C. Sakondhavat et al., "Promoting Condom-only Brothels through Solidarity and Support for Brothel Managers," *International Journal of STS & AIDS* 8(1) (1997): 40–43.

CHAPTER SIXTEEN

The Role of Communication in the Integrated Management of Childhood Illness: Progress, Lessons Learned, and Challenges in Latin America

Rafael Obregon

Chapter Questions

1. What are the major communication challenges for the Integrated Management of Childhood Illness (IMCI) and child health?
2. In what ways can communication and promotion be improved at the service and community levels in the implementation of IMCI?
3. What are the implications of improved IMCI communications for behavior change promotion and the adequacy and effectiveness of care for children?
4. What are potential new conceptual and methodologic approaches for applying communication strategies within the framework of IMCI?

Introduction

Nearly eleven million children under five years of age died globally in 2003, although over 50 percent of these deaths could have been avoided using simple and low cost but effective measures.[1] In Latin America alone, nearly half a million children under five years of age die each year and about a quarter of a million of these deaths can be easily prevented through integrated care and access to primary health services; greater involvement of local actors and networks; and effective communication with families and communities. This chapter focuses on the lessons learned and on the challenges faced by health professionals and health communicators in the context of the Integrated Management of Childhood Illness (IMCI), a strategy designed to combat the main causes of mortality and morbidity among children five years old and younger.

While IMCI focuses on a larger set of issues that includes the functioning of health systems, the performance of health workers, and the promotion of healthy practices at the community and family levels, communication plays a key role in the implementation of IMCI both at the service and community levels. At the health service level, effective communication between health professionals and parents and caretakers of children is critical to ensure adequate and effective care both at health centers and at home. At the community and family levels, health promotion and health communication activities centered on key family practices for healthy growth and development of children rely primarily on the effective design and application of multiple, integrated communication and mobilization strategies to promote behavior change.

This chapter starts with the epidemiologic context on child mortality in the region, followed by an overview of the basic concepts pertaining to the full implementation of IMCI, and some achievements in the implementation of IMCI. The discussion then turns to the role of communication in IMCI with several examples of communication interventions documented through various operational research activities and studies. Based on regional meetings held over the past years, challenges are identified along with their implications for health communication. While IMCI has been implemented worldwide, this chapter focuses on what has been learned in the implementation of the strategy in Latin America, particularly from the experience of the Pan American Health Organization (PAHO). PAHO is the oldest technical cooperation agency, with 102 years of operation, and serves as the Regional Office for the Americas of the World Health Organization (WHO).

Child Mortality in the Region of the Americas

Considerable progress has been made to reduce child mortality in the region of the Americas (the United States and Canada) over the years, especially on deaths caused by diarrhea and respiratory infections (Figure 16–1). It is estimated that between 1998 and 2000 overall mortality was reduced by 22 percent in the American hemisphere, a reduction that was even larger in the case of intestinal infectious diseases, which caused 32 percent fewer deaths in 2000 than in 1998. However, PAHO estimates that approximately half a million boys and girls die every year before ever having reached their fifth birthday, with 27 percent of these deaths due to

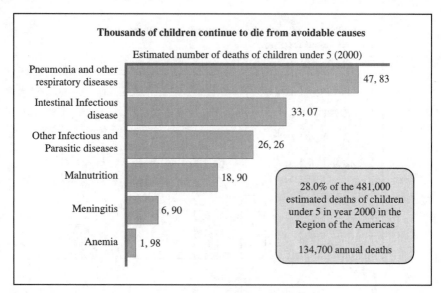

Figure 16–1. Current Situation of Mortality in Children under Five

infectious diseases and nutritional deficiencies.[2] These represent more than 150,000 annual deaths of children under five in the American hemisphere, with respiratory diseases—mainly pneumonia—and diarrheal diseases (DDs) as the leading causes of mortality.

Similarly, there are considerable differences in the distribution of deaths between countries, and within countries, in the region, which constitutes an example of the existing inequities in child health in the American hemisphere. While in some countries infectious diseases, respiratory diseases, and malnutrition no longer represent a problem of large magnitude, in others they continue to cause a sizable number of annual deaths. For instance, five countries (Haiti, Bolivia, Ecuador, Guatemala, and Paraguay) concentrate 10 percent of children under five years old in the region, but contribute 40 percent of deaths, while other five countries (United States, Canada, Costa Rica, Chile, and Trinidad and Tobago) concentrate 30 percent of the population under five but only 1.4 percent of deaths.

Along with these trends, neonatal mortality has emerged as a critical area in need of increased and effective action if child mortality is to be consistently reduced over the next years. According to PAHO, 60 percent of deaths among children under one year of age in 10 selected countries in the Americas occur during the neonatal period, and 41 percent of neonatal deaths in 16 countries are mainly due to complications during pregnancy and childbirth. Figure 16–2 shows the main

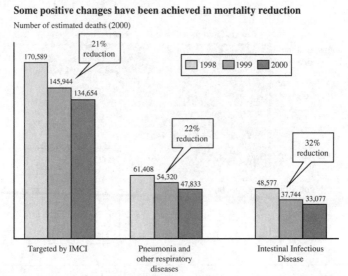

Figure 16–2. Evolution of Mortality in Children from Some Specific Causes

causes of death among children under one year with neonatal complications, mainly neonatal asphyxia and sepsis.

Despite these significant improvements over the past years, the majority of infectious diseases that continue to affect children's health *can be prevented or effectively treated through the application of simple, low-cost interventions.*[3] However, thousands of families still do not have access to these interventions, receive low-quality care, and/or lack

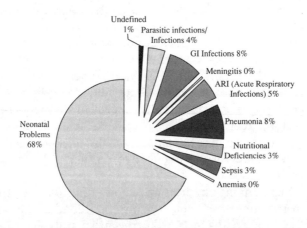

Figure 16–3. Causes of Death of Children under One Year in Ten Latin American Countries, 1998

the knowledge and skills that would enable them to apply some of these interventions both at home and in their community.

While in the past, vertical programs such as standardized management of DDs and acute respiratory infections (ARIs) made important contributions to reductions in child mortality and morbidity,[4] there has been an increasing need to provide an integrated response to main causes of disease and mortality among children five years of age and younger. However, it must be noted that interventions such as immunization programs have remained strong and continue to be a key aspect of health systems in most countries. Interest in integrated interventions was particularly fueled by the fact that children who are taken to a health center are sometimes affected by comorbidity—the presence of two or more conditions, for example, diarrhea and pneumonia, although in principle only one cause might be the reason for the visit.[5] For instance, a study conducted at Hospital Emilio Coni, in Santa Fe, Argentina, showed that two-thirds of children taken to this center were affected by a second health problem, in addition to the original condition that led mothers and caretakers to visit the center.[6]

In 1996, WHO and the United Nations Children's Fund (UNICEF)[7] took the lead in designing a strategy that integrated key interventions for prevention, treatment, and health promotion to help reduce child mortality and morbidity, and to promote better conditions for child health and development during the first five years of children's life. This strategy has been known as *IMCI—Integrated Management of Childhood Illness*.

The Integrated Management of Childhood Illness (IMCI) Strategy

The IMCI strategy focuses on the integrated care of children under five years of age, not only in terms of the diseases that primarily affect them but also in regard to children's overall health status. Thus, IMCI takes advantage of each opportunity—children's visit to health centers, for early detection and treatment of diseases that can escape the attention of both parents and health workers, with the consequent risk of the illness or condition worsening, and complications arising. In addition, it uses those opportunities to educate mothers and caretakers about appropriate care for children at home.

While it has been argued that in its original conception IMCI tended to focus on treatment and prevention of disease, it rapidly incorporated a strong health promotion component that seeks to improve knowledge and practice of health of families and communities, subsequently contributing to children's healthy growth and development. The implementation of the

IMCI strategy has three components that operate synergistically to achieve the desired results. These components are:

- Improvement of the performance of health workers (health worker component)
- Improvement of the organization and overall functioning of health care services aiming at efficient, good-quality care (health service component)
- Improvement of knowledge and use of key practices of families and communities for the care of boys and girls at home and in the community (community component)

Thus, IMCI works both at the health systems level and at the family and community level. At the health systems level, IMCI assesses the overall condition of the child. The assessment comprises the recognition of warning signs that require immediate attention (signs include lethargy, vomiting, persistent diarrhea, fever, and inability to drink or to be breastfed), and assessing conditions associated with main causes of death and morbidity. These can include DDs, ARIs, nutrition, and immunization status. Finally, the assessment of the child's overall condition includes examining the education level of mothers and the caretakers who provide care at home. At the family and community levels, using a social networks approach, IMCI seeks to mobilize communities, local organizations, and social actors to promote the key family practices for healthy growth and development of children. These practices are organized into four areas: mental and physical growth and development; prevention of diseases; adequate care at home; and seeking opportune care. The key family practices, developed by WHO and UNICEF and based on scientific evidence, are listed in Table 16–1.[8] They serve as an organizing framework that helps communities decide what practices to target in a specific community as a result of a participatory planning process. Also, at the community level these 16 practices can be modified to accommodate inclusion of other practices that are considered critical by communities, hence allowing their incorporation in the set of priority practices and into the plan of action that communities develop to improve child health.

Families and communities play a vital role in detecting warning signs early enough to seek care in a timely manner; in applying early treatment; and in fostering healthy lifestyles, that is, practices and behaviors that contribute to optimal child growth and development. Improving quality of care in health centers through effective interpersonal communication and counseling, and strengthening the role of communication in the community component of IMCI is of foremost importance for a broader dissemination of the key family practices. Empowering families

Table 16–1. Key Family Practices for the Healthy Growth and Development of Children

For physical growth and mental development

1. Breastfeed infants exclusively for at least six months. Mothers found to be HIV positive require counseling about possible alternatives on the basis of norms and recommendations by WHO/UNICEF/UNAIDS about HIV infection and infant feeding.

2. Starting at six months of age, feed children freshly prepared energy and nutrient-rich complementary foods while continuing to breastfeed up to two years or longer.

3. Ensure that children receive adequate amounts of micronutrients (vitamin A and iron in particular), either in their diet or through supplementation.

4. Promote mental and social development by responding to a child's needs for care through talking, playing, and providing a stimulating environment.

For disease prevention

5. Take children as scheduled to complete a full course of immunizations (BCG, DPT, OPV, and measles) before their first birthday.

6. Dispose of feces, including children's feces, safely; wash hands after defecation, before preparing meals, and before feeding children.

7. Protect children in malaria-endemic areas by ensuring that they sleep under insecticide-treated bed nets.

8. Adopt and sustain appropriate behavior regarding prevention and care for HIV/AIDS affected people including orphans.

For appropriate home care

9. Continue to feed and offer more fluids, including breast milk, to children when they are sick.

10. Give sick children appropriate home treatment for infections.

11. Take appropriate actions to prevent and manage child injuries and accidents.

12. Prevent child abuse and neglect and take appropriate action when it has occurred.

13. Ensure that men actively participate in providing childcare and are involved in the reproductive health of the family.

For seeking care

14. Recognize when sick children need treatment outside the home and seek care from appropriate providers.

15. Follow the health worker's advice about treatment, follow-up, and referral.

16. Ensure that every pregnant woman has adequate antenatal care. This includes having at least four antenatal visits with an appropriate health care provider, and receiving the recommended doses of the tetanus toxoid vaccination. The mother also needs support from her family and community in seeking care at the time of delivery and during the postpartum and lactation period.

and communities to achieve greater ownership of the key family practices for improving their own health is a central tenet of IMCI. From a
community standpoint, the continued occurrence of a high number of
deaths of children from easily preventable diseases, is related to a combination of factors such as failure to identify early warning signs to seek
care; lack of access to either institutional or community health services,
poor quality of care; and unnecessary or inadequate use of certain practices that delay the process of recovering from disease or maintaining a
good health status.

Between 1997 and 2002, IMCI became an official strategy in 17
countries in Latin America and the Caribbean,[9] while in other countries
it has been an important tool that often sets the standards for childcare
interventions. Some countries such as Bolivia, the Dominican Republic,
and Ecuador have made IMCI their key strategy for health care provided
to children five years old and younger, while in countries such as Peru
and El Salvador IMCI protocols and methodologies have been incorporated into their integrated health care models. In Bolivia, for instance,
IMCI was introduced as the key strategy in the SUMI (Universal
Insurance for Maternal and Child Health), created by law in 2003.

Since its inception dating from 1996 in the region, IMCI has contributed to a continuing decline in child mortality rates in the region.
Figure 16–4 shows child mortality rates from 1998 to 2000 in the
Americas, data gathered as part of the monitoring of PAHO's initiative
Healthy Children 2002, which sought to avoid 100,000 deaths in four
years. In the meantime, reduction of deaths in the neonatal mortality
period has been minimal at best. For instance, it has been documented
that reductions in the neonatal period (0 to 28 days) almost have

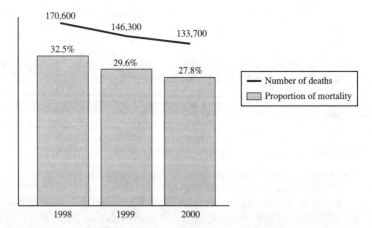

Figure 16–4. Trends in Child Mortality Due to Diseases Targeted by IMCI in the Region
of the Americas

remained flat over the past years. Thus, countries face a serious challenge to sustain reduction of child mortality rates across different age groups (neonatal and post-neonatal mortality).

The sustained and effective implementation of the IMCI faces various challenges. For instance, low training rates in countries—despite efforts made to create a critical mass of health workers trained in the strategy — mean that the number of staff trained still represents a small proportion of the volume of personnel that must be trained to provide universal access to the strategy. In addition, there is high staff turnover at the first level of care in health systems in some countries. Turnover demands new training of personnel, follow-up after training, and also makes subsequent periodic supervision difficult to carry out. Finally, these activities require a degree of organization and an availability of resources that are not always within the reach of all countries or districts within a country.

Recent studies conducted to evaluate the impact of IMCI in various countries across the world (WHO's Multicountry Evaluation, known as MCE;[10] the Analytical Review of IMCI;[11] and the Lancet series on child survival[12]) have shown that while IMCI is a comprehensive and effective strategy, it needs relatively strong health systems for the strategy to work adequately. This is of particular relevance to Latin America and the Caribbean, a region where health systems are generally more advanced than their counterparts' in other regions of the developing world.

However, with a couple of exceptions, these studies provide few details about specific aspects of the communication component of IMCI. For instance, one of the few mentions is found in the MCE, which indicates that there seems to have been a decline in the intensity of communication efforts of IMCI when compared with previous experiences in the context of vertical programs such as DDs and ARIs. Thus, this chapter is also an attempt to bring greater attention to the communication issues in the context of IMCI in the region of the Americas. In doing so, it is expected that aspects of this discussion will transcend the specifics of IMCI and will spill over the broader considerations of public health communication.

The Role of Communication in IMCI

Expansion of IMCI in the Region of the Americas heavily depends on a continuous interaction of activities aimed at strengthening, scaling-up, and sustaining IMCI through the provision of better health care service, and through activities designed to empower communities and families aimed at improving child health in and out of their homes with the support of the different levels of the health system. Figure 16–5 presents

Americas

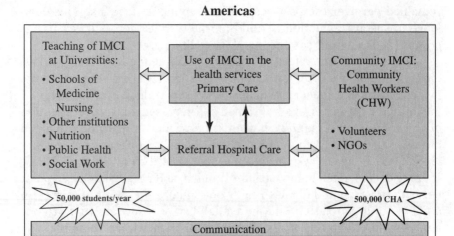

Figure 16–5.   PAHO's Framework for Expansion of IMCI in the Region of the Americas

PAHO's framework for expansion of IMCI including the various areas, organizations, and individuals working on child health to ensure scaling up of the IMCI strategy. It includes the work to be done with schools of medicine and other health-related schools as well as with the half a million health volunteers and community agents that contribute in various ways to the health needs of the region.

Within this framework, communication is a crosscutting element that plays a critical role in strengthening all aspects of the strategy. For practical reasons, the three components of the strategy—health systems, health workers, community—are often grouped into two categories: clinical (health systems and health workers) and community. The role of communication in the IMCI strategy is organized around these two broad priority areas. First, improvement of the quality of communication processes is needed among health providers and users of health services and the broader community. Second, facilitation of a process of individual and collective ownership of key family practices and messages by families and communities is necessary to lead to adoption of healthy behaviors. Table 16–2 shows each component of the strategy and the corresponding specific focus of communication to ensure greater effectiveness of the strategy.

Behavior change communication includes the use of interpersonal and community-based communication activities, as well as the use of various communication materials that range from counseling cards to educational guides to educational games. At the health service level, key communication activities include counseling of mothers before, during,

Table 16–2. IMCI Components and Communications Focus

IMCI COMPONENT	COMMUNICATION FOCUS
Performance of health workers to provide better care to children under five years of age and their mothers, caretakers, and families	• Competencies of health workers for effective interpersonal communication and counseling • Process to improve the quality of communication between health personnel and users of health services • Mobilization of families and communities for improved quality of health services with a focus on IMCI
Organization and functioning of health services to provide adequate and quality care	• Communication and social marketing strategies for greater use and demand of health services • Communication strategies that link up actions at the health and community levels
Promotion of key family practices for child health	• Behavior change communication strategies to contribute to the creation of enabling environments and to the adoption of healthy behaviors • Communication and advocacy strategies to promote changes in the social, economic, and environmental contexts to facilitate the adoption of healthy behaviors

and after their visits to clinics or health centers; and exposure of mothers and caretakers to key messages while they wait in health centers through videos, audiotapes, talks, and informal discussions. Similarly, at the community level, health community agents and volunteers conduct home visits and carry out counseling and education sessions with mothers and caretakers in an effort to ensure adequate care of children at home. These volunteers and agents typically are members of the community who are recognized as community and opinion leaders and can communicate easily with mothers and caretakers in what is considered a form of homophilous communications. Print materials such as guides and brochures highlighting warning signs, immunization schedules, and adequate breastfeeding, seek to reinforce key practices and messages and are handed out to mothers and caretakers of children.

Conceptual and methodologic approaches to communications in IMCI have changed over time. Communication in IMCI originally tended to focus on changing people's behaviors through improvements in knowledge, attitudes, and practices of mothers and caretakers, relying heavily on improving the communication skills of health providers (an effort that has required considerable in-service training). However, communication in IMCI is increasingly moving toward greater participatory approaches focusing on mobilization of social networks and actors and toward the use of natural communication spaces by involving local actors such as teachers, community leaders, women's groups, community health agents, and other community volunteers.[13] This shift in focus takes advantage of the various opportunities that bring mothers and caretakers into contact with these local actors; to use these opportunities to promote key family practices and messages to improve children's health; and to facilitate greater participation of communities and families in responding to a community's needs on child health.[14]

Accordingly, implementation of IMCI at the community level starts with a participatory diagnostic process in which local actors and networks work together toward the identification of priority issues using the key family practices as a basic framework that leads to community consensus. This exercise is followed by the preparation of a plan of action that draws on the mapping of community resources available and those additional resources that are needed. This plan of action includes various areas such as advocacy and communication components, with detailed activities, indicators, and community members responsible for the execution of such activities, creating a greater sense of ownership and facilitating sustainability of interventions.

Selected Results of IMCI Communication Interventions in Latin America and the Caribbean

While the impact of IMCI is often assessed in its broader context, studies conducted in Latin America and the Caribbean illustrate how communication contributes to progress made in child health through IMCI. This operational research focuses on the communication component of this progress and the type of results achieved. These include studies conducted by PAHO and some of its partner organizations such as UNICEF, BASICS II, and other international and national nongovernmental organizations (NGOs) (Project HOPE, CARITAS, PROCOSI-Bolivia) that have participated in the implementation of IMCI across the region.

A study conducted with 80 families in three rural, poor communities in Bolivia—Altiplano Valle Sur, Valles Crucenos, and Chiquitania Centro—between 1997 and 1999, showed an increase of 37 percentage points among mothers who were able to correctly describe how to administer oral medicines (such as oral rehydration solutions) to their children. In addition, there was an increase of 63 percent among mothers who were able to recognize at least two warning signs in children that would require immediate care from a health worker. These results, measured before and after implementation of IMCI, came up after health providers counseled mothers and caretakers during their visits to health centers.[15]

Similarly, a study as part of the implementation of IMCI was conducted by Project HOPE in the Dominican Republic between 1998 and 1999 in marginal areas of the country's capital, Santo Domingo. The results showed consistent improvements in knowledge and practices among mothers and caretakers of children.[16] Some of the key results included increased recognition of at least two warning signs (48% to 78%); knowledge of key practices for care at home, for example, provision of oral rehydration therapy (78% to 92%); how to maintain feeding during episodes of diarrhea (66% to 91%); adequate administration of liquids to control dehydration (33% to 77%); and increased practice of exclusive breastfeeding before and after implementation of the strategy.

An intervention led by Adecap, a local NGO, and the Ministry of Health of Peru, with support from PAHO, in Huancavelica, Peru, worked with indigenous, Quechua-speaking communities. Evaluation results showed sizable improvements among mothers and caretakers who were able to recognize the most important warning signs that would cause immediate risk for children and that would require immediate care from a health worker.[17] Table 16–3 shows results about recognition of warning signs before and after implementation of IMCI. While more common warning signs such as vomiting, fever, and diarrhea were relatively known beforehand, other signs such as fast breathing, difficulty to

Table 16–3. Knowledge of General Warning Signs in Children under Five, Indigenous Communities, Districts of Colcabamba, Tayacaja—Huancavelica, Mayo 2003

WARNING SIGNS	PRE N = 84		POS N = 92	
	N°	%	N°	%
Cannot drink/be breastfed	37	44.0	90	97.8
Fever/vomit/diarrhea	65	77.4	89	96.7
Fast breathing	6	7.1	72	78.3
Difficulty to breath	8	9.5	33	35.9
Bloody stools	9	10.7	80	87.0
Lethargy	12	14.3	64	69.6
Moves less than normal	2	2.4	51	55.4
Convulsions	0	0.0	52	56.5
Other (Specify)	20	23.8	65	70.7
Do not know/ Do not recognize	3	3.6	0	0.0

breathe, and convulsions were hardly known by mothers and caretakers. These results also were consistent across recognition of danger signs related to pregnancy and postpartum. While recognition of warning signs does not guarantee that mothers will seek the immediate help of a health worker due to various factors that include traveling long distances, lack of transportation, and lack of economic resources, among others, it does guarantee a greater level of awareness about warning signs and of the need to take immediate action, which constitutes the first step in saving a child's life.

While these results show improvements in recognition of warning signs, a field study conducted by BASICS II in Honduras also looked at whether mothers applied what they learned in caring for their children at home.[18] This intervention focused on five key practices (monitoring of child growth and development; breastfeeding and complementary feeding; home management of respiratory infections; hygiene; and home management of DDs). Three communities were monitored in their role as experimental groups. Those communities were then compared to three other communities that were not exposed to the communication activities included in the intervention and were monitored as control groups. Results showed that the number of mothers who only breastfed their children during the baby's first six months and the number of mothers who adequately administered oral rehydration therapy to their children almost doubled, with increases from 27 to 49 percent and 8 to 16 percent respectively.

Unlike the first experiences summarized in the preceding paragraph, which relied primarily on interpersonal communication activities held in health services, the experience in Honduras was characterized by a more comprehensive communication strategy. This package included integrated communication interventions: mass media through the use of radio dramas, radio jingles, and print; reminder materials; interpersonal communication through counseling; group activities; the participation of church leaders; and community activities such as the distribution of radios to mothers so that they could listen at the workplace. The process included a series of methodologic steps that integrated formative research, strategy design, pretesting of materials, implementation, and monitoring and evaluation of activities—steps that are generally acknowledged as essential in health communication planning.

This experience also left various lessons learned such as the importance of promoting consistent messages through each of the various communication channels used. In the context of child health it is relatively common to find that different organizations deliver messages that differ on certain aspects, thus creating confusion among the audience. In the context of child health, mixed messages have unexpected, negative consequences for the health of children and the well-being of families. Other important lessons included the need to bring together various organizations that work toward the same goals, thus maximizing existing resources and strategies.

These examples illustrate some of the important contributions that communication makes to achieve the expected results in the implementation of IMCI. However, health professionals and communicators working in child health must pay special attention to various challenges in the process of making IMCI a more effective strategy. While challenges are found across each of the three components of IMCI, the next section focuses on a set of communication-related challenges that have been identified so far, including some recommendations for future action and their implications for the practice of public health communication in the context of child health.

Communication Challenges for IMCI and Child Health

Challenges identified in this section are based not only on the previous discussion but also on results that have been identified throughout the implementation of the strategy. As a matter of synthesis, it must be said that each challenge discussed here responds to a specific lesson learned. Most of these were identified at regional workshops conducted in Quito, Ecuador,[19] Lima, Peru,[20] and Tegucigalpa, Honduras, between 2002 and 2003.[21] Also, it is important to take into account that while these challenges focus on communication, they are closely interconnected with some of the larger challenges that underline the implementation of IMCI.

Communication Strategies for Integrated Promotion of Key Family Practices

At a technical meeting convened to discuss further implementation of IMCI, Winch and others[22] clearly indicated that the integrated promotion of the key family practices pose a challenge for implementers of IMCI:

> BCC has been most successful with the programs promoting single behavioral objectives (e.g., ORT use) or clusters of closely-related behavioral objectives (e.g., family planning), and their effectiveness has been demonstrated. The major challenge for BCC in IMCI is how to promote several very different sets of behavioral objectives in one integrated package while maintaining the effectiveness of communication programs that promote single objectives. (p. 47)

The integrated promotion of the key family practices remains a critical challenge for health communicators working in IMCI, and whose development will have important implications for public health communication. The notion of promoting several practices that involve several behaviors as part of the same communication strategy is almost counter to what traditional behavior change communication teaches practitioners of this field. However, this notion comes as an opportunity to public health practitioners to push the boundaries of health communication by searching for new, innovative approaches. PAHO is currently implementing 30 small community IMCI projects in 10 countries across the region,[23] which should provide important lessons for the future of the strategy and the practice of health communication. Also, the emergence of neonatal mortality as a priority brings into the equation another set of warning signs as well as key practices for prevention of neonatal mortality and promotion of neonatal health.

The dominance of behavior-centered health communication approaches has been the subject of long debates over the past few years, which in turn has led to considerable discussion and debate about whether certain communication approaches (behavior change communication, social marketing, participatory communication, etc.) are more appropriate than others. Clearly, there is neither a magic formula nor easy solutions. Yet, the integrated promotion of key family practices emerges as another challenge, and it should provide important lessons on how this integrated approach can work.

Communication as an Element of Integration of IMCI's Components

Another important challenge faced by health communicators working in IMCI is the need to achieve a more effective articulation of its three components. In this respect, communication must play a vital and more visible role as an integrating element. Some organizations have implemented specific components of IMCI (i.e., NGOs often decide to implement only the community component of IMCI if difficulties within, or with, the health system component prevent the full implementation of the strategy). While this is an understandable position, efforts must be made to ensure the articulation of all IMCI components. Communication can play an important role in creating the necessary conditions and commitment on behalf of authorities. Thus, communication must be thought of, and integrated, in the implementation of IMCI from the very beginning.

Repositioning the Strategy among Policy and Decision Makers

At a regional workshop held in Quito, Ecuador in 2003, with the participation of nearly 25 health and communication professionals working in IMCI in different countries of the region, it was concluded that the strategy could benefit from being repositioned among those policy and decision makers responsible for implementation of IMCI, particularly in regard to allocation of resources and political commitment to move forward with the strategy. It was suggested that IMCI needs to provide decision makers with the necessary evidence that illustrates how the implementation of IMCI will give them benefits at the economic, social, and political levels, thus creating a more favorable environment for its implementation. The clear implication of this recommendation is that even if certain strategies encompass a series of technical strengths, communication and advocacy efforts targeting key decision and policy makers still are needed to ensure implementation of an otherwise sound strategy.

A Rights-based Communication Approach

Along with the focus on decision makers, it was strongly recommended that efforts be made to promote a rights-based approach as part of the implementation of IMCI. This rights-based approach must have a stronger focus on the rights of mothers and caretakers of children so that they can demand integrated care, a process in which communications must play a key role. Until now, efforts have been made at persuading health professionals about the importance of using this integrated approach. However, promoting the notion of integrated care among mothers and caretakers of children will ensure that the application of the principles of IMCI will no longer be simply an option but rather a demand of users. This will ensure widespread application of the key aspects of IMCI.

Focus on Intercultural Communication

Under the notion of equity that underlines PAHO's implementation of IMCI, many interventions take place in poor communities, often of indigenous backgrounds. Thus, it is strongly recommended that communication strategies take firm steps toward increased efforts aimed to introduce a stronger intercultural communication approach that will help health workers respond more effectively to the needs of mothers, caretakers, and family members to facilitate a communication process that is centered on greater understanding of cultural differences.

From Individual Change to Family and Community Change

The design, implementation, and evaluation of communication strategies for the promotion of key practices in the context of IMCI must have as a departing point the fact that behavior change does not depend solely on interventions that target individuals. It is critical to recognize the role played by contextual issues and those aspects that affect possibilities of changing behavior, leading to the development of strategies that will work at different levels (individual, family, community, institutional, and policy), and consider the use of systematic and articulated actions that include advocacy, social mobilization, participatory communication, and interpersonal and mass communication, among others.

Evaluation Issues

Evaluation remains as an important challenge. Evidence of what contributions communication makes to the adoption of healthy practices by communities, families, and individuals needs to be shown in a rigorous way in order to strengthen the role of communication in the implementation of the IMCI strategy and in public health communication as a whole. However, the increasing trend toward new participatory approaches demands a broader focus in this sense, and evaluators will need to look at processes of empowerment, participation, leadership, and social norms, and not only at more classic indicators traditionally used such as knowledge, attitudes, and practices. This will require greater integration of qualitative and quantitative indicators with communities playing an active role to truly understand the process of empowerment and change in community and family settings. Also, what types of changes take place in the social structures of communities need to be considered, recognized, and analyzed beyond the exclusive focus on the indicators related to the epidemiological indicators.

The need to document and systematize the contribution of communication to the achievement of the IMCI objectives emerges as another important challenge. The different experiences that are generated through the implementation of projects at the local level, either financed by ministries of health or by international institutions that work in children's health, must provide important lessons for the future practice of IMCI. Hence, efforts must be made to guarantee that these experiences are documented systematically.

Adaptability of the Strategy

Finally, it is of utmost importance for IMCI to remain a strategy flexible enough to accommodate new technical elements, and to get adjusted to the new challenges imposed by social and economic changes at the international level, which will certainly have an impact on the prioritization of health issues and current trends in the responses provided to social problems. For instance, the need to work in neonatal health brings with it specific challenges such as making the health of the newborn a lot more visible.[24] IMCI shows that, if implemented with a minimum of resources and with strong political support, it can be an effective strategy.

By Way of Conclusion

Arguably, some or most of these lessons learned and challenges ahead might have been identified in other areas of health communication. However, there are many experiences in health communication for child health in the region that have not been adequately evaluated and documented, and whose lessons have not been brought into the discussion of communication and health. Thus, it is necessary to continue working toward the identification of these experiences in order to analyze them and to gather new lessons that will help public health communication practitioners and academics work toward more effective communication interventions for the health of children. Only this type of approach will help identify new conceptual and methodologic approaches for communication strategies within the framework of IMCI.

This chapter provides an overview of the IMCI strategy and the role communication plays in its implementation. While IMCI is a technically sound strategy that has shown positive results in a handful of communication experiences documented to date, it is clear that several challenges remain for health communication professionals who work on its implementation. However, responding to these challenges must be seen as a tremendous opportunity to expand knowledge of the role of communications in the implementation of the strategy and in health communication in general.

Notes

1. "The World's Forgotten Children," *The Lancet* 361: 1.
2. Pan American Health Organization, *Health in the Americas* (Washington, DC: Pan American Health Organization, 2002).
3. The Bellagio Study Group on Child Survival, *The Lancet* 361 (2003): 323–327.
4. World Bank, *World Development Report 1993: Investing in Health* (Washington, DC: The World Bank, 1993).
5. R. Black, S. Morris, and J. Bryce, "Where and Why Are 10 Million Children Dying Every Year?", *The Lancet* 361 (2003): 2226–2234.
6. INER "Emilio Coni," *Investigacíon Operativa Sobre la Implementacion de AIEPI*, Santa Fe, Argentina, 1999.
7. World Health Organization, *Improving Child Health&IMCI: The Integrated Approach* (Geneva: World Health Organization, 1997).
8. Z. Hill, B. Kirkwood, and K. Edmond, *Family and Community Practices That Promote Child Survival, Growth, and Development: A Review of the Evidence* (Geneva: World Health Organization, 2002).
9. Y. Benguigui, "Current Status of the IMCI Strategy in the Region of the Americas: Progress, Results, Challenges, and Prospects," in *Technical Advisory Group IMCI (TAG-IMCI): Report of the Second Meeting* (Washington, DC: Pan American Health Organization, 2003), 9–17.
10. World Health Organization, *Multi-Country Evaluation of IMCI Effectiveness, Cost, and Impact (MCE): Progress Report May 2002–April 2003* (Geneva: World Health Organization, 2003).

11. World Health Organization, *Analytical Review of the IMCI Strategy* (Geneva: World Health Organization, 2003).

12. P. R. Kowal and A. D. Lopez, "Child Survival," *The Lancet* 362 (2003): 915.

13. J. Nkum, *Communication Approach for Community IMCI* (UNICEF, 2002).

14. P. Winch et al., *Reaching Communities for Child Health and Nutrition: A Framework for Household and Community IMCI* (Washington, DC: Basics II/CORE Group/USAID, 2001).

15. BASICS II/Ministry of Health of Bolivia, *Health Facility Surveys 1997–1999, Altiplano Valle Sur, Valles Crucenos and Chiquitania Centro* (Arlington, VA: BASICS II).

16. T. Narvaez, "Programa de Atención Primaria en Salud," Noticias sobre AIEPI, December 2000, 7–9.

17. Adecap/Ministerio de Salud Peru, Organización Panamericana de la Salud 2004, *Informe Final, Campana: Juntos Podemos Salvar a Los Ninos* (Huancavelica, Peru: Adecap, 2004).

18. V. Alvarado, *Programación Multimedia Focalizada en Conductas Clave en Honduras*. Presented at the Regional Workshop, Estrategias Comunitarias papa la Salud del Recién Nacido (Tegucigalpa, Honduras, 2004).

19. "Experiences in Communication and Child Health: Lessons Learned, Challenges and New Directions," International Workshop (Quito, Ecuador: Pan American Health Organization, June 2002).

20. "A Communication Strategy for IMCI," Regional Workshop (Lima, Peru: Pan American Health Organization, October 2002).

21. "Community Approaches to Newborn Care," Regional Workshop (Tegucigalpa, Honduras: BASICS II, April 2003).

22. Winch et al., *Reaching Communities for Child Health and Nutrition: A Framework for Household and Community IMCI*.

23. *Proyecto Regional AIEPI Comunitario: Taller de Trabajo Técnico* (Washington, DC: Pan American Health Organization, 2001).

24. BASICS II, *Final Report of the Regional Workshop, Community Strategies to Newborn Care* (Arlington, VA: BASICS II, 2004).

CHAPTER SEVENTEEN

Linking Communication for Campaign and Routine Immunization: In Need of a Bifocal View

Silvio Waisbord

Chapter Questions

1. What are the major challenges for communication related to immunization programs?
2. What are possible ways in which communication activities for immunization campaigns and routine immunizations can be integrated?
3. How might the combination of media and interpersonal communication inform caretakers and increase compliance with health care regimens?
4. How can communication activities provide information while reinforcing cultural norms that legitimize immunization as well as build sustainability of immunization programs?

Introduction

Much has been debated about the impact of eradication efforts on routine immunization (RI) systems. Some points of contention include whether eradication campaigns develop separated immunization infrastructures or whether they strengthen, add, or divert resources from routine services.[1-5] In this chapter, I want to examine communication aspects of the debate that have not received sufficient attention. My intention is neither to revisit the debate nor to add another commentary to a long-lasting polemic. Rather, I am interested in exploring how it is possible to integrate communication activities for immunization campaigns and RI.

The analysis draws examples from the Polio Eradication Initiative (PEI). The World Health Assembly launched the PEI in 1988. Much progress has been made since then. The number of global cases of polio fell from approximately 300,000 to 483 in 2001. The number of cases was 1,925 in 2002 and 677 in 2003. The Americas, Europe, and Western Pacific have been declared polio-free. Despite enormous progress, the original goal of eradicating polio by 2000 has not been met. The goal has been reset for 2005. Polio remains endemic in six countries in the world (Nigeria, India, Pakistan, Egypt, Niger, and Afghanistan). During the PEI, communication focused on campaigns at the expense of other strategies such as RI and surveillance. The PEI has designed a four-prong strategy: campaigns, routine immunization, surveillance, and mop-ups. Most communication programs have focused on the National Immunization Days.

This trend raises an interesting question about whether the focus on campaign communication (and the concomitant lack of balanced attention across strategies) is inevitable due to programmatic design and funding availability, or if it can be corrected if a different approach is taken. This chapter aims to answer this question.

Because at the heart of the debate is the question of sustainability of immunization campaigns, it is necessary to examine the long-term impact of communication interventions during eradication campaigns. Finding answers to this question could help us understand better whether communication programs implemented during eradication initiatives necessarily have short-term impact or if they can contribute to promoting immunization practices, in general. Because sustainability remains a crucial and difficult issue in international health projects, this question has implications for theory and practice of health communication more broadly. Although there is plenty of evidence showing short-term impact of a variety of communication interventions in international health programs, we are still grappling with the difficulty of understanding and measuring sustainable impact.

My argument is that as long as communication is based on informational and individualistic premises, it would be difficult to grasp the ways in which "campaign" and "routine" communication can be integrated. Communication is more than information delivery. Although a substantial literature already demonstrates this point, it has not been sufficiently incorporated into the design of communication strategies for immunization programs, which continue to have an informational bias. One cannot doubt that information is necessary, but sustainable immunization requires specific institutional conditions and social practices. Information activities have a time horizon that is much shorter than the duration of social factors that are conducive to optimal immunization.[6–7]

Therefore, the task is twofold: to get communication to delineate its informational parameters and to link communication to institutions, and establish norms that influence immunization practices. An ecologic approach that focuses on institutional and social factors that facilitate immunization practices gives us a more inclusive perspective to assess the actual and potential synergies between communication for eradication and RI. It allows us to understand the factors that determine immunization practices at different levels (individual, family, community, policy). If those factors are not properly identified and considered in planning communication interventions, opportunities to link communication for campaigns and RI will continue to be missed. In what follows, I suggest that a bifocal view of campaign and RI communication needs to see how programs contribute to sustaining social conventions underlying immunization practices, improving vaccine supply and delivery, and mobilizing communities in support of vaccination programs.

Raising Demand, Changing the Norm

Communication is typically expected to raise demand for immunization services during both campaign and routine interventions. The expectation is that communication programs for eradication initiatives drum up and channel demand for immunization services. If demand is not present or is very low, it is hoped that communication instills the right expectations and cultivates correct practices. The underlying premise is that through learning the value of immunization for a specific disease, populations become aware and knowledgeable of immunization in general. In this way, campaign communication, presumably, has effects beyond its contribution to disease eradication. If demand is latent but actual use of services is less than optimal, then campaign communication stirs up demand through publicity and interpersonal communication.[8]

Studies indicate that, in general, communication programs have done a relatively good job achieving those goals for the majority of the population.[9–11] Information activities during campaigns are usually effective in creating awareness about vaccination days, and getting people to bring their children to vaccination booths during fixed-site campaigns (or wait for vaccinators teams at home during home-to-home campaigns). By many accounts, communication interventions in support of polio eradication have made caretakers aware of immunization days and contribute to getting children vaccinated.

It is incorrect to expect that short-term information activities per se create long-term demand for immunization services. They can effectively mobilize into action caretakers already favorably predisposed to get children immunized, but it is not obvious that providing brief information messages builds sustainable demand. Long-term demand is not based on off-and-on information messages, but rather on underlying permanent factors that make immunization *qua* social practice sustainable.

Engaging communities in one-time behavior (e.g., getting children vaccinated during campaigns) is different and more complicated than promoting habitual practices. The former is more likely if, as happens during vaccination campaigns, it is shored up by a number of concurrent communication activities including media messages and communication with community mobilizers. However, success in mobilizing people to get vaccinated a few times a year does not necessarily guarantee that the practice will become routine or accepted. For "campaign" behavior to become "routine" behavior, communication has to play a different role. Ideally, verbal and written reminders (such as counseling from health workers and immunization cards) should be sufficient to trigger practices. If immunization requires a constant and intense publicity blitz, then sustainability is weak.

The success of communication to raise and maintain sustainable demand is more likely when three conditions exist.

First, when populations have already practiced or regularly engage in a behavior, the task of communication is easier than when people are asked to engage in a completely new practice. Exceptions do exist, when individuals are reluctant to repeat a practice because of bad past experiences. For example, mothers who were mistreated by health workers in the past would be understandably hesitant to return to health posts for vaccinations. However, if the practice is sustained by an influential norm, people could repeat the behavior ("return to health posts for vaccination") if problems are satisfactorily addressed and solutions/improvements are properly communicated.[12]

Long-term effectiveness of information cues should rest on whether caretakers (and their surrounding group/community) believe and self-enforce norms that legitimize vaccination. Messages to this effect might include: "Vaccination is good"; "Good mothers get their children vaccinated"; or "The life of any child is valuable." When individuals and communities strongly support and impose these values (by sanctioning those who violate them), interventions have better chances to communicate effectively messages such as, "Get children vaccinated," and "Try vaccination again." However, when the expected practice is absent or does not resonate with legitimate and enforced beliefs, the task of communication is more complicated. It needs to persuade caretakers to engage in new practices and/or to generate new cultural norms that are conducive to immunization.

This is related to a second condition: Demand and sustainability are more likely when a practice is socially approved and encouraged by cultural precepts, particularly by reference groups whose opinions are relevant to individual decisions. Practices that conform to social norms are more likely to be maintained through time. Social norms provide the supportive environment that promotes and encourages, accepts and tolerates practices. In the case of immunization, the weight of social norms is different among different groups of mothers: Illiterate mothers are more likely to get children immunized in order to comply with norm than better schooled mothers, who tend to make decisions based on knowledge of vaccines.

In cultures where the idea of preventive medicine is absent, successful communication interventions have tapped into existing local beliefs (such as the need to get "protection" from disease) to convey the value of immunization.[13] In many communities, the opinion of mothers and mothers-in-law carries a great deal of influence among young mothers' decision to vaccinate their children.

In contrast, if cultural/religious norms prohibit vaccination or reference groups disapprove it, then different strategies are needed. Changing deep-seated cultural beliefs and social expectations is not impossible, but it is certainly more challenging than promoting behaviors that resonate with preexisting norms. Changing practices in a short period of time without transforming long-standing cultural norms upon which those practices rest is not implausible. Gerry Mackie's analysis of the rapid extinction of China's century-old practice of foot-binding is particularly illuminating.[14] This issue, however, has not been sufficiently explored analytically and programmatically to draw definite conclusions and define courses of action. Health communication is better at explaining how new practices that conform to existing cultural norms can emerge rather than accounting for how enduring cultural norms gradually or quickly change and bring about new behaviors. For example, this is one of the central ideas of social marketing applied to health programs: persuade individuals and communities to engage in a certain behavior to conform to accepted social norms. When cultural norms that are conducive to vaccination are present and enforced, communication's path is already outlined: It needs to appeal to conformity to those conventions to make immunization sustainable. When those norms are missing and immunization has little "cultural traction" (or cultural inertia is unreceptive to new practices), communication faces the more demanding task of engineering cultural transformation.

Third, behavior sustainability is more likely when "external" obstacles between present and expected practices are few.[15] When vaccination sites are far away and hard to access and vaccine shortages are common, then sustainability is more difficult. In cases of "infrastructural" problems, the issue at stake is not purely (or even mainly) communicational. In some cases, strong social norms can offset some of the problems caused by infrastructural barriers (that are not uncommon in large swaths of the developing world). It has not been unusual that caretakers, convinced about the need of vaccination, decide to get their children vaccinated despite transportation difficulties and bad experiences at health posts (erratic hours, lack of vaccines, long lines).

What these conditions suggest is that as long as campaign communication focuses on inducing one-time practices, based on large-scale media efforts and consisting of ephemeral messages (e.g., the date, place, and hours that a clinic specifically offers vaccinations), its contribution to sustainable practices is doubtful. The PEI confirms that the combination of media and interpersonal communication is effective to inform caretakers and increase compliance. However, after years of polio campaigns worldwide, the impact of campaign communication on sustainable practices remains unknown. Communication interventions are effective in making people aware of campaigns, but we do not know whether campaign communication substantially improves knowledge or builds long-standing practices.[16] Nor do we know whether messages promoting multi-agent immunization are confusing or effective in informing populations about diseases and vaccines. We also lack information on whether house-to-house campaigns build the wrong set of expectations and practices, namely, conveying the sense that vaccines are always "home delivered" and immunization does not require active participation.

The existence of a social norm does not guarantee the sustainability of immunization behavior. Some problems are, in fact, essentially informational. A case in point is dropout in completing coverage of children's immunization schedule (especially after receiving OPV3 and DPT3), a problem that has been observed in many countries. Among other factors, the fact that caretakers lack information or have incorrect information about needed doses accounts for failure to comply with full immunization.

Another example is the case of dropping rates caused by rumors about vaccine safety, a problem that has challenged immunization programs. Anti-vaccination rumors and suspicions are not new, neither in the North nor in the South. The history of the vaccination movement has been filled with opposition (based on political and religious reasons), and questions about the effects and effectiveness of vaccines. The difference is that, today, anti-vaccination information can travel faster and more easily reach a large audience who might be already skeptical of immunization; is interested in exploiting rumors for political purposes; or is misinformed and confused about the effects of vaccines. The recent controversy about the links between the measles, mumps, and rubella vaccine and autism, and ongoing conflicts about the effects of polio vaccine in several states in Northern Nigeria are examples of the challenges that immunization supporters confront in a new media landscape.

The global information environment has become more diverse with the proliferation of news and pseudo-news on the Internet. Health news has gained more presence in the media. However, the fact that some news organizations have a penchant for sensationalizing the coverage of health issues, highlighting "bad news" and "out-of-control" risks and failing to distinguish the reliability and quality of different information sources, presents challenges for immunization. In these conditions, programs are more likely to confront "informational" difficulties in developed and developing countries. If anti-vaccination groups have been savvy in using new communication opportunities, how can immunization partners intelligently take advantage of information technologies to bolster their position, build trust, and achieve higher immunization coverage?

In summary, information issues and cultural issues affect sustainability. Communication strategies need to be aware of both issues: How do information activities build sustainability? How can communication activities provide information while changing and reinforcing cultural norms that legitimize immunization? Campaign communication could make important contributions by adopting a bifocal view: drumming up demand during National Immunization Days while promoting and reinforcing social norms that support RI.

This is why perspectives that examine how ideas, practices, and norms become disseminated provide useful insights. "Tipping point," "social networks," "through contagion" approaches, for example, explain how information affects behavioral trends and is integrated within social dynamics that underlie the adoption and maintenance of specific beliefs and practices. Conventional message-oriented, transmission-centered communication approaches, which are mainly concerned with the production of information, pay little attention to the processes by which information is integrated in everyday social practices and cultural norms. Communication interventions need to keep in mind that the ultimate goal is to contribute to information processes that become crystallized in sustainable practices.

Building Demand *and* Supply

Although communication has been typically assigned the task of creating demand, recent experiences show that communication can accomplish more than that. The PEI demonstrates that communication can make important contributions to building and maintaining vaccine supply.

Through advocacy activities, communication interventions can mobilize and sustain political leadership and support. The importance of political will for the success of vaccination programs (or any other public health intervention, for that matter) has been increasingly accepted in international development. Without it, access and quality of services suffer. Unfortunately, immunization supply in many developing countries continues to be plagued by several problems such as cold chain breakage, insufficient fixed facilities, lack of vaccines and equipment, shortage of health staff, and poor transportation resources. Improving these problems, let alone resolving them, seems unlikely without considerable commitment from political will at global, regional, national, and local levels.

Advocacy to strengthen vaccine supply at these four levels is necessary. Although immunization and infectious diseases are commonly defined as "global issues," they require a variety of actions at all levels from several actors. Also, because immunization activities in developing countries typically involve the collaboration among public, civic, and private actors, advocacy plays a key role in building and sustaining partnerships. Until recently, only a handful of actors such as national governments, a few international organizations (i.e., World Health Organization, United Nations Children's Fund), and vaccine manufacturers carried primary responsibilities for vaccine programs. Today, instead, the booming numbers and participation of civic associations, private voluntary organizations (PVOs), and nongovernmental organizations (NGOs) have opened up new possibilities and challenges for active collaboration in immunization.

The availability of a wealth of monetary, institutional, and human resources makes it possible to reach more communities with vaccines and messages. Rotary International and the Red Cross, for example, play key roles in the eradication of polio and measles, respectively. In countries where the government's health infrastructure fails to reach a large percentage of the population, international and national NGOs and PVOs fill gaps through the supply of RI services, to the point that services could come to a complete halt without them. This arrangement has obvious short-term benefits, particularly where health systems have collapsed or continue to experience substantial difficulties. However, a heavy reliance on global partners and funders does not lead to sustainability. It is a good, temporary solution, but a dangerous one if it becomes permanent. As international organizations shift priorities and reduce or withdraw funding, long-term problems are likely to emerge unless national governments and community organizations take full ownership.

Because global partnerships bring together actors whose interests perhaps only strategically and momentarily converge, advocacy is indispensable to ensure support at different levels. If the involvement of more actors is a boon to immunization initiatives, it also generates tensions that required constant negotiation among partners.

A sensitive issue is the dissimilar power of global partners to set goals and assign resources.[17] Because decisions (particularly about eradication programs) are made at the global level, bringing national (heads of state, ministers of health) and sub-national actors (governors and religious leaders) on board is necessary. Commitment from regional and even national institutions is not always sufficient to guarantee undivided support for eradication initiatives. National governments, for example, might be willing to support global programs by attending high-profile events, but are reluctant to commit human and monetary resources to those programs. Rhetorical commitments do not necessarily translate into key decisions that affect the functioning of vaccine supply systems. Also, support from national leaders does not always trickle down to all government levels. The troubles that the PEI currently faces with authorities who do not support polio vaccination in India and Nigeria are two glaring examples of this situation. Moreover, it is not unusual for immunization initiatives (again, the experience of the PEI is quite telling) to confront situations that require well-honed advocacy skills such as leaders and communities demanding other vaccines (and health services) they consider more urgent or opposing vaccination for a variety of reasons.

Moreover, the undergoing process of decentralization of health systems presents new challenges to immunization programs that heighten even further the role of advocacy. In the past, central governments had a strong influence on local decisions basically because they monopolized resources. This was particularly the case in countries where centralized government structures coexisted with authoritarian rule. Such political arrangement had a strong institutional affinity with vertical immunization programs. Today, as decentralization gains momentum and democracies are replacing dictatorial regimes, a new decision-making scenario is emerging.[18] Top-down decisions are prone to face obstacles that were less likely to exist in the past, especially where the following conditions exist: federalism and decentralization grants margins of autonomy to state and local leaders; immunization programs cannot remain above the fray and are trapped in power plays between central and local authorities; and cultural politics (that appear as or are based on religious and ethnic conflicts) bitterly divide countries. Because current political conditions are less favorable to vertical immunization programs, it is a tactical mistake to assume that advocacy at the top is sufficient to obtain political will at all levels. Decades ago, such as during the eradication of smallpox in the 1960s and 1970s, getting top-level commitment could have been enough to carry out large-scale immunization programs, but today it is insufficient. Consequently, segmented, localized advocacy strategies are needed.

Advocacy affects both infrastructural and normative and behavioral aspects of immunization. On the one hand, advocacy among national and local leaders has a crucial impact where "the rubber hits the road," that is, where vaccine supply meets demand. Global partners wield power to determine goals and mobilize structures and funds, but cannot alone carry out immunization programs in every community. For better or worse, government structures are still key in making vaccine supply systems functional either in terms of having access to communities or through the provision of services (no matter their quality). Even in cases where state failure renders those structures ineffective (such as in war-torn countries), global partners cannot implement programs without getting some form of commitment from local leaders.

On the other hand, advocacy among political, religious, and medical authorities who wield influence on people's attitudes and practices indirectly contributes to sustaining immunization practices. Advocacy is a means not only to strengthen vaccine supply but also to cultivate demand through working with leaders (e.g., governors/mayors, priests/imams, traditional birth attendants, healers, medical staff). Advocacy among authorities who have the power to influence practice through nonpersuasive means (ordering, coercing, jawboning) to have communities get vaccinated and among opinion leaders willing to endorse immunization as a desirable practice helps to change and maintain cultural norms.[19] Here, I am not endorsing any specific means as legitimate or more desirable to influence immunization. This is a subject that deals with complex ethical issues that fall outside the scope of this chapter. Regardless of what ethical position we take, it is necessary to acknowledge that coercive immunization has been widely and successfully used in vaccination campaigns and RI in determining behavior.

What has emerged is a more complex institutional network that articulates different aspects of vaccine supply. Because consensus among partners that manage and fund different parts of that network is not automatic (their agendas might tangentially coincide), regular consultation and advocacy are needed. Advocacy perhaps is not a standard communication strategy in the health communication toolkit. It is traditionally closer to political communication than to communication interventions in health. But similar to other strategies that originated in other fields (social marketing and social network come to mind), it is increasingly important for communication for immunization to approach health policy and social issues that affect conventions and practices.

By opening up ways to connect institutional resources—such as Rotary International—with the supply of immunization services and communication campaigns, we can develop an alternative to traditional reductionist approaches. Traditional approaches tend to reduce the target of communications (that promote supply creation and immunization-seeking behavior) to simply individual psychological factors. Rather, we can produce greater behavioral impact by incorporating the organizational factors that affect positive health practices into communications campaigns for immunization.

Communication for Community Mobilization

The third challenge for communication for immunization is to make community mobilization (CM) sustainable. Community-centered approaches in health communication have questioned central premises of the individualistic, information-driven paradigm that dominated the field. Those approaches revealed a number of analytical blindspots in conventional health communication analysis and programs that prevent us from grasping the factors that influence health behavior and the role of community empowerment in bringing better health conditions. Several studies have attributed low immunization coverage to poor social mobilization, among other reasons. What is needed is to recognize the practical implications of CM for immunization programs.

CM needs to be understood as the linchpin between vaccine supply and demand. While it builds up supply through mobilizing people to work on several activities (managing the cold chain, transporting vaccines, vaccinating children), CM also strengthens demand through providing information, developing skills, and promoting a sense of ownership among caretakers and citizens in general.

In theory, CM promotes the idea that immunization is a communal, public good. It assumes that success depends on a combination of efforts and local actions rather than on government-run, vertical programs. It appeals to the idea that CM helps to build social capital, that is, "dense horizontal local networks" to enable social changes and community empowerment.[20] In times of political decentralization and the acceptance of community approaches in health and development communication projects, traditional top-down immunization programs are anachronistic.

Vertical immunization programs run against the grain of today's conventional idea in public health and development circles that CM is ideologically desirable and pragmatically effective. Carrying the baggage of outmoded authoritarian models (including the ethically questionable experiences of enforced immunization), they stand in contrast to demands for autonomy.[21] Chances of top-down programs failing or having to be retooled are greater when communities feel entitled to set health goals and to allocate resources and empowered to question goals and strategies decided elsewhere. Vertical immunization interventions have always rested on problematic ethical premises according to which a handful of international/national actors dictate the goals of a vast number of communities. What has changed is that the acceptance of community empowerment as both goal and strategy coupled with democratization is antithetical to key ethical, universalistic justifications underlying global immunization programs.[22] CM is put forth as a necessary corrective to the historical vertical bias of vaccination programs. By putting communities at the center, community-based communication turns immunization into a health issue that simultaneously necessitates and promotes political democracy.

In reality, the links between CM and immunization programs are more complex than what some CM arguments (especially in their more romantic versions) assume. How community empowerment contributes to increasing coverage rates is a difficult issue that still awaits careful analysis of several questions.

First, it is open to discussion whether communities would choose preventive medicine interventions such as childhood immunization, no matter what its health benefits and cost-effectiveness. Other demands and calculations might prevail over plans to immunize against specific diseases. Like on any other public goods issues, free-rider situations are possible. Although vaccine-preventable diseases are conventionally defined as global risks that ignore territorial boundaries and that require concerted global efforts, communities can opt not to invest in vaccination programs. Perhaps they do not define these risks as "their" risks. They speculate that other actors would pay the bill for "public good" issues. They might choose to prioritize other health interventions due to a variety of reasons (impact, political benefits, etc).

Second, there is also the question of when and why CM needs to take place in immunization programs. The PEI shows that vertical programs and CM are not antithetical as long as communities are mobilized for implementing rather than for deciding goals and strategies. This raises an interesting issue, particularly for community-oriented interventions in health communication. Among other reasons, community-based health programs have been justified on the grounds that they promote participatory and democratic goals. The premise is that community participation and ownership are good not only for the sustainable well-being of its members but also for democratic life.

However, as immunization campaigns suggest, CM is not synonymous with community, democratic participation. CM activities during immunization days have been central to the PEI. Without the vast mobilization of government and community resources, it would have been difficult to run successful campaigns. CM activities have involved government offices (Ministry of Health, Ministry of Education, Ministry of Information, Armed Forces, the police department, and others) and a variety of civic organizations (NGOs, PVOs, churches, mosques) and leaders (political, religious) in coordinating activities to ensure that oral polio vaccine would be available and children will be brought to vaccination booths or wait for vaccinator teams at their homes.

Why is it worth putting so much time and money into CM? CM has symbolic and instrumental goals. It symbolizes community participation and support for PEI. It signals the commitment of political authorities, particularly in countries where CM around major events is ingrained in the political culture of the country. It provides a moral booster to fatigued and underpaid health workers and vaccinators. It renews support for PEI, especially after many years of campaigns. Also, CM has instrumental goals, namely, to deliver polio vaccines to hard-to-reach populations. Hard-to-reach populations are those who are not reached either by the health system or conventional communication interventions. The fact that the health infrastructure is too distant or fails to provide services partially accounts for levels of coverage lower than the national average, and large numbers of zero-dose children.

Still, these actions do not necessarily contradict top-down programs. In fact, one could argue that there has been a sort of functional necessity between them. It remains questionable whether the uses of CM for vertical programs foster community ownership in ways that make support for immunization sustainable.

This brings us to a third issue: The idea that CM and immunization coverage are positively correlated needs to be critically examined. Centralized and authoritarian health systems (such as in socialist regimes), which were not exactly inspired by ideals of community empowerment, achieved some of the highest immunization rates worldwide. Nor does it seem obvious that differences across countries and regions can be attributed completely or partially to different degree/intensity of CM. The relationship between CM and optimal coverage is not straightforward. Evidence seems to indicate that CM is a useful strategic tool under specific institutional conditions. Rather than concluding that CM is always effective or is unrelated to coverage rates, we need to understand when it makes a difference. Rather than taking CM as an article of faith or dismissing it, we need to assess more rigorously when and why CM positively contributes to immunization.

A fourth and last question is: Why has CM been successful during campaigns but has rarely been used for RI? Again, the case of the PEI offers important lessons. CM in support of polio eradication has generated excitement, participation, and goodwill. However, neither the social/political commitment nor the organizational capital that CM energized has been mobilized to improve RI and surveillance problems. Polio partners, for example, have not capitalized on CM during immunization days for strengthening RI and surveillance. Why? Has it been an inherent bias of the design of eradication programs? A conscious strategic decision? A result of the difficulty of mobilizing communities on a regular basis? Can CM be sustainable? What does noncampaign communication for CM look like? If two and three rounds of National Immunization Days during many years prove to drain out community energies and result in fatigue and apathy, how is it possible to institutionalize long-term CM?

Concluding Remarks

Because a variety of international and national interests will continue to favor eradication campaigns in the next years, "campaign" communication is likely to remain a fixture of immunization programs. It is not difficult to understand why campaigns (and related communication activities) will remain popular while raising support for communication for RI will continue to be challenging. "Campaign" communication fits the strategic designs of powerful international agencies whose mission is to eradicate and control infectious diseases. It is attractive for political leaders interested in reaping publicity and credibility from high-profile media events. It offers monetary incentives for underpaid and poorly motivated health workers to participate. It gives opportunities for local media organizations to get contracts. Organizing campaigns twice or thrice a year can be extenuating for all parties involved because they consume extraordinary amounts of time, energy, and money. However, campaign communication has important built-in attractions that are missing in communication activities in support of RI.

The challenge for communication for immunization programs is to find ways to utilize the tremendous energies mobilized for campaigns to benefit routine services. This chapter has suggested that this is possible if we move away from an approach that reduces communication to information transmission, and instead, take a perspective that links communication to interventions to enable and maintain social conditions that favor immunization practices. The production and dissemination of information are certainly important, especially when problems are related to knowledge and perceptions (such as rumors and misinformation) or to the apparent "invisible" individual and collective benefits of practicing immunization (information messages need to make tangible the positive results of behavior compliance). Addressing informational issues is necessary, but an informational mindset should not guide the diagnosis and prescription of communication programs. Communication interventions could make long-lasting contributions to immunization programs if they seriously consider how to promote specific social norms and build political support that affect immunization infrastructure and practices.

Notes

1. R. B. Aylward et al., "Global Health Goals: Lessons from the Worldwide Effort to Eradicate Poliomyelitis," *The Lancet* 362 (2003): 909–914.

2. S. Gloyd, J. Suarez Torres, and M. A. Mercer, "Immunization Campaigns and Political Agendas: Retrospective from Ecuador and El Salvador," *International Journal of Health Services* 33(1) (2003): 112–128.

3. C. Gounder, "The Progress of the Polio Eradication Initiative: What Prospects for Eradicating Measles?" *Health Policy and Planning* 13(3) (1998): 212–233.

4. M. M. Khanm and J. Ehreth, "Cost and Benefits of Polio Eradication: A Long-run Perspective," *Vaccine* 21 (2003): 702–705.

5. R. Steinglass and R. Fields, "Immunization: Challenges and Opportunities," *Global HealthLink: The Newsletter of the Global Health Council*, May–June 2000, 103.

6. K. Stretfield and M. Singarimbun, "Social Factors Affecting Use of Immunization in Indonesia," *Social Science and Medicine* 27(11) (1988): 1237–1245.

7. S. J. Sheldon and C. Alons, "A Study to Describe Barriers to Childhood Vaccination in Mozambique," USAID/MOH Mozambique/The CHANGE Project/Project HOPE, 2003.

8. M. Rasmusson, *Sustaining EPI: What Can Communication Do?* (Washington, DC: HEALTHCOM, 1990).

9. K. Bhattacharyya and R. Khanam, *Process Evaluation of the First National Immunization Day in Bangladesh* (Washington, DC: BASICS, 1998).

10. E. N. L. Browne et al., "Factors Influencing Participation in National Immunization Days in Kumasi, Ghana," *Annals of Tropical Medicine & Parasitology* 96(1) (2002): 93–104.

11. H. Harmanci et al., "Reasons for Non-vaccination during National Immunization Days: A Case Study in Istanbul, Turkey," *Journal of Public Health* 117 (2003): 54–61.

12. R. W. Porter et al., "Role of Health Communicates in Russia's Diphtheria Immunization Program," *Journal of Infectious Diseases* 181 (2000): 220–227.

13. UNICEF, A Critical Leap to Polio Eradication in India, 2003: 1–84.

14. G. Mackie, "Ending Footbinding and Infibulation: A Convention Account," *American Sociological Review* 61(6) (1996): 999–1017.

15. D. McKenzie-Mohr and W. Smith, *Fostering Sustainable Behavior* (New Society Publications, 1999).

16. *Communication for Immunization and Polio Eradication: Five Sub-Saharan Country Case Studies* (WHO/UNICEF/USAID/BASICS/CHANGE, 2000).

17. R. Dogson and K. Lee, "Global Health Governance: A Conceptual Review," in eds. R. Wilkinson and S. Hughes, *Global Governance: Critical Perspectives* (London: Routledge, 2002), 92–110.

18. P. Khalegian, *Decentralization and Public Services: The Case of Immunization*. World Bank Policy Research Working Paper 2989, 2003.

19. P. Greenough, "Intimidation, Coercion and Resistance in the Final Stages of the South Asian Smallpox Eradication Campaign, 1973–1975," *Social Science and Medicine* 41 (1995): 633–645.

20. C. Campbell, "Social Capital and Health: Contextualizing Health Promotion within Local Community Networks," in eds. S. Baron, J. Field, and T. Schuller, *Social Capital* (Oxford: Oxford University Press, 2000), 182–196.

21. D. Banerji, "Crash of the Immunization Program: Consequences of a Totalitarian Approach," *International Journal of Health Services* 20(3) (1990): 501–510.

22. C. Taylor, F. Cutts, and M. Taylor, "Ethical Dilemmas in Current Planning for Polio Eradication," *American Journal of Public Health* 87 (1997): 922–916.

CHAPTER EIGHTEEN

Communication Campaigns for Chronic and Emergency Health Problems

Leslie B. Snyder and Mark Cistulli

Chapter Questions

1. What are the areas of activities for a health communications campaign?
2. How can the model for communication campaign activities be applied to emergencies?
3. How does consideration of the target audience play a role in each activity area?

Introduction

Communication campaigns can efficiently change the health behaviors of large numbers of people. Campaigns addressing chronic health issues, such as lifestyle diseases, the need for checkups, alcohol, drug, and cigarette use prevention, and family planning, benefit from social marketing and advocacy approaches. Campaigns addressing emergency health issues such as Sudden Acute Respiratory Syndrome (SARS), immunizations for emerging epidemics, bio-terrorism, environmental emergencies, and sanitation crises benefit from public relations approaches. The purpose of this chapter is to review some state-of-the-art recommendations for communication campaign design for both chronic and emergency health problems.

Communication campaigns consist of a set of organized communication activities, involving a particular type of person, designed to achieve a particular goal in a specified length of time.[1] Health communication campaigns often draw on many different traditions to maximize the chance of success, including marketing, communication, psychology, anthropology, and public health. For example, social marketing campaigns are communication campaigns using marketing techniques to promote a behavior that will improve society or the individual.[2] Health advocacy campaigns aim to change the policies of the government or an organization to improve health by directly targeting policy makers and indirectly trying to change public opinion.[3] Communication campaign goals can also include fundraising, recruitment, election of a particular candidate, and commercial marketing.

A Bit of History

Health campaigns have a long history in the United States. Cotton Mather used interpersonal communication and pamphlets to promote his smallpox immunization campaign in 1721.[4] Advocacy campaigns in the 1800s used grassroots organizing, legislative testimony, books, and confrontational events to get news coverage to promote the abolition of slavery, limit alcohol sales, and push for women's rights. By the late 1800s, the advent of inexpensive newspapers enabled "muckraking" campaigns by newspapers and individual journalists to campaign for sanitation issues and against child labor. By the early 1900s, sanitation and anti-tuberculosis campaigns were sponsored by governmental agencies and nonprofit health organizations, using mass media, promotions such as Easter Seal stamps, pamphlets, and home visits.

After World War II, there was an increase in government-sponsored campaigns both in the United States and overseas. Topics ranged from dental hygiene to AIDS to family planning. There was also an increase by nongovernmental organizations such as the March of Dimes and the American Cancer Society in campaigns for fundraising and behavior change. Campaigns can be waged with very large budgets or very small ones.

Today, communication campaigns are an accepted way to get messages across to the population. Congress has directly mandated two campaigns—the $1 billion Anti-Drug Campaign coordinated by the National Institute on Drug Abuse, and the Youth Physical Activity Campaign run by the Centers for Disease Control and Prevention (CDC). Court settlements have also mandated campaigns, including the anti-tobacco campaign run by the Legacy Foundation with funds from the tobacco industry, and a Sport Utility Vehicle safety campaign run by a coalition of State Attorney Generals with money from Ford Motor Cars.

Profile of a Campaign

Most communication campaigns address chronic health issues. Meta-analyses show that communication campaigns can be successful in changing health behaviors related to long-term health issues.[5–8] Youth campaigns prevent, on average, 3 percent to 8 percent of youth from adopting a harmful behavior, by using school-based outreach or media or a combination of both.[9–11] Media campaigns vary in their success based on the topic of the campaign, ranging from changing 2 percent to 17 percent of the population.[12] Clinic-based outreach can have a higher average effect than mediated campaigns aimed at adults,[13] but can be quite expensive per capita.[14] Campaigns have a greater rate of success when they include messages about the imminent enforcement of a law or regulation about the health behavior (e.g., seat belt checkpoints), include information that is new to the audience, and have greater reach.[15] Advocacy campaigns are also successful at changing policies.[16]

Fifty years of research on communication campaigns have led to recommendations about how to plan and execute them. Some critical points are outlined as follows.

Campaign Activities

There are many tasks that campaign designers need to complete.[17] While some authors refer to the steps or stages of campaigns, we prefer to think about the areas of activities that a health communicator engages in when creating and implementing communication campaigns. Some of the activities happen concurrently, and some are revisited after engaging in other activities. Each activity is discussed in turn.

Research. The initial task is research, because it is important to know as much as possible about the resources available for the campaign, the people the campaign hopes to reach (the target groups), and the behavior that is being considered. It is also critical to understand the context of the social, political, economic, organizational, and legal contexts of the campaign and behavior. At this stage, campaigners conduct focus groups with members of the potential target groups, interview health professionals and community leaders, observe health service settings where people interact about the health issue, test the feasibility of the advocated behavior with members of the target group, and search the literature and use interpersonal networks to locate existing, relevant studies on the topic or about the target groups. When it is important to know with more precision about the distribution of a problem or perceptions of the target groups, surveys can be conducted. As a result of what is learned in the research phase, initial conceptions about what behavior to promote can change, as can decisions about whom to target.

Creating the communication plan. The second activity, which is often conducted on an ongoing basis while conducting the pre-campaign research, is to create the communication plan. The core of the plan consists of well-specified goals and objectives. Most health communication campaigns aim to promote a healthy behavior, prevent an unhealthy one, or help people cease an unhealthy behavior. The behavior can be something one can do by oneself (e.g., brushing teeth or voting on a referendum); with a partner, friend, or family member (e.g., using a condom or talking with children about drugs); or involving a health professional (e.g., getting a mammogram). In advocacy campaigns, the goal can be to change a policy with the expectation that the policy change will support population-based behavior change. Examples of laws that have led to health behavior change include mandatory seat belt laws, restrictions on cigarette sales to teens, raising the minimum age for alcohol consumption, and increasing taxes on alcohol and tobacco.

In the past, it was common for campaigns to see their goal as merely providing people with information. However, we have seen that behavior change can be quite complicated, and merely knowing that one should or should not engage in a particular behavior often does not lead to behavior change. Simple informational messages that say smoking is bad and exercise is good are not sufficient to cause behavior change. Rather, it is better to understand the mechanisms of behavior change for that particular behavior with the particular target group, and use that information to design appropriate messages. By the same token, interventions occasionally choose their channels and communication strategy unreflectively, whether based on habit, unfamiliarity with other channels, or personal preference. It is better to understand the communication patterns of the target group and weigh the features of different channels against one another in order to select a combination of channels that are best suited to the particular message.

The goals and objectives stated in the communication plan should include precisely defined target groups and target behaviors. Good objectives are measurable, stating the percentage of the targets that will change their behavior within a specified time period. An advocacy campaign can state the number of decision makers ready to approve the policy change by a particular date or the date by which a policy will be adopted. AIDS campaigns that had more specific goals were also more likely to have higher execution quality.[18]

A communication plan should also include a *persuasive strategy* to convince people to change their behavior. A campaign's persuasive strategy should be based on knowledge of the target audience and theories of behavior change and persuasion. Theories and models that are currently used include: the Information Processing Model;[19] Social Learning Theory;[20] Health Belief Model;[21] Theory of Reasoned Action;[22-23] the Stages of Behavior Change Model;[24-25] child development theories;[26] extended parallel processing model,[27] social capital,[28-29] and diffusion of innovations.[30-31]

A communication plan needs to include a *communication strategy* to reach the target groups. Communication strategies are concerned with exactly how and when the communication will take place with members of the target groups. The communication activities can be quite varied, such as one-on-one counseling, distribution of flyers, broadcasting public service announcements, marching in parades with placards, sending letters to the editor, playing video games with imbedded health messages, and wearing t-shirts or baseball caps with messages printed on them, to name a few. Communication can be mediated or occur interpersonally. Opportunities for communication also arise at events (e.g., performances, festivals, and sporting events), and in particular places (e.g., a bathhouse, public square, or health center). Channel choice depends on the target group. For example, a campaign might use newspaper coverage to put pressure on local politicians, messages imbedded in popular music to reach youth, and counseling by health professionals to reach patients.

Research on how different audiences respond to different channels can inform channel choice. Novelty is an important part of gaining attention for a message, so campaigners should not rely on using the same channels time after time. Campaigns also need to "refresh" themselves by using new materials after a period of time. Campaign slogans and symbols can be a reminder for a more complicated message, communicating it succinctly to people who already have some familiarity with the campaign. The communication strategy needs to take into account persuasive strategy and timing. When are the optimum times to communicate with people in order to increase the probability of behavior change? Which channels should be used to communicate with people at different times?

The process of designing a communication plan is iterative, and decisions about the communication strategy and persuasive plan can have implications for the goals and targets. When part of the communication strategy is to have other people communicating with the primary targets, then those people become secondary targets for the campaign. For example, an oral rehydration campaign in The Gambia communicated with religious leaders to ensure they would publicly support the campaign in their communities.[32] Similarly, a persuasive strategy can specify the antecedents to behavior change. Secondary targets and the antecedents to behavior change can be incorporated specifically into the goals and objectives of the campaign.

Finally, a campaign design should include plans for *monitoring the implementation of the campaign* and *evaluating* whether or not the campaign is achieving the goals. Monitoring and evaluation will be discussed further.

Creating the management plan. The third type of activity is creating the management plan. Management plans include personnel, resources, timetables of activities, and plans for how to integrate the campaign with other organizations, events, and campaigns. Knowledge of available resources that the campaign can potentially draw on is necessary to plan the campaign, and budgeting those resources is part of the planning process. The management plan depends in part on the communication strategy, and the communication strategy is limited by budget, personnel, and other resource considerations. Partnerships can be formed with organizations that share similar goals. Community advisory boards can be created to sustain an ongoing mechanism for cooperation and communication with community leaders. Partners and advisory boards need to participate in the creation of the communication plan.

Preparing messages and services. Once the plans are established, the fourth type of activity—preparing messages and services—can begin. Using the research conducted earlier, develop sample messages, pretest them with members of the target group, revise them accordingly, and then produce them. Train the people who will act as interpersonal channels to communicate directly with members of the target group. Make sure that services are prepared for any increase in demand that will be caused by the campaign, and that any improvements in services vital to campaign success have been implemented.

Implementing and monitoring. When the messages and services are ready, the campaign can be implemented. During the implementation phase of the campaign, it is important to *monitor all activities*. The campaign manager can then respond quickly to the inevitable glitches that happen during implementation.

Evaluating and adjusting. The final type of campaign activity is *to evaluate and adjust* the campaign communication plan, persuasive strategy, or management plan. Evaluation provides the campaign with feedback that can be used to improve the campaign (if it has not yet concluded) and future campaigns. Campaigners that do not evaluate their programs will instead make decisions based on their biases, and can be destined to repeat mistakes. If the evaluation involves measuring baseline levels of the behavior in the target group, then evaluation activities need to begin prior to implementation of the campaign. For other types of evaluation designs, evaluation begins during the campaign or after it is over.

It is important to note that communication campaigns including all of these activities have a better chance of success. Campaigns that create media materials but do not have comprehensive communication and persuasive strategies will not be as effective. Campaigns that are not evaluated are less likely to have a realistic sense of what worked and what needs to be adjusted within the communication plan.

Emergency Health Issues

Recently in the United States and elsewhere, considerable attention has turned to health crises, including emerging insect-borne diseases, new contagious diseases, and bio-terrorism. Emergencies need to be dealt with in a timely manner, before crises escalate. Research shows that new scientific findings that require an immediate behavior change can be successfully communicated with the public, as happened with Reye's Syndrome.[33] Similarly, immunization campaigns that deal with emerging health problems have the potential to be very successful, especially when built on the success of many prior immunization campaigns.[34-36]

Public relations and crisis communication are especially important during health emergencies. This raises the question: How does the model of campaign activities change for emergencies?

First, there are probably more people who need to be targeted in the early stages of an emergency communication campaign than in a campaign to counteract a chronic problem. Target groups during health emergencies often include (1) people who have been affected by the problem, (2) people at immediate personal or familial risk, (3) those likely to be unaffected by the health problem, and (4) health and emergency professionals.

Second, as with any campaign, each target group in an emergency needs very different messages. People with the problem need to be connected with the appropriate treatment procedure, and perhaps cautioned about how to avoid spreading a disease. Research suggests that information dissemination through effective public relations decreased during the time between symptom onset and hospitalization in China during the 2003 SARS crisis.[37]

People at risk need to know how to avoid the problem. The messages can be crafted following the principles of communication campaigns dealing with chronic health behavior problems.

As news of a health crisis spreads, many people will unnecessarily believe that they are at risk. It is important to communicate very quickly with those unaffected by the problem in order to reassure them; control rising panic; and prevent some from overreacting to the threat and taking inappropriate or even dangerous actions. The first AIDS pamphlet widely issued by the U.S. government was successful in reducing perceptions of risk by those not, in fact, at risk.[38]

The last target group, health and emergency professionals, need to know appropriate procedures for the particular crisis. To maintain credibility, messages need to be crafted so that the target groups consider them reasonable, consistent, and truthful. For example, right after the September 11, 2001, terrorist attacks and through the anthrax crises in the United States in September and October of 2001, "first responders" stayed on alert and needed up-to-date information about the threats.

Third, there is less time for creativity in planning message design and channel choice. With an increased level of public concern around an emerging health crisis comes an increased willingness by the press to cover the story. This is both an opportunity for inexpensive media exposure and a challenge to ensure that the public health message is the correct communication, as opposed to inappropriate advice by other groups. Channels that are often used to communicate quickly with the press and the public are: press releases, press conferences, Web site updates, and hotlines for the public and for press inquiries. It is imperative to work with newspapers, magazines, the Internet, and television and radio outlets to provide the public with accurate and up-to-date information. Once they begin to cover an issue, the media will look for as much information as possible to keep their constituencies updated, and sometimes turn to less reliable sources if official news is lagging.[39]

Information is often incomplete during a crisis, and communications professionals must work with the best information possible, sharing information about the extent of uncertainty. Statements later perceived as dishonest can compromise credibility. In the middle of the anthrax crisis, for example, when a coalition of public health and law enforcement officers were deciding whether to close all postal plants, a Washington, D.C. Health Commissioner recalled, "I think it's time for us to stop needing to say we know and let people know what we don't know . . . Because if we don't do that they won't believe us when we come to say we know stuff, and that's critical."[40]

For example, a diverse array of effective public relations tools was used for getting the public the information it needed about SARS in Beijing. Press conferences, health seminars, billboards, bus ads, television, a 24-hour SARS hotline, educational pamphlets, and even traditional red neighborhood banners bombarded the public with health and safety information.[41] Worldwide, the CDC reported that there were more than 2.6 million visits to their Web site by people seeking information about SARS.[42]

To deal with the anthrax threat, the CDC held tele-briefings every day in the month of November updating the media on the ongoing anthrax investigations. From October 1, 2001, to January 19, 2002, the CDC released 44 press releases, handled over 7,000 press calls, and responded to 18,000 public inquiries. Other methods of public relations included audio and video news releases, interviews with CDC experts, press conferences, and satellite training for the staff.[43]

When crises endure a long time or become cyclical, they move into chronic status such that the public health community has time to become more creative and find new channels. A rheumatic fever campaign in Guadeloupe and Martinique took four years to bring rates down and continued through two more minor resurgences for a total of 10 years.[44]

Fourth, emergency communication campaigns can still benefit from target group research to craft effective messages for different groups and get feedback about the adequacy of relevant health and emergency services. Unfortunately, it is often not done for acute problems, perhaps because of the time pressure at the beginning of a crisis, or perhaps because crisis communication is more often patterned after current public relations practices than chronic communication campaign practices. After the first few days of an emergency, it is possible to have some "quick and dirty" feedback from different target groups about the messages that the targets are exposed to from different sources, the channels of communication, and adequacy of services received. Armed with such feedback, public health officials know whether their initial panic control and behavior change messages struck a chord with the targets, and can adjust them accordingly. The feedback can also uncover misconceptions about the issue that need to be addressed in the public discourse, as well as problems related to service delivery that should be addressed.

Fifth, the management task is often very complex. Sometimes it is necessary to set up new institutional structures to deal with a new type of crisis. It is important to coordinate both within-institution and between-institution communication. Responsibilities and lines of authority need to be clear. In Hong Kong, for example, better coordination between the Department of Health and the Hong Kong Hospital Authority and health experts would have helped communicate the SARS threat more effectively.[45]

Local, state, national, and international organizations sometimes need to be involved, each with their own communication staff. In the United States, the CDC has the task of monitoring health threats and communicating about them to the public, and typically must work with state and local public health officials in threatened areas. For bio-terrorism, law enforcement agencies join health and emergency agencies in dealing with the crisis. For example, because the threat of anthrax was nationwide, individual states needed to create communication plans in addition to CDC's national coordination. Despite being geographically isolated from the threat that originated on the eastern seaboard of the United States, Idaho's public health communication system handled 133 calls regarding suspicious powders thought to be anthrax. Each threat was evaluated by a joint effort between public health officials, medical staff, police, and communication professionals. After the substances were tested, public health officials informed the public and the media.[46]

Sixth, in a related point, the "sources" of communication need to be coordinated. Which organizations will spearhead communication with the press and public? Which spokespeople will become the "face" of official information? The spokespeople should be viewed by the various target groups as credible and part of the senior decision-making team.[47] It is imperative to keep the communication staff in all concerned organizations prepared with accurate and current information.[48]

International health organizations can play a critical role in defining a public health crisis. The Global Outbreak Alert and Response Network was established by the World Health Organization (WHO) in 2000 to analyze potential threats due to periodic epidemics and "deliberate" epidemics caused by biological and chemical weapons. WHO was crucial in alerting the press to the SARS threat. In March of 2003, WHO issued a global alert about SARS in Vietnam, Hong Kong, and China, which caused an increase in press coverage around the world. In Italy, for example, the number of stories about SARS jumped from zero before the alerts to 759 articles by May 2003, almost 10 percent of which appeared on the front page of the highest circulated newspapers.[49]

Seventh, evaluating the process of communication and crisis management is particularly helpful for emergency communication situations, because of the complexity involved in managing crises. Noting the lessons learned from past crises should enhance future preparedness. For example, it was valuable for the 9/11 Commission and the agencies involved to analyze New York City's emergency responses to the September 11 terrorist attacks.

Summary

Communication campaigns are an important tool for sharing health information with the public. Campaigns on chronic health issues have been successful in the past. Professionals conducting health campaigns typically engage in the following activities in order to increase the chances of meeting the campaign goals: research; campaign planning (including goals, persuasion strategy, communication strategy, monitoring plan, and evaluation plan); creating the management plan; creating the messages; implementation and monitoring of the plan; and evaluating and modifying the campaign. With some caveats and modifications, the model can be used to communicate with the public during health emergencies. Special attention will need to be paid to the target groups; messages for each target group; channel choice; quick research with the target groups for feedback on messages, channels, and access to resources; management in light of the large number of agencies and organizations typically involved in crises; selecting appropriate spokespeople; keeping the communication staff informed of breaking developments, and providing them with adequate background information; and conducting an evaluation of the communication process in order to improve management strategies prior to the next crisis.

Notes

1. E. M. Rogers and J. D. Storey, "Communication Campaigns," in eds. C. R. Berger and S. H. Chaffee, *Handbook of Communication Science* (Newbury Park, CA: Sage Publications, 1988).

2. P. Kotler and G. Zaltman, "Social Marketing: An Approach to Planned Social Change," *Journal of Marketing* 33 (1971): 10–15.

3. L. Wallack et al., *Media Advocacy and Public Health: Power for Prevention* (Newbury Park, CA: Sage Publications, 1993).

4. W. J. Paisley, "Public Communication Campaigns: The American Experience," in eds. R. E. Rice and W. J. Paisley, *Public Communication Campaigns* (Beverly Hills, CA: Sage Publications, 1981), 15–40.

5. L. B. Snyder, "How Effective Are Mediated Health Campaigns?" in eds. R. Rice and C. Atkin, *Public Information Campaigns,* 3d ed. (Thousand Oaks, CA: Sage Publications, 2001), 181–190.

6. L. B. Snyder, N. Diop-Sidibé, and L. Badiane, *A Meta-analysis of the Effectiveness of Family Planning Campaigns in Developing Countries.* Paper presented at the annual meeting of the International Communication Association, San Diego, California, May 2003.

7. L. B. Snyder and M. A. Hamilton, "Meta-analysis of U.S. Health Campaign Effects on Behavior: Emphasize Enforcement, Exposure, and New Information, and Beware the Secular Trend," in ed. R. Hornik, *Public Health Communication: Evidence for Behavior Change* (Hillsdale, NJ: Lawrence Erlbaum Associates, 2002), 357–383.

8. L. B. Snyder et al., "A Meta-analysis of the Effect of Mediated Health Communication Campaigns on Behavior Change in the United States," *Journal of Health Communication* 9(1) (2004): 71–96.

9. S. T. Ennett et al., "How Effective Is Drug Abuse Resistance Education? A Meta-analysis of Project DARE Outcome Evaluations," *American Journal of Public Health* 84(9) (1994): 1394–1401.

10. B. L. Rooney and D. M. Murray, "A Meta-analysis of Smoking Prevention Programs after Adjustment for Errors in the Unit of Analysis," *Health Education Quarterly* 23(11) (1996): 48–64.

11. Snyder et al., "A Meta-analysis of the Effect of Mediated Health Communication Campaigns on Behavior Change in the United States."

12. Snyder et al., "A Meta-analysis of the Effect of Mediated Health Communication Campaigns on Behavior Change in the United States."

13. P. D. Mullen et al., "A Meta-analysis of Trials Evaluating Patient Education and Counseling for Three Groups of Preventive Health Behaviors," *Patient Education and Counseling* 32 (1997): 157–173.

14. Snyder et al., "A Meta-analysis of the Effect of Mediated Health Communication Campaigns on Behavior Change in the United States."

15. Snyder and Hamilton, "Meta-analysis of U.S. Health Campaign Effects on Behavior: Emphasize Enforcement, Exposure, and New Information, and Beware the Secular Trend."

16. Wallack et al., *Media Advocacy and Public Health: Power for Prevention.*

17. N. K. Weinreich, *Hands-on Social Marketing* (Thousand Oaks, CA: Sage Publications, 1999).

18. J. Kiwanuka-Tondo and L. B. Snyder, "The Influence of Organizational Characteristics and Campaign Design Elements on Communication Campaign Quality: Evidence from 91 Ugandan AIDS Campaigns," *Journal of Health Communication* 7 (2002): 1–20.

19. W. McGuire, "Theoretical Foundations of Campaigns," in eds. R. E. Rice and W. J. Paisley, *Public Communication Campaigns* (Beverly Hills, CA: Sage Publications, 1981).

20. A. Bandura, *Social Foundations of Thought and Action* (Englewood Cliffs, NJ: Prentice-Hall, 1986).

21. N. Janz and M. Becker, "The Health Belief Model: A Decade Later," *Health Education Quarterly* 11 (1984): 1–47.

22. I. Ajzen and M. Fishbein, *Understanding Attitudes and Predicting Social Behavior* (Englewood Cliffs, NJ: Prentice-Hall, 1980).

23. M. Fishbein et al., "Using a Theory-based Community Intervention to Reduce AIDS Risk Behaviors: The CDC's AIDS Community Demonstration Projects," in eds. S. Oskamp and S. C. Thompson, *Understanding and Preventing HIV Risk Behavior, Safer Sex and Drug Use* (Thousand Oaks, CA: Sage Publications, 1996), 177–206.

24. E. Maibach and D. Cotton, "Moving People to Behavior Change: A Staged Social Cognitive Approach to Message Design," in eds. E. Maibach and R. L. Parrott, *Designing Health Messages: Approaches from Communication Theory and Public Health Practice* (Thousand Oaks, CA: Sage Publications, 1995), 41–64.

25. J. O. Prochaska and C. C. DiClemente, "Stages and Processes of Self-Change of Smoking: Toward an Integrative Model of Change," *Journal of Consulting and Clinical Psychology* 51 (1983): 390–395.

26. E. W. Austin, "Reaching Young Audiences: Developmental Considerations in Designing Health Messages," in eds. E. Maibach and R. L. Parrott, *Designing Health Messages: Approaches from Communication Theory and Public Health Practice* (Thousand Oaks, CA: Sage Publications, 1995), 114–144.

27. K. Witte, "Putting the Fear Back into Fear Appeals: The Extended Parallel Process Model," *Communication Monographs* 59 (1992): 329–349.

28. N. Lin, *Social Capital: A Theory of Social Structure and Action* (NY: Cambridge University Press, 2001).

29. R. D. Putnam, "Bowling Alone: America's Declining Social Capital," *The Journal of Democracy* 6(1) (1995): 65–78.

30. E. M. Rogers, *Diffusion of Innovations* (NY: Free Press, 1962, 1995).

31. R. Rice and C. Atkin, eds. *Public Information Campaigns*, 3d ed. (Thousand Oaks, CA: Sage Publications, 2001), 181–190.

32. D. Foote et al., *Mass Media and Health Practices Evaluations in the Gambia: A Report of the Major Findings* (Menlo Park, CA: Applied Communication Technologies, 1985).

33. S. B. Soumerai, D. Ross-Degnan, and J. S. Kahn, "Effects of Professional and Media Warnings about the Association between Aspirin Use in Children and Reye's Syndrome," *Milbank Quarterly* 70(1) (1992): 155–182.

34. V. Balraj and T. J. John, "Evaluation of a Poliomyelitis Immunization Campaign in Madras City," *Bulletin of the World Health Organization* 64 (1986): 861–865.

35. R. Grilli et al., "Mass Media Interventions: Effects on Health Services Utilization (Cochrane Review)," *The Cochrane Library, 4* (Oxford: Update Software, 1999).

36. L. B. Snyder, "Development Communication Campaigns," in ed. B. Mody, *International and Development Communication: A 21st Century Perspective* (Thousand Oaks, CA: Sage Publications, 2003), 167–188.

37. X. Pang et al., "Evaluation of Control Measures in the Severe Acute Respiratory Syndrome Outbreak in Beijing, 2003," *Journal of the American Medical Association* 290 (2003): 3215–3221.

38. L. B. Snyder, "The Impact of the Surgeon General's 'Understanding AIDS' Pamphlet in Connecticut," *Health Communication* 3(1) (1991): 37–57.

39. K. Golan, "Surviving a Public Health Crisis: Tips for Communicators," *Journal of Health Communication* 8 (2003): 126–127.

40. E. Lipton and K. Johnson, "Tracking Bio-terrorism's Tangled Course," *New York Times*, December 26, 2001.

41. Pang et al., "Evaluation of Control Measures in the Severe Acute Respiratory Syndrome Outbreak in Beijing, 2003."

42. P. Arguin et al., "Health Communication during SARS," *Emerging Infectious Diseases* 10(2) (2004): 377–380.

43. Golan, "Surviving a Public Health Crisis: Tips for Communicators."

44. J. F. Bach et al., "A 10-Year Educational Programme Aimed at Rheumatic Fever in Two French Caribbean Islands," *The Lancet* 347 (1996): 644–648.

45. S. J. Marshall, "Expert Committee Finds Little Fault in Hong Kong's Response to SARS," *Bulletin of the World Health Organization* 81 (2003): 11.

46. L. Tengelsen et al., "Coordinated Response to Reports of Possible Anthrax Contamination, Idaho, 2001," *Emerging Infectious Diseases* 8(10) (2004): 1093–1095.

47. J. Koplan, "Communication during Public Health Emergencies," *Journal of Health Communication* 8 (2003): 144–145.

48. Tengelsen et al., "Coordinated Response to Reports of Possible Anthrax Contamination, Idaho, 2001.

49. G. Rezza et al., "SARS Epidemic in the Press," *Emerging Infectious Diseases* 10(2) (2004): 381–382.

CHAPTER NINETEEN

Communication-for-Behavioral-Impact (COMBI): A Review of WHO's Experiences with Strategic Social Mobilization and Communication in the Prevention and Control of Communicable Diseases

Elil Renganathan, Everold Hosein, Will Parks, Linda Lloyd, Mohammad Raili Suhaili, and Asiya Odugleh

Chapter Questions

1. Why was the COMBI approach chosen for the two communicable diseases in India and Malaysia?
2. How is COMBI used to mobilize the community in this case study?
3. What lessons can be learned from applying COMBI for current IEC and BCC strategies?

Introduction

One-third of the world's deaths are due to communicable diseases. Together, HIV/AIDS, tuberculosis, and malaria claimed 5.7 million lives in 2002.[1] "Neglected" diseases such as lymphatic filariasis and leprosy that do not kill nevertheless silently bleed the health and wealth of a nation, causing high levels of suffering, disability, and economic deprivation. Effective prevention and treatment strategies have long been available to control these diseases, yet this is only part of the equation. Along with improving health service provision and access, a continuing dilemma for health professionals has been finding effective ways to encourage the adoption of healthy behaviors at individual, household, community, and societal levels. Many different approaches have been used in the past. While there have been some successes, there has also been enormous frustration at not being able to achieve more at a faster rate.

The Genesis of COMBI at WHO

Among the agencies focused on public health, the United Nations Children's Fund (UNICEF) traditionally had a lead role in assisting national communicable disease programs with strategic social mobilization and communication. Recently, however, UNICEF has moved away from disease-focused programs toward broader social determinants of children's health (as embodied in the Child Rights Convention).[2] The World Health Organization (WHO) has increasingly relied on its own resources and other development partners (such as national agencies) to blend technical interventions with social mobilization and communication initiatives.

COMBI is social mobilization directed at the task of mobilizing all societal and personal influences on an individual and family to prompt individual and family action with respect to specific healthy behaviors. It is a process that strategically blends a variety of communication interventions intended to engage individuals and families in considering recommended healthy behaviors and to encourage the adoption and maintenance of those behaviors. Developed and tested over a number of years, COMBI incorporates the lessons learned from five decades of public health communication and draws substantially from the experience of private sector consumer communication.

WHO, through its regional and country-level partners, has been applying COMBI in a range of the communicable disease programs (Table 19–1).

In developing COMBI, social mobilization and communication specialists at WHO drew on three core fields: Public Health Communication; Social Mobilization; and Integrated Marketing Communication (IMC). Such a combination is not necessarily a comfortable theoretical mix and can be even harder to achieve in reality. IMC and public health communication, in particular, are often seen in opposition, and communicators sometimes set up unnecessary barriers between their various fields. Elements of all three fields, however, are often required to achieve and sustain development gains in public health.

Public Health Communication

The field of public health communication has passed through different periods in its development. Conventional "Information-Education-Communication" (IEC) programs in health have been able to increase awareness and knowledge but have not been as successful at achieving behavioral results. Increased awareness and education about health behaviors have been insufficient bases for action, though they are essential steps in the process toward behavioral impact. COMBI

Table 19–1. COMBI Programs (2001–2004)

TARGETED DISEASE	BEHAVIORAL OBJECTIVES (EXAMPLES ONLY)	COUNTRY (STATE/REGION)	YEAR/S

Lymphatic filariasis	• Prompt, x no. of people to swallow 4–6 tablets at home in the presence of a Filaria Prevention Assistant (or go to the distribution point) on Filaria Day	Zanzibar
		Sri Lanka
		India (Tamil
		   Nadu/Orissa)
		Kenya
		Philippines
		   (Region 5)
		Nepal
			2001–2003
			2002–2003
			
			2002–2003
			2002–2003
			
			2003
			2003

Dengue fever	• (Depending on ecology of *Aedes*) weekly inspection of all potential larvae breeding sites and cleaning containers/emptying/ changing/treating the water
	• Have fever? Assume it is Dengue Fever and seek immediate diagnosis and treatment
	• Weekly scrubbing of large cement water storage containers
		Malaysia
		   (Johor Bahru)
		Lao People's
		   Democratic
		   Republic
		   (Vientiane
		   Municipality)
		Nicaragua
		Guatemala
			
			2001–2003
			
			2003
			2003
			2003–2004

Leprosy	• Check your skin often for early signs of leprosy and seek diagnosis at the nearest health center	Mozambique India (Bihar)	2002–2003 2002
Tuberculosis	• Coughing, coughing, coughing, then go to the nearest designated TB center for a free sputum test	Kenya India (Kerala) Bangladesh	2003–2004 2003–2004 2003–2004
Malaria	• Families to consistently sleep under insecticide-treated bed nets during the malaria transmission season • Re-treatment of bed nets before the malaria transmission season	Afghanistan Sudan	2003–2004 2003–2004

attempts a seamless connection between these steps and those needed to prompt desired behavioral results.

Social marketing is a population-wide strategy for changing behavior that assembles the best elements of traditional approaches to social change in an integrated planning and action framework and makes use of advances in communication technology and marketing (product, price, placement, promotion).[3–6] Social marketing or program communication can be defined as the process of identifying, segmenting, and targeting specific groups or audiences with particular strategies, messages, products, or training programs through various mass media and interpersonal channels, both traditional and nontraditional, with the objective of creating consumer demand for a product or services. While social marketing programs often entail careful consumer research, there is frequently an absence of strategy for creating societal ownership.

Social marketing is often based on an appeal to the individual—if he or she can be reached. Yet in many countries, reaching individuals with new ideas or products is the most difficult thing to do. COMBI, as an example of strategic communication for behavior change, adds an element of social mobilization to the social marketing model so that the products, concepts, or innovations will be widely diffused and lead to an accelerated process of diffusion and acceptance.

Social Mobilization

The concept of "social mobilization" arose from the Alma Ata conference in 1978.[7] Following the declaration of "Health for All by the Year 2000"[8] at the Thirty-fourth World Health Assembly in 1981, UNICEF took up the challenge with a set of activities dubbed "social mobilization," involving the creation of a social movement in support of a particular program. A definition of social mobilization could read as follows:

> Social mobilization is the process of bringing together all feasible and practical inter-sectoral allies to raise people's awareness of and demand for a particular development programme, to assist in the delivery of resources and services and to strengthen community participation for sustainability and self-reliance.[9]

Social mobilization evolved out of UNICEF's earlier interest in community participation as an essential ingredient for delivering services to the poorest sectors of the urban and rural populations.[10] Social mobilization expands the concept of "community" to include not just householders, villagers, or urban settlements, but many other social allies such as heads of state and other political leaders, various ministries, district and local government authorities, community and religious leaders, businesses, environmentalists, nongovernmental organizations, service clubs, journalists, filmmakers, artists, and entertainers, to name the most common examples.

Social mobilization campaigns have often been used to mobilize local resources around a proposed social or health action, whether it is undertaking a service-related activity such as drug distribution or immunization, satisfying a community-identified need, or correcting societal injustice.[11]

COMBI differs from traditional social mobilization in at least two ways:

- It is more concerned with reducing the burden of particular diseases rather than with building national consensus and carrying out a broad educational process that should energize and uplift people.
- In addition to analysis of societal structures, it is concerned with attempting to achieve behavioral impact by researching and communicating specific messages to specific target audiences.[12]

COMBI can thus often be considered as disease-oriented social mobilization, always with a behavioral focus. Adding the behavioral focus to the mobilization model ensures that programs get value for money—with budgets and human resources that are usually very limited—in terms of actual behavioral results.

Integrated Marketing Communication (IMC)

In the private sector, experience over 100 years in successfully using marketing communication with consumer behavior (for products both awful and superb) points to an approach applicable to health and social development. One of the most interesting recent developments in commercial marketing theory is the development of IMC. Increasing evidence shows that consumers mostly rely on their perceptions of what they believe to be important or true (how they select, process, and store information in memory and then access, add to, retrieve, and use this stored information) or of what they think is right or correct, rather than on solid, rational, economically derived information.[13] A perception might not be correct but it is what consumers know, and what they know is all they need to know:

> As we have increased the flow and volume of data, consumers have been forced to find ways to cope with the cacophony of information around them. What they apparently have decided to do is simply to skim the surface, gather bits and pieces, weave the bits and pieces into some sort of knowledge or decision fabric, and be on their way. In other words, people today take in and process enough information to allow them to understand or muddle through on most subjects. They limit their information to the least they need to know. Thus, while consumers know a little bit about many things, they don't know very much about anything. They know just enough to get by.[14]

This new "sound bite" approach to gathering information places increasing demands on health programs. Statements about healthy behaviors, products, or services need to be clear, consistent, and comprehensible. An integrated and coordinated approach with credibility is vital. Integration does not occur at the level of the agency or of the media. Integration takes place with *consumers*; therefore, IMC *begins with the consumer*. The critical dimension is not what health programs or services think they deliver but what clients or consumers *believe they receive*. IMC requires that planners and health workers radically shift from thinking "inside out" (what we have to promote, what we have to say), to "outside in" (what consumers tell us about themselves, their needs, wants, and lifestyles). It is about looking at the development process from the consumer's point of view.

IMC is based on the need for a continual exchange of information between the mobilizer and the consumer or beneficiary. IMC is thus about better management of the communications/mobilization or marketing process so that all messages about a product/service/organization to which a consumer is exposed are coordinated.[15] IMC provides greater consistency, reduces waste, and gives a product/service/organization a competitive advantage. IMC also requires zero-based communications planning. In other words, preconceived notions of what was done in the past should be discarded to allow planners the freedom to choose what skills and resources they need, based on fresh market research and situation analysis.

COMBI in Action

WHO technical staff and consultants trained in COMBI planning apply a 10-step process in developing a COMBI Plan.[16] Two key principles underpin COMBI planning. First: Do nothing—produce no T-shirts, no posters, no leaflets, no videos, until you have set out clear, precise, specific behavioral objectives. Second: Do nothing—produce no T-shirts, no posters, no leaflets, no videos, until you have successfully undertaken a situational "market" analysis in relation to those preliminary behavioral objectives. Consequently, a large percentage of COMBI planning time is spent in "situational market analysis" to define and field test the appropriate behavioral objectives for the program. Once these objectives are established, COMBI helps program managers and partners choose, modify, monitor, and evaluate a judicious blend of advocacy, communication, and mobilization actions in a massive, repetitive, persistent, and engaging manner to increase healthy behaviors among those at risk and healthy policy action among decision makers.[17]

Now, consider two brief case studies of COMBI in action.

The Five Integrated Communication Action Areas

1. *Political Mobilization, Public Advocacy, and Public Relations,* for putting the particular healthy behavior on the public and administrative/program management agenda via the mass media: news coverage, talk shows, soap operas, celebrity spokespersons, discussion programs; meetings/discussions with various categories of government and community leadership, service providers, administrators; official memoranda; partnership meetings.

2. *Community Mobilization,* including use of participatory research, community group meetings, partnership meetings, traditional media, music, song and dance, road shows, community drama, leaflets, posters, pamphlets, videos, home visits.

3. *Media/Advertising,* via radio, television, newspapers, and other available media, engaging people in reviewing the merits of the recommended behavior vis-à-vis "cost" of carrying it out. Incentives such as free samples and small gifts are used to motivate people to consider the suggested behavior, branding the behavior or associated product/service, and promoting the brand.

4. *Interpersonal Communication/Counseling,* at the community level, in schools and involving school children as "personal sellers," in homes and particularly at service points, with appropriate informational literature and additional incentives, and allowing for careful listening to people's concerns and addressing them.

5. *Point-of-Service Promotion,* emphasizing easily accessible and readily available solutions to health problems.

Dengue Fever in Johor State, Malaysia

In anticipation of a dengue outbreak in early 2001 in the State of Johor, Malaysia, the Western Pacific Regional Office of WHO (WHO/WPRO) requested the assistance of WHO in helping the State Ministry of Health (MoH) design a COMBI program to involve the community in the district of Johor Bahru in dengue prevention. A key challenge for the State MoH staff was to define the behavioral results expected of the community to avert a dengue outbreak, avoiding the temptation to revive the old communication strategy, which was limited to a few posters and a radio jingle urging the population to eliminate the *Aedes* mosquito. This process of delineating anticipated behavioral results led to a list of 25 possible behavioral objectives targeted at individuals, families, the community at large, business owners, and industrial plants. In the end, the COMBI Plan focused on just two behavioral goals: (1) Get all families, totaling a quarter million, to check their homes for a half an hour every Sunday for mosquito breeding sites over a 12-week period, with recommended actions on what to do if sites are found; and (2) Get everyone with a fever to presume that it is dengue and go to the health clinic for diagnosis and treatment.

Information gathered as part of a very quick market situational analysis, including field visits to various local communities and interviews with household members that explored knowledge, attitudes, and behavioral tendencies with respect to dengue, led to the design and circulation of a draft COMBI Plan for a three-month campaign.

The plan proposed a strategic blend of COMBI's basic five communication action areas with considerable mass media advertising, posters, banners and street danglers, press coverage and featured articles, and administrative mobilization activities (memos and staff meetings), among other actions.

All of these focused on the two behavioral themes cited earlier and stated why the recommended behaviors were of value in relation to the effort involved. Three uniquely combined components of the plan were actions described as personal selling and community mobilization efforts.

- One component involved 200,000 school children ages 9 to 12 taking home a single page "Worksheet" about dengue and the recommended behavior of the 30-minute Sunday household check to be carried out by all family members. The worksheets, first reviewed in the classroom with the teacher's help, were to be read aloud at home and signed by parents after each one of the 12 household checks was completed.

- A second component created a group of riders called "D'Riders" (Dengue Riders), dressed in a red vest and cap with the dengue prevention logo and the two behavioral messages cited earlier. These riders rode into different communities every Sunday morning and created a stir with their presence and their encouragement to families to do the household checks.

- A third component was the creation in various community groups of dengue voluntary inspection teams, consisting of local volunteers who met every Sunday morning and walked around their residential area encouraging the weekly household checks, checking on mosquito breeding sites outside homes, and taking appropriate action.

The budget for the three-month campaign was $270,000 (a little over one dollar per household). However, only $100,000 was ultimately allocated: The WHO Regional Office funded the COMBI Plan to the amount of $76,000, and the MoH provided an additional $24,000 on top of staff and other in-kind contributions. Futher small amounts were raised from the private sector.

WHO supported the State MoH in identifying competent local advertising agencies to help with implementation and after interviews eventually selected one agency. The State MoH, the lead implementing partner, had not previously worked with an advertising agency. One of the tasks of the selected agency was to secure private sector support of the campaign in consultation with the MoH. This led to considerable discounts for many of the items produced (such as ballpoint pens decorated with the behavioral themes for the school children) and cash grants in exchange for placement of a company/product logo (nonpharmaceutical) on promotional and educational materials.

Preliminary analysis by the State MoH shows that in Johor Bahru the three-month COMBI Program resulted in 85 percent of households in sampled areas reporting that they had carried out the desired behavioral task of inspecting the inside and outside of their homes for mosquito breeding sites every Sunday for the 12-week duration of the program. Additional behavioral results were reported in terms of increased treatment-seeking for fever, as well as volunteer groups who continued to visit vacant plots and unkempt public areas on a weekly basis. Data from standard larval indicators and ovitraps were collected and analyzed. Organizational changes were noted, such as new linkages between the program and the community at large, new structures within the program, and new partnerships.

Leprosy in Bihar State, India

WHO staff made a short preliminary visit to India in June 2000 to explore the design and implementation of a leprosy COMBI Plan with the WHO South-East Asia Regional Office and the Indian MoH. The decision was made to design and implement a COMBI leprosy plan in the State of Bihar, one of the country's most highly endemic regions for leprosy. Over the course of two field visits, WHO and MoH staff visited several health centers in Bihar State, conducting extensive interviews with patients and health staff and walk-throughs in various health centers to grasp the process involved in visiting a health center for leprosy diagnosis and treatment. The Leprosy COMBI Plan for the State of Bihar was designed on the basis of these exercises. Defining the desired behavioral outcome was a key challenge in developing the COMBI Plan. In thinking about communication action, colleagues who worked on leprosy behavioral impact communication would often hit upon dealing with stigma as their immediate goal. Their view was that changing the "image" of leprosy was the pre-eminent communication goal.

The COMBI approach, however, calls first for defining a specific behavioral goal. So when colleagues pointed to the stigma issue, a follow-up question was: Why is this behaviorally important? What does one expect would happen behaviorally if stigma was altered? Other communication goals raised were: to inform people that leprosy is curable and that the multi-drug therapy (MDT) is free and readily available. Again, a follow-up query related to the behavioral importance of the message. These lines of questions and exploration with leprosy staff in Bihar focused attention on what were the expected behavioral outcomes. Staff felt that if stigma was lowered and people knew that leprosy was curable and that MDT was free, then people would rush to the health centers for diagnosis and treatment. Further reflection on this rationale, however, suggested that this would not be the case. Stigma associated with leprosy can be reduced (presuming that anything can be done about stigma), and people can be informed that leprosy is curable and MDT is free, but they still might not show up at the health centers for any number of reasons such as lack of time, other household priorities, or simply forgetfulness.

"Walking around research" in various communities and further exploration with leprosy staff eventually led to the conclusion that a more fundamental behavioral goal of getting people with early signs of leprosy to "self-report" to a health center for treatment and diagnosis was desired: the earlier they came in, the better it would be for treatment of the disease. In follow-up discussions during the design of the COMBI plan, the goal of getting people with early signs of leprosy to "self-report" to the health centers was broken down into steps, including the need to be able to tell whether or not an individual had early signs of leprosy. And as this was further discussed, it was realized that early signs of leprosy were recognizable only if one checked one's skin, a habit that observational research showed was not common. Indeed, many homes had no full-length mirrors. Men took showers outdoors partially dressed and hardly looked at their skin as they soaped-up and threw buckets of water over their heads. Women at home might have only a small mirror for face make-up. Couples were not in the habit of checking each other's skin or seeing each other naked, even in moments of intimacy.

These findings led to the realization that if people were to self-report with early signs of leprosy, they first needed to get into the habit of checking their skin for early signs of leprosy. This behavior had less to do with stigma or knowing that leprosy was curable and that MDT was free. It had to do with one's attitudes toward oneself. Of course, if the desired behavior change was to have people check their skin for early signs of leprosy, they first needed to be told why it was important and then within that framework, the discussion could turn to the fact that leprosy was indeed curable and that MDT was free. So, the first behavioral task became: Check Your Skin (CYS) for Early Leprosy Signs (ELSI). Out of this process, came the behavioral goal of getting everyone in Bihar to "CYS for ELSI." The Leprosy COMBI Plan was designed around this behavioral goal, with an integrated blend of the five COMBI communication areas that included: 200,000 posters; 84 radio spots and 41 newspaper advertisements (in concentrated issues); 68 vehicles used for community microphone announcements over the course of 3 days; 400,000 school children taking home worksheets; 3,000 banners and dangler flags at service centers; and 22,000 badges worn by staff.

The COMBI Plan was intended to be a one-year plan covering the entire state, using start-up funds from the Nippon Foundation. Action on this plan, however, was postponed indefinitely because the India MoH/Leprosy Program decided to focus exclusively on the multi-million dollar World Bank-financed All-India Leprosy Communication Program. It was felt that to focus on a $50,000 pilot COMBI effort in Bihar would distract from the national effort.

In due course, ongoing discussions with the India MoH/Leprosy Program nevertheless led to a decision to pilot a COMBI Program but to limit focus to a few districts in the State of Bihar rather than covering the entire state. The COMBI Plan was revised to cover only three districts with a budget of $46,750. Implementation of the COMBI Plan began in June 2002, and the program was formally launched in October 2002. Case data of the numbers of people coming to clinics for skin ailments (self-reporting) were taken as the primary method of impact evaluation for the COMBI plan. Data collected before, during, and after the campaign showed that there was a 69 percent overall increase in the number of skin cases attending the clinics, with a 73 percent increase in the number of female skin cases self-reporting and a 90 percent increase in the number of child skin cases. The number of diagnosed leprosy cases increased by 23 percent.

Lessons Learned

- **Strategic COMBI Planning as a Pre-requisite to Materials Production**

  It is important to wean disease program managers off the view that health education, health communication, and health IEC consists of producing posters, pamphlets, and T-shirts. These communication materials might or might not be needed; it all depends on the behavioral results intended and the market situational analysis.

- *The Importance of Behavioral Goals*

  Without explicit behavioral goals driving program planning, implementation, and evaluation, many social mobilization and communication programs struggle to coordinate the activities of different stakeholders and usually fail to provide evidence of tangible impact. Behavioral goals, created through broad stakeholder consultation, negotiation, and market research, serve as unifying statements of program purpose and allow for more transparent program evaluation. Changes in knowledge or attitudes, while useful proxy measures, do not allow stakeholders to gauge whether health programs are actually achieving the behavioral results that ultimately lead to better health outcomes.

- *Implementation Commitment*

  However excellent a strategic social mobilization plan seems to be in design, it comes to nothing if there is not a keen level of commitment for implementation on the part of senior staff and officials of an MoH. Without this commitment, plans will be implemented half-heartedly, if at all. A critical requirement of COMBI plans is what is called the "administrative mobilization" that aims to secure the active and focused participation of political leaders and, more important, to galvanize the civil service and government bureaucracy into action at all levels.

- *Organizational Adaptation*

  The structures of existing organizations often have to be adapted so that the mechanisms needed to implement a COMBI plan can be put in place and that new alliances and networks stimulated by COMBI can be maintained. Usually COMBI plans have to operate within a broad existing organization. COMBI programs therefore confront the challenge of finding a way to ensure integration into an organization as a legitimate philosophy and organizational unit. Such integration can be said to evolve in three stages: an initial "resistance" stage, a growth and "acceptance" stage, and a mature or "established" stage. Specific organizational change strategies—whether implemented through a "program-centered" approach (e.g., supervised by a disease control program manager) or a "stakeholder-centered" approach (e.g., supervised by an intersectoral committee)—must be applied at each stage of COMBI's integration and at different organizational levels, from headquarters to field operations to program support levels.[18] Organization change strategies might imply the design of a modified organizational structure by identifying and delineating new responsibilities; the creation of new positions (if necessary); the setting up of teams and committees; the training, mobilization, and supervision of a field workforce; and the setting up of management procedures, benchmarks, and feedback or tracking mechanisms.[19]

- *Working with Competent Local Advertising Agencies*

  Government offices and global, intergovernmental agencies currently manage and design a large share of health promotion and communications activities. With so many forces cautiously encouraging staff to embrace the status quo, many government health programs end up conducting "tepid" health promotion strategies designed to cause the least offense to the smallest number of people. Our experience so far suggests that it is possible to establish superb working relationships with competent local advertising and marketing communication agencies in implementing COMBI plans. Advertising agencies bring a refreshing creativity to program design and implementation as well as the opportunity to mobilize new private sector partners drawn from the client-base of advertising agencies that deal with the commercial world. Our experience also suggests that such relationships have to be diligently managed and guided. When this is done, however, the overall impact on behavioral results can exceed expectations.

Conclusion

Medical and technical solutions for the major communicable diseases exist. The real challenge is to mobilize political and social capital and ensure these interventions are used widely and well. The commercial marketing sector long ago learned an important lesson. It takes a major effort in terms of research, creativity, alliance building, funds, and other resources to achieve and sustain behavioral impact. In the public health sector, we have only to look at immunization and anti-smoking campaigns to appreciate this. A major global and national commitment recognizing that this enterprise goes far beyond poster production must fund these initiatives in a far more substantial and sustainable way than has been the case to date.

COMBI currently falls into the selective disease approach and can thus be the target of criticism, particularly with failure to tackle the broad social determinants of health such as inequity, injustice, and poverty.[20] Unless disease-focused programs are allied to wider societal change, "disease-replacement" runs the risk of negating the inroads made against selected diseases; injustice and inequality will remain. Furthermore, vertical approaches are difficult to integrate within overstretched, poorly resourced health systems and sustained without massive external contributions. COMBI by itself cannot generate development. Its advocates, however, argue that disease problems cannot wait for overall economic and social development to generate solutions. While systematic development is important, our efforts in one problem area can energize people to move on to integrated approaches. In addition, addressing communicable diseases removes a significant obstacle that keeps people in poverty, makes progress against the most formidable childhood killers, and can strengthen health services.

What remains clear is that in most developing countries, health promotion, in whatever guise, continues to be undervalued and underresourced.[21] COMBI has raised the profile of social mobilization and communication, and in so doing stimulated resource investment in a technical area that has traditionally been given a very low priority. COMBI's style appeals to planners and program managers anxious to get more "behavioral impact for their buck" and is alluring for technical health specialists involved in a systematic approach to development because all stages of the program can be mapped out with clear objectives and targets. COMBI prevents communicable disease programs from throwing their scarce resources into a "tornado" of poorly targeted public appeals and organizational processes. It helps program managers and partners choose, modify, monitor, and evaluate a blend of advocacy, communication, and mobilization actions to increase healthy behavior among those at risk and encourage health policy action among decision makers.

Unfortunately, COMBI confronts the same internal barriers (e.g., turf battles among health promotion and communication practitioners) and external barriers (e.g., institutional egos, lack of knowledge about more than one communication area, loss of motivation, and lack of funds and skilled creative professionals) that IMC faces in the commercial sector as well as resource competition for projects and longer-term programs.[22]

Our experiences have nevertheless shown that COMBI:

- Delivers a clear, consistent message that is both more efficient and more effective in stimulating a behavioral response
- Cuts through the increasingly cluttered development landscape
- Fosters a two-way dialogue between clients and services/organizations that, in turn, leads to long-term client-organization relationships
- Gets rid of the "same-old same-old" approach that has not been working; it keeps the things that are working moderately well, improves them, and adds some new ideas and techniques. This combination of improvement and innovation assists in creating a new organizational culture of staff enthusiasm for the task, which is itself a scarce and vital resource.

COMBI presents a new paradigm for behavioral impact. It is the way forward for those who seek to engender the adoption and maintenance of healthy behaviors. Our experiences have shown that this can be achieved with the right partnerships at country level.

Acknowledgments

The authors gratefully acknowledge the efforts of national staff and partners in the dengue and leprosy programs in India and Malaysia who were largely responsible for implementation of the COMBI programs described here. The invaluable support of colleagues at the WHO Regional Offices of South-East Asia and of the Western Pacific and in the Communicable Diseases Control, Prevention and Eradication department at WHO headquarters is greatly appreciated. The credit for the ultimate success of any COMBI program is due to the individuals, families, and local communities who have embraced these activities and who dedicate time and effort to their implementation.

Notes

1. *Scaling Up the Response to Infectious Diseases*, WHO/CDS/2002.7.
2. United Nations General Assembly resolution (November 20, 1989): Resolution 44/25.
3. P. Kotler and E. L. Roberto, *Social Marketing: Strategies for Changing Behavior* (New York: The Free Press, 1989).
4. A. R. Andreasen, *Marketing Social Change: Changing Behavior to Promote Health, Social Development, and the Environment* (San Francisco: Jossey-Bass Publishers, 1995).
5. R. C. Lefebre and L. Rochlin, "Social Marketing," in *Health Behavior and Health Education: Theory, Practice and Research*, eds. K. Glanz, F. M. Lewis, and B. K. Rimer (San Francisco: Jossey-Bass Publishers, 1997), 384–402.
6. M. Siegel and L. Doner, *Marketing Public Health: Strategies to Promote Social Change* (Gaithersburg, MD: Aspen Publishers, 1998).
7. World Health Organization, *Report of the International Conference on Primary Health Care*, "Health for All" Series, No. 1, 1978.
8. World Health Organization, Thirty-Fourth World Health Assembly: Resolution WHA34.36, 1981.
9. World Health Organization, Thirty-Fourth World Health Assembly.
10. N. McKee, *Social Mobilization and Social Marketing in Developing Countries: Lessons for Communicators* (Penang: Southbound, 1992), 4.
11. United Nations Children's Fund, *A Strategy for Basic Services* (New York: UNICEF, 1977).

12. A. Berjemo and A. Bekui, "Community Participation in Disease Control," *Social Science and Medicine* 36(9) (1993): 1145–1150.

13. McKee, *Social Mobilization and Social Marketing in Developing Countries: Lessons for Communicators*.

14. D. Schultz, S. I. Tannerbaum, and R. F. Lauterborn, *The New Marketing Paradigm: Integrated Marketing Communications* (Chicago: NTC Business Books, 1994), 22.

15. Schultz, Tannerbaum, and Lauterborn, *The New Marketing Paradigm: Integrated Marketing Communications*, 23.

16. T. L. Harris, *Value-Added Public Relations: The Secret Weapon of Integrated Marketing* (Chicago: NTC Business Books, 1998).

17. WHO/WMC, *Mobilizing for Action: 2004*, 3.

18. WHO/WMC, *Mobilizing for Action: 2004*, 2.

19. Andreasen, *Marketing Social Change: Changing Behavior to Promote Health, Social Development, and the Environment*.

19. P. Kotler and A. R. Andreasen, *Strategic Marketing for Nonprofit Organizations*, 3d ed. (Englewood Cliffs, NJ: Prentice-Hall, 1987).

20. Andreasen, *Marketing Social Change: Changing Behavior to Promote Health, Social Development, and the Environment*.

21. D. Werner and D. Sanders, *The Politics of Primary Health Care and Child Survival* (Palo Alto, CA: Health Wrights, 1997).

22. L. W. Green and J. Raeburn, "Contemporary Development in Health Promotion. Definitions and Challenges," in *Health Promotion at the Community Level*, ed. N. Bracht (Newbury Park, CA: Sage Publications, 1990).

CHAPTER TWENTY

State of the Art in Crisis Communication: Past Lessons and Principles of Practice

Scott C. Ratzan and Wendy Meltzer

Chapter Questions

1. Based on the examples given, what are some of the negative outcomes that result from a lack of effective risk communication? How can the Risk Management/Communication Framework (RMCF) be applied to these cases to achieve better results?
2. What is the role of public trust during a crisis? How can public trust be gained through crisis communication using the RMCF process?
3. What is the value of working with stakeholders before a crisis occurs?

Introduction

In this age of the 24-hour news cycles, public health organizations are often in the position of responding to a crisis as it unfolds, sometimes with the spokesperson learning the facts simultaneously with the public. Communicators must instantly impart vital information in order to mitigate panic and fear, while fostering the trust and confidence that are critical in a crisis situation.[1]

There are many challenges in how we communicate risk, especially risks to health. Few areas continue to stir debate more than advances in medicine and biotechnology. Even public health successes that have decreased morbidity and mortality—such as vaccination, air bags, and fluoridation—have been surrounded by controversy. Stem cell research, vaccine development, and genomic manipulation join recent "scares'" of Bovine Spongiform Encephalopathy (BSE), Sudden Acute Respiratory Syndrome (SARS), and anthrax. Scientific and health literacy requires understanding, but the incremental and imprecise nature of science and experimentation that contribute to defining risk thrives on doubts, criticism, and debate, which often translate into only theoretical causality and "risk." Furthermore, scientifically valid information is not absolute and can change over time.

Translating theoretical (imprecise and incomplete) and changing knowledge of causality and risk has developed into its own body of knowledge called "risk communication." According to a U.S. National Research Council report, risk communication "emphasizes the process of exchanging information and opinion with the public."[2] No matter the crisis, whether it is a terrorist attack, a dangerous weather condition, or a health epidemic, those filling the role of crisis communicator can benefit from studying incidents past to identify the gold standard of risk communication during a crisis. "The objective remains the use of effective communication to avoid or avert a crisis in the first place, but if, for whatever reason crisis proportions have been reached, then that crisis must be handled—*managed*—until equilibrium can be restored."[3]

Luckily, or unluckily, there is now a substantial history of crises from which to take lessons. In the United States the anthrax crisis of 2001 resulted in a plethora of research that provides communicators with a "how-to" of what and what not to say and do during such a crisis. The United States is now practicing the lessons learned to respond to new crises around Mad Cow disease and influenza. In Europe, there have been multiple crises including acrylamide, the Belgian Coca-Cola scare, and most famously, BSE. Also, the recent SARS and avian flu epidemics will undoubtedly provide lessons. These events lay the groundwork for future successful crisis communication.

Recognizing the challenges to health progress that lie in the communication process, not in the laboratory, this chapter was developed to provide principles for practice of risk and crisis communication in health. Although the examples are about communicating health risks, the principles are transferable to other types of risk, such as environmental risk. The overarching goal is to provide a brief overview and best practice from the body of published knowledge and ongoing practical applications relating to risk communication from multiple perspectives. In addition, as the decision-making burden of risk, while often on the shoulders of consumers, is also under increased scrutiny by policy makers, a comprehensive science-based approach to risk—

the Risk Management/Communication Framework (RMCF)—is presented in this chapter.

Use of such terms such as "infinitesimal," "negligible," and "probable" in defining risk places a great responsibility on those who determine what information is valuable and salient for their audience. A high ethical standard has thus become necessary for the purveyors of health—whether they are in government, academia, marketing, publishing, news media, or other fields of public address. To facilitate optimal decision making, finding ways to increase the quality of information becomes more important than increasing the quantity of information. Ideally, this article and the principles of practice will contribute to better understanding of risk and actions that advance communication with salient, valuable, factual, and ethical risk information.

Crisis and Risk Communication: One and the Same?

Risk communication has been defined by a variety of groups as any two-way communication between stakeholders about the existence, nature, form, severity, or acceptability of risks.[4] It is vitally important to understand the basic concepts of risk communication to ensure that the critical components are integrated into any risk management process. Since the mid 1980s, the focus of risk communication has evolved from concern about how to most effectively inform the public about the technical aspects of risk assessments to a process of ensuring early and ongoing dialogue among various stakeholders. While guidelines for risk communication have been developed by a number of experts, translating these principles into practical application has become a long-term, challenging process requiring considerable resources, time, and effort.

The terms crisis communication and risk communication are inextricably linked and often used interchangeably. Crisis communication is often characterized as one of four types of risk communication.[5] Crisis communication occurs when the risk is high hazard and affects a large audience that is very upset. He states that in this case, everyone is a stakeholder looking for information. Unlike the three other types of risk communication he defines—public relations, stakeholder relations, and outrage management—crisis communication focuses on helping the public weather the fear, anger, misery, and stress that accompany crises. Crisis communication has also been defined as the verbal, visual, and/or written interaction between an organization and its public prior to, during, and after a negative event.[6] In both cases, communication is the conduit to define risk to a large group of concerned persons. Most of these persons are not experts (some possibly not even aware) on the specific concern.

Illustrating the importance of developing effective crisis communication is easiest when looking at examples of poor risk communication. When risk communication goes awry, risk and crisis management can be greatly hindered. Many negative outcomes are possible, including refusal by vulnerable populations to follow a recommended preventive or treatment regimen. This was evident during the U.S. anthrax situation in which reactions to governmental communication resulted in inappropriate use of prophylactic antibiotics, a decline in public confidence in experts' assessment of risk, and an unforeseen increase in panic within affected communities. Scott Lillibridge, Director of the Bioterrorism Preparedness and Response Program, Centers for Disease Control and Prevention (CDC), stated, "We knew that communications would be important, but I don't think we knew it would be this dominant in the response."[7] This event demonstrates the failure to adequately prepare government and public health officials to engage in productive information exchanges and partnerships with potentially targeted populations, health care providers, first responders, and the news media. The obvious effect of ill-preparedness is the compromise of a country's ability to address the devastating medical, psychosocial, and economic outcomes that could result from a health crisis such as a biological attack.

Real People Are Different Than Experts or Social Scientists

Social scientists have studied the ways in which average citizens perceive risks and have shown clearly that the public tends to view risks differently than "experts" (i.e., the scientific and policy-making communities). While consumers do perceive risks differently than experts, this does not necessarily signify that their "different" perspective is the "wrong" perspective. These two audiences receive different information, process it in unique ways, and respond to conclusions based on their own set of circumstances and concerns. Scientists and regulators tend, for a variety of good reasons, to focus on measurable, quantifiable attributes of risks. The nonexperts, who are often the average consumers, receive different information from the media that tends to focus less on the quantitative aspects of risks, but rather on the qualitative, value-laden attributes of risks— such as fairness and controllability. (This often means the public responds quite differently from the intentions of the experts.)

Principles of Practice for Risk Communication

This chapter integrates Maxims for Effective Health and Risk Communication derived by the author as part of a World Health Organization consultation on Transmissible Spongiform Encephalopathies in 1998[8] with Best Practices in Public Health Risks and Crisis Communication developed by Vincent Covello in 2003, along with the myriad of publications and presentations on this topic throughout the world. These six principles are subsequently described:

I. Listen to and partner with stakeholders.
II. Establish, build, and maintain trust.
III. Work with the media.
IV. Develop your message.
V. Be honest, clear, and compassionate.
VI. Think before you speak.

Each principle uses recent examples to illustrate the pitfalls and/or successes of crisis communication and the lessons that were learned in the aftermath of an event. These examples allow us to glean state-of-the-art crisis communication methods and learn from the past what works best in a crisis situation.

I. Listen to and Partner with Stakeholders

In a crisis, the category of "stakeholder" expands to include anyone and everyone touched by the event. Embracing these groups as partners in the situation is an advantage in managing the reaction to the crisis. Some guidelines to identifying and involving these stakeholders include:

- Involve all parties that have an interest in the crisis at hand.
- Demonstrate respect for those affected by decisions and include them early in the process.
- Use a wide range of communication channels.
- People will hold you ethically accountable. Recognize that fact and use the highest ethical standards.[9]

These partners can have a different view of the situation, and listening is key to recognizing cultural and other variables.

- Empathize with your audience and try to put yourself in their place.
- Try to assess needs and public opinion through polls, surveys, interviews, and other formative research.
- Recognize cultural, economic, and political considerations that can complicate risk communication.[10]

Partnering with credible sources, whether it is with the media, large corporations, trade associations, or politicians, is a valuable tool to get a unified message out to the concerned public. For example, during the 1996 BSE crisis in the United Kingdom, there was no strategy to elicit relationships with key factions. One result was that McDonalds decided to eliminate British beef from its U.K. menu and in effect set a policy for other countries and corporations to follow. Two days later British beef was banned worldwide. A relationship that involved McDonalds perhaps could have prevented the devastating economic blow that followed.[11]

The appropriate level of stakeholder involvement depends on the situation. The U.S. Presidential/Congressional Commission on Risk Assessment and Risk Management offers the following factors to consider in determining the nature and extent of stakeholder involvement:

- The complexity, uncertainty, impact, and level of controversy associated with the decision to be made;
- The urgency with which the problem must be addressed; and
- The extent to which participants can have a genuine influence on the decision.[12]

A stakeholder analysis provides the decision maker with a profile of potential stakeholders for consideration in decision making and communication processes. Analysis includes the following information for each stakeholder group: needs, interests, issues, and concerns and underlying values; risk perceptions; level of interest and knowledge of the issue(s); knowledge gaps and misconceptions; trusted information sources and communication preferences. The profile is verified and updated through dialogue with stakeholders throughout the risk management process (for example, through group meetings, focus groups, as well as telephone and one-on-one interviews).

II. Establish, Build, and Maintain Trust

The process of involving and identifying stakeholders is just one step toward the ultimate goal of building trust and credibility. These two go hand-in-hand toward reducing fear and mistrust from interested parties during a crisis. During the anthrax crisis of 2001, the CDC decided to issue a recommendation for postal workers to begin prophylactic antibiotic use of doxycycline. This was different from the earlier recommendation to the Capitol Hill workers to take prophylactic ciproflaxin. This decision outraged postal workers who felt that they were being treated less well than their "executive" counterparts. The CDC was aware of new information that doxycycline worked as effectively as ciproflaxin, but with less side effects. However, this information was not broadly communicated before the recommendation was issued. If the CDC had anticipated such a reaction and included postal workers in the discussion, this information could have been disseminated with the new recommendation.[13]

Following the BSE crisis of 1996, a survey conducted in the United Kingdom found that three-fourths of people surveyed felt that it was hard to know if government advice was free of political pressure. The same survey found that the government was less trusted by the public than the food industry.[14] In June 1999, 26 children from one school in Belgium reported illness after drinking bottled Coca-Cola. Hundreds of people contacted the National Poison Center to report complaints after drinking Coca-Cola beverages. Cases of "poisoning" were also reported from northern France. Ultimately the illness was attributed to mass sociogenic illness. This was the subject of intense media coverage. However, it was a full week before Coca-Cola addressed the public about possible health risks, possible causes of the problems, and the actions undertaken. Coca-Cola's delay in addressing the public and informing health authorities seemed like a suspicious evasion. Government and health practitioners did not receive detailed information from the company until nearly 10 days after the crisis began. Because of a lack of information about what was happening and in an effort to shore up public confidence, the national health authorities banned the sale of all Coca-Cola products. This led to the largest product recall in Coca-Cola's history, involving the recall of about one hundred million packages and a loss of around 99 million Euro.[15]

Research shows that if a low trust source (i.e., a tabloid) criticizes a high trust source (i.e., the government), then the low trust source will lose.[16] If a high trust source supports a low trust source, the likelihood for the low trust source to win a crisis rises significantly. High trust institutions receive more media attention than low trust institutions. This puts certain conditions on how a high trust institution can and should communicate to media and the public.

Trust is, at its essence, a measure of how the public perceives competence and credibility.[17] Each time a nation is faced with a crisis, the degree of trust should build and not erode. These examples underscore the importance of credible communication with the public during a crisis. This is in agreement with the caution to be honest and open because communication blunders have long-lasting effects. "Once lost, trust and credibility are almost impossible to regain. Never mislead the public by lying or failing to provide information that is important to their understanding of issues."[18]

III. Work with the Media

While personal face-to-face communications during a crisis can be more accurate and effective, the reality is that one of the most important nonmedical sources of health information involves mass media news reports.[19-20] The public may receive 85 percent of health information from media sources.[21] During the U.S. anthrax crisis, survey respondents were asked where they had gone for information, and the top choices were local television and radio stations and cable and network news channels.[22] Therefore, the information that the media disseminates must be accurate and reliable in order to prevent any public misperceptions.

Media attention is swift and prevalent. For example, in Sweden, after acrylamide was announced to be a possible carcinogen found at high levels in fried foods, from April 23 to May 16, the four leading Swedish papers had a total of 112 articles on the scare. During the first few days after the press conference headlines such as "Cancer poison found in food," "Alarm about cancer poison in common foods," and "Potato chips can give you cancer" appeared on the front page. The acrylamide scare was a major news item on the evening news, making the top news story two days in a row, and receiving major coverage on morning and evening talk shows over the first two days.[23]

Media reach people quickly and can either help or hinder a crisis situation. During the BSE crisis the continuous media attention had a large, highly negative effect on consumer behavior.[24] The question was raised as to whether the media hyped up the public or informed them. Inaccuracies reported during that time heightened public fear, forced the government's hand to a severe reaction that had devastating economic repercussions, and led to public skepticism regarding the government's competence, which has lasted to this day. An examination of the coverage of BSE in the *Financial Times* found that the "media filled a void and became the primary health disseminator, drawing conclusions regarding health risks; the media engendered fear over BSE; the media misinterpreted scientific data about BSE; and the government was portrayed as unreliable and incompetent in dealing with the BSE crisis."[25] In the United States, news coverage led to consumers unnecessarily stockpiling antibiotics and purchasing bioterrorism kits.[26]

Today's media have a need for constant information updates to fill 24-hour broadcasts. Crisis communicators need to be aware that if they do not supply information, the media will report what they have. There are effective ways to embrace the media and enlist them as partners in reporting critical information during a crisis.

- Request that reporters disseminate specific pieces of information.
- Communicate to news media the importance of attributing information to its source.
- Be accessible to reporters and aware of deadlines.
- Prepare key messages and repeat them during press interactions.
- Say only what you want the media to repeat.
- Focus on what you know and reassure the media you will find out what you do not know.
- Provide background materials about complex issues.

IV. Develop Your Message

When communicating with the public is necessary, developing and testing (if time permits) your messages is of great importance. This recommendation stems from the need for a strategic approach to crisis communication. In an ideal world all messages would be pre-tested and consistently broadcast throughout the crisis. Obviously due to the emergent nature of crises, this is not always possible. However, some pre-planning should allow for some standards to follow when crafting your message.

The CDC usually develops messages for a variety of audiences. Pre-testing, and audience research are standard steps in this development process. During the anthrax crisis the CDC used communication monitoring as a proxy for audience input as the CDC continuously shaped its messages throughout the crisis.[27] Because bioterrorism was new to the CDC, there were no existing messages and materials to use with nonscientific audiences; today there would be some material available. The CDC used communication inputs from field staff, media briefings, public inquiries, Web sites, and opinion polls to determine what the major messages needed to address. In the case of anthrax, messages regarding exposure and necessary precautions were needed to combat public fears. This method of message development had flaws and barriers to success, but the CDC was able to take some lessons that can prove useful in future crises:

1. Communication monitoring must be a dynamic activity that senior leadership finds useful when planning communication strategies for key audiences.
2. Communication monitoring results must be presented to senior leadership daily and with the same status as information about the ongoing crisis and response.
3. Daily noncrisis communication monitoring needs to be an agency priority if it is going to be a priority in an emergency.

4. Communication monitoring must expand to include not just news media clippings but also media inquiries, public inquiries, field reports, and poll data. A quick guide to communication monitoring must be available to staff brought in from other areas to help in a crisis.

5. Communication monitoring can be done broadly or narrowly. If you have limited time and resources, be selective about the number and type of news sources that you monitor.

6. Because audience research and message pre-testing are not possible in most emergency situations, communication monitoring can be an important proxy for audience input for organizations as they shape and re-shape messages that address public questions and concerns.[28]

Besides communication monitoring, the CDC found opinion polls to be valuable. In a short time health officials were able to determine what the Americans knew, what they believed, and whom they trusted. In a survey following the anthrax crisis, health officials were the top choice as a trusted source of reliable information.[29] This was obviously helpful in determining who should deliver the messages created.

During the BSE crisis not enough emphasis was placed on message development prior to the major crisis. Although there had been some debate over the link between eating beef and the risk of contracting Creutzfeldt-Jakob disease, messages addressing the actual risk were not created. Instead of concise messages about the safety of beef, the public received repetitive messages created by media more interested in sensationalism than facts.[30]

V. Be Honest, Clear, and Compassionate

There are many variables beyond the control of the policy maker or risk communication planner. One example of a common variable that predisposes individuals and multiple publics to vulnerability and poor health outcomes is literacy. Literacy disparities are of concern because low-literacy consumers/patients who do not understand health professionals' instructions will be less apt to make the best decisions or receive high quality care. To reach all people effectively, information must be provided in a variety of formats and reading levels. In calm times, this can be achieved with planning and forethought. In times of crisis, thoughts of public literacy are overshadowed by the need to release information quickly.[31]

As risk communications both inform and provide reassurance, attention to clarity will pay dividends in public trust and health. What can be done in times of crisis? The U.S. Institute of Medicine suggests including members of the intended audience when crafting the message. A review process can include members of the lay public. Principles of plain-language communication and easy-to-read formats should be familiar to organizations prior to a crisis. Attention to literacy in relation to language, format, and structure of message will help broaden their reach.[32]

Besides clarity, connecting with your audience with compassion, empathy, and reassurance are the key elements to public communication in a crisis. This is the exact reason that Mayor Giuliani was so successful at managing a citywide crisis. Because city residents believed that his caring was genuine, he earned public confidence. "Even when the only message is uncertainty, admitting that 'we don't know' is a tried way to earn long-term public confidence."[33]

There are no absolutes in risk management, so one must be wary of over-reassurance, trivializing, and speculating while portraying empathy. Good examples of over-reassurance that backfired include the British Minister of Agriculture encouraging his child to eat a hamburger during the BSE crisis and, more recently, Ann Veneman, Secretary of the U.S. Department of Agriculture, stating that despite the discovery of BSE in the United States, she was having beef for Christmas dinner. These actions alienated people rather than garnering their confidence. To connect with your audience:

- Let your emotions show. Leaders who seem to be without emotion are useless as role models for a public trying to cope with its emotions.

- Let your compassion show, not just for the most obvious victims and their families, but also for less directly affected people.

- Letting your emotions show is not the same thing as describing them. Your language, demeanor, and nonverbal communication should match the situation.

- Fear and sadness are normal responses to many kinds of emergencies. You can best help by showing that you are feeling these emotions, too; that you can recognize, accept, and bear them; and that you are still doing what needs to be done.

- Talk about yourself—though not to the point where you seem to think the most interesting thing about the emergency is that you're on the scene.[34]

VI. Think Before You Speak

Communicating with understandable language, refined and consistent messages, and communicating only what you know are critical. Equally important is the person and method selected to put out the messages on behalf of an administration or organization.

Based on experiences with crises in Belgium, Anthonissen outlined key elements of crisis communication: background information, details about the incident, actions undertaken, sympathy, and consumer reassurance.[35] If these elements are addressed quickly, there is a better chance of avoiding a large-scale scare. Consumer reassurance, however, can hardly be provided immediately because it will be successful only when based on scientific evidence resulting from careful investigation.[36]

The events that led up to the Swedish acrylamide scare offer an example for planned risk communication. The sentinel event in the Swedish acrylamide scare was a planned press conference. Swedish National Food Administration (SNFA) was aware of a soon-to-be-published study conducted by researchers at Stockholm University, and they jointly decided to head off a scare by holding a press conference on the subject. They sent out a carefully worded, but somewhat cryptic, invitation to the press to attend the briefing. A press conference was selected as the best communication tool to deliver their message because they felt it would circumvent any unnecessary miscommunications with journalists and members of the public. In fact, SNFA had held only one press conference in the past 10 years and the researchers had not participated in a press conference, nor did they have media training. The end result was a press conference that perhaps created the scare rather than prevented one.[37]

What began as a well-planned event ended up providing media and communication experts fodder for criticism. The cryptic press invitation coupled with a significant delay before the press conference led to information vacuums and caused rumors and speculation. Although the decision to hold a press conference was made carefully, key questions regarding the purpose of the event were not asked, nor was thorough analysis of available alternatives. In ideal circumstances, both the press invitation as well as the press conference itself should have been pretested. "The most kind thing one can say is that one handled it this way because of a lack of knowledge, that one did not [realize] what signals one sent out when it was done this way."[38]

Based on his analysis of the acrylamide experience, Lofstedt concludes the following :

- Never amplify risks that are, in their very nature, attenuated. Amplifying such risks will lead to public confusion, and in many cases public and media backlash, as happened here.
- High trust institutions will receive more media attention than low trust institutions. This puts certain conditions on how a

high trust institution can and should communicate to media and the public.

- In any communication message, focus on the aspects that are certain and avoid those that are uncertain, if possible. Communicating uncertainty, particularly when it is not necessary, affects the outcome of how the message being communicated will be interpreted by the receiver.

- Finally, one must not forget that risk and science communication is never easy. There is no such thing as a "one size fits all" solution to any communication problem.[39]

In contrast with the Swedish experience and press conferences, New York City was well-prepared to deal with the anthrax crisis through press conferences and media briefings. New York had implemented a routine of twice-daily press conferences since September 11. The Mayor stood at the forefront of the crisis, surrounded by health and public officials, asking the public to trust in his leadership. Because of his experience in this role, the public did trust his statements and supported by other communication vehicles such as broadcast faxes, an updated Web site, and constant communication with the community, the city weathered the crisis better than most cities would have.[40]

Applying Risk Management Theory: The Risk Management/Communication Framework (RMCF)

Overarching Principles and Roles

In 1997, the Presidential/Congressional Commission on Risk Assessment proposed a model for risk management that encompassed processes for identifying and assessing the risks of specific health hazards, implementing activities to eliminate or minimize those risks, communicating risk information, and monitoring and evaluating the results of the interventions and communications. The Food and Drug Administration enhanced that model to the current system for managing risks from medical products, illustrated in Figure 20–1. The activities and elements in the model are still under agency development.

In this chapter the authors have synthesized the evidence base supporting the model from other credible sources. The new RMCF presents the current state of the art and science of how to approach risk.

A key element of the model is the integration of a systems framework in the area of greatest interest to the FDA: medical product risk

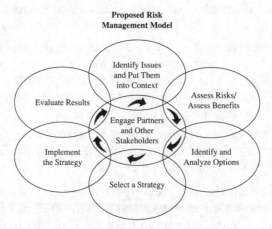

Figure 20–1. FDA Model for Risk Management

management. In the complex system of risk management, the FDA acknowledges that it is only one agency among numerous other groups participating in decision making related to the use of medical products. A systems framework for risk management enables a better integration of all the involved parties' efforts. This approach also facilitates a more comprehensive knowledge base of both the risks involved in using medical products and the sources of those risks.

The proposed RMCF (Figure 20–2) identifies the components of risk management and offers guidance with questions and considerations for each step and stage of the enhanced framework. This framework builds on those models previously cited and developed for managing the risks

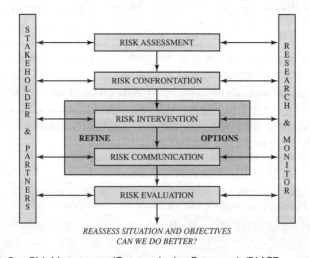

Figure 20–2. Risk Management/Communication Framework (RMCF)

associated with other health and safety issues. The model encompasses the basic processes that are used to identify and assess the risks of specific health hazards and confront the hazard with activities to eliminate or minimize those risks, communicate risk information, and monitor and evaluate the results of the interventions and communication. This new framework encourages a much greater integration of risk management efforts than the current system.

The RMCF builds directly on the framework originally embraced by the FDA. Each step of the framework is guided by concepts that the FDA, Presidential Commission, and external risk communication experts have defined. These are:

1. *Risk Assessment:* Estimation and evaluation of risk
2. *Risk Confrontation:* Determining acceptable level of risk in a larger context
3. *Risk Intervention:* Risk control action
4. *Risk Communication:* Interactive process of exchanging risk information
5. *Risk Management Evaluation:* Measure and ensure effectiveness of risk management efforts.

Stakeholders and Partners

One activity that is clearly articulated in the literature but is often missing in risk management entails engaging health care partners and other stakeholders in risk-benefit analyses. All stakeholders in the risk management system have a role in minimizing the risks for adverse events and damages from improper use of medical products. Stakeholders should collaborate to determine how better data on risks could be collected and shared, so that efforts and interventions can be targeted to the most serious problems, and the effects of interventions can be evaluated.

Second, community-based problem solving that actively involves relevant stakeholders in the decision-making process is critical. For example, the FDA Task Force suggests that risk confrontation is a key element that needs to be a part of any new risk management framework. The RMCF includes stakeholder involvement and concerns at each step. Furthermore, key questions that should be addressed at each step have been adapted from the National Research Council's "Ensuring Completeness: Risk Message Checklist."

The RMCF is also a systematic approach in which stakeholders are engaged throughout the risk management process. Stakeholders include the FDA, industry, health care provider organizations, health care practitioners, professional/consumer organizations, patients, and the public.

Examining the roles of these various participants can identify gaps and misallocation of efforts where improvements can be made. These stakeholders and partners are integrated in future efforts to build trust, mitigate risk, and maximize benefits.

The criteria for selecting stakeholders in RMCF are based on four basic principles:

1. That the participation is sufficiently broad;
2. That the selection process is fair, open, and perceived as fair;
3. That participants who presumably represent interested and affected parties are acceptable to those parties as representative; and
4. That participants bring to the process the kinds of knowledge, experience, and perspectives that are needed for the deliberation at hand.

Organizing appropriately broad deliberation presents significant challenges including managing scarce resources, setting realistic expectations, identifying all the parties that should be involved, and nurturing the process. As often is the case in risk involving industry and government with high stakes and low trust, organizations need to make special efforts to ensure that the interested and affected parties accept and understand key underlying assumptions about the risk-generating processes and risk estimation methods.

Benefits of the RMCF Process

Communities and agencies often have very different notions of what level of public participation is appropriate. A theme that is a central part of the popular literature on public risk perception relates to "trust." Trust is the process by which individuals assign to other persons, groups, agencies, and institutions the responsibility to work on certain tasks. The risk management literature defines the components of trust to include: perceived competence; objectivity; fairness or procedural equity in decision making; consistency, and faith (a perception of goodwill in composing information).

When citizens participate in a risk management decision, they are more likely to accept it for three principal reasons:

1. They have instituted changes that make it objectively more acceptable.
2. They have moved past the process issue of control and mastered the technical data on risk; that is, they have learned why the experts consider it acceptable.

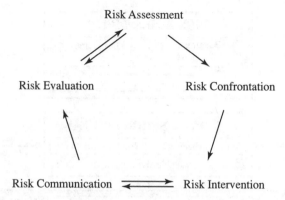

Risk Assessment

Risk Evaluation   Risk Confrontation

Risk Communication ⇄ Risk Intervention

Figure 20–3. Inter-relationships among Assessment, Confrontation, Intervention, Communication, and Evaluation of Risks

3. They have been heard and not excluded, and therefore can appreciate the legitimacy of the decision even if they continue to dislike the decision itself.

The appropriate level of stakeholder involvement depends on the situation. The Presidential/Congressional Commission on Risk Assessment and Risk Management offers the following factors to consider in determining the nature and extent of stakeholder involvement:

1. The complexity, uncertainty, impact, and level of controversy associated with the decision to be made;
2. The urgency with which the problem must be addressed; and
3. The extent to which participants have a genuine influence on the decision.[41]

In the RMCF, each element is interrelated: for example, poor risk assessment cannot be overcome with excellent risk communication. RMCF has key questions as well as considerations that are critical for developing solutions and strategies. Step one identifies the issue or hazard, its context, and the perceptions held by the stakeholders. Step two focuses on assessing the risks versus the benefits associated with the issue. Step three identifies options and presents analysis so that actions can be developed. Step four selects and implements strategies, while step five focuses on evaluating the first four steps in the process. The double arrows in the RMCF pentagonal diagram (Figure 20–3) represent the element of trust.

The following flowchart (Figure 20–4) represents some of the questions for illustrative purposes:

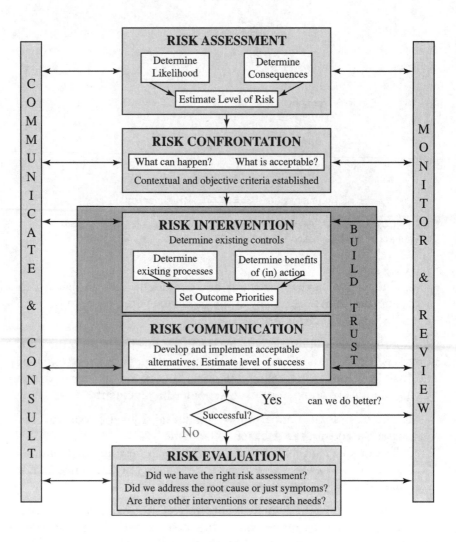

Figure 20–4. Detailed Flowchart of the RMCF

Lessons Learned

The information presented here, including the six principles and the RMCF, summarize the lessons learned by past communication efforts during crises, and introduce a framework for applying them. As we have seen, the acrylamide crisis presents the pitfalls of uncertainty about message and the need to cultivate relationships with the media. The BSE scare demonstrates the necessity of involving stakeholders at an early stage and the importance of maintaining credibility as an organization. The Coca-Cola crisis illustrates the need for fast provision of adequate, reliable, and sufficient information to consumers.[42] The threat of anthrax is a prime example of the importance of establishing trust and the necessity of constantly monitoring the public's reaction to the crisis. September 11 taught the United States that a crisis can occur without warning and the need to communicate with the public can be instantaneous. Planning for these communications is the overarching lesson.

Conclusion

It can be simple to find flaws in past crisis communications. Those in charge worked under pressure, often without full knowledge of the facts and did their best to communicate what they knew. What we can take from the past are the lessons and results and build them into planning for future crises. There is a gold standard of communication. It is based on a strategic approach, one that works with stakeholders to deliver a strong and consistent message, all the while building public confidence and trust. There are guidelines and frameworks presented by those who were faced with crises past. It is up to the health administrations to plan and prepare for the future by training staff and building these tenets into their communication policy.

Notes

1. V. Covello et al., "Risk Communication, the West Nile Virus Epidemic, and Bioterrorism: Responding to the Communication Challenges Posed by the Intentional or Unintentional Release of a Pathogen in an Urban Setting," *Journal of Urban Health: Bulletin of the New York Academy of Medicine* 78 (2001): 382–391.

2. P. C. Stern and H. V. Feinberg, eds., *Understanding Risk: Informing Decisions in a Democratic Society* (Washington, DC: National Research Council, Committee on Risk Characterization, 1996), 27.

3. M. Chamberlain, "Avoiding, Averting and Managing Crisis: A Checklist for the Future," in *The Mad Cow Crisis: Health and the Public Good*, ed. S. Ratzan (New York University Press, 1998), 169–175.

4. National Research Council, *Improving Risk Communication* (National Academy Press, 1989).

5. P. Sandman, http://www.petersandman.com/.

6. K. Fearn-Banks, "Crisis Communication: A Review of Some Best Practices," in *Handbook of Public Relations*, ed. R. Heath (Thousand Oaks, CA: Sage Publications, 2000), 479–485.

7. S. G. Stolberg and J. Miller, "A Nature Challenged: Medicine; Bioterror Role an Uneasy Fit for the CDC," *The New York Times 1A* (2001): 1.

8. World Health Organization: Emerging and Other Communicable Diseases, Surveillance and Control. Global Surveillance, Diagnosis, and Therapy of Human Transmissible Spongiform Encephalopathies: Report of a WHO Consultation. Geneva, Switzerland (1998).

9. V. Covello, "Best Practices in Public Health Risk and Crisis Communication," *Journal of Health Communication* 8(1S) (2003): 5–8.

10. Covello, "Best Practices in Public Health Risk and Crisis Communication."

11. S. Ratzan, "Strategies for Attaining Public Health," in *The Mad Cow Crisis: Health and the Public Good*, ed. S. Ratzan (New York: University Press, 1998), 182–208.

12. Presidential/Congressional Commission on Risk Assessment and Risk Management, *Framework for Environmental Health Risk Management—Final Report* 1 (1997).

13. M. Vanderford, "Communication Lessons Learned in the Emergency Operations Center during CDC's Anthrax Response: A Commentary," *Journal of Health Communication* 8(1S) (2003): 11–13.

14. S. Hughes, "Protecting Health: Can the U.K. Do Better?" in *The Mad Cow Crisis: Health and the Public Good*, ed. S. Ratzan (New York: University Press, 1998), 111–117.

15. W. Verbeke and P. Van Kenhove, "Impact of Emotional Stability and Attitude on Consumption Decisions under Risk: The Coca-Cola Crisis in Belgium," *Journal of Health Communication* 7(5) (2002): 455–472.

16. R. E. Lofstedt, "Good and bad examples of siting and building biosafety level 4 laboratories: A Study of Winnipeg, Galveston, and Etobicoke," *Journal of Hazardous Materials* 93(1) (2002): 47–66.

17. D. Shore, "Communicating in Times of Uncertainty: The Need for Trust," *Journal of Health Communication* 8(1S) (2003): 13–14.

18. V. Covello and F. Allen, *Seven Cardinal Rules of Risk Communication* (Washington, DC: U.S. Environmental Protection Agency, Office of Policy Analysis, 1988).

19. D. McCallum, S. Hammond, and V. Covello, "Communication about Environmental Risks: How the Public Uses and Perceives Information Sources," *Health Education Quarterly* 18 (1991): 349–361.

20. M. Bunn, "Aspects of Consumer Search for Health Information: A Framework for Structuring Information Problems," *Health Marketing Quarterly* 11 (1994): 75–98.

21. M. S. Wilkes, "The public dissemination of medical research: Problems and solutions," *Journal of Health Communication* 2(1) (1997); 3–15.

22. W. E. Pollard, "Public Perceptions of Information Sources Concerning Bioterrorism before and after Anthrax Attacks: An Analysis of National Survey Data," *Journal of Health Communication* 8(1S) (2003): 93–103.

23. Lofstedt, "Good and bad examples of siting and building biosafety level 4 laboratories: A Study of Winnipeg, Galveston, and Etobicoke."

24. W. Verbeke, J. Viaene, and O. Guiot, "Health Communication and Consumer Behavior on Meat in Belgium: From BSE until Dioxin," *Journal of Health Communication* 4(4) (1999): 345–357.

25. D. Dornbusch, "An Analysis of Media Coverage of the BSE Crisis in Britain," in *The Mad Cow Crisis: Health and the Public Good*, ed. S. Ratzan (New York: University Press, 1998), 138–152.

26. F. Mebane, S. Temin, and C. Parvanta, "Communicating Anthrax in 2001: A Comparison of CDC Information and Print Media Accounts," *Journal of Health Communication* 8(1S) (2003): 50–82.

27. C. Prue et al., "Communication Monitoring: Shaping CDC's Emergency Risk Communication Efforts," *Journal of Health Communication* 8(1S) (2003): 35–49.

28. Prue et al., "Communication Monitoring: Shaping CDC's Emergency Risk Communication Efforts."

29. Pollard, "Public Perceptions of Information Sources Concerning Bioterrorism before and after Anthrax Attacks: An Analysis of National Survey Data."

30. Ratzan, "Strategies for Attaining Public Health."

31. R. Rudd, J. Comings, and J. Hyde, "Leave No One Behind: Improving Health and Risk Communication through Attention to Literacy," *Journal of Health Communication* 8(1S) (2003): 104–115.

32. Rudd, Comings, and Hyde, "Leave No One Behind: Improving Health and Risk Communication through Attention to Literacy."

33. J. P. Koplan, "Communication during Public Health Emergencies," *Journal of Health Communication* 8(1S) (2003): 144–145.

34. Sandman, http://www.petersandman.com/.

35. P. F. Anthonissen, "Murphy was een optimist: Hoe ondernemingen door crisiscommunicatie in leven bleven" [Murphy was an optimist: How companies survived thanks to crisis communication]. (Tielt, Belgium: Uitgeverij Lannoo, 2001).

36. Verbeke and Van Kenhove, "Impact of Emotional Stability and Attitude on Consumption Decisions under Risk: The Coca-Cola Crisis in Belgium."

37. R. E. Lofstedt, "Science communication in the Swedish acrylamide 'alarm'," *Journal of Health Communication* 8(5) (2003): 407–432.

38. I. Hedlund, "Larmet a"r oserio" st." [The alarm is not serious], *Expressen* (April 25, 2002): 1.

39. Lofstedt, "Science communication in the Swedish acrylamide 'alarm'."

40. S. Mullin, "The Anthrax Attacks in New York City: The 'Giuliani Press Conference Model' and Other Communication Strategies That Helped," *Journal of Health Communication* 8(1S) (2003): 15–16.

41. Presidential/Congressional Commission on Risk Assessment and Risk Management, *Framework for Environmental Health Risk Management—Final Report*.

Appendix I: Maxims for Effective Communication on Health and Risk Issues

I. Develop a theme/goal with common interests (e.g., "We are interested in the health and safety of our community").
- Identify clear and explicit objectives (short-term and long-term).
- Establish a common agenda while recognizing political/economic interests and hidden agendas.
- Base information on needs assessment and ethical community values.

II. Identify all parties that have an interest in the issue (nongovernmental organizations, trade associations, media, government, public, etc.).
- Build coalitions/partnerships with those integral for successful delivery of information.
- Work with other credible sources.
- Recruit competent spokespeople with your participants.
- Establish roles for the media, advocacy groups, organizations, the public, etc.

III. Identify the intended audiences, their concerns, and the potential mechanisms to reach them.
- Listen and understand your audience, including cultural variables.
- Measure public opinion—survey, polls, baseline, etc.
- Conduct formative research—focus groups, observational studies, survey/baseline.
- Identify communication patterns of the audience (e.g., how do they get information)

IV. Develop a strategic approach to communicate with public(s).
- Open communication channels immediately in crisis.
- Choose a competent spokesperson, recognize emotions, speak clearly and understandably.
- Choose a message, pre-test and adapt it, and establish tracking mechanism(s).
- The actual audience perhaps cares more about fairness, competence, and empathy than data and statistics.
- Build trust with honest and open disclosure—never lie.
- Use objective criteria, standards, and benchmarks for your planning and implementation.

V. Communicate a consistent and credible message.
- Create inter- and intra-organizational mechanisms for delivery of messages.
- Consult with appropriate parties before making major decisions or announcements.
- Use risk comparisons to help put risks in perspective; avoid comparisons that trivialize.
- Focus on credibility with a high-level, consistent messenger.

VI. Establish mechanisms for direct public/audience communication.
- Utilize existing media with openness and accessibility.
- Establish trust and interactivity—news media, radio call-in, free calls, bulletin boards, etc.
- Tell people what your limitations are; you cannot do everything.
- Discuss actions underway or to be taken.
- If in doubt, share more rather than less information.

VII. Maximize your communication effectiveness.
- Acknowledge and respond to emotions.
- Avoid instant, abstract, or harsh language about deaths, injuries, and illnesses.
- Speak with compassion, using simple, nontechnical language.
- Use visual, vivid, and vocal images that connect at a personal level.
- Use examples and anecdotes that are culturally sensitive and make data come alive.
- Create a relationship with the public(s) by offering realistic, compliance-prone actions.

VIII. Evaluate your interventions/efforts on intended audiences.
- Tracking: Did your audience make the desired decision? Assess and evaluate with outcome and impact measures.
- Did you build relationships with key participants?
- Are you more prepared for the next intervention? Next steps?

Source: Available at http://www.who.int/emc-documents/tse/docs/whoemczdi989.pdf.

Appendix II: Best Practices in Public Health Risks and Crisis Communication

Best Practice 1. Accept and Involve Stakeholders as Legitimate Partners
Guidelines

- Demonstrate respect for persons affected by risk management decisions by involving them early, before important decisions are made.
- Involve all parties that have an interest or a stake in the particular risk.
- Include in the decision-making process the broad range of factors involved in determining public perceptions of risk, concern, and outrage.
- Use a wide range of communication channels to engage and involve stakeholders.
- Adhere to the highest ethical standards; recognize that people hold you professionally and ethically accountable.
- Strive for mutually beneficial outcomes.

Best Practice 2. Listen to People
Guidelines

- Before taking action, find out what people know, think, or want done about risks.
- Use techniques such as interviews, facilitated discussion groups, information exchanges, availability sessions, advisory groups, toll-free numbers, and surveys.
- Let all parties with an interest or a stake in the issue be heard.
- Let people know that what they said has been understood and tell them what actions will follow.
- Empathize with your audience and try to put yourself in their place.
- Acknowledge the validity of people's emotions.
- Emphasize communication channels that encourage listening, feedback, participation, and dialogue.
- Recognize that competing agendas, symbolic meanings, and broader social, cultural, economic, or political considerations can complicate risk communication.

Best Practice 3. Be Truthful, Honest, Frank, and Open
Guidelines

- Disclose risk information as soon as possible; fill information vacuums.
- If information is evolving or incomplete, emphasize appropriate reservations about its reliability.
- If in doubt, lean toward sharing more information, not less—or people can think something significant is being hidden or withheld.
- If you don't know, or are unsure about an answer, express willingness to get back to the questioner with a response by an agreed-upon deadline. Do not speculate.
- Discuss data and information uncertainties, strengths, and weaknesses—including those identified by other credible sources.
- Identify worst-case estimates as such, and cite ranges of risk estimates when appropriate.
- Do not minimize or exaggerate the level of risk; do not over-reassure.
- If errors are made, correct them quickly.

Best Practice 4. Coordinate, Collaborate, and Partner with Other Credible Sources
Guidelines

- Coordinate all inter-organizational and intra-organizational communications.
- Devote effort and resources to the slow, hard work of building partnerships and alliances with other organizations.
- Use credible and authoritative intermediaries between you and your target audience.
- Consult with others to decide who is best able to take the lead in responding to questions or concerns about risks. Document those decisions.
- Cite credible sources that believe what you believe; issue communications with or through other trustworthy sources.
- Do not attack individuals or organizations with higher perceived credibility.

Best Practice 5. Meet the Needs of the Media
Guidelines

- Be accessible to reporters; respect their deadlines.

- Prepare a limited number of key messages before media interactions; take control of the interview and repeat your key messages several times.

- Keep interviews short. Agree with the reporter in advance about the specific topic of the interview and stick to this topic during the interview.

- Say only what you want the media to repeat; everything you say is on the record.

- Tell the truth.

- Provide background materials about complex risk issues.

- Provide information tailored to the needs of each type of medium. For example, provide sound bites and visuals for television.

- If you do not know the answer to a question, focus on what you do know and tell the reporter what actions you will take to get an answer.

- Be aware of, and respond effectively to, media pitfalls and trick questions.

- Avoid saying "no comment."

- Follow up on stories with praise or criticism, as warranted.

- Work to establish long-term relationships with editors and reporters.

Best Practice 6. Communicate Clearly and with Compassion
Guidelines

- Use clear, nontechnical language appropriate to the target audience.

- Use graphics and other pictorial material to clarify messages.

- Personalize risk data. Use stories, narratives, examples, and anecdotes to make technical data come alive.

- Avoid embarrassing people.

- Respect the unique communication needs of special and diverse audiences.

- Express genuine empathy. Acknowledge, and say, that any illness, injury, or death is a tragedy to be avoided.

- Avoid using distant, abstract, unfeeling language when discussing harm, deaths, injuries, and illnesses.

- Acknowledge and respond in words, gestures, and actions to emotions that people express such as anxiety, fear, anger, outrage, and helplessness.

- Acknowledge and respond to the distinctions that the public views as important in evaluating risks.
- Use risk comparisons to help put risks in perspective; make sure those comparisons take into account the distinctions the public considers important.
- Identify specific actions that people can take to protect themselves and to maintain control of the situation at hand.
- Always try to include a discussion of actions that are underway or can be taken.
- Be sensitive to local norms, such as speech and dress.
- Strive for brevity, but respect requests for information and offer to provide desired information within a specified time period.
- Promise only what you can deliver, then follow through.
- Understand that trust is earned—do not ask or expect to be trusted by the public.

Best Practice 7. Plan Thoroughly and Carefully
Guidelines

- Begin with clear, explicit objectives—such as providing information, establishing trust, encouraging appropriate actions, stimulating emergency response, or involving stakeholders in dialogue, partnerships, and joint problem solving.
- Identify important stakeholders and subgroups within the audience; respect diversity and design communications for specific stakeholders.
- Recruit spokespersons with effective presentation and personal interaction skills.
- Train staff—including technical staff—in basic, intermediate, and advanced risk and crisis communication skills. Recognize and reward outstanding performance.
- Anticipate questions and issues.
- Prepare and pre-test messages.
- Carefully evaluate risk communication efforts and learn from mistakes.
- Share what you have learned with others.

Source: Vincent T. Covello, Ph.D., Director, Center for Risk Communication, New York, New York. Published in *Journal of Health Communication*, 8 (2003):5–8. Copyright (c) Taylor & Francis Inc.

CHAPTER TWENTY-ONE

Emergency/Risk Communication to Promote Public Health and Respond to Biological Threats

*Gary L. Kreps, Kenneth Alibek, Linda Neuhauser,
Katherine E. Rowan, and Lisa Sparks*

Chapter Questions

1. What makes a health message credible? What are some ways to enhance the credibility of messages?
2. What are the challenges to making emergency communications relevant and understandable to various sub-groups of society? How can the Biodefense Communication Model address these challenges?
3. What are the key elements of the Biodefense Communication Model?

Introduction

Communication is a critical component of efforts to prevent, prepare for, and respond to biological threats. Effective emergency communication facilitates sharing essential information and coordinating activities among priority interdependent policy makers, security personnel, health care providers, and members of the general public who need to work together in times of crisis.[1-3] A report from the Institute of Medicine concludes,

> Efforts to improve the global capacity to address microbial threats should be coordinated with key international agencies such as the World Health Organization (WHO) and based in the appropriate U.S. federal agencies (e.g., the Centers for Disease Control and Prevention [CDC], the Department of Defense [DOD], the National Institutes of

Health [NIH], the Agency for International Development [USAID], the Department of Agriculture [USDA]), with active communication and coordination among these agencies and in collaboration with private organizations and foundations. Investments should take the form of financial and technical assistance, operational research, enhanced surveillance, and efforts to share both knowledge and best public health practices across national boundaries.[4]

Increasingly, it is essential for mutually dependent groups of policy makers, security personnel, health care workers, and the public to gather information to discover potential risks for biological contamination, to understand the nature of such threats, to identify incidences of contamination, and to guide development of the best strategies for responding to and minimizing harm from such problems.[5–7]

In times of biological threat, it is important to have successful communication across agencies and to disseminate timely and accurate information with the public, especially with those individuals who are most at risk. Public information about biological threats must be carefully developed into messages that key groups can clearly understand and use. These messages have to be strategically disseminated through communication channels that these groups can easily access. The messages should be presented by sources the specific intended audiences trust.[8–9] Carefully gathered and interpreted information is of utmost importance in times of emergency to quickly and accurately gauge the nature and intensity of potential threats, and to determine the best strategies for response.[10]

Information must be presented quickly and meaningfully about serious biological hazards to many diverse groups of people, who differ greatly in their education, expertise, and capacities to understand and act on complicated health threats. The fears and apprehensions surrounding biological hazards can be minimized by providing the public with sound, sensible information that is both accurate and reassuring, reducing risks of mass hysteria, public panic, and loss of confidence in the authorities.[11] Risk information must be presented to reduce panic, promote understanding, motivate compliance with important life-preserving recommendations, and encourage broad collaboration with community representatives, and health and safety workers. National health information systems can help support the communication demands of responding effectively to serious biological emergencies.

Information Credibility

According to Pollard, biodefense information must be presented by trusted, expert, and credentialed information sources to be believable.[12] For example, public health information can be presented by important health professionals representing major public agencies (such as the Surgeon General, the Director of the CDC, or local public health officials). Likewise, the most credible sources of security information might be leading officials (such as the Director of the FBI, local police chiefs, or military leaders). One difficulty is that audiences often differ in their judgments about which sources are most credible on specific issues. Therefore, biological threat information sources should be selected based on their perceived credibility by the intended audiences for the messages. Using opinion surveys to find out who people trust can be very helpful to guide official communication strategies.[13] Studies indicate that during disease outbreaks most Americans prefer to receive health advice from their personal physicians. Such findings point to the importance of enlisting primary care physicians, if possible, as sources of health information dissemination in times of biological threat.[14–15] Most U.S. county health departments have now established biological risk information networks for local physicians.

Another strategy to improve the credibility of messages is to reinforce people's efforts to understand warning messages. Disaster research finds that although people often initially respond with denial, they subsequently spend significant time confirming the accuracy of the message, arriving at a warning belief, and assessing their own personal risk.[16] Community members are more likely to interpret warnings constructively when their initial confirmatory efforts are supported.[17–20] Effective support strategies include creating hotlines to answer questions and providing background information on emergent risks at Web sites. In non-emergency times, hosting "open houses" at facilities perceived as susceptible to threat can help community members identify local individuals whom they perceive as credible.[21] Crisis spokespersons can also help by analyzing and responding to the stories people develop as they attempt to make sense of crises.[22]

Consistency is another important feature of credible emergency communication. Biological risk information must be consistent across the range of messages and communication channels. Otherwise, messages can conflict and result in confusion, frustration, and misinformation. Because it is often necessary to customize information to the regional, occupational, or other needs of specific different groups, it is important to specify the exact guidance for each group or situation. Due to the complexities of responses required for various biological threats, key messages can need to be repeated and clarified using different message content and communication channels. Message redundancy must be calibrated so that it clarifies complex messages, without overwhelming or irritating key audiences. For example, if there are too many messages sent, recipients often cope with the overload by blocking out the alarm or trivializing it.

Communication Channels

Selecting the appropriate communication channels to disseminate biological threat information is essential to effective risk communication. In the same way that different groups perceive the credibility of information sources differentially, they are also likely to have preferences for specific channels of communication for health-related messages. For example, new information technologies can be used effectively to communicate biodefense information and to protect public health in times of crisis.[23–25] Technologically sophisticated groups of people might prefer to receive biological risk updates via e-mail, because they check their e-mail several times per day. For those who are not connected to the Internet, this is not a viable option. Radio and television can provide emergency information in a very dramatic way to many people, but the messages are fleeting and information can be missed.[26] It is difficult to know which audiences were exposed to and impacted by radio and television messages. Because such a large and diverse audience has access to radio and television, these channels can be best for providing general information and not necessarily for providing unique messages appropriate only to specific groups. More personalized channels of communication, such as mail, telephone, and face-to-face personal communication can be necessary when there are concerns about information privacy or specificity.[27]

Two-way interaction between senders and receivers is important to ensure the most successful communication.[28] This requires that there be feedback channels for different groups of people to determine how well diverse groups understand emergency communication. Feedback channels can provide answers to people's questions and thus help clarify information received by diverse audiences. Telephone hotlines, interactive Web pages, and e-mail contacts are effective feedback channels. As for one-way communication channels, these feedback channels must be familiar and easy-to-use for the target audiences. It is important to carefully analyze the different audiences for emergency messages to determine the best message strategies, information sources, and channels for communicating effectively with unique groups.

Currently, there are major barriers to meeting the biodefense communication needs of subgroups who vary with respect to language, culture, literacy, disability, and information connectivity.[29–31] Most health and safety information in the United States is presented in English, and secondarily in Spanish, restricting access for those who speak other languages. For example, although Web sites are often a preferred channel to provide constantly updated biological emergency information, 98 percent of U.S. Web sites are in English.[32] There is some evidence that state agencies are addressing this issue. It is encouraging that a Public Health Preparedness Survey conducted by the U.S. Association of State and Territorial Health Officers (ASTHO) found that the state risk communications plans addressing language differences increased from 38 percent to 73 percent during 2002.[33]

Another issue is that cultural differences are particularly important in the communication of biological emergency information, and this can invoke strong feelings of vulnerability and mistrust in certain audiences. For example, cultural differences in expressing grief and responding to death make it important to tailor communication about biological crises.[34] Studies show that if communication is not culturally appropriate, it can provoke distrust or hostility toward the official communicators and even cause a setback in emergency efforts.

Low literacy is another barrier. The National Adult Literacy Survey found that an estimated one-half of Americans are functionally or marginally illiterate.[35] In contrast, most health-related materials typically require high school, college, or graduate reading levels. Further, risk communication often involves complex vocabularies that are not familiar to the average person. Although online information is often used for crisis communication, only 1 percent of this information is usable by people with low literacy. "Multiple literacies"—using browsers, spelling, selecting from a large database, and even typing—are often required for people using Internet communication. Unfortunately, literacy barriers affect those vulnerable populations that are most in need of good communication.

Similarly, disability issues require that risk communication be carefully disseminated. Learning and cognitive disabilities can limit people's reading abilities at an elementary school level, and a great deal of information is inaccessible to people with eyesight limitations. People who are deaf or hard of hearing can have difficulties with emergency communication that is received by automated phone calls from health and safety agencies. People with disabilities that prevent typing and using a mouse often have trouble accessing the Internet. The U.S. Department of Commerce[36] found that people with disabilities were much less likely to use computers or the Internet, and about 30 million Americans with disabilities have restricted access to Internet information.

Socio-demographic differences also affect access to communication channels. An estimated 42 percent of Americans lacked access to the Internet in 2002.[37] The "digital have-nots" are primarily from low income, minority, older, and disabled populations who are the hardest to reach for preparedness and crisis response. Such groups require other media channels for biological risk communication. An underlying factor that contributes to the weaknesses of communication for diverse and vulnerable populations is that members of these groups are rarely involved in the design and testing of communication.[38] Community-based approaches involving key audiences are critical in risk communication efforts.

Prevention, Preparation, and Response to Biological Threats

Kreps and his colleagues developed a relevant three-stage "Strategic Biodefense Communication Model," as seen in Figure 21–1, of preventing, preparing for, and responding to biological threats that applies nicely to our analysis of emergency communication during biological risks. The model builds on Dudley's conclusion that effective biodefense efforts depend on coordinating communications to promote awareness, surveillance, mobilization, and response.[39] The model focuses on prevention of biological threats as the central and constant communication activity for biological emergency efforts. All other emergency communication efforts are built on initial prevention efforts. However, even the best prevention efforts cannot help avert all biological threats, and communication activities must also be geared toward preparing key groups to mobilize actions to respond effectively to biological hazards. Strategic communication is needed to prevent, prepare for, and respond effectively to biological threats.

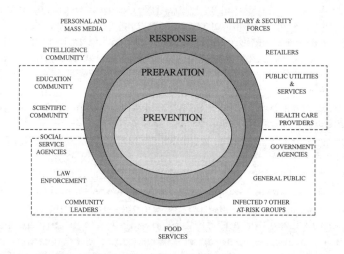

Figure 21–1. The Strategic Biodefense Communication Model

The outer circle of the model describes the critical communication activities needed to respond effectively to biological hazards once such problems occur. Generally, these response activities are intended to activate the plans developed in the preparation. However, emergency response communication must be able to adjust to changing conditions. Scholars of chaos theory suggest that in times of crisis, logical planning does not always reflect the unpredictable and equivocal nature of crises, and crisis communications must take into account unexpected events and suggest novel strategies for responding to crises.[40] Surrounding the concentric circles of the "Strategic Biodefense Communication Model" are examples of the many interdependent groups who must coordinate activities and share information in biodefense efforts.

Communicating to Prevent Biological Threats

The first step in biodefense prevention is coordinated in-depth intelligence-gathering efforts to identify potentially important health risks before they are imminent.[41–42] Intelligence-gathering activities involve actively seeking regular updates from extensive networks of informants and organizational contacts to uncover threatening plans and activities.[43] Biohazard intelligence is also gathered through close (and often unobtrusive) surveillance of group activities and environmental conditions that might identify risk factors and indicators, including monitoring communications among terrorist groups, tracking any unauthorized or suspicious access to contagious substances, and identifying epidemiologic evidence of biological contagion and disease from around the world.[44–45]

The prevention stage also seeks to increase public safety by monitoring information about ways that biohazards might be delivered to citizens, as well as identifying and closing down potential access points that can introduce contagious bio-agents. Examples of access points include, for example, food sources and distribution sites, the water supply, air and ventilation sources, various modes of transportation, border crosspoints, airports, and other transportation centers. Information gathered can inform development of and refinement of security measures to minimize opportunities for the introduction of biohazards.

Communicating to Prepare for Biological Threats

Careful planning is needed to organize many interdependent activities proactively to enable effective responses biological threats if they occur.[46–47] For example, medical personnel need to have adequate medical supplies, equipment, and services available to respond to potential health hazards.[48–49] Concerted planning is required to educate infection control personnel about the specific etiology of contagious substances and the best responses to them.[50]

Communication is the primary tool for disseminating information to these groups of professionals about the best strategies to protect the public from bio-contamination. A key communication approach is the development and dissemination of guidelines for key health and safety personnel for concerted response to biological threats. Similarly, communication processes are needed to support community planning for emergencies, such as creating simulated response drills to aid rapid responses to biological emergencies.[51–52] Public education about potential biological threats is essential, especially due to heightened fears of bioterrorism after the events of September 11, 2001, and the subsequent anthrax scare.[53–54] Federal agencies, such as the CDC and the Federal Emergency Management Association have developed plans for guiding coordinated responses to biological emergencies.[55]

Another communication challenge is to quickly and effectively disseminate results of research about infectious disease detection, vaccination, and treatment to practitioners.[56] Web sites that can be easily updated are an effective way to make this information available to key health and safety communities.[57] Rosen, Koop, and Grigg advocate for a "cybercare" information system that can enable rapid mobilization of health care resources wherever needed.[58]

The Center for Community Wellness at the University of California, Berkeley has developed a promising approach to reach diverse audiences with preparedness information (www.ucwellness.org). The intervention involves incorporating emergency preparedness advice and community, state, and national referrals into general health guides that go to millions of households each year. The guides are collaboratively developed by and tested with groups of people from multiple socioeconomic, cultural, and linguistic backgrounds and disability conditions. The resources are produced in hard copy, Braille, audio, and online formats.

Communicating to Respond to Biological Threats

There is a dramatic need to use communication to effectively mobilize efforts and implement coordinated responses among interrelated health and safety officials and the affected publics in the event of significant biological hazards. Yet, the ASTHO report on preparedness suggests a lack of guidance for public health officers on principles and practical processes for developing communication for multiple audiences. People who are at the greatest risk from the biohazards must be contacted and provided with the best available prevention, treatment, and response information.[59] Public responses can be informed by automatic infectious disease surveillance systems, and electronic sensors to detect biological hazards can quickly detect cases of biological emergency.[60–61]

Responsive communication in times of biological emergency demands development of a coordinated plan for media relations to promote the most accurate and strategic coverage of biological emergencies.[62] This means coordinating media coverage via numerous news channels, including television, radio, newspapers, the Internet, magazines, news wire services, and many other news information sources. Effective news coverage can provide basic information, identify key communication channels for follow-up information, and help to reassure the public in emergencies. Ineffective news coverage can have many negative effects, such as increasing confusion, spreading misinformation, and even causing public panic. Local, regional, national, and even international media can be effective at disseminating relevant information if key media representatives (such as reporters) are provided with the latest and most accurate information, and treated as important and respected partners in biodefense efforts. The CDC has taken the lead to provide accurate and quickly updated information (http//:www.cdc.gov and http://www.bt.cdc.gov/) about biodefense and other health emergencies directly to U.S. state health and safety agencies through its Health Alert Network. The CDC's credibility makes it a trusted information source for the general public. In addition, most states have now also developed their own sites for professionals and the public. However, there is still a significant challenge to make this information accessible to people who are not digitally connected or have barriers related to literacy, language, culture, or disability.

Further research is needed on science, health, risk, and crisis communication to guide efforts to build effective media relations.[63–67] A government publication offering research-based tips for crisis and risk spokespersons is a notable resource. There are an increasing number of Web sites that offer reporters in-depth, accessible explanations of the science behind news events. For example, the University of Wisconsin's Why Files (http://whyfiles.org) offers news stories with explanations of relevant biological hazards. Research on the Why Files and other interactive sources designed to help journalists suggests that these resources deepen users' understanding of complexities and can enhance coverage quality.[68–69]

Conclusions

Communication is a critical process in preventing, preparing for, and responding to serious biological threats and emergencies. Effective risk communication requires a high degree of government and community collaboration and poses special challenges to developers and practitioners. Communication is essential to coordinate groups of health and safety professionals affected by biological threats. Biodefense communication requires advance preparation and constant and accurate updating during crises. Multiple channels of human and mediated communication (including the use of new information technologies) must be strategically coordinated to help prevent biological threats, identify the risks of such threats, prepare for biological hazards, and coordinate effective, evidence-based responses to biological emergencies. Audiences must be carefully analyzed, messages finely crafted, and channels appropriately selected to meet the needs of diverse groups. Care must be taken to identify credible spokespersons and work cooperatively with media representatives to ensure that accurate and timely information is delivered to those most affected.

Notes

1. V. T. Covello, "Best Practices in Public Health Risk and Crisis Communication," *Journal of Health Communication* 23 (2003): 164–193.
2. B. Riley, "Information Sharing in Homeland Security and Homeland Defense: How the Department of Defense Is Helping," *Journal of Homeland Security* 2003. Accessed January 15, 2004, from: http://www.homelandsecurity.org/journal/articles/displayArticle.asp?article=97.
3. P. C. Tangm, "AMIA Advocates National Health Information System in Fight Against National Health Threats," *Journal of the American Medical Informatics Association* 9(2) 2002: 123–126.
4. M. S. Smolinski, M. A. Hamburg, and J. Lederberg (eds.), *Microbial Threats to Health Emergence, Detection, and Response* (Washington, DC: The National Academy Press, 2003).
5. G. L. Kreps et al., "The Critical Role of Communication in Preparing for Biological Threats: Prevention, Mobilization, and Response," in *Communication, Communities, and Terrorism*, eds. D. O'Hair, R. Heath, and G. Ledlow (Westport, CT: Praeger Publishers, in press).
6. T. May and R. Silverman, "Bioterrorism Defense Priorities," *Science* 301(5629) (2003): 17.
7. L. A. Talbot, "Biological Threats to America's Health," *Biological Research for Nursing* 4(4) (2003): 241–243.
8. W. W. Pollard, "Public Perceptions of Information Sources Concerning Bioterrorism before and after Anthrax Attacks: An Analysis of Survey Data," *Journal of Health Communication* 8 (2003): 93–103.

9. D. A. Shore, "Communicating in Times of Uncertainty: The Need for Trust," *Journal of Health Communication* 8 (2003): 13–14.

10. J. M. Teich et al., "The Informatics Response in Disaster, Terrorism, and War," *Journal of the American Medical Informatics Association* 9(2) (2002): 97–104.

11. A. Moscrop, "Mass Hysteria Is Seen as Main Threat from Bioweapons," *British Medical Journal* 323(7320) (2003): 1023.

12. Pollard, "Public Perceptions of Information Sources Concerning Bioterrorism before and after Anthrax Attacks: An Analysis of Survey Data."

13. R. J. Blendon et al., "Using Opinion Surveys to Track the Public's Response to a Bioterrorist Attack," *Journal of Health Communication* 8 (2003): 83–92.

14. R. J. Blendon et al., "The Impact of Anthrax Attacks on the American Public," *Medscape General Medicine* 17(4) (2002): 1.

15. A. Kittler et al., "The Internet as a Vehicle to Communicate Health Information during a Public Health Emergency: A Survey Analysis Involving the Anthrax Scare of 2001," *Journal of Medical Internet Research* 6(1) (2004): e8. URL: http://www.jmir.org/2004/1/e8/.

16. T. E. Drabek, "Disaster Warning and Evacuation Responses by Private Business Employees," *Disasters* 25 (2001): 76–94.

17. R. R. Dynes and T. E. Drabek, "The Structure of Disaster Research: Its Policy and Disciplinary Implications," *International Journal of Mass Emergencies and Disasters* 12 (1994): 5–23.

18. R. W. Perry and M. K. Lindell, "Understanding Citizen Response to Disasters with Implications for Terrorism," *Journal of Contingencies and Crisis Management* 11 (2003): 49–60.

19. K. E. Rowan et al., "The "CAUSE" Model: A Research-Supported Guide for Physicians Communicating Cancer Risk," *Health Communication* 15 (2003): 239–252.

20. P. M. Sandman, *Responding to Community Outrage: Strategies for Effective Risk Communication* (Fairfax, VA: American Industrial Hygiene Association, 1993).

21. R. L. Heath, "Corporate Environmental Risk Communication: Cases and Practices along the Texas Gulf Coast," in *Communication Yearbook* 18, ed. B. R. Burleson (Thousand Oaks, CA: Sage Publications, 1995), 255–277.

22. R. L. Heath, "Telling the Story: A Narrative Approach to Crisis," in *Responding to Crisis: A Rhetorical Approach to Crisis Communication*, eds. D. P. Millar and R. L. Heath (Mahwah, NJ: Lawrence Erlbaum Associates, 2004), 167–188.

23. G. Eysenbach, "SARS and Population Health Technology," *Journal of Medical Internet Research* 5(2) (2003): e14.

24. M. J. Mastrangelo, "Biodefense Communications," *Journal of Homeland Security*, 2001. Retrieved from: http://www.homelandsecurity.org/journal/articles/displayArticle.asp?article=23.

25. E. Ortiz and C. M. Clancy, "Use of Information Technology to Improve the Quality of Health Care in the United States," *Health Services Research* 38(2) (2003): xi–xxii.

26. L. Neuhauser and G. L. Kreps, "The Advent of E-health: How Interactive Media Are Transforming Health Communication," *Medien and Kommunikationswissenschaft* 51 (2003): 541–556.

27. J. Bruce, "Bioterrorism Meets Privacy: An Analysis of the Model State Emergency Health Powers Act and the HIPAA Privacy Rule," *Annals of Health Law* 12(1) (2003): 75–120.

28. R. Lundgren and A. McMakin, *Risk Communication: A Handbook for Communicating Environmental, Safety and Health Risks* (Columbus, OH: Battelle Press, 1998).

29. R. M. Parker and J. A. Gazmararian, "Health Literacy: Essential for Health Communication," *Journal of Health Communication* 8 (2003): 116–118.

30. R. E. Rudd, J. P. Comings, and J. N. Hyde, "Leave No One Behind: Improving Health and Risk Communication through Attention to Literacy," *Journal of Health Communication* 8 (2003): 104–115.

31. C. Zarcadoolas, A. Pleasant, and D. Greer, "Elaborating a Definition of Health Literacy: A Commentary," *Journal of Health Communication* 8 (2003): 119–120.

32. W. Lazarus and F. Mora, "Online Content for Low-income and Underserved Americans: The Digital Divide's New Frontier," 2000. Retrieved from: http://www.childrenspartnership.org/.

33. Association of State and Territorial Health Officers, "Public Health Preparedness: A Progress Report—The First Six Months," 2003. Retrieved from: http://www.astho.org/?template=public_health_preparedness.html.

34. CDC, "Crisis and Emergency Risk Communication." Retrieved January 15, 2004, from: http://www.cdc.gov/communication/emergency/cerc.htm.

35. R. Logan et al., *Adult Literacy in America: A First Look at the Results of the National Adult Literacy Survey* (NALS 2004) (Washington, DC: U.S. Department of Education).

36. U. S. Department of Health and Human Services, *Communicating in a Crisis: Risk Communication Guidelines for Public Officials* (Washington, DC: Substance Abuse and Mental Health Services Administration, 2002) (publication SMA02-3641). Retrieved January 15, 2004, from www.samhsa.gov.

37. A. Lenhart, *The Ever-Shifting Internet Population* (Washington, DC: The Pew Internet and American Life Project, 2003). Retrieved January 15, 2004, from: http://www.pewinternet.org/reports/toc.asp?Report=88.

38. L. Neuhauser, "Participatory Design for Better Health Communication: A Statewide Model in the USA," *Electronic Journal of Communication/La Revue Electronique de Communication* 11(3 and 4) (2001). Retrieved January 15, 2004 from: http://www.cops.org/wwwejc/v11n3.htm#design.

39. J. P. Dudley, "New Challenges for Public Health Care: Biological and Chemical Weapons Awareness, Surveillance, and Response," *Biological Research for Nursing* 4(4) (2003): 244–250.

40. T. L. Sellnow, M. W. Seeger, and R. R. Ulmer, "Chaos Theory, Informational Needs, and Natural Disasters," *Journal of Applied Communication Research* 30(4) (2003): 269–292.

41. P. P. Mortimer, "Anticipating Smallpox as a Bioterrorist Weapon," *Clinical Medicine* 3(3) (2003): 255–259.

42. L. D. Rotz et al., "Bioterrorism Preparedness: Planning for the Future," *Journal of Public Health Management Practice* 6(4) (2000): 45–49.

43. M. Sawyer, "Connecting the Dots: The Challenge of Improving the Creation and Sharing of Knowledge about Terrorists," *Journal of Homeland Security*, 2003. Retrieved January 15, 2004, from: http://www.homelandsecurity.org/journal/articles/displayArticle.asp?article=93.

44. U. Fisher, "Information Age State Security: New Threats to Old Boundaries," *Journal of Homeland Security*, 2001. Retrieved January 15, 2004, from: http://www.homelandsecurity.org/journal/articles/displayArticle.asp?article=25.

45. W. D. Stephenson, "Homeland Security Requires Internet-based Thinking—Not Just Technology," *Journal of Homeland Security*, 2002. Retrieved January 15, 2004, from: http://www.homelandsecurity.org/journal/articles/displayArticle.asp?article=28.

46. J. M. Haas, "Addressing Bioterrorism: What Ethical Issues and Questions Surround Potential Responses to Bioterrorist Attacks?" *Healthcare Executive* 18(3) (2003): 76–77.

47. A. J. Heightman, "The Need to Address New Threats," *Journal of Emergency Medical Services* 28(4) (2003): 12.

48. J. G. Bartlett, "Mobilizing Professional Communities," *Public Health Reports* 116 (Suppl. 2) (2001): 40–44.

49. H. E. Rippen, E. Gursky, and M. A. Stoto, "Importance of Bioterrorism Preparedness for Family Physicians," *American Family Physician* 67(9) (2003): 1877–1878.

50. D. M. Manassaram, M. F. Orr, and W. E. Kaye, "Counterterrorism Planning Using the Hazardous Substances Events Surveillance System," *Disaster Management and Response* 1(2) (2003): 35–40.

51. D. A. Ashford et al., "Planning against Biological Terrorism: Lessons from Outbreak Investigations," *Emerging Infectious Diseases* 9(5) (2003): 515–519.

52. C. DiGiovanni et al., "Community Reaction to Bioterrorism: Prospective Study of Simulated Outbreak," *Emerging Infectious Diseases* 9(6) (2003): 708–712.

53. K. L. Brooks and S. A. Dauenhauer, "The Anthrax Team: A Novel Teaching Approach to Increase Anthrax and Bioterrorism Awareness," *American Journal of Infection Control* 31(3) (2003): 176–177.

54. M. S. Dworkin, X. Ma, and R. G. Golash, "Fear of Bioterrorism and Implications for Public Health Preparedness," *Emerging Infectious Diseases* 9(4) (2003): 503–505.

55. G. Fiedelholtz, "Responding to Biological Terrorist Incidents: Upgrading the FEMA Approach," *Journal of Homeland Security*, 2003. Retrieved January 15, 2004, from: http://www.homelandsecurity.org/journal/articles/displayArticle.asp?article=91.

56. A. S. Fauci, "Bioterrorism: Defining a Research Agenda," *Food Drug Law Journal* 57(3) (2002): 413–421.

57. V. L. Yu, "Bioterrorism Web Site Resources for Infectious Disease Clinicians and Epidemiologists," *Clinical Infectious Diseases* 36 (2003): 1458–1473.

58. J. M. Rosen, C. E. Koop, and E. B. Grigg, "Cybercare: A System for Confronting Bioterrorism," *The Bridge* 32(1) (2002). Retrieved January 15, 2004, from: http://www.nae.edu/nae/naehome.nsf/weblinks/CGOZ-58NLKL? OpenDocument.

59. T. Slezak et al., "Comparative Genomics Tools Applied to Bioterrorism Defense," *Briefings in Bioinformatics* 4(2) (2003): 133–149.

60. J. A. Higgins et al., "A Handheld Real Time Thermal Cycler for Bacterial Pathogen Detection," *Biosensors and Bioelectronics* 18(9) (2003): 1115–1123.

61. M. L. Popovich, J. M. Henderson, and J. Stinn, "Information Technology in the Age of Emergency Public Health Response: The Framework for an Integrated Disease Surveillance System for Rapid Detection, Tracking, and Managing of Public Health Threats," *IEEE Engineering Medical Biology Magazine* 21(5) (2002): 48–55.

62. L. Garrett, "Understanding the Media's Response to Epidemics," *Public Health Reports* 116 (Suppl. 2) (2001): 87–91.

63. S. M. Friedman, S. Dunwoody, and C. L. Rogers (eds.), *Communicating New and Uncertain Science* (Mahwah, NJ: Lawrence Erlbaum Associates, 1999).

64. K. Rowan, "Effective Explanation of Uncertain and Complex Science," in *Communicating New and Uncertain Science*, eds. S. Friedman, S. Dunwoody, and C. L. Rogers (Mahwah, NJ: Lawrence Erlbaum Associates, 1999), 201–233.

65. L. Sparks, "Social Identity and Mass-Mediated Representations of Terrorist Groups: An Intergroup Communication Approach to Terrorism," in *Communication, Communities, and Terrorism*, eds. H. D. O'Hair, R. Heath, and G. Ledlow (Westport, CT: Praeger Publishers, in press).

66. M. F. Weigold, "Communicating Science: A Review of the Literature," *Science Communication* 23(2) (2001): 164–193.

67. W. T. Coombs, *Ongoing Crisis Communication: Planning, Managing, and Responding* (Thousand Oaks, CA: Sage Publications, 1999).

68. S. Dunwoody, "Studying Users of the Why Files," *Science Communication* 22 (2001): 274–282.

69. M. Tremayne, S. Dunwoody, and J. Tobias, "Interactivity, Information Processing, and Learning on the World Wide Web," *Science Communication* 23 (2001): 111–134.

CHAPTER TWENTY-TWO

Health Communication Challenges of an Anthrax Vaccination Program

Skye K. Schulte and J. Gregory Payne

Chapter Questions

1. What can be learned from risk communication efforts surrounding West Nile Virus and SARS? How can these lessons be applied to an anthrax vaccination program?
2. What are some strategies for successfully addressing public fear?
3. What are the specific communications challenges and issues unique to anthrax? How can these issues be addressed through risk communication?

I. Risk Communication: Lessons Learned

Bioterrorism and Emerging Diseases

The public health challenges of implementing a nationwide vaccination program are both numerous and complex. Fortunately, there is precedent for successful vaccination programs that address both the intentional and unintentional introduction of pathogens into our communities. Case studies like the West Nile virus epidemic in the United States are useful in designing and implementing a successful anthrax vaccination program. By learning from our past experiences, both in the United States and abroad, we can address the many communication challenges inherent in protecting the public from the potential risk of anthrax and implementing a nationwide vaccination should it be needed. Our purpose here is to discuss some of the pertinent issues and communication strategies that must be addressed by health professionals regarding an anthrax health crisis.

Though it is generally believed that the risk communication efforts around West Nile Virus have been comprehensive and successful, there are still many lessons to be learned, especially related to understanding the target audiences and the various stakeholders that can play a role in the success of communication efforts. The following recommendations suggested for improving future risk communication efforts concerning the West Nile Virus epidemic can also be included as part of a strategy for an anthrax vaccination program.

Lessons Learned: Key Target Areas of Risk Communication Overlooked during the West Nile Virus Epidemic[1]

1. Measure and analyze stakeholder judgments of major risk perceptions factors.
2. Expand circle of stakeholders beyond the obvious medical, political, and legal groups—try to predict what they can do.
3. Deliver easily digestible messages (e.g., not too many, not too complicated).
4. Use various communication methods and channels to appeal to the greatest number of people (e.g., use charts, graphs, and audiovisual aids where possible and make sure materials are at a reading and interpretation level that is appropriate for the audience).
5. Pay attention to the balance of the Negative Dominance Model where individuals give more weight to negative messages than neutral or positive messages (see Table 22–1).

The international Sudden Acute Respiratory Syndrome (SARS) crisis in 2003 also provided many lessons for implementing a nationwide anthrax vaccination program. SARS is somewhat different, however, in that it is transmitted from person to person—anthrax is not contagious in this way. The fear and health communication challenges are similar to those experienced during the anthrax attacks of 2001. Both SARS and anthrax cases documented the widespread fear among the public—a major challenge to health professionals in addressing such crises. The SARS outbreak witnessed thousands in Asia snapping up facemasks, as whole cities were shut down in order to quarantine the disease. As will be further discussed in this chapter, the post September 11, 2001, anthrax attacks resulted in a crisis in credible information among the public seeking valid answers to their concerns on what measures should be taken as a means of protection.

Table 22–1. Overview of Theoretical Models for Risk Communication

THE RISK PERCEPTIONS MODEL	THE MENTAL NOISE MODEL
Understanding the levels of concern of different individuals and groups, and how those perceptions of risk can be addressed through leadership communication and other activities.[2–3]	Understanding how people process information in stressful situations and how these processes can affect communication and the adoption of suggested courses of action.[4]
THE NEGATIVE DOMINANCE MODEL	THE TRUST DETERMINATION MODEL
Understanding the disproportionate value that individuals give negative messages and how that effect can be counterbalanced with positive messages and/or utilized for the best strategic result. [5]	Understanding the elements of building and maintaining trust and how this affects actions and risk communication efforts.[6]

The Government of Hong Kong implemented a comprehensive strategy to address the SARS outbreak. These efforts included establishing three separate committees that (1) addressed overall cleansing campaigns and environmental improvements, (2) set up programs to revitalize the economy of areas hardest hit by the epidemic and the negative effect it had on tourism and business, and (3) promoted community involvement in the public health and civic environment.[7] Another important component of the SARS health communication effort was the successful use of attention-getting public service announcements that helped allay the fears of the Chinese public.

In the event of another use of the anthrax agent, it is hoped that a strategy would include these considerations, in addition to all of the components of a general vaccine dissemination program. Contraction of anthrax probably would be the result of a deliberate release of the anthrax spores into the population. Anthrax is different from other potential bioterror agents such as smallpox and influenza because transmission of the anthrax spores is limited to the "primary exposure point," that is, anthrax is not contagious person-to-person except by physical transmission of the spores.

In any educational campaign, the public must be aware of these differences and how they can prevent or limit their exposure to the spores and the risk of developing anthrax. Should an event occur, it might not be reasonable or medically recommended to vaccinate the entire population. Instead, the personal education component could be crucial for successful efforts to limit an individual's exposure to risky situations and environments.

Vaccination Programs and the Safety and Efficacy of the Anthrax Vaccine

Even though the flu causes thousands of deaths each year, there is not the same public fear and lack of understanding about this communicable disease (though this could be a serious threat that is inflicted as a bioterror agent). The public fears what it does not understand. Unlike the flu, of which the public has some understanding, anthrax is a relatively unknown entity among the public. It is popularly viewed solely as a deadly disease that the public is exposed to through malicious and calculated means. Vaccines are available for both the flu and anthrax. Yet, given the lack of knowledge about the disease and controversy surrounding the vaccine, suffice it to say that an anthrax vaccination program would not have the public support of the yearly flu shot campaigns. The major reason for this is the lack of understanding and the past credibility issues that surrounded the sources of information concerning anthrax.[8]

Currently the anthrax vaccine is given to members of the military and is recommended for other people who can be exposed to *Bacillus anthracis* spores, the biological component that causes anthrax. The treatment and post-exposure prevention of anthrax are the antibiotics ciprofloxacin or doxycycline. Administering the anthrax vaccine after exposure to anthrax spores is not sufficient for the prevention of the disease, so vaccination at this juncture is also accompanied by 60 days of antibiotic therapy.[9] The intensive medical care and risk of death associated with the contraction of anthrax makes vaccinating against the disease an attractive preventive option in the event of a bioterrorist event.

While it could be an important part of a coordinated anthrax health communication campaign addressing the concerns about anthrax being used as a biological weapon, administration of the anthrax vaccine to the U.S. military to even a relatively small and limited group of soldiers has not been without controversy. For example, fears over being required to have the anthrax vaccination have been cited as one reason U.S. reservists were being driven away from service.[10] Scientific articles have raised concerns about the efficacy of the vaccine in an anthrax attack. For instance, there is concern about the off-label use of the anthrax vaccine to protect against aerosol exposure to anthrax, which is likely to be the way the spores are "weaponized" during a biological attack.[11] The current Food and Drug Administration approval was based only on the vaccine's efficacy against cutaneous anthrax.

In addition, some researchers report parallels between Gulf War Syndrome and adverse effects reported from the anthrax vaccine.[12] Other studies charge that the military's Anthrax Vaccine Immunization Program was a "well-intentioned but over-wrought response to the threat of anthrax as a biological weapon."[13]

Side effects, such as an increase in joint symptoms, have also been reported when comparing anthrax vaccination with vaccinations against diseases such as Hepatitis A.[14] These and other legitimate as well as unsubstantiated beliefs among the public have to be addressed as we attempt to improve the safety profile of the existing anthrax vaccine. Although symptoms like joint pain would not invalidate the use of the existing vaccine during a biological attack, its use as a prophylactic vaccine should be further examined. Many questions like, "Can the existing vaccine be improved for use in the general population?" will need to be addressed before any initiatives take place in the general population. There is also a very real fear that widespread vaccination of a population might lead terrorists and potential producers of biological weapons to develop new strains of anthrax not covered under the current vaccine. Therefore, health professionals need to ponder these and other concerns in the effort to implement regional and national vaccination programs.

Within the scientific community there has been additional debate about the safety and efficacy of the anthrax vaccine.[15-16] Yet, the negative assertions about the vaccine are countered by evidence supporting the safety and use of the vaccine as it currently stands. The result is that the Institute of Medicine currently recommends continued improvements and analysis before the anthrax vaccine is widely used in the general population.

In some respects, this medical debate is somewhat secondary. If the public, for whatever reason, does not have confidence in the safety and the efficacy of the vaccine, any anthrax vaccination program is not likely to be successful. In a military setting there is some expectation that people will "follow orders" and receive the vaccination, but in a civilian population there are many additional considerations. Within the general public, there is no meaningful authoritative directive or fear of job reprisals like in the military. Persuasive efforts must be addressed in a sustained campaign that addresses the information needs of the public.

For example, calculating the actual risk of exposure to the general public is difficult for any pre-event vaccination program. This is why many experts recommend against pre-exposure vaccination for groups where a calculable risk cannot be determined. In other words, public health professionals would wait to vaccinate a group of people until risk of exposure to anthrax spores is imminent. As one might expect, this presents many logistical and timing issues concerning disseminating the vaccine and follow-up antibiotic therapy when and where it is needed most. This is why risk communication before, during, and after a potential anthrax bioterror attack is such a vital component of the communication process.

One major challenge we witnessed after the anthrax attacks in 2001 was that misinformation, especially on the Internet, can be rampant when people are not fully educated on the facts. These first anthrax attacks in the United States forced the Centers for Disease Control and Prevention (CDC) to examine the flow of information from the agency to the public, and to reassess how its personnel had communicated with the media. Studies find that this event led to new work practices, tools for performing that work, and a greater understanding of what it takes to handle communications during a terrorism-related crisis.[17] Researchers also examined systems for developing an effective communication response during a crisis such as this one.[18]

Other research addresses the need for standardized health and risk communication protocols that deal with suspected or actual bioterrorist attacks.[19] Protocols such as this would also be useful in confronting some of the barriers and misinformation that are likely to occur during the education and implementation stages of an anthrax vaccination program.

Efforts related to the successful implementation of an anthrax vaccination program need to be part of a comprehensive, coordinated, and integrated effort—involving many different agencies and health organizations and facilitating efficient communication among these stakeholders. One strategy of the CDC in currently trying to facilitate this cooperation is through the Health Alert Network, which electronically links health agencies around the country. Using existing systems such as this can help to facilitate the necessary interagency communication needed for a successful vaccination program.

In addition, continued efforts to gauge public perception and understanding of bioterrorism (specifically related to anthrax) can help to distinguish between real information and unsubstantiated rumors, deal with barriers, and address other challenges that can exist in the event that a local, regional, or national anthrax vaccination program is necessary.[20] Gathering this type of information can help health officials to determine how best to deal with their constituents.

Addressing the Public's Fears: Components of a Successful Communications Program

The greatest challenges in planning and implementing an anthrax vaccination program is addressing the fears that the public can have about an anthrax attack, as well as the anthrax vaccination program itself. Fear can be a powerful motivator, but the focus and manifestation of that fear can be unpredictable, especially when facing a new threat like a biological attack. For instance, during the 2001 anthrax attacks, thousands of people took broad-spectrum antibiotics to prevent a possible anthrax infection, even though such a practice was ineffective. Fear drove these people to try anything they reasoned might decrease their risk, though unfortunately practices like this can often be *more* harmful—in this instance promoting the growth of antibiotic-resistant bacteria.

What is called for is a well-planned, risk communication educational effort to help people keep a healthy perspective on their fears and embrace practices that *do* protect them. Effective communication about the anthrax vaccine—its strengths and its limitations, how it is contracted and how it is not—can help to promote the understanding of how individuals can protect themselves in the event of a bioterrorist attack using anthrax.

Implementation in such a coordinated effort requires the health communication professional to consider psychological, behavioral, and societal reactions to biological warfare.[21] Any successful vaccination program against a biological agent like anthrax must address these pertinent issues.

When addressing the fears and challenges faced by a public exposed to a bioterrorist attack, one must also look at the population as co-active allies, as partners, in the joint efforts to carry out a successful vaccination program. Forgetting to involve the public as a key partner could have serious negative implications on credible efforts to promote and facilitate an anthrax vaccination program. Glass and Schoch-Spana propose five guidelines for involving the public in bioterrorism response planning:[22]

1. Treat the public as a capable ally in the response to an epidemic
2. Enlist civic organizations in practical public health activities
3. Anticipate the need for home-based patient care and infection control
4. Invest in public outreach and communication strategies
5. Ensure that planning reflects the values and priorities of affected populations

A successful anthrax vaccination program utilizes various communication techniques and theories required to address the public's fears and give them the necessary tools and information to protect themselves and their families. To become credible and accepted by the public, the effective anthrax program must convince the public in various communication venues and utilize various strategies so that the public is educated in a timely manner, and so that trust is instilled in the public health infrastructure and programs that are in place—should an anthrax attack occur and a vaccination program be necessary.

II. Logistics of Vaccination and Risk Communications Concerning Anthrax

There are numerous logistical concerns with implementing a local, regional, or national anthrax vaccination program. Ideally, information and vaccine dissemination strategies would be in place long before a biological attack with anthrax would occur. The logistics of an anthrax vaccination program can vary widely depending on the population, communication channels, medical and public health infrastructure, and other factors. The following questions highlight some of the issues that may need to be addressed and researched in each individual effort:

- When does vaccinating the public become necessary and who has the authority to make that decision?
- What barriers or gaps in knowledge exist among decision makers and those involved in the anthrax vaccination program?
- What barriers to getting the vaccination are expected in the target population?
- How will those barriers be addressed?
- What organizations and groups should be involved in decision making?
- What could go wrong with this vaccination program and how likely is that to occur?
- What do we do in childhood populations? Is this vaccine safe for children?
- How do we keep track of who has received the vaccine and who has not?
- What public health, medical, and other infrastructure must be in place for local, regional, or national anthrax vaccination programs?
- Who distributes the vaccine?
- How is the vaccine distributed?

- What training and information is needed for the health care professionals implementing the program and giving the vaccine to the public?
- How will the anthrax vaccination program and anthrax vaccines be funded?
- What legal issues can arise with this program and how will those be dealt with?
- How will the desires of the individual be balanced with the needs of the population?
- What communication channels will be used?
- Who will be the spokesperson?
- How will the public's questions and concerns be addressed?
- In what other ways will the public be protected?
- How will we conduct surveillance and other ongoing research?
- How will risk communication training for health care workers be provided?
- What steps are necessary to improve the systems for sharing of information?
- How will the success of any programs or campaigns be measured?
- What risk communication efforts will be used?

III. Planning Risk Communication for the Public

In the case of an anthrax vaccination program, effective risk communication is essential to help all those involved. For a successful risk communication program, evaluation studies show that it is necessary to (1) provide knowledge and access to tools for making informed decisions about risk, (2) facilitate trust among stakeholders, and (3) build cooperation and consensus by promoting fluid communication and negotiation. Additional barriers such as lack of coordination and planning, inadequate preparation, and limited resources can also factor into the success of a risk communication program and must be addressed.

Health agencies and organizations must move beyond a model of "decide, announce, defend," and work with other organizations and their constituents to determine the most effective leaders, messages, and channels during a risk communication program. The four theoretical models (as shown in Table 22–1) on which risk communication is based should be employed by these stakeholders to put together good risk communication programs.

Past surveys of the U.S. public highlight the importance of effective communications about anthrax and the need to use all of the mass and interpersonal communication resources available. One result of these surveys is the desire on the part of the public to have both local and national health officials as spokespersons during a bioterrorist attack and any subsequent public health efforts.[23] One must always remember that like in politics, to be effective all health communication should be local.

After the 2001 anthrax attacks in the United States, information about the public's response indicated that even a month afterward, people were still dealing with fear related to the attacks and were making medical demands for antibiotics and vaccines when this was medically unnecessary. Any anthrax vaccination program should be a cooperative effort with current and future hospital preparedness activities. Research in other countries shows that when faced with a bioterrorism crisis, the majority of patients chose their family physician or the health authorities over the hospital emergency department.[24] There is a need to better understand where those living in the United States would most trust getting their health care and information about bioterrorism.

Effective and credible communication is at the core of any public health effort. Nowhere is this more important than in a potential crisis situation such as a bioterrorist event that necessitates mass vaccination from a disease like anthrax. It is important to have a consistent message delivered by a trusted source in a timely manner. By giving the public actionable knowledge, it is possible to reduce the negative impact that fear can have in a population. Public health officials can also question whether the medical community should implement a nationwide vaccination program for anthrax when an epidemic of the disease is not imminent.

One of the challenges of a nationwide anthrax vaccination program is determining the specific channels that will be the most effective in disseminating both the vaccine and any related health communication messages. Hospitals, public health organizations, schools, civic organizations, and other stakeholders too numerous to mention would need to be involved in such a large-scale effort. The communication efforts of all these organizations—Internet, print, audio, interagency, interpersonal, etc.—would also need to be coordinated via a trusted centralized system.

The CDC's "Emergency Operations Center," which was designed to promote faster and more coordinated responses to public health emergencies, will be useful in addressing some of the barriers to a successful anthrax vaccination program. This organization can help to gauge if and when the threat of exposure to anthrax is enough to warrant the vaccination of the general public. The Emergency Operations Center includes 85 workstations, nine team rooms, a central command station, high-frequency radio support, and geographic information system (disease mapping) capabilities.[25]

Researchers who have simulated bioterrorism-related crisis events have found that different groups, and in fact specific individuals within those groups, can respond very differently to the same crisis. The human factor and the variable autonomy within each of us affects the crisis equation and predictable reactions in such instances in innumerable ways. For instance, in a simulation of an intentional outbreak of Rift Valley fever, researchers observed that the local journalists showed considerable personal fear and confusion during the hypothetical crisis. It is imperative to learn from these simulated cases the importance of pivotal communication sources and appropriate channels. How do we enhance the respective credibility of agents, channels, and venues utilized in disseminating prescriptive messages during such crises?[26]

The numerous needs and challenges in the event of a bioterrorist attack, and subsequent implementation of an effective anthrax vaccination program, will require sustained efforts to mend some of the existing gaps in the public health infrastructure.[27] The medical, social, economic, environmental, and legal issues surrounding a bioterrorist attack have widespread impact on the social and political fabric: hospital emergency departments are overwhelmed; those who are "exposed" are stigmatized; businesses are ruined or stunted; lawsuits follow as victims seek understanding and retribution; and there are impacts on civil norms and laws.[28]

Responding effectively to a bio-crisis and being able to protect the public with measures like vaccination and risk communication programs can help decrease the negative effects of such an event.

Effective communication and education can empower the public in a crisis with direction on how they can protect themselves and their families. Effective risk communication and a detailed crisis communication plan can provide a needed roadmap and understanding in the event a tragedy strikes. For instance, warning the public to stay away from areas that are contaminated and recommending the vaccine if it is available can be effective risk communication efforts. Doing so will decrease panic during a potential attack or crisis.

An effective campaign will also strategize where the public can go for additional information and care without overburdening the health care system and public health infrastructure during a crisis. Vaccines and information could be distributed at local pharmacies, churches, schools, malls, and other areas that do not overburden health care workers and systems that provide acute care for those directly exposed to the bioterrorist event. These teaching moments are also a great opportunity to educate the public about general terrorist attacks and how they can help prevent these events and protect themselves and their families if an attack does occur.

In any event, those trained to implement the anthrax vaccination program should be sure that they (1) do not provide inappropriately reassuring information, (2) do not downplay uncertainty, and (3) do not delay the release of information. Doing so could undermine the trust and confidence that is needed for the public to accept a program of this nature.

IV. The Big Picture

Since the aftermath of September 11 and the use of anthrax as a bioterror agent in the United States, many questions about planning for other public health emergencies have arisen. Both naturally occurring infectious diseases and deliberate acts of bioterrorism threaten the public health. What is the public to do to protect themselves?

With the medical and physical issues associated with anthrax, many legal issues also appear. The Model State Emergency Health Powers Act provides some useful insight into planning for and responding to bioterrorism and naturally occurring infectious disease. This act was drafted by The Center for Law and the Public's Health at Georgetown and Johns Hopkins University and discusses five basic public health functions that could be facilitated through legislation and law:[29]

1. Preparedness including comprehensive public health emergency planning
2. Surveillance that measures and detects emerging public health threats
3. Management of property such as ensuring adequate availability of vaccines, pharmaceuticals, and hospitals
4. Protections like the power to compel vaccination, testing, treatment, isolation, and quarantine when clearly necessary
5. Communication that provides credible, accurate, and useful information to the public.

Cooperation and communication among many different local, regional, and national organizations is imperative for a successful anthrax vaccination program aimed at patient, personnel, and community safety.[30] These initiatives must involve the media, public health, medical, law enforcement, government, and other helpful organizations such as churches, schools, and other places where people congregate and get information. A grassroots effort at the community level, involving opinion leaders and the latest in Internet technology and notification strategies, should also be a major priority.

Working on bioterrorism and public health surveillance with emerging diseases should all be done in concert with all parties and with a clear chain of command and designated credible leadership at all levels. As our world gets smaller and technologically more advanced, it is imperative to remember that our future depends on all of us working together, especially in a crisis situation. Public health is our number one shared objective.

Involving key stakeholders is essential. It must begin at the local level and include appropriate community, national, and global agencies: for example, CDC, the World Health Organization, and the health ministries of other countries. Given our past and the terrorist cloud that characterizes our present, the U.S. public health infrastructure must adopt a proactive posture. We must continue to lay the groundwork for effective communication about anthrax and a potential vaccination program—perhaps by promoting the work already done with the U.S. military and possible implementation of a voluntary anthrax vaccination program in our general civilian population. Though the health communication and other challenges of implementing an anthrax vaccination program are numerous, with thoughtful and cooperative planning an effective program can be implemented.

Notes

1. V. T. Covello et al., "Risk Communication, the West Nile Virus Epidemic, and Bioterrorism: Responding to the Communication Challenges Posed by the Intentional or Unintentional Release of a Pathogen in an Urban Setting," *Journal of Urban Health* 78(2) (2001): 382–391.

2. G. O. Rogers, "The Dynamics of Risk Perception: How Does Perceived Risk Respond to Risk Event?" *Risk Analysis* 17(6) (1997): 745–757.

3. A. Wildavsky and K. Dake, "Theories of Risk Perception: Who Fears What and Why," *Daedalus* 112 (1990): 41–60.

4. K. Neuwirth, S. Dunwoody, and R. J. Griffin, "Protection Motivation and Risk Communication," *Risk Analysis* 20(5) (2000): 721–733.

5. V. T. Covello, "Risk Perception, Risk Communication, and EMF Exposure: Tools and Techniques for Communicating Risk Information," in *Risk Perceptions, Risk Communication, and Its Application to EMF Exposure: Proceedings of the World Health Organization/ICNRP International Conference* (ICNRP 5/98), eds. R. Matthes, J. H. Bernhardt, and M. H. Repacholi (Vienna, Austria: International Commission on Non-Ionizing Radiation Protection, 1998), 179–214.

6. P. Slovic, "Trust, Emotion, Sex, Politics, and Science: Surveying the Risk-Assessment Battlefield," *Risk Analysis* 9(4) (1999): 689–701.

7. L. S. Hung, "The SARS Epidemic in Hong Kong: What Lessons Have We Learned?" *Journal of the Royal Society of Medicine* 96(8) (2003): 374–378.

8. M. Haider, personal communication.

9. S. R. Kimmel, M. C. Mahoney, and R. K. Zimmerman, "Vaccines and Bioterrorism: Smallpox and Anthrax," *Journal of Family Practice* 52(Suppl. 1) (2003): S56–61.

10. F. Charatan, "Fears over Anthrax Vaccination Driving away U.S. Reservists," *British Medical Journal* 321(7267) (2000): 980.

11. M. Nass, "The Anthrax Vaccine Program: An Analysis of the CDC Recommendations for Vaccine Use," *American Journal of Public Health* 92 (2002): 715–721.

12. *The Department of Defense Anthrax Vaccine Immunization Program: Unproven Force Protection* (Washington, DC: Committee on Government Reform; April 3, 2000). Available at http://www.house.gov/reform/ns/reports/anthrax1.pdf. Accessed February 19, 2002.

13. D. A. Geier and M. R. Geier, "Anthrax Vaccination and Joint Related Adverse Reactions in Light of Biological Warfare Scenarios," *Clinical & Experimental Rheumatology* 20(2) (March-April 2002): 217–220.

14. V. W. Sidel, M. Nass, and T. Ensing, "The Anthrax Dilemma," *Medical Global Survival* 5 (1998): 97–104.

15. M. Nass, "The Department of Defense's Anthrax Vaccine Experiment," *Maine Progressive*, December 1998. Available at: http://www.mainprogressive.org/121998/anthrax.htm. Accessed September 13, 2002.

16. S. J. Robinson and W. C. Newstetter, "Uncertain Science and Certain Deadlines: CDC Responses to the Media during the Anthrax Attacks of 2001," *Journal of Health Communication* 8 (Suppl. 1) (2003): 17–34.

17. M. Haider, personal communication.

18. J. A. Mott et al., "Call-tracking Data and the Public Health Response to Bioterrorism-Related Anthrax," *Emerging Infectious Diseases* 8(10) (2002): 1088–1092.

19. R. J. Blendon et al., "Using Opinion Surveys to Track the Public's Response to a Bioterrorist Attack," *Journal of Health Communication* 8 (Suppl. 1) (2003): 83–92.

20. A. E. Norwood, H. C. Holloway, and R. J. Ursano, "Psychological Effects of Biological Warfare" [Review], *Military Medicine* 166(Suppl. 12) (December 2001): 27–28.

21. T. A. Glass and M. Schoch-Spana, "Bioterrorism and the People: How to Vaccinate a City against Panic" [Review], *Clinical Infectious Diseases* 34(2) (January 2002): 217–223.

22. W. E. Pollard, "Public Perceptions of Information Sources Concerning Bioterrorism before and after Anthrax Attacks: An Analysis of National Survey Data," *Journal of Health Communication* 8 (Suppl. 1) (2003): 93–103.

23. E. Kahan, Y. Fogelman, E. Kitai, and S. Vinke, "Patient and family physician preferences for care and communication in the eventuality of anthrax terrorism," *Family Practice* 20(4) (2003); 441–444.

24. B. Vastag, "CDC Unveils SARS Plan: Emphasizes Rapid Identification, Communication," *Journal of the American Medical Association* 290(19) (2003): 2533–2534.

25. C. DiGiovanni, Jr., B. Reynolds, R. Harwell, E. B. Stonecipher, F. M. Burkle, Jr. "Community Reaction to Bioterrorism: Prospective Study of Simulated Outbreak," *Emerging Infectious Diseases* 9(6) (June 2003): 708–712.

26. E. Salinsky, "Will the Nation Be Ready for the Next Bioterrorism Attack? Mending Gaps in the Public Health Infrastructure," *NHPF Issue Brief* 776 (June 12, 2002): 1–19.

27. K. C. Hyams, F. M. Murphy, and S. Wessely, "Responding to Chemical, Biological, or Nuclear Terrorism: The Indirect and Long-term Health Effects May Present the Greatest Challenge," *Journal of Health Politics, Policy & Law* 27(2) (April 2002): 273–291.

28. L. O. Gostin et al., "The Model State Emergency Health Powers Act: Planning for and Response to Bioterrorism and Naturally Occurring Infectious Diseases," *Journal of the American Medical Association* 288(5) (August 2002): 622–628.

29. J. M. Miller, "Agents of Bioterrorism. Preparing for Bioterrorism at the Community Health Care Level," *Infectious Disease Clinics of North America* 15(4) (December 2001): 1127–1156.

CHAPTER TWENTY-THREE

Cancer Communication Research for Health Promotion at the National Cancer Institute: A Case Study

Gary L. Kreps

Chapter Questions

1. How can each of the cancer communications research initiatives outlined in this chapter contribute to reduce the burden of cancer on society?
2. How are disparities in different populations addressed through NCI's health communications research?
3. What is the role of new technologies in cancer communications? How can new technologies be applied to different cancer programs?

Introduction

Communication is a central human process that has great relevance for health promotion, providing information to guide individual and collective adaptation to health threats.[1-2] Cancer poses a particularly complex array of health challenges that demand effective communication to encourage cancer prevention; inform cancer detection and diagnosis; guide cancer treatment; support successful cancer survivorship and quality of life; and promote optimal end-of-life care. [3-6] Two Institute of Medicine reports conclude that cancer communication is a central part of quality of cancer care.[7-8] There is a great need for cancer communications research to fill gaps in current knowledge about communication processes and information needs in cancer prevention and control, as well as to capitalize on the unique opportunities presented by the advent of advanced communication technologies to help achieve cancer prevention and detection goals. A significant expansion in the cancer communications research enterprise is warranted to increase knowledge and identify practical strategies to enhance cancer communications and improve prevention and control of cancer.

The National Cancer Institute's Investment in Communication Research

The National Cancer Institute (NCI) identified cancer communications as one of its higher scientific priorities for cancer research, identifying cancer communications as an area of extraordinary opportunity.[9] (See http://plan2002.cancer.gov/.) This is an unprecedented large-scale commitment to apply communication research to the promotion of public health. The NCI has begun implementing a comprehensive research strategy for introducing powerful new communication initiatives to expand health communication knowledge, lead to more effective interventions across the cancer continuum through prevention to end-of-life, and influence public health policies and practices. In the next sections of this chapter we will outline several of these initiatives.

1. Digital Divide Pilot Projects

In conjunction with the NCI Cancer Information Service (CIS), this program established the groundwork for the CIS network to form collaborative partnerships with researchers, technology experts, and organizations serving underserved populations in need of relevant cancer information. The NCI awarded close to $1 million to help develop research and development projects to increase understanding and help to narrow the digital divide that exists among many underserved populations in accessing and utilizing cancer information on the Internet. The Digital Divide has been identified as a special problem in health care that can lead to disparities in care.[10] Many studies show that certain ethnic minorities and low-income, less-educated populations suffer a disproportionate cancer burden and have limited access to electronic information about health.[11] However, too little is known about their interest in and use of cancer information tools. The funded projects attempt to increase understanding of why barriers to information and knowledge exist, and use the data gleaned from the pilot projects to design programs that can lead to better health care decisions and adherence to recommended health behaviors. These four pilot projects will serve as models for larger scale efforts.

CIS New York State (Memorial Sloan-Kettering Cancer Center, N.Y.) worked with a consortium of nonprofit and private sector organizations, including the Urban League, Harlem YMCA Cyberlab, and the Bell Atlantic Technology Education Center, to make basic cancer information accessible in community computer centers located in Harlem, New York.

CIS North Central and Mid-West Regions (University of Wisconsin, Madison, Wis., and Karmanos Cancer Center, Mich.) expanded the Comprehensive Health Enhancement Support System Program (CHESS) that puts personal computers and Web-based support resources into the homes of low-income breast cancer patients. The program reaches rural women in Wisconsin and urban African-American women in Detroit. The Markle Foundation has provided supplemental funding to extend subject recruitment and analysis for this demonstration project.

CIS New England Region (Yale Cancer Center, Conn.) worked with Head Start in inner city New Haven to bring computer skills and access to cancer information to Head Start workers and the parents of the children they serve. The goals are to determine what cancer information is most useful to the community and to leave a legacy of computer access in the Head Start center and in the homes of Head Start families.

CIS Mid-South Region (Markey Cancer Center, Ky., and the Louisiana State University Health Sciences Center, La.) introduced computer technology at meal sites in 10 senior centers in low-income areas of Louisiana. The goal is to provide cancer information in a format that is useful to senior citizens and overcomes limitations in literacy skills within this target population. (For more information about NCI's Digital Divide Pilot Projects, see: http://dccps.nci.nih.gov/eocc/ddpp.html.)

2. Health Information National Trends Survey

The NCI administered the first wave of the biennial Health Information National Trends Survey (HINTS) in 2003 to examine the American public's access to and use of cancer information. This representative national survey (n = 6,000) will establish important baseline data about cancer communication practices and preferences across the United States. The need for such a survey was endorsed strongly at a meeting sponsored by the NCI on Cancer Risk Communication in 1999.[12] The survey will clarify our understanding of the public's perceived needs for relevant cancer information, their current usage of cancer information, and the impact of that information on their lives.

The survey will identify the specific cancer information topics the American public is most concerned about and specify important directions necessary for effective national dissemination of cancer information. In addition, data will be collected about public perceptions about cancer risks as related to particular hazards (e.g., smoking), and perceptions about specific risks for particular cancers (e.g., breast cancer). The survey will identify public preferences for specific cancer information channels and sources, credibility of sources, as well as the relationships between cancer information access and cancer-related health beliefs, attitudes, and behaviors, such as engaging in cancer screening behaviors.

The data gathered in the surveys will be used to identify the information needs of different key audiences for cancer communication to help target cancer information dissemination efforts. The NCI intends to make the data from the HINTS surveys available quickly and widely to enable others to use these data for research and development of health promotion programs. The surveys will also provide important evaluation data about the relative impact of the NCI's and other health promotion organizations' information dissemination programs and services. (For more information about HINTS see: http://dccps.nci.nih.gov/hcirb/hints.html.)

3. Centers of Excellence in Cancer Communications Research

The NCI established four national Centers of Excellence in Cancer Communication Research (CECCRs) in late 2003 at institutions that made strong institutional commitments to the organization and conduct of interdisciplinary programs of cancer communication research. The centers are expected to provide the essential infrastructure needed to facilitate rapid advances in knowledge about cancer communication, including the development of new theories of health and cancer communication that are appropriate to underserved populations, development of evidence-based strategies and tools for cancer communication, training of tomorrow's health communication scientists, and promotion of collaboration with government agencies, advocacy groups, industry, and commercial endeavors. We also expect that these centers will spur the development of new evaluation methods appropriate for the new interactive health communication technologies.

The centers will be population-based information delivery test beds that encourage and facilitate theoretical and applied health communication research. They will conduct basic and applied research to answer fundamental questions and develop strategies to improve the penetration, efficacy, effectiveness, and dissemination of relevant cancer information. They will answer questions about the mechanisms by which cancer messages exert influence, including the mediators of cancer risk communication and the most effective channels to use. Other potential topics of research include: the role of culture; increasing the understanding of how people search for and use cancer information; identification of optimal formats for communicating cancer risks to different populations; examination of how to integrate cancer communications into the continuum of cancer care; dissemination of best practices; communication of uncertainty about risks; and reduction in disparities in demand for, access to, and use of cancer communication. Centers of Excellence should also respond to important practical issues, such as helping people respond to cancer scares and introducing tested research products quickly into the public domain. Studies can focus on one-to-one communication, mass media, news media or combinations thereof, as well as examine current NCI cancer communication systems, such as the CIS, CancerNet, the NCI designated Cancer Centers, and other existing systems.

The centers' interdisciplinary scientific staff, representing different areas of expertise, will collaborate on projects to promote understanding and improvements in cancer communication. Each Center of Excellence must also provide career development opportunities for new and established investigators who wish to pursue active research careers in interdisciplinary cancer communication research; provide developmental funds for innovative pilot projects; and participate with other Centers of Excellence on a regular basis to share information, assess scientific progress in the field, identify new research opportunities, promote discovery, and resolve areas of scientific controversy. The four CECCR research programs include:

1. *The University of Michigan Center for Health Communications Research (UMCHCR).* This will develop an efficient, theory-driven model to generate tailored health behavior interventions that can be generalized across health behaviors and sociodemographic populations. The research conducted by this Center will advance the evidence base, methodologies, technologies, and conceptual frameworks relevant to developing and implementing tailored Web- and print-based cancer prevention and control materials. The UMCHCR will support three research projects. Project 1 will aim to facilitate smoking cessation; Project 2 will focus on promoting fruit and vegetable intake among African-American adults; and Project 3 will develop a decision aid to help women decide whether to undergo tamoxifen prophylaxis for breast cancer prevention. All projects will employ a resolution IV fractional

factorial design to determine the potential active ingredients of tailoring, including, but not limited to, communication factors such as message content, message framing, message source, and graphics presentation; individual factors such as culture and sociodemographics; and psychometric factors such as motivation and self-efficacy.

2. *The University of Pennsylvania Effects of Public Information in Cancer (EPIC) Center.* This will examine how people make sense of the complex public information environment and how it affects the behavioral choices they make, relevant to cancer. The effects of the public information environment occur in the context of individuals' personal knowledge, skills and characteristics, their social relationships, and their contact with health professionals and health institutions. The EPIC Center brings together scholars with a range of disciplinary backgrounds and conceptual frameworks for each project and core, including communication science, medical science, public health, and social, cognitive, and clinical psychology. This primary focus on research will complement careful attention to the development of new research and research approaches in the area, the training of researchers in the area of cancer communication, and the dissemination of results in ways that influence practice. The three Penn Center research projects include studies of information scanning and searching behavior about prostate, breast, and colon cancer-related decisions, differential responsiveness to anti-tobacco advertising varying in content and format among high and low sensation-seeking young adults, and how the framing of news media information about genetic risk for nicotine addiction influences smoking-related cognitions and behaviors.

3. *The St. Louis University Center of Excellence in Cancer Communications Research.* This research will enhance the effectiveness of cancer communication among African Americans. It will help identify strategies for integrating cancer communication within the cultural norms, values, and beliefs of various groups of African Americans; evaluate the effects of these strategies; and explain the mechanisms through which they influence cancer-related beliefs and practices. The Center consists of three major studies. Project 1 will capture on videotape the stories of 80 African-American breast cancer survivors, examine the effectiveness of these stories in promoting mammography in 900 African-American women, and test a new

explanatory model of narrative cancer communication effects. Experience-based communication through storytelling is deeply rooted in the culture of African-American women and is promising for cancer communication. Project 2 will conduct the first ever national study of black newspapers to determine the frequency and nature of their coverage of cancer-related stories, then develop and test a computer-based intervention to enhance cancer coverage in black newspapers by providing them with community-specific stories and data on cancer. Black newspapers are largely untapped as a channel for cancer communication, but promising because they are read, trusted, and valued by African Americans, attentive to issues in the local black community, and provide information and perspectives that are largely missing from the general media. Project 3 will compare the effectiveness of three different approaches to cultural appropriateness on affective, cognitive, and behavioral responses to a series of colorectal cancer risk reduction magazines. Learning more about these three approaches—peripheral, evidential, and sociocultural—will help develop a theory of cultural cancer communication and assist practitioners in developing more effective programs and materials.

4. *The University of Wisconsin (UW) Center of Excellence in Cancer Communication.* This Center is designed to advance interactive cancer communication systems (ICCSs) to improve the quality of life of patients and families facing cancer across the disease spectrum—with special emphasis on underserved populations. The CHESS program developed at UW is an ICCS that pioneered the use of interactive computer technology for cancer patients. Specific goals of this center are to extend the reach of interactive health communication systems to include new skills in managing distress; relating as couples; providing help for caregivers and patients facing the end of life and bereavement; tailoring sophisticated systems to individual needs; understanding the mechanisms of the effect of a successful ICCS; measuring the cost and outcomes of integrating interactive computer technology with NCI's CIS telephone information service (serving as cancer mentors); learning the impact on patient and caregiver quality of life when clinicians are informed electronically about patient's health status and patient and caregiver levels of distress; determining how partner/caregivers are affected by ICCSs; developing cost-effective ICCS for the underserved; and building an interdisciplinary

structure that supports creative discourse, understanding, and modeling of pioneering cancer communication technologies. The Web site at Project 1 shows a controlled trial to examine whether breast cancer patient outcomes change as different types of conceptually distinct CHESS services (information, social support, and skills training) are systematically added to a patient's treatment resources. The Web site at Project 2 is a fully crossed design to test the efficacy of CHESS and a human Cancer Mentor against a control condition in which patients are given only access to the Internet (rapidly becoming a de facto standard information care situation). Another Web site, Project 3, evaluates whether CHESS improves palliative care and the impact of sharing patient information with clinicians. (For more information about the CECCR research program please see: http://dccps.nci.nih.gov/eocc/ceccrs_index.html.)

4. The Multimedia Technology/Health Communication Grants Program

The NCI also supports Small Business Innovation Research (SBIR) and Small Business Technology Transfer Research (SBTTR) grants as part of its Multimedia Technology/Health Communication (MT/HC) Grant Program. This program encourages small businesses and nonprofit collaborators to create innovative approaches to translate cancer research into practice by developing and applying a wide array of media technology interventions, programs, systems, networks, or products needed by health care professionals and/or the public that will reduce the risks of cancer, provide treatment options, or address the needs of cancer survivors.

The MT/HC grants support the development of novel health communication products and technologies for introduction into markets where they can provide relevant health information to key populations. For example, these grants have been used to promote the use of media technology to translate cancer research into information that educates primary care providers and the public about cancer risk reduction activities, and health promotion of cancer survivors. They have been used to promote creative and appropriate uses of computer or Web applications, expert systems, advanced telephone technologies, videotext, cable or broadcast television, radio, virtual reality, animation, or imaging to inform or educate target populations. These grants have also helped to promote education and training in the use of media technology to help different individuals and groups translate science and research into practical communication applications. (For more information about this SBIR/SBTTR program, see: http://dccps.nci.nih.gov/hcirb/sbir/.)

5. The Cancer Information Service Research Consortium

The Cancer Information Service Research Consortium (CISRC) is an innovative multi-initiative program project that supports health communication research projects utilizing the NCI's CIS network as a laboratory to examine new strategies for disseminating cancer information, reaching diverse audiences, and influencing important health behaviors. Unlike the other initiatives described here, the CISRC was conceived and developed by the principal investigators with support from NCI. The goal of the CISRC is to expand knowledge about new cancer communication strategies and processes, while innovating the health communication policies and practices of the CIS by providing evidence-based health communication strategies to disseminate cancer information, influence relevant cancer behaviors (e.g., risk assessment, decision making, screening and detection, clinical trial accrual, and adjustment to cancer), and generally meeting the public's need for accurate cancer information. CISRC projects are described by Morra[13] and Rimer and colleagues.[14]

6. The Health Communication Intervention Research Program

The Health Communication Intervention Research Program is a targeted group of health communication field research projects funded by the NCI. Seven multi-year research projects are studying innovative strategies for communicating cancer information to diverse high-risk populations. Researchers are evaluating new health communication design and delivery strategies, such as message tailoring, message framing, and Internet-delivered health messages to promote cancer screening, risk assessment, and behavior changes (such as dietary, exercise, and smoking interventions) across several different cancer sites and stages in the continuum of cancer care (prevention, detection, diagnosis, treatment, survivorship, end of life). While these research projects are still in progress, there is great promise that they will lead to important new knowledge about cancer communications and applications for cancer prevention and control.

7. Making Quality Count for Consumers and Patients Research Program

The NCI and the Agency for Health Care Research and Quality jointly sponsored a new research funding initiative, as part of an interagency agreement, in support of the Department of Health and Human Services in its broad-ranging "Quality of Care" initiative. The research program supported by NCI and administered by the Health Communication and Informatics Research Branch as part of this initiative is currently developing and testing materials that help consumers interpret and understand health risks. To understand the important health risks they face and whether they can do anything to reduce these risks, people need data that are intrinsically quantitative and probabilistic. Unfortunately, there is evidence that people have trouble with the basic skills required to understand such data: working with probabilities, recognizing the additional information needed to give probability meaning, and making basic assessments about data quality.[14]

The study funded under this initiative involves development of new educational materials that will cover what to look for in statements about risk, how to put cancer risk and treatment benefit in perspective, how to make sense of changes in risk, and quality of evidence. The new materials are designed to facilitate the communication of data by putting risk into context. Three basic risk communication tools will be developed and evaluated to supplement the tutorial: *cancer risk charts*—tables containing age-specific mortality rates for a range of diseases plus all-cause mortality; *prevention benefit charts*—tables presenting the mortality benefit of various preventive strategies; and *standard disease summary templates*—a standard format to present information about a specific disease. This study addresses an important topic and could be the groundwork for a body of research on consumer understanding of health statistics. It has the potential to demonstrate an inexpensive and effective method to improve people's ability to understand and interpret probability data about their health.[15]

8. Unsolicited Health Communication Grant Applications

The NCI actively supports a vibrant program of investigator-initiated research projects that reflect current and emerging health communication research interests. Applications are supported under a broad range of funding mechanisms for these unsolicited grant applications, including P01 (program project grants); R01 (research project grants); R03 (small research grants); and R21 (exploratory/innovative research grants). (See http://www.nci.nih.gov/research_funding/ for information about NCI research funding opportunities.) The NCI's unsolicited health communication and informatics research portfolio now supports innovative research on a broad range of topics, including provider/consumer relations; new communication technology interventions for health promotion; health risk communication; Internet-based dissemination of health information; and Web-based health risk assessment and prevention counseling. Unsolicited grant applications provide health communication scholars with a wonderful opportunity to gain support for rigorous and important health communication inquiry.

NCI staff are developing several new research initiatives to complement these programs. The plan is to establish a broad range of communication research projects to examine the powerful role of human and mediated communication in cancer prevention and control across many important settings; with different relevant populations; and across key communication channels and media. The cancer communications research program will encompass interpersonal, group, organizational, and societal levels of communication, and will include examinations of a broad range of communication delivery systems, including mass media and new media. There is much to learn about the processes of communication in health care, and especially in cancer prevention and control. NCI's initiatives provide a rich model for stimulating investigation, building new knowledge, and guiding health communication policy and intervention. In many cases, these initiatives are being developed in partnership with other National Institutes of Health as well as nongovernmental foundations and agencies.

Conclusion

Health communication has the great potential to help reduce cancer risks, incidence, morbidity, and mortality, while enhancing quality of life across the continuum of cancer care (prevention, detection, diagnosis, treatment, survivorship, and end-of-life care). Yet, the role of communication in cancer prevention and control is complex. Research is needed to untangle the complexities of cancer communications and identify strategic applications across the continuum of cancer care. The NCI's development of an ambitious program of cancer communications research to examine the influences of health communication in confronting cancer and promoting important health outcomes has the potential to significantly increase knowledge about the role of communication in cancer prevention and control, and direct strategic communication interventions to help reduce the burden of cancer on society.

Notes

1. G. L. Kreps, "The Pervasive Role of Information in Health and Health Care: Implications for Health Communication Policy," in *Communication Yearbook* 11, ed. J. Anderson (Newbury Park, CA: Sage Publications, 1988), 238–276.

2. G. L. Kreps, "The Evolution and Advancement of Health Communication Inquiry," in *Communication Yearbook* 24, ed. B. Gudykunst (Newbury Park, CA: Sage Publications, 2001), 232–254.

3. I. Byock, "Completing the Continuum of Cancer Care: Integrating Life-prolongation and Palliation," *CA: A Cancer Journal for Clinicians* 50 (2000): 123–132.

4. M. Hewitt and J. V. Simone, *Ensuring Quality Cancer Care* (Washington, DC: National Academy Press, 1999).

5. R. A. Hiatt and B. K. Rimer, "A New Strategy for Cancer Control Research," *Cancer Epidemiology, Biomarkers, & Prevention* 8 (1999): 957–964.

6. G. L. Kreps, "The Impact of Communication on Cancer Risk, Incidence, Morbidity, Mortality, and Quality of Life," *Health Communication* (2003).

7. Institute of Medicine, *Crossing the Quality Chasm: A New Health System for the 21st Century* (Washington, DC: National Academy of Sciences, 2001).

8. Institute of Medicine, *Speaking of Health: Assessing Health Communication Strategies for Diverse Populations* (Washington, DC: National Academy of Sciences, 2002).

9. National Cancer Institute, *The Nation's Investment in Cancer Research: A Budget Proposal for Fiscal Year 2003* (Washington, DC: NCI, 2001).

10. Science Panel on Interactive Communication and Health, *Wired for Health and Well-Being: The Emergence of Interactive Health Communication*, trans. ed. D. H. Gustafson (Washington, DC: U.S. Department of Health and Human Services, U.S. Government Printing Office, 1999).

11. Institute of Medicine, *The Unequal Burden of Cancer: An Assessment of NIH Research and Programs for Ethnic Minorities and the Medically Underserved* (Washington, DC: National Academy of Sciences, 1999).

12. B. K. Rimer and J. P. Van Nevel (eds.), "Cancer Risk Communication: What We Know and What We Need to Know," *Journal of the National Cancer Institute* 25 (1999): 1–185.

13. M. Morra, ed., "The Impact and Value of the Cancer Information Service: A Model for Health Communication," *Journal of Health Communication* 3 (Suppl.) (1998).

14. B. K. Rimer et al., eds., "Cancer Information Research Consortium: 1993–1997," *Preventive Medicine* 27 (Suppl.) (1998).

15. S. Woloshin, L. M. Schwartz, and H. G. Welch, "Risk Charts: Putting Cancer in Context," *Journal of the National Cancer Institute* 94(11) (2002): 799–804.

CHAPTER TWENTY-FOUR

Content Analysis of Anthrax in the Media

Muhiuddin Haider and Nisha P. Aravindakshan

Chapter Questions

1. What are the possible reasons that the public received misinformation through the media regarding anthrax?
2. What were the reasons for increases in media coverage of anthrax at different periods in 2003? What were the consequences of increased media coverage?
3. Who do you think should be responsible for disseminating information during bioterrorism events? How can accuracy and credibility be ensured when it is necessary to respond rapidly?

Introduction

A mere mention of anthrax spread fear and paralysis throughout the population. The anthrax threat rips through the lives of Americans nationwide, eliciting panic and concern among the population. These fears are amplified by the media, which have taken on the daunting role of the bearer of bad news. The anthrax outbreak in 2001 arose amid a great deal of controversy regarding the nation's preparedness for a biological attack. The security and welfare of the people seemed to be in jeopardy despite the fact that this was not the first blow to the integrity of national security. The Manchester anthrax outbreak of 1957 at the

Arms Textile Mill in Manchester, New Hampshire, spurred the beginnings of vaccination experiments for the deadly spores.[1] Although the epidemic was not the result of a terrorist attack, it did warrant the attention of the Centers for Disease Control (CDC), which then initiated an experimental vaccination campaign on uninfected mill workers.

Mention of the anthrax outbreak only recently came to light with the October 5, 2001, intentional anthrax release in Florida.[2] This episode was classified as a bioterrorist attack, calculated to cause fatalities among thousands of unsuspecting Floridians. The question to raise here is why the media resurrected the Manchester case that took place over 40 years earlier? The opportunity to point a finger and designate the blame on the nation's nonexistent bioterrorism defense team is a possibility. The goals of the media are not always well intended and are often premature as the purveyors of truthful information to the public.

The media saturate the public with extraneous information such as the lethality and number of spores, which an individual must be exposed to in order to become infected.[3] Realistically, such information has no practical application for the individual at risk of exposure. These details merely complicate fears and escalate the threat of anthrax, which then becomes an esoteric issue that the media paint as the responsibility of the government to protect the helpless population. This case study will discuss the presentation of anthrax in the media and analyze the effect of this information on the public's opinion of the anthrax threat and the government's response to the biological agent and the public's concerns.

Biological Brief

Anthrax infections can be contracted several ways. These include inhalation, cutaneous entry, and gastrointestinal intake, making it one of the most potentially threatening diseases to public health. Though not contagious, the versatility of the anthrax bacteria to infect inanimate and live hosts heightens the concern over its ability to be transmitted effortlessly from person to person or even from animals to humans. The various manifestations of anthrax help to classify its origin as one of natural or unnatural production. The latter situation is indicative of an intentional threat to the health and safety of the intended targets. The former condition has not elicited as much fear as the latter but should be regarded as an equal threat to public health.

Cutaneous anthrax is contracted through direct exposure to anthrax spores or through contact with infected animals. Anthrax spores can exist on a surface or in the atmosphere indefinitely until appropriately disinfected. Gastrointestinal anthrax is uncommon except for a few international cases. Consumption of infected meat results in 25 percent to 65 percent fatality rate. Inhalation anthrax is the most fatal of the three forms and perhaps the most difficult form to detect. Furthermore, antibiotic treatment is not always appropriately administered or successful. This creates the potential breeding of new drug-resistant strains.

Public Health Threats

The Food and Drug Administration (FDA) of the United States predicted possible contamination of the food supply by anthrax in the fall of 2003. Despite this warning, no visible precautions have been taken. In light of the bovine spongiform encephalitis, commonly known as Mad Cow disease, protection of the vulnerable food supply appears to be of the utmost concern. However, the ill-preparedness of the government to handle a nonterrorist threat against our food supply revealed its further inadequacy in quelling fears over a deliberate attack. The FDA has emphasized the fatal nature of anthrax and botulinum toxins if disseminated into the food supply. The relative ease of its ability to contaminate upon contact makes it particularly difficult to contain and detect without the proper methods or mechanisms in place. Internationally, livestock face the threat of gastrointestinal and cutaneous anthrax, which can later be passed on to humans. The contamination of horsemeat and cattle in Kazakh[4] and West Bengal,[5] respectively, has raised concerns about the risk involved in handling contaminated meat.

Reports of contaminated textiles as in the Manchester case and of infected livestock as in India and Kazakh generated minimal significance in the eyes of the media, which focused all of their energy on the terrorist threat of anthrax. The key element to recognize in this disparity of attention is that anthrax is equally fatal in cases of natural and unnatural exposure. In fact, the former is more manageable by the public, which can take preventive measures and identify and isolate suspicious infections before they spiral out of control. The most action that can be taken to prevent unnatural exposure is to be vaccinated. However, the media have generated the idea that additional efforts can be taken by the biodefense taskforce to prevent anthrax infection. It is the fulfillment of these promises or lack thereof that has left many Americans wondering if the government is capable of protecting them.

Is This Threat Visible to the Public?

The anthrax attack in the District of Columbia posed a major threat to virtually all U.S. Postal Service customers. The threat turned junk mail into potential parcels of danger. The psychological impact of the anthrax scare created a wave of concern over the actual risk to individuals in the event of mass contamination.[6] The methods of risk communication during the attack are often criticized for not conveying sensitivity to the psychological welfare of the public and not managing the threat in a cautious and considerate manner. Exclusion of the public's trust as a foundation toward execution of an efficient and flawless containment protocol resulted in alarm and confusion, which was followed by lack of cooperation.

The media play a pivotal role in establishing the psychological management of the population. In 2001 the media failed to deliver relevant and credible information to the public immediately following the attacks. The common trend found in media messages elicited fear and resentment due to the government's lack of preparedness. The blame, however, does not rest solely on the shoulders of print and broadcast media. The medical and scientific community also failed to quell the public's fears, mostly due to their own ignorance. These two factors together fueled the growth for widespread ignorance about the potential dangers of anthrax. Without accurate and reliable information, the public depended on myth and hearsay to determine the ill effects of anthrax. The consequences of this were illuminated almost immediately when fear caused the public to refuse inoculation against potentially fatal diseases such as smallpox.

The 2003, Sudden Acute Respiratory Syndrome (SARS) outbreak elicited a parallel response when many who fled China to escape from the disease inadvertently put others at risk of contracting the contagious illness. Clear, accurate, and manageable information is necessary to prevent panic and encourage cooperation among the population.[7] In an effort to achieve this crucial element, various organizations have set forth campaigns to communicate the risk posed by biological agents. The efforts of organizations such as the Partnership for Anthrax Vaccine Education seek to dispel common myths about anthrax and its vaccine and provide scientifically sound and relevant information via electronic media. The challenges to communication risks are similar to those faced by general emergency care situations. Both must consider the psychological impact of the crisis situation and replace inaccurate beliefs with scientific facts.

Analysis: Presentation of Anthrax through the Media

If the government collaborated with the private media on how best to disseminate information, the question that remains is, Who would ultimately authorize decisions?[8] With the scientific community stretching across the globe, it is important to recognize its important role in communicating and assessing the true risks posed by biological agents. The management of information, myths, and rumors should be a bilateral effort between the government and public health leaders. This is key to avoid conflicting plans of action that lead the public to question the credibility of authority.[9] Lack of an information system infrastructure led to the confusion over anthrax vaccine efficacy and safety. Anxiety over the potential side effects of the vaccine deterred many postal employees and military personnel from being inoculated. The failure to communicate the benefits of inoculation is evident here. Elicitation of fear itself did not convince those at the highest risk of threat to risk the side effects of the vaccine. Communication is principal to increasing and maintaining security. An informed and confident society will be more responsive to the introduction of technology and tactics designed to protect the public from bioterrorism threats in the future.[10]

Methodology and Analytic Framework

The research methods involved content analysis of periodical news articles featuring anthrax and bioterrorism information during the year 2003. The newspapers involved in the study included *the New York Times, Wall Street Journal, USA Today, The Washington Post, The Washington Times,* various local papers, international sources, and selected releases from the Associated Press. Both quantitative and qualitative methods were used to analyze the articles with respect to the frequency and potential impact of the news media coverage.

News items selected for the study were print articles from periodicals written for the distinct purpose of communicating news related to anthrax or bioterrorism. Next, the news articles were classified based on their relevance to bioterrorism and anthrax. All articles with content relating to awareness, information-seeking, instruction, risk communication, or persuasion were included.

Content analysis of media sources, especially periodicals, reveals that extreme biases are involved in the selection of news material. Sponsorship and censorship regulations filter the news before it is printed or broadcast to the public. The literacy level of potential readers, as well as the audience range, differs for each publication. Considering that one in five Americans is functionally illiterate and 51 percent report frustration and challenge when interpreting scientific or health information.[11] it is important to recognize that this will affect their decision on where to obtain their information and what sources they trust. Additionally, 21 percent of Americans do not read newspapers, creating a surge in the usage of the Internet as a major source of health information.

The communications utilized thus far have included news media on television and published reports that are not designed for low literacy groups. A substantial amount of information is confined to scholarly journals, which are often not accessible or popularized in the general public. The use of Internet sources is becoming commonplace and a primary source for instant information. The ability to regulate and filter this information for accuracy is limited.[12]

Analysis of the coverage trends shows an overwhelming amount of local papers carried more anthrax articles than national papers such as *The New York Times, Washington Post, and Wall Street Journal* (see Figure 24–1).

The responsibility of maintaining journalistic integrity during a time of potential crisis is key to the success of any media distributor in gaining the support and trust of the target audience. Ultimately, no matter what audience is targeted, the best types of communication use a balance of fear and evidence-based appeals to raise awareness and instruct the audience on how to modify behavior and adapt to the environmental changes.

Coverage Trends

In October of 2003, Dr. Julie Gerberding, director of the CDC, cited anthrax among a number of public health threats that required the use of fast, credible communication.[13] The acknowledgment of

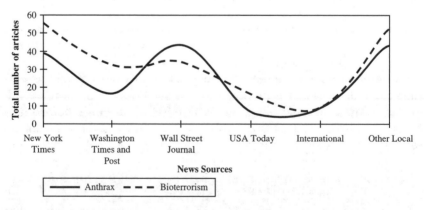

Figure 24–1. Comparison of Bioterrorism and Anthrax Frequency in the News

anthrax as a biological threat that demands a rapid response is now evident in light of the frequency and potential threat of attacks. Barriers to monitoring and evaluating the quality of health risk communications need to be addressed. CDC cites this as a major obstacle to improving the effectiveness and efficiency of communications.[14] The CDC blames the inadequacy of threat communication on the sheer lack of resources, appropriate protocol, and appropriate personnel to execute the task of gathering the necessary data and analyzing the response of the public to the media. It is this lag in developing adequate protocol for data collection and dissemination that plagued the minds of Americans throughout 2003.

The coverage of anthrax and bioterrorism reflects the public's desire to know more because article publication is often fueled by periodical sales. The frequency of articles indicates that the fear of anthrax was still strong from January to June of 2003 (see Figure 24–2).

Because the popularity of articles can influence the decision to print subsequent articles, an important question remains: Are the media creating a bigger threat than that which actually exists? Media coverage following the anthrax attacks was coupled with a subsequent rise in the number of over-the-counter and prescription drug requests.[15] Media coverage shapes the public's perception of events and how to respond to a given situation. It can establish norms or influence attitudes toward a particular issue. Considering the response to media coverage, it can be said that it was unnecessary to create this

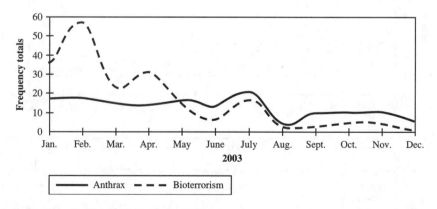

Figure 24–2. Frequency Comparison of Bioterrorism and Anthrax Articles throughout 2003.

much fear when it was reciprocated by unattainable demands. The government's response was limited, and the public labeled this response as a result of complete lack of preparedness.

The contents of articles on bioterrorism ranged from concerns over mass contamination by agents such as smallpox, which has already been eradicated globally, to toxins such as botulinum. Stories on vaccine refusal were matched by those discussing rampant demand. An increase in the number of potential identified threats identified was complemented by a surge in articles and public fears (see Figure 24–3).

The spikes of media coverage in May 2003 can be attributed to the increase in awareness about Mad Cow disease and SARS. Recurring fears that vaccines posed a great risk to the health of individuals hindered vaccination campaigns, especially among the military and health care workers. Most of the media coverage focused on this factor and perhaps only reinforced or contributed to concerns about the safety and benefits of vaccination. Local papers tended to cover anthrax more frequently and covered a large variety of issues. The more academic papers tended to focus on research and funding as key concerns and offered little information regarding what the public themselves could do (see Figure 24–4).

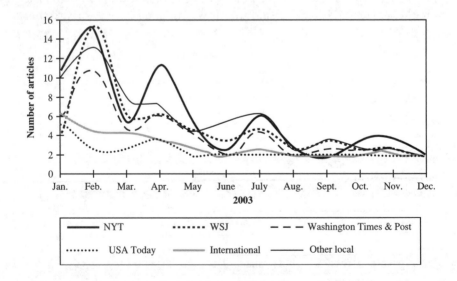

Figure 24–3. Frequency of Bioterrorism Articles in 2003 News Clippings

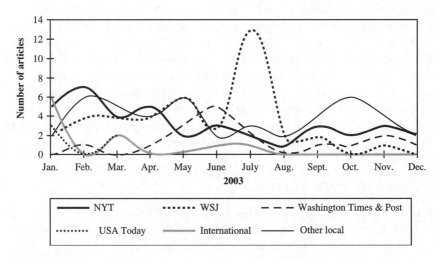

Figure 24–4. Frequency of Anthrax Articles in 2003 News Clippings

Analysis: Key Issues

Threats initiated from foreign terrorist groups were predominant in media coverage. Despite the finding that most of the postal threats were locally initiated, the media conjured the notion that foreign terrorists would seize the opportunity to play on the fear and weaknesses in national security. Whether or not these claims were legitimate did not stop the general public from envisioning life-threatening scenarios in which they were left unprotected and helpless. The threat of anthrax was reinforced by media coverage that emphasized the fatal outcome of exposure to even minute amounts of the toxic spores. This coverage, however, was not paralleled or countered by providing relevant prevention and safety measures. Vaccination methods were discussed frequently in news articles but these options did not apply to the general public. Inoculation options were restricted to first responder emergency and military personnel and those who were potentially exposed to anthrax. Furthermore, the aversion toward inoculation exhibited by these groups who are at high risk of exposure did not quell the public's fears on the potential danger of anthrax exposure.

There are of course limits to a campaign's effectiveness because there is potential for boomerang effects or desensitization from overexposure to extreme or inaccurate information. In the case of anthrax, psychological responses were not carefully considered before releasing the information. The clear purpose for communicating information about anthrax to the public was also blurred. Was it to encourage demand for the vaccine? This seems self-defeating because adequate stocks of vaccines and antibiotics are not available for the general public and were limited to those considered at the highest risk. Anthrax demands international attention because it has the versatility of being directed at individuals and whole populations; therefore international response protocol for risk communications should be developed.

Vulnerable Populations

Due to a lack of licensed treatment options, certain groups including pregnant women, children, the elderly and immunocompromised individuals are particularly vulnerable to biological threats. Providing people with accurate methods of protection or cautionary measures they can take, such as storing water, masks, and disaster kits, is vital. It is also important to correct misinformation. For example, stockpiling pharmaceuticals and plastic sheeting will not help against a threat like anthrax. Furthermore, the treatment options for individuals should be clearly communicated so that in the event of exposure, they can be immediately treated. Those who have been exposed or may have family members that are exposed need to know the facts of treatment and symptoms to recognize. In the event of a biological threat, there should be resources available so people can have in-home detection methods to ensure safe drinking water and an environment clear of toxins. Also, due to the virulent nature of anthrax, it can exist in the environment for long periods of time. Therefore, reoccurring contamination should be carefully monitored.

The susceptibility of livestock, crops, and animals to anthrax and other toxins has yielded only more safety concerns. These concerns however, have not yet been met by an adequate response. The Federal Emergency Management Administration guidelines for protecting this vulnerable population are vague and limited in scope of prevention. The concern of pet owners for their pets' welfare is also met with little response from the scientific community. Speculation on developing toxin-resistant breeds of livestock was a reoccurring theme in most articles that discussed research on bioterrorism. This is not unwarranted, however, because spores can exist after decontaminating livestock and can be recirculated into the environment.

The question that currently stands is whether investment in surveillance and technology is going to be enough to protect us from a real threat. A recent reduction in public health and emergency first responder preparedness is being sacrificed for the purpose of funding more research. This is quite alarming, because lack of preparedness for an unpredictable attack is what spurred fears in the first place.

Treatment Options

A 60-day antibiotic treatment was prescribed as a precaution for those potentially exposed during the 2001 anthrax attacks. Despite concern over the exposure severity, there was more than 40 percent failure to adhere to the extensive treatment. One contributing factor was that many individuals did not experience any symptoms of illness and, therefore, discontinued treatment.[16] This is commonplace because the perceived threat of an illness is low or nonexistent. A consequence of this is the need for even more extensive countertherapy for those who fail to finish the course of therapy or who are exposed to higher levels than others. Furthermore, those who do survive have the potential to suffer during post-treatment.

The quest to decontaminate, neutralize, and eradicate the threat of anthrax has been pursued by various public and private sector agencies. Project Bioshield has invested heavily in developing a new generation of vaccines and antibiotics to prevent and potentially cure anthrax infections.[17] Avanir Pharmaceuticicals has developed an antibody that neutralizes the key toxin in anthrax.[18] This option alone or in combination with other antibodies provides immunity to those exposed or those who might have been exposed. In comparison to the BioThrax,™ which requires six injections over an 18-month period, this new technology provides a rapid treatment. This is a crucial option during a situation where, if an outbreak should occur, the public will be reassured that an instant cure exists. Due to the varying types of exposure and different degrees of severity, treatment options must be tailored to meet needs on a case-by-case basis.

The BioThrax™ vaccine is FDA-licensed for individuals between 18 and 65 years old. However, as previously mentioned, those who are at potentially greater risk, are children and the elderly. Prevention and treatment options have not yet been tested to address this issue. The effects on children, a population largely neglected to this point, and the risk they face in the event of exposure are completely different than that of adult exposure. There needs to be a component addressing the symptoms and effects on children. Anything that can be done in case exposure occurs to a child should be included. Treatment of children, the elderly, and the immunocompromised requires more intensive action in developing the correct dosage requirements, and no such standard has yet been established.

Additionally, treatment of livestock or crops has not yet been discussed in the public arena as an area of concern. In light of the Mad Cow outbreaks, this avenue should be explored further. It is possible that the public is unaware that the gastrointestinal and cutaneous forms of anthrax can be contracted through contaminated meat. The decision to inoculate livestock and domesticated animals should be factored into potential vaccine campaigns. If the efforts of the government are visible to the public, this will alleviate fear of ill-preparedness during future attacks.

The need to develop technology, which can quickly detect anthrax spores, is crucial to developing a rapid response system. New York University and other innovative researchers are eager to develop handheld devices, which would allow for rapid detection of anthrax and other potentially harmful microbes.[19] These highly anticipated devices are expected to be available within the next five years. The public sector anticipates the development of such products, which will alleviate concerns regarding early detection and responsiveness to future threats.[20]

Fast, Credible Communication

Risk communication should convey salient, comprehensible, and credible knowledge.[21] Primary exposure to inaccurate or skewed data will leave individuals misinformed regarding the potential risks involved in exposure to a biological antigen. Standard policy for informing the public of biological threats is to disseminate information regardless of the potential for panic or worry. If a rapid response is not carried out, the likelihood of myths and rumors circulating as supplementary information is potentially greater. Fischoff and colleagues[22] found that initial risk communications following the anthrax scare failed to deliver accurate information. The study found that nearly 28 percent of those surveyed believed anthrax to be contagious and 19 percent held other false beliefs about anthrax.

The effect of misinformation can be critical in the event of a real threat. Without a proper understanding of how the antigen is transmitted, individuals can inadvertently be putting themselves at risk. For example, instead of remaining indoors to protect themselves from inhalation or cutaneous exposure, panicked individuals might flee or evacuate a contaminated area, as in the case of the SARS epidemic.[23] Fischhoff and colleagues identified three mistakes that would result in failure of risk communication: facts missing from messages that reached the public, facts lost in the clutter of messages, and poor communication of facts.[24]

Communication between various sectors is also critical during responses to infectious diseases or biological threats. Ensuring that frontline medical responders are accurately informed about the clinical aspects of a biological threat is key to containing and eliminating the threat. The methods of dissemination used to brief medical personnel differ from those used to address the general public. In fact, electronic information systems are relied on heavily to distribute information rapidly among health care facilities.[25] Providing specific protocols in preparation for an anthrax attack is necessary for ensuring threat precautions. These protocols, however, should also devise a proper strategy for communicating risks and recommendations.

While the electronic media distributed to health providers and first responders contain accurate and pertinent information, the electronic media available to the general public are not always as credible. The use of the Internet as a source of information has become increasingly popular. The standard time for a posting on electronic media without proper editing is 24 to 48 hours after the announcement of a threat.[26] Is this standard appropriate in a time of crisis when hours or even minutes can be crucial to protecting oneself from a threat that can be inhaled in seconds? Major newspapers, Web sites, and encyclopedias can all be accessed with just a few clicks of a mouse. The disadvantage of this is the tendency for unedited, inaccurate information to be accessed. Under the protection of the First Amendment, little can be done to regulate the content of the Internet regardless of its validity and accuracy. As a result, millions of Internet users depend on the information published by sometimes questionable sources.

The anthrax outbreaks highlighted the need to create a biological threat protocol that would minimize fear and anxiety while maximizing cooperation. The 2003 SARS outbreak revealed how this need for emergency protocol was fulfilled. The SARS threat was met with a rapid and clear response to the public's inquiries. Although the SARS threat was not as immediate as the anthrax threat because of its seclusion to the Asian region, many Americans felt threatened by its potential to cross borders undetected. Coincidentally, this theme reoccurred in the media coverage during the SARS outbreak, suggesting that the media were fueling the fears of Americans.

Eliciting Fear

One of the take-home lessons from the 2001 anthrax attacks and the current SARS and Mad Cow disease coverage is that the most crucial period to disseminate verifiable and reliable information is during the announcement/definition stage of media coverage.[27] This involves a strategy designed to allow the public to respond to the information and raise concerns that will then be systematically addressed. The main concerns of the media during this crisis focused on assignment of blame and not on dispelling myths and raising prevention awareness.

The anthrax scare has been criticized as being overly dramatized in the sense that little could be done to control future threats; whereas for Mad Cow disease the agriculture and livestock industry was able to enhance protection of the food supply.[28] As with the Mad Cow disease crisis, it is questionable as to whether the media played a pivotal role in exaggerating the crisis and pointing blame at the U.S. Department of Agriculture.

The high volume of information presented to the public did not appear to have clear underlying purpose with regard to prevention. The ability to communicate anthrax information effectively signifies an understanding of human nature and the demand for accurate and practical knowledge. The trends in data and content of the news coverage during 2003 did not reflect that the media had a clear understanding of the importance of this innate relationship.

Mad Cow disease was able to gain more attention and financial response perhaps because the overflow of momentum from the anthrax scare fueled an urgency for investment in prevention. The second opportunity to win the public's trust and to covertly apologize for lack of preparedness previously during the anthrax attacks was immediately seized. Perhaps the Mad Cow threat garnered more attention because the capacity to protect against it did exist, unlike anthrax. The Mad Cow scare also increased the budget for vaccine stockpiles and upgraded funding for anthrax vaccine reserves for the public.

Avoiding partial responsibility for the effects of the information released is a key skill of the media in a crisis. Inaccuracies are often responsible for eliciting fear. Should this be remedied by allowing only the government to dispense knowledge as it sees fit to ensure accuracy? Are we then susceptible to the government's incompetence during times of crisis when it fails to give the public fair warning? Balancing media and government responsibility is wrought with difficulty. However, this must be achieved to ensure public health success. It is critical to evaluate and monitor the success and failure of these campaigns for the future.

Predictability plays a pivotal role in determining the necessary precautionary measures to be taken; in the case of anthrax, future threats are virtually unpredictable, leaving the public vulnerable and defenseless. The only hope the public has in such a situation is the security of accurate information delivered in a timely manner.

Notes

1. Pam Belluck, "Anthrax Outbreak of '57 Felled a Mill but Yielded Answers," *New York Times,* October 27, 2001.

2. "Bioterrorism-Related Inhalation Anthrax: The First 10 Cases Reported in the United States," *Emerging Infectious Diseases* 7(6) (November–December 2001): 933–944.

3. *Protecting Americans Against Anthrax: The Need for an Effective Disease* (Bioport Corporation, October 2002).

4. "Kazakh Anthrax Linked to Horse Meat," July 19, 2003. http://www.theage.com.au/articles/2003/07/19/1058545616107.html.

5. "Anthrax Fear Grips West Bengal Village," India Express Bureau, October 17, 2001. http://www.indiaexpress.com/news/regional/bengal/20011017-0.html.

6. M. J. Hall et al., "The Psychological Impact of Bioterrorism," *Biosecurity and Bioterrorism: Biodefense Strategy, Practice and Science* 1(2) (2003): 139–144.

7. "Kazakh Anthrax Linked to Horse Meat."

8. E. R. Parker and L. G. Jacobs, "Government Controls of Information and Scientific Inquiry. The Psychological Impact of Bioterrorism," *Biosecurity and Bioterrorism: Biodefense Strategy, Practice and Science* 1(2) (2003): 83–95.

9. Hall et al., "The Psychological Impact of Bioterrorism."

10. R. Carlson, "The Pace and Proliferation of Biological Technologies," *Biosecurity and Bioterrorism: Biodefense Strategy, Practice and Service,* 1(3) (2003): 203–214.

11. National Center for Education Statistics (NCES), U. S. Department of Education. 1992 National Adult Literacy Survey. A Program of the National Assessments of Adult Literacy (NAAL) conducted by the NCES.

12. J. Hobbs et al., "Communicating Health Information to an Alarmed Public Facing a Threat Such as a Bioterrorist Attack," *Journal of Health Communication,* 9(1) (2004): 67–76.

13. "CDC Focuses on Public Health Threats," *New York Times,* October 29, 2003.

14. C. E. Prue et al., "Communication Monitoring: Shaping CDC's Emergency Risk Communication Efforts," *Journal of Health Communication* 8(1) (2003): 35–49.

15. F. Mebane, S. Temin, and C. F. Parvanta, "Communicating Anthrax in 2001: A Comparison of CDC Information and Print Media Accounts," *Journal of Health Communication* 8(1) (2003): 50–82.

16. "Longer Anthrax Therapy May Be Needed," *The Washington Post,* A05, July 29, 2003.

17. "New Bugs: 'Project Bioshield,'" *The Washington Post,* July 15, 2003.

18. "AVANIR Reports on Xenerex Technology," *The Wall Street Journal,* February 12, 2003.

19. "Handheld Bio-Terror Detectors in Works," *USA Today*, July 10, 2003.

20. "Firm Detects Profits in Chip-based Tests," *Chicago Tribune*, July 7, 2003.

21. B. Fischhoff et al., "Evaluating the Success of Terror Risk Communications," *Biosecurity and Bioterrorism: Biodefense Strategy, Practice and Science* 1(4) (2003): 255–258.

22. Fischhoff et al., "Evaluating the Success of Terror Risk Communications."

23. Fischhoff et al., "Evaluating the Success of Terror Risk Communications."

24. Fischhoff et al., "Evaluating the Success of Terror Risk Communications."

25. N. M. M'Ikanatha et al., "Sources of Bioterrorism Information among Emergency Physicians during the 2001 Anthrax Outbreak," *Biosecurity and Bioterrorism: Biodefense Strategy, Practice and Science* 1(4) (2003): 259–265.

26. P. Potter, "Electronic Journal Publishing in the Age of Bioterrorism: How Fast Is Fast?" *Journal of Health Communication* 8(1) (2003): 9–10.

27. J. G. Payne, "Media Coverage of the Mad Cow Issue as in Health and the Public Good," *Journal of Health Communication*, ed., S. C. Ratzan, 1997.

28. G. Parker, "4.5m Cows May Face Slaughter: U. K. Seeks to Restore Confidence in Beef, Tougher E. U. Controls Expected," *The Financial Times* 25 (1996): 1.

CHAPTER TWENTY-FIVE

Developing a Theoretical Model of Rapport Building: Implications for Medical Education and the Physician-Patient Relationship

Gretchen R. Norling

Chapter Questions

1. What verbal and nonverbal factors lead to enhanced rapport within a medical encounter?
2. Why are some physicians able to develop rapport with their patients while some are unable to do so? How does rapport develop in a client-provider interaction?
3. How can a skill such as rapport, which is difficult to define, be accurately measured and evaluated? What are its behavioral indicators?

Notes from the Field

Rapport has been identified as an important aspect of the physician-patient relationship. However, a review of the extant literature reveals that rapport has been defined, both conceptually and operationally, in an inconsistent manner within health communication research and medical education texts. Further, there is little theory guiding the research. Consequently, medical educators have little to guide their instruction and evaluation of communication skills in the classroom. Given that communication skills are now being incorporated into the national board certification process, it becomes even more important (especially for evaluation purposes) to identify some of the measurable components of rapport.

Focusing on rapport also offers us an opportunity to gain insight into the physician-patient relationship. Finally, the development of The Rapport Development Model (RDM) provides us with a starting point to begin to understand the complexities of the rapport-building process.

In order to begin to address these challenges, this project focused on how rapport was defined in the literature, how patients defined rapport, and the development of a theoretical model of rapport building. The formal research questions for this project included: (1) Which nonverbal and verbal factors improve rapport building within the medical encounter? (2) Which nonverbal and verbal factors lead to decreased rapport building within the medical encounter? For the purposes of this chapter, brief summaries of the findings along with the RDM will be presented.

A Review of the Literature

A thorough review of health communication, medical education, and related literature found that there was no consistent definition of rapport. Further, there was no agreement regarding what the components of rapport were or how to measure them. Two of the outcomes of this project were to define rapport conceptually, as well as operationally. Drawing on the existing literature and formative research findings, rapport was conceptually defined for this project as, "*a feeling of connectedness and emotional support between physicians and patients.*"[1] Further, based on prior research[2-3] and the development of the current theoretical model, rapport was operationally defined as the following:

> Rapport is built through specific behaviors. Positive rapport behaviors are comprised of rapport-initiating and enhancing behaviors, which can lead to positive rapport. Negative rapport behaviors are comprised of rapport-terminating behaviors, which can lead to no rapport or negative rapport. Ultimately, positive rapport should lead to increased patient comfort (reduced anxiety), increased self-disclosure, and increased patient trust of their physician, whereas, negative rapport should lead to reduced patient comfort (increased anxiety), decreased self-disclosure, and decreased trust.[4]

Formative Research

In addition to identifying components of rapport from the literature, the researcher drew on the experiences of real patients who had recently interacted with their physician(s). The purpose of the focus groups was twofold: (1) to identify any additional verbal, nonverbal, and paraverbal behaviors related to rapport building not found in the literature; and (2) to ascertain which behaviors patients identify as important to rapport-building (both physician and patient behaviors). These findings informed the development of the theoretical model.

The following questions were asked of the participants to initiate discussion regarding prior physician-patient communication:

1. Please recall a medical encounter with a physician where you felt there was high rapport. Specifically, what did the physician do or say that made you feel that he or she cared about you, your illness, or your concerns?
2. Please recall a medical encounter with a physician where you felt there was low rapport. Specifically, what did the physician do or say that made you feel that he or she did not care about you, your illness, or your concerns?

As the literature review showed, rapport is difficult to define. This was the case, as well, for the focus group participants. One participant defined rapport as a personal connection between the physician and the patient. Another thought rapport was "whether or not the doctor can communicate with the patient without the patient becoming offended or washed out because of too much information or the wrong kind of information." Other participants thought rapport was about "feeling at ease" or a "comfortableness" with your doctor so "you can talk to them no matter what the topic is." Still another participant thought it had to do with the "attitude of forming a relationship with people...not specifically with people who are close to you but people whom you are caring for." Overall, defining rapport included words like empathy, compassion, comfort, trust, and caring for the patient. Similar terms were found in the literature.

In sum, the content analysis of the focus groups supports the earlier review of the literature. It appears that everyone knew rapport when they saw it; however, no one really knew how to define it. Additionally, all agreed that rapport was made up of both verbal and nonverbal components; however, sometimes it was easier for the participants to identify the things that detracted from rapport than those behaviors that built rapport. Ultimately, as the formative analysis shows, the focus groups offered specific suggestions on what physicians can do (and not do) to improve rapport with their patients. Specifically, physicians should be attentive to their patients, respond with understanding, maintain appropriate eye contact, and listen. A physician should not dismiss symptoms or concerns, be mechanical in communication, or assume that he or she knows what the patient is going to say and interrupt. A number of these suggestions were used to create the theoretical model.

The Rapport Development Model (RDM)

The development of the theoretical model was informed by the literature review, the focus groups, the communication competence model, and personal observations from day-to-day interactions on the part of the researcher (who had considerable experience in the medical system as a patient). The model, as seen in Figure 25–1, is an attempt to describe the process of rapport development and to explain why some physicians are able to develop rapport with their patients while some are unable to do so as well or even at all.

Additionally, the model is one of process, one that recognizes that building rapport is developmental. There are certain behaviors that initiate rapport development and those that continue to enhance it once it has begun. Typically, once the initiating behaviors have occurred, they are not revisited within the primary care visit. Some of the behaviors can be repeated during the next visit (e.g., shaking hands, establishing initial eye contact), but the behaviors would not be implemented over and over again during one visit, as enhancing behaviors would be.

As was noted in the literature review, both physicians and patients agree that physicians are responsible for the relational communication within the doctor-patient relationship.[5] Therefore, the physician is shown initiating the rapport-building process in the model. However, the patient has an important role in the rapport-building process as well, and this is illustrated in the model.

Within the model, rapport behaviors are separated into three categories: initiating, enhancing, and terminating. The literature review revealed that some behaviors would be done only one time during the course of the medical interview (e.g., shaking hands and introducing themselves). Thus, these behaviors were considered to be *initiating* behaviors.

Rapport *enhancing* behaviors are those that improve rapport once it has been initiated (e.g., asking open-ended questions, allowing the patient to talk uninterrupted, and using supportive statements). Alternatively, behaviors deemed opposite of the enhancing behaviors are rapport terminators (e.g., asking only closed-ended questions, interrupting the patient, and not using supportive statements).

Overall, there are four parts to the RDM: (1) physician motivation to build rapport, (2) rapport behaviors (initiating, enhancing, and terminating), (3) patient feedback, and (4) outcomes.

Motivation. Emerging from the communication competence model and focus group data, the first component of the model is motivation. Is the physician motivated to establish rapport to begin with? If yes, the

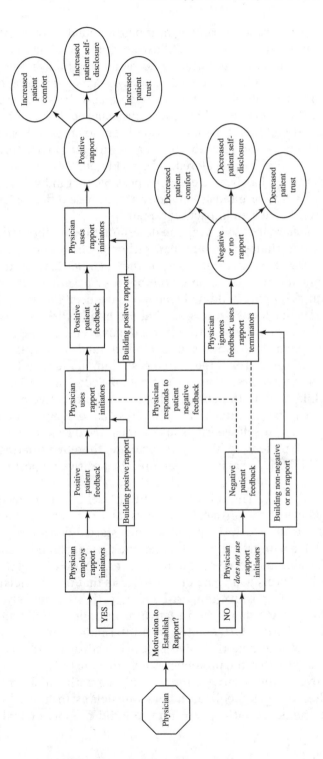

Figure 25–1. Rapport Development Model (RDM) during the Initial Primary Care Medical Encounter

building of positive rapport can begin. If no, the building of negative or no rapport can begin. As the model illustrates, it is possible that physicians who start off on the negative or no rapport path have opportunities during the interaction to change negative rapport-building behaviors, with an end result of building positive rapport. However, it is also possible that the reverse could be true. Physicians could begin building positive rapport and then for some reason begin to employ rapport terminating behaviors and end up building negative rapport. However, because that scenario is considered to be highly unlikely, it is not illustrated in the model. Lastly, it is certainly possible that individual physicians vary in quality or intensity of motivation. These differing levels of motivation would have an impact on rapport.

Rapport behaviors. Following the determination of motivation, the model indicates that physicians can either begin building rapport through the use of rapport initiators, or they can not employ the rapport initiators and risk developing no rapport or negative rapport. For example, initial rapport-building behaviors have been identified in the literature and the focus groups as shaking hands with the patient, addressing the patient by his or her formal name, and having good eye contact. Physicians who are not motivated to build rapport might not introduce themselves (or forget), avoid shaking hands, and call the patient by his or her first name or not acknowledge the patient at all (possibly while reading the chart). Therefore, the negative or no rapport process can begin. Alternatively, a physician can enter the room, introduce him or herself clearly, shake hands, have good eye contact, and address the patient by his or her surname, thereby initiating positive rapport-building behaviors. Therefore, the positive rapport process can begin.

Patient feedback. The third part of the model is patient feedback. Whatever behaviors the physician employs, he or she *should* be monitoring patient feedback. If the physician has started down the positive rapport-building path from the beginning, the patient should seem relatively comfortable and relaxed, and disclose information (i.e., give positive feedback). At this point, the model suggests that the physician simply remains on this positive rapport-building path. Alternatively, if the physician has started down the negative or no rapport-building path, the patient can be less forthcoming with information, and can appear nervous or uncomfortable (i.e., give negative feedback). At this point, the model suggests that the physician is able to adjust his or her behaviors and move to the positive rapport-building path. In short, being aware of the patient's feedback allows physicians to move forward through the model to either continue to build rapport or make the appropriate communication behavior changes to facilitate positive rapport building. The forward movement is illustrated within the model by the continued use of rapport-enhancing behaviors on the part of the physician, which should continue to build positive rapport with patients. Of course, a physician who has started down the negative or no rapport-building path might not attend to the patient's negative feedback—either as a result of not recognizing the negative feedback or choosing to ignore it. In that case, the model suggests that the physician simply will remain on the negative or no rapport-building path.

Outcomes. The fourth and final component is outcomes. The model suggests that there are three additional outcomes related to positive rapport development: increased patient comfort (reduced anxiety); increased patient self-disclosure; and increased patient trust. Alternatively, the model suggests that negative or no rapport can lead to decreased patient comfort (increased anxiety), decreased patient self-disclosure, and decreased patient trust. Testing the relational outcomes identified in the model was beyond the scope of this project. It is an area, however, for future research.

Discussion and Implications for Public Health Communication

The timeliness of this project is important due to the earlier mentioned trend in medical education of incorporating communication skills into the board certification process. As such, one of the biggest challenges the American Medical Association will face is accurately and uniformly measuring and evaluating communication skills. Given these challenges, this research contributed not only to some theoretical underpinnings of rapport that can guide future research, but also identified some specific behaviors, which could lead to more uniform evaluation for medical educators.

The challenges in tackling relational concepts such as rapport are many, but that should not stop researchers. Although rapport is hard to define, it is clearly a critical component of the provider-patient relationship and one we should not ignore. Further, as diagnostic and treatment technologies become more and more sophisticated, communication and the presence of rapport can be one of the few things that keep patients and their health care providers connected on a human level. Therefore, it is critical not only to continue exploring factors related to relational communication but also to find ways to make sure they remain an integral part of the medical experience.

Notes

1. G. R. Norling, *Developing and Testing a Theoretical Model of Rapport Building: Implications for Medical Education and Physician Patient Communication*. Unpublished doctoral dissertation, University of Kentucky, 2004.

2. J. Grahe and F. Bernieri, "The Importance of Nonverbal Cues in Judging Rapport," *Journal of Nonverbal Behavior* 23(4) (1999): 253–269.

3. L. Tickle-Degnen and R. Rosenthal, "Nonverbal Aspects of Therapeutic Rapport," in *Applications of Nonverbal Behavioral Theories and Research*, ed. R. Feldman (Hillsdale, NJ: Lawrence Earlbaum Associates, 1992), 143–164.

4. Norling, *Developing and Testing a Theoretical Model of Rapport Building: Implications for Medical Education and Physician Patient Communication*.

5. D. Cegala, D. Socha McGee, and K. McNeilis, "Components of Patients' and Doctors' Perceptions of Communication Competence during a Primary Care Medical Interview," *Health Communication* 8 (1996): 1–27.

CHAPTER TWENTY-SIX

Understanding and Challenging HIV Stigma: Toolkit for Action

Sue Clay, Gayle Gibbons, Ross Kidd, Jessie Mbwambo, and Anton Schneider

Chapter Questions

1. In what ways can the anti-stigma toolkit be adapted for different audiences and settings?
2. In what capacities were community members involved in participatory learning? What types of exercises are instrumental in challenging HIV-related stigma?
3. What are the major causes, manifestations, and consequences of HIV and AIDS-related stigma and discrimination?
4. Identify essential components of programs that successfully address stigma.

Notes from the Field

We often do the same old things in our workshops—brainstorm and discuss, brainstorm and discuss—and participants get bored. What I liked about this approach is the methods kept changing. We had no time to be bored!

PARTICIPANT, ETHIOPIAN TOOLKIT WORKSHOP, MAY 2003

What Is the Toolkit?

The toolkit was developed to fill the need for educational materials about stigma. It is a resource for trainers to use with community groups to help people understand why stigma is an important issue, what the root causes are, and how to develop strategies to challenge stigma and discrimination.

The toolkit was written by AIDS activists from over 50 nongovernmental organizations and is based on research by the International Center for Research on Women and research partners in Ethiopia, Tanzania, and Zambia. More than 100 group exercises were developed in participatory, interactive workshops.

A strength of the toolkit is that it can be adapted for different audiences and settings. The exercises can be used with health care professionals, faith-based organizations, employers, media/journalists, youth groups, and women's organizations.

The toolkit is organized into three sections:

1. Tackling the root causes of stigma—awareness and denial, ignorance and fear, and shame and blame
2. Working with affected groups—children, people living with HIV and AIDS and their families
3. Stopping stigma—ways frontline workers and communities can mobilize

Resource for Participatory Learning

The toolkit is a resource for raising awareness and promoting action to challenge HIV stigma. The idea is to get participants learning through doing—sharing feelings, concerns, experiences, discussing issues, solving problems, and taking action. It is not a step-by-step guide for a single training course or workshop. Instead, trainers can select those exercises that suit the needs of their group and use them to create a training program, or they can select exercises and integrate them into an existing training program, or they can adapt an exercise to make it more appropriate for the local context. The exercises are user-friendly and each exercise includes easy-to-follow instructions so it can be adapted and translated into local languages.

From Research to Programs

The toolkit is based on research by the International Center for Research on Women in partnership with Miz Hasab Research Center (Ethiopia); Muhimbili University College of Health Sciences (Tanzania); and ZAMBART and Kara Counseling and Training Trust Zambia.

The research project (2001 to 2003) investigated the causes, manifestations, and consequences of HIV- and AIDS-related stigma and discrimination and made recommendations for programs.

Five critical elements were identified to help programs address stigma.

1. Create greater recognition of stigma and discrimination
2. Enhance knowledge about all aspects of HIV and AIDS through a participatory and interactive process
3. Provide forum to discuss the values and beliefs about sex, morality, and death that underlie stigma
4. Find common language to talk about stigma
5. Involve people with HIV and AIDS

These elements were applied in the development of the toolkit.

Copies of the research report "Disentangling HIV and AIDS Stigma in Ethiopia, Tanzania and Zambia" are available from the International Center for Research on Women, 1717 Massachusetts Avenue NW, Washington, DC 20036 or online at: www.icrw.org.

Methods and Materials

The toolkit uses a problem-based approach and links learning directly to behavior change—focusing on practical solutions. For example, through drama and role playing, participants act out how stigma is manifested in their communities. Then each participant in the drama responds from a personal perspective—"How did that make you feel when he said that?" The group explores how these issues and problems can be addressed at the community level. Presentations are kept to a minimum and used only in summarizing sessions or to explain a technical topic.

The toolkit uses a wide variety of participatory training methods and materials including:

- *Buzz groups*
  Two people sitting beside each other can jump-start participation. It is hard to be silent in a group of two people.

- *Report backs*
  A technique to bring ideas together after small group sessions or buzz groups. Often "round robin" reporting is used—one new point is added from each group going around the circle.

- *Card-storming*
  This is a quick way to get ideas out and get participants involved. Participants working individually or in pairs write single points on cards and tape them on the wall. The cards are then organized into categories and discussed.

- *Rotational brainstorming*
  Each small group is given a starting topic and records points on a flipchart. After two to three minutes, the group moves to a new topic and points.

- *Stop-start drama*
  The drama starts and stops for discussion to analyze the issues.

- *Skills practice with feedback*
  A way for participants to practice skills needed to mobilize action against stigma, such as facilitating discussions and giving presentations.

Using the Toolkit

Kenya

The toolkit was introduced at the thirteenth International Conference on AIDS and STIs in Africa, held in Nairobi in September 2003, as part of skills building workshops sponsored by the Positive Action Program of GlaxoSmithKline. Participants took part in a series of exercises including analyzing different images of stigma; an exercise on participants' experience of being stigmatized and stigmatizing others; a stigma simulation game; and a problem tree analysis on the forms, effects, and causes of stigma.

Zambia

I have heard that "Base Bano Bayo" is known as the stigma anthem in several Southern African countries, thanks to Ross Kidd, creator of this uplifting song, and Clement Mfuzi, one of Zambia's leading AIDS activists who is spreading the anti-stigma word through the toolkit.
—Sue Clay, Kara Counseling and Training Trust, Zambia

The toolkit is yet another training manual, but the workshops that result from it are more than just another training session. Song, dance, drama, and personal reflections are all key elements of the anti-stigma training, ensuring that workshops are lively, relevant, soulful, and life-changing. The aim after all is to change attitudes, raise awareness, and change lives.

In April 2004, CHANGE ran a four-day workshop called "Training of Stigma Trainers." The workshop was for Kara Counseling's Kanayaka Community REACH Project, and the aim was to train a group of outreach workers and community leaders to carry out anti-stigma education using the toolkit. *Kanayaka* is a term of insult used in Zambia to

Next Steps | 419

describe a person living with HIV/AIDS. It literally means *the warn-ing light is on.* The participants were active in HIV work in their two communities (a township in Lusaka and a village in Southern Province) and were committed to the Kanayaka Project.

The course was a mix of facilitation skills and exercises from the toolkit, following the sequence of steps in anti-stigma education. "Naming the Problem" begins by using pictures of stigma. Pairs of participants choose a picture and discuss the stigma they see. This simple exercise is powerful, due mainly to the clarity and detail of the pictures: a landlord evicts a family from their house; a man sits eating alone in the corner, while the rest of the family share a bowl of *nshima*; an orphan faces a mound of dirty dishes while others jeer at her. Every time we do this exercise, people see new things or come up with yet more interpretations. It really illustrates the complexity and many layers of stigma. There are always gasps of realization as participants recognize the scenarios. *"This is stigma."*

Moving through the toolkit, participants pick exercises from each chapter, try out new ones, and discuss how they could be used in different settings. Memorable moments from the workshop included creative stop-start drama to explore the stigma about using condoms; a detailed problem tree made to analyze the stigma that children face; human sculptures of stigma and freedom; one woman's story about her brother who was locked up in his room when he fell sick (this arose in a discussion on stigma in the family); and the numerous energizers and songs that the participants taught everyone.

The emphasis was on participation, participation, participation: you cannot change stigma by telling people to change. Through the participants' own presentations on the final day, it was clear that by the end of the course everyone was in full agreement.

Next Steps

Nongovernmental organizations and other institutions use the toolkit to train their staff and others in their communities. The Community REACH project uses the toolkit with grantees, and CORE group members share it with partners. Workshops have been organized in Botswana, Tanzania, Uganda, and Zambia and a workshop using the toolkit is being planned with journalists in Nigeria.

The Swedish International Development Cooperation Agency supports the establishment of a regional anti-stigma training program that uses the toolkit to train trainers in Southern and Eastern Africa. The project will be hosted by the International AIDS Alliance at Alliance Zambia.

The toolkit is also being adapted in Vietnam by the Institute for Social Development Studies.

The toolkit is available electronically at: www.changeproject.org.

Research and development of the toolkit was supported by the U.S. Agency for International Development.

A limited number of CD-ROMs are available from:

The CHANGE Project
Academy for Educational Development
1825 Connecticut Ave NW
Washington, DC 20009
changeinfo@aed.org

CHAPTER TWENTY-SEVEN

Epilogue

Muhiuddin Haider and Ranjeeta Pal

Future Roads in Public Health Communications: Focused Behaviors, Innovations, and Organizations

Communication strategies can be used to impact individual behavior, health decisions, and ultimately the quality of life. It is therefore important to consider different approaches that are well tailored to target audiences and their social, political, economic, environmental, and health circumstances. The best fit between health communication programs and their intended beneficiaries arises from a combination of focused behavior, innovations, and organizations. Health programmers are generally well versed in the organic or biologic factors that contribute to disease burden. The often significant role of behavioral factors in public health problems and solutions, however, is overlooked. The connection between individual behavior and health outcomes must be one focus of the health programs that are aimed at alleviating problems affected by behavior. Properly focused messages will only result from focused behavior and thereby target the risk factors or behaviors ultimately responsible for compromised wellness. The use of messages that promote favorable health behaviors, as alternatives to ones that propagate illness, offers target audiences with behavioral tools to adopt healthful habits and make healthy choices.

Focused innovations and organizations play key roles in targeting behavioral contributors to health promotion and disease prevention. Innovations that are tailored to suit specific audience segments and are marketed through proper media channels have a greater likelihood of being adopted by individuals and groups. Organizations that aim specifically to foster behavior change through health communications can concentrate their efforts on identified needs of the consumer as part of a consumer-oriented paradigm.

Major Lessons Learned and Implications for Future Applications

Throughout many of the examples presented in this book, the importance of active community participation cannot be underestimated. Community groups, faith-based organizations, and educational institutions can be leveraged to maximize the reach of communicated messages and information to the intended beneficiaries. Other lessons include integrating communication with delivery of services, such as providing skilled birth attendants to help mothers recognize and seek care for obstetric complications; using public-private partnerships (PPPs) to facilitate objectives; and building capacity across multiple sectors to foster collaboration for improved results. Another important theme that emerges is the need to improve risk communication for emergency preparedness. Also worth prioritizing is the advancement of health literacy among the public—a significant prerequisite in the effectiveness of all health communications.

Continuing Challenges

Some of the common themes seen across the case examples presented in this book highlight the continuous challenges in affecting behavior change through communications campaigns. In order to build on the evidence presented in this book and beyond, it is essential to focus on results-oriented approaches that integrate analyses and interventions within a socioeconomic context. First, it is important to understand and apply the theories and research that help public health professionals make vital connections between health, communication, and behavior. The examples outlined in the introductory chapters demonstrate how public health programs employ the body of research and theories in the fields of public health, communications, and behavior change. This analysis is the foundation for creating effective health communications interventions. Figure 27–1 represents this process of analysis in drawing fundamental connections between health, communication, and behavior. Employing theories to display the interaction of these elements is the foundation for developing effective health communication interventions.

As a complement to the theoretical approach represented in the analysis phase, Figure 27–2 represents the intervention level of health communication. It shows the methodologic aspects of planning and implementation that are required to create an effective intervention. At the intervention level, the focus is on the interaction of promotion, prevention, and disease. Many of the chapters demonstrate the interplay among the elements of promotion, prevention, and disease to create health outcomes.

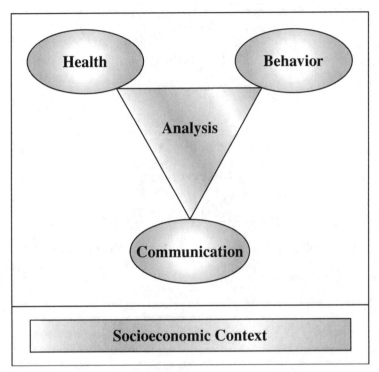

Figure 27–1. Triangular Interaction among Health, Behavior, Communication, and SES

In Figure 27–3 the two models are combined and the crucial inter-action is evident between analyses (linking health, behavior, and com-munication) and interventions (combining burden of disease, preven-tion, and promotion activities). Some of the examples in this text focus on only the analysis stage while others focus on the intervention. Several chapters combine all or many of the elements of these stages together when presenting case examples. As the models illustrate, shift-ing priorities and resources onto any one component of this overall interaction will inevitably affect the other components. This stresses the importance of carefully assessing the validity and predictability of associative relationships among the different components and strategi-cally implementing programs that have the greatest potential in maxi-mizing impact on the quality of life. The evidence presented in this book implies that, when viewed together, the two models illustrate how the interaction between analyses and interventions needs to be further examined in light of dynamic socioeconomic contexts.

The examination of this interaction leads to a few lessons learned. In reviewing the lessons from the broad spectrum of examples pre-sented in the book, several themes emerge. Among these are common

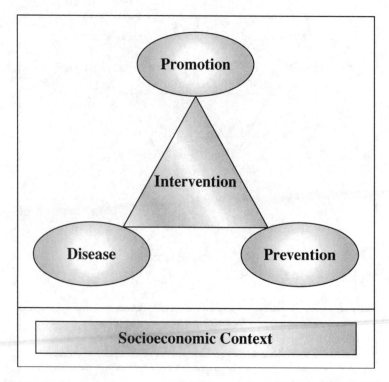

Figure 27–2. Triangular Interaction among Disease, Prevention, Promotion, and SES

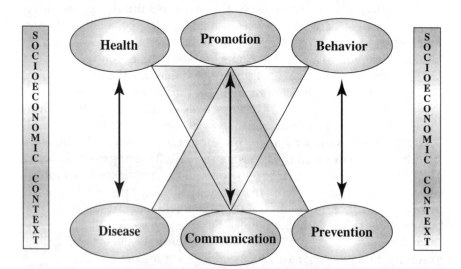

Figure 27–3. Comprehensive Interaction between Analyses and Interventions within a Socioeconomic Context

challenges of designing and implementing health communications interventions. Some of these shared challenges are presented as follows.

Process

The example of the Philippines in Chapter 15 illustrates the ongoing challenges involved with organizing, planning, and managing an intervention. In this case, which outlines an STI/HIV/AIDS prevention program, the authors demonstrate that it is difficult to align different interests toward common goals while removing barriers and designing appropriate incentive systems. As is often the case, identifying certain intervention strategies can come only after a program has been implemented for some time and anecdotal evidence comes in from the field. Here, the program planners were able to adapt the intervention to the changing needs and context of the targeted population by using evidence-driven strategies throughout the planning and implementation of the intervention. In facing the challenges, such as addressing the barrier of the price of condoms, it is important to implement strategies that include careful planning and ongoing monitoring of the process, impacts, and outcomes of the health intervention. The following pages outline other results-oriented strategies that can also greatly enhance the chances for a successful intervention.

Implementation

The variables from concept to implementation require identification of indicators. Without identifying specific, measurable indicators of health outcomes, theoretical variables cannot be translated into useful measures. The implementation process requires much more than research and data analysis. Two important questions to ask are the following. Were theoretical models maintained throughout program design and activities? Were the findings able to be generalized to the populations of interest? For example, in Chapter 5, observational research is used to define problems and to formulate research questions. This illustrates an optimal case where proper operational integration of qualitative variables is crucial in adequately assessing the needs of a given population, and developing appropriate interventions to address them. Chapter 6, which uses social mobilization as a tool for HIV/AIDS outreach programs, demonstrates the importance of setting clear indicators for behavioral and social determinants of health and outcomes.

Impact

It is a continuous challenge to assess the impact of public health programs, particularly in developing countries. In Chapter 14, the authors point out that social marketing monitoring practices have not kept pace with the increased sophistication of social marketing programs in reproductive health. They recommend tracking additional indicators that focus on the unique aspects of social marketing programs in addition to standardized indicators for evaluating reproductive health programs. This solution can apply to interventions outside of social marketing as well. Ongoing monitoring and evaluation that employs the most appropriate indicators and tracking techniques is essential to properly measure the impact of any health intervention.

Sustainability

The challenge to achieve sustainable behavior change is another ongoing theme throughout this text. In all stages of planning and implementing a health communications campaign, consideration must be given as to whether the program is sufficient to sustain the behavior change. In Chapter 12, The Goli ke Hamjoli program to promote low-dose oral contraceptives in India illustrates how a comprehensive strategy requires a long-term sustained effort. This campaign reached a critical mass to achieve positive attitudes and acceptance use. But only time will tell whether long-term sustainability can be achieved. In order to meet the challenge of achieving sustainability in public health programs, long-term strategies and follow-up are important to be able to adapt to changed attitudes and needs of the target population.

Cultural Sensitivity

A text on global public health communication would not be complete without mentioning the role of cultural sensitivity in designing health interventions. From Tanzania to Romania, Latin America to Bangladesh, the examples in this book encompass cultures across the globe. In working with vastly different cultures in many communities of the world, cultural sensitivity is a consistent challenge for practitioners of global public health. In Chapter 5, the authors underscore the challenge of remaining nonjudgmental when observing practices that might not be the norm in the researcher's culture. Whether conducting observational research or designing a health intervention, it is vitally important to act without ethnocentrism, as Margaret Mead did when she first researched the sexual behavior of adolescent women in Western Samoa.

Simply defining the role of cultural sensitivity is not enough. Building capacity of health care institutions, organizations, and health care workers to use cultural competencies requires more than an exercise in analysis. Social marketing strategies can be used to position health-promoting messages in the context of culture. Cultural considerations must also be taken into account in providing access to services and ensuring the quality of health care.

The four specific health-related Millennium Development goals are to eradicate extreme poverty and hunger; reduce child mortality; improve maternal health; and combat HIV/AIDS, malaria, and other diseases. In all of these cases, communication programs that aim to change behavior, educate, or inform people face challenges in their processes, impact, and sustainability. Experience mandates the need for thorough evaluation of any health communication program to improve its planning, organization, and management; to sustain its long-term effects on poverty, child mortality, maternal health, and infectious diseases; and to ensure its adaptability to different people, places, times, and situations.

Guidelines for Best Practices and Needs for Further Research

Best practices can be based on the health communication interactions model presented in this book. These practices must incorporate research on the interaction among health, behavior, and communication into interventions combining disease prevention and health promotion. Finding associative relationships—such as those between behavioral factors and health outcomes as well as between communication and behavior change—will assist in formulating research questions on causality and complexities. This will allow proper determination of true cause-and-effect relationships and their differentiation from confounding effects. Complexities, or relationships whose nature is not immediately clear, require control of confounder variables as well as tracing of primary and secondary linkages among associated variables.

The interaction between analyses (linking health, behavior, and communication) and interventions (combining burden of disease, prevention, and promotion activities) needs to be further examined in light of dynamic socioeconomic contexts. As Figure 27–3 illustrates, shifting priorities and resources onto any one component of this overall interaction will inevitably affect the other components. This stresses the importance of carefully assessing validity and predictability of associative relationships among the different components and strategically implementing programs that have the greatest potential in maximizing impact on the quality of life.

There are several aspects of health communication programs that need further research. Each of these must apply the interactive model when in the process of being put into operation, from concept to implementation. Clear and measurable indicators must also be defined for purposes of their process, outcome, and impact evaluations.

The following areas of health communications require more extensive research and development of best practices. Some summary guidelines are provided here.

A. *Results-oriented Approaches*

Results-driven interventions on a community level involve developing effective programs with the outcomes in mind. These can affect change through education, communication, and policy decisions. As an added benefit, while designing such interventions, a participatory approach can promote community involvement and ownership of a health issue facing those concerned. Emphasis should be placed on how to achieve optimal, specific, evidence-based, and measurable results.

Specific goals must be established prior to program implementation; results must be measured at regular intervals; and corrective mid-course action, if necessary, must be undertaken efficiently. Results-oriented approaches must also include proper evaluation and monitoring components in their strategic frameworks. This would serve to determine the degree to which given results are actually attributable to intervention activities, or to external factors or confounding variables.

As an example, Performance Improvement Programming (PIP) is a results-oriented approach to project review that involves stakeholders in a process of evaluation and planning to improve project performance. PIP can be used as a practical, low-cost, participatory method for midterm project review and planning. It engages partners in refocusing and strengthening the organizational, technical, managerial, and impact capacity of projects. Benefits of PIP include:

Clarification of project objectives; refinement of objectives if required

A shared vision of project success among partners

Better utilization of local experience and resources

Improved coordination among implementing agencies

Strengthened local capacity for program implementation

A flexible, rapid, and low-cost approach

Source: "Social Impact," http://www.socialimpact.com/INPIP.html

B. *Integrating Communication with Service Delivery*

Communication campaigns must be closely linked with the delivery of services that promote the health behaviors or knowledge being promoted. Services include education; care at health facilities; prevention and treatment measures; financing schemes such as insurance or community fund-pools; and market health products.

For example, communicating the need for voluntary counseling and testing for HIV/AIDS is futile without having modes of treatment in place so that those who test positive can seek care. In the case of condom promotion, effective means of condom distribution and quality assurance must already be established prior to message dissemination. Otherwise, those who are ready to change their behavior will encounter avoidable barriers to acting upon their readiness simply due to lack of a product. Services must also be made accessible to marginalized groups that are hardly reached, such as those who lack transportation or face literacy challenges.

C. *Building Indigenous Capacity to Maximize Expertise in Supporting Multimedia and Multi-sector Initiatives*
The most sustainable programs and progress in public health are those that rely on local capacity to be developed and implemented. Thus, such a capacity that does not rely on external intervention must be built in a way that involves multiple sectors that will be responsible for overseeing and managing the planning, implementation, and evaluation of health initiatives. Sectors that must be actively involved are health, education, finance, social welfare, technology, and civil service. Local capacity must also be developed to take advantage of multimedia channels such as radio, television, print publications, Internet, and live entertainment education in promoting behavior change and wellness.

D. *Public-Private Partnerships (PPPs)*
Public-private partnerships are becoming a common approach to achieving social and behavioral change. These partnerships can be more effective than the public and private organizations that operate separately for various reasons, which stem mainly from the specific skills that each brings to the PPP. A public organization frequently has the mandate and financial resources for the task it is assigned through government appropriations and other multilateral funding sources, but it frequently lacks the know-how to effectively manage the project. Here, the private organization can usually be key to providing the managerial expertise and processes that it has carefully honed over years of supplying its customers

with products and services. This specialized expertise can be in any of the functional areas of business—human resources, operations, finance, or marketing. In the area of marketing, for example, the field of "social marketing" has developed from the realization that marketing principles followed by commercial organizations can be applied, with some modifications, to situations where the product of interest is to bring about planned social and behavioral change in a variety of settings—education, environment, and public health.

Further research is needed to answer questions about how to create PPPs; motivate public and private organizations to engage in and sustain partnership with each other; and monitor and evaluate the process efficacy and outcome effectiveness of PPPs in achieving program objectives.

One area where the potential of PPPs to make a difference has yet to be fully harnessed is HIV/AIDS prevention. Public and private organizations can tap into their combined potential to develop and implement effective programs that use education, media advocacy, and behavior change to prevent HIV/AIDS transmission and reduce its prevalence. For example, nongovernmental and faith-based organizations can work with ministries of health to promote behavior change; risk avoidance through abstinence, mutual monogamy or fidelity; delay of sexual debut; and risk reduction in high-risk groups via consistent condom use.

E. Emergency Preparedness and Communications

Successful communication strategies are vital to prevent, detect, and respond to biological threats. Preparing for and coping with public health crises require building partnerships among government agencies, academic and research institutions, businesses, industries, and communities. The capacity of nations to address threats such as microbial weapons and infectious epidemics depends on successful coordination of efforts with local and global key players, such as World Health Organization, Centers for Disease Control and Prevention, National Institutes of Health, Department of Defense, ministries of health, and international development agencies. Each of these stakeholders can contribute specialized technical capacity, human resources, and expertise. Collaboration among these groups in the processes of surveillance, planning, implementation, and evaluation is crucial to their ability to avert or control health crises. Equally important is the dissemination of timely, credible, and accurate information to the public, who must be able to easily access and use the information to reduce their risk of exposure.

F. *Responsiveness and Communication of National Governments,
Donors, and Implementation Agencies in Public Health Agenda*
National governments and their ministries, global donors, policy
setters, and health programmers must communicate clearly and
consistently in any efforts to establish public health agendas.
These agendas may involve health systems reform, health education campaigns, surveillance, communication initiatives, and disease prevention and treatment. The needs and concerns of targeted or intended beneficiaries, not the donor's agenda, must be
foremost and prioritized in making implementation decisions in
their best interest. This is critical to responsiveness.

Conclusion

Future horizons for health communications present challenges for producers and consumers of health information. However, strategies to
meet them are not elusive. The answers to many of the questions lie in
the grasp of health programmers, health care workers, policy makers,
leaders, and community members themselves. The potential of each of
these stakeholders must be tapped in any endeavor to communicate
messages that promote healthy behaviors for public wellness. Each has
an indispensable role to play.

In a global society where the public is bombarded daily with numerous messages of both benign as well as insidious natures, the act of communicating accurate, credible, and useful information about health
issues continues to be a challenge. The advent of information systems
such as the Internet, health literature, and mass media creates potential
for not only the dissemination of factual health-promoting messages,
but also the harmful propagation of myths and misleading information.
Systematic checks must be established to ensure the publication and
posting of peer-reviewed or authority-approved information and prevent falsities from being accepted as fact when the public's health is at
stake.

Augmenting these stated challenges is the issue of linking communication support with delivery of services. For example, in the case of
HIV/AIDS, behavioral change communication about the need to use
condoms or seek voluntary counseling and testing (VCT) must be complemented by accessible and affordable VCT services and condom distribution. Building communication support without ensuring the provision of services creates the risk of discouragement and frustration for
intended beneficiaries and results in the futility of promotion efforts.
Also, having optimal health services available without communication
tools to promote them to potential clients does not make sense, since

those who could be helped most by such services may be the hardest to reach. Thus, communication infrastructure and service considerations such as costs and benefits must go hand-in-hand to effectively impact the health of the audiences concerned.

Fortunately, the experiences and practical guidance presented in this book offer several tools to confront such grave challenges—by empowering individuals; integrating communication with service delivery; building the capacity of health sector infrastructures; and promoting multisectoral responsiveness of national governments to the health needs of its citizens. Communication, through various modes and methods, holds considerable promise for the future of health promotion and disease prevention efforts.

In the interest of achieving focused behaviors, innovations, and organizations, the concept of FOMENT introduced in the first chapter of the book can be linked to this aim. To recapitulate, the six components of FOMENT are: "*focus* on a specific behavior change; *organization* of the behavior change program; *management* that supports and approves of the behavior change plan; *environment* that is conducive to behavior change; *network* to diffuse innovations at individual and organizational levels; and *technology* available to diffuse innovations." Given that an optimal match between health communication programs and their intended beneficiaries arises from a combination of focused behavior, innovations, and organizations as explained earlier, applying components of FOMENT to the communication of health messages will contribute to their success in promoting behavior change and healthful practices among audiences of interest.

FOMENT has the power to build capacity for organization and planning of health communication programs at a management level and optimize diffusion of innovations (DOI) on the level of whole organizations, aside from that of the individual. As FOMENT is a synergistic complement to DOI, it can facilitate the efficacy of the innovation (whether the innovation is an idea or behavior) in the organizational setting. For example, FOMENT aims at adoption of an innovation at the group level, whereas DOI focuses on the individual level. Haider explains that modifying a behavior change innovation for a group is easier than for an individual. Moreover, FOMENT analyzes interventions before implementation of a program, whereas DOI examines the intervention after the program is already implemented. Thus, FOMENT minimizes problems in applying the intervention prior to its implementation, and thereby can maximize its effectiveness.

Index

A

absences in research notes, 81

access to information. *See also* data collection; message
  distribution of (CAMS model), 167
  as indicator of success. *See* knowledge
  information overload, 204
  information sharing, 166
  levels of awareness, 132–133
  noise in communication, 124, 365
  rumors. *See* rumors

access to leadership, 159–160

activities
  collective action, 62–64, 107, 110–111
  social mobilization, 95, 98–99

adaptability
  COMBI (Communication-for-Behavioral-Impact), 315–316
  evidence-driven, 251–252
  IMCI strategy, 272

administration, DOI theory recommendations, 13

adoption of change, 2, 44. *See also* behavior change; social change
  DOI theory and, 4–5
  PPFF (push and pull factors), 47–64
    broad-base communication strategy, 52–56

advisory committees, 143

advocacy. *See also* partnerships and stakeholders
  marketing vs., 34–35
  vaccine supply, 279

AIDS. *See* HIV/AIDS pandemic

analysis of data, 82–87

anthrax, 298–299. *See also* crisis and risk communications
  media representation of, 391–404
  response to 2001 attacks, 157
  vaccination programs, 363–375, 401–402. *See also* vaccinations
    controversy over, 366–368

anthropological methods, 69–71

anti-stigma toolkit for HIV, 415–420

approaches to communication. *See* channels of communication

archetypes, 128

assessment. *See* evaluation

attention-grabbing, 131

attitudes
  adoption of behavioral change, 51
  assessing (example), 195

audience, 3, 44, 54
  channels of communication, 55–56, 298
    anthrax, media representation of, 391–404
    bio-crises and attacks, 352–354, 357, 373
    choosing, 295
    crisis and risk communications, 328, 346
    feedback channels, 352
    oral contraceptives in India (case study), 187–189
  compassion, 330–331, 346
  credibility of message, 31, 345, 402
    biological threat response, 350–351
    crisis and risk communications, 327. *See also* trust
    media representation of anthrax, 391–404
    rapport building, 407–413
  crisis and risk communications, 297–298, 324
  motivating change. *See* change agents
  public fears of, addressing
    media representation of anthrax, 391–404
    vulnerability to misinformation and fear, 400
  segmentation of, 55, 224–225
    sales data and, 221
    in social marketing, 27, 37
    targeted surveys, 231